THE INTERIOR DESIGN BUSINESS HANDBOOK

Second Edition

MARY V. KNACKSTEDT, ASID

with Laura J. Haney

JOHN WILEY & SONS, INC.

New York • Chichester • Weinheim • Brisbane • Singapore • Toronto

First published by the Whitney Library of Design in 1988

This book is printed on acid-free paper. ⊖

Copyright © 1988, 1992 by Mary V. Knackstedt. All rights reserved

Published by John Wiley & Sons, Inc.

Published simultaneously in Canada.

This publication is designed to provide accurate and authoritative
information in regard to the subject matter covered. It is sold with the
understanding that the publisher is not engaged in rendering professional
services. If professional advice or other expert assistance is required, the
services of a competent professional person should be sought.

Library of Congress Cataloging-in-Publication Data:

Knackstedt, Mary V.
    The interior design business handbook / Mary V. Knackstedt, with
Laura J. Haney.—2nd ed.
        p.   cm.
    Includes bibliographical references and index.
    ISBN 0-471-28484-X
    1. Interior decoration firms—United States—Management—
Handbooks, manuals, etc.   2. Interior decoration—United States—
Marketing—Handbooks, manuals, etc.   I. Haney, Laura J.
II. Title
NK2002.K57   1992
729'.068—dc20   91-41326

Printed in the United States of America

This book is dedicated to all designers, especially to those who call me with questions or to share information. Together, we can continue to raise the standards of the field of interior design and to increase our ability to serve our clients.

ACKNOWLEDGMENTS

My goals in writing this book and in sharing business information have been to help create a professional standard for the interior design field and to try to ensure that there are rewards enough to keep all the bright young designers working in this field. Without the help and encouragement of many special people, I could never have completed a book of this scope and complexity.

Special thanks to the late Samuel Ledger for teaching me to understand accounting procedures.

to Robert Herr, Sr., for valuable information on insurance;

to John Purcell, Jr., for updating legal information;

to Gwen Richards of the CCNB bank for current banking practices;

to Linda Chubb for assistance on a multitude of forms;

to Lee Bethel for typing the several reams of paper used in writing and revising the manuscript;

to Lee Kolker for all her encouragement;

to all my designer friends and fellow members of ASID for posing questions that inspired research and for sharing their views on a variety of issues;

to the consultants and business friends who helped develop ways to improve professional business practices for designers, and who are part of the Design Business Monthly team;

to Julia Moore, Cornelia Guest, and Laura J. Haney for refining the book's concept and working long and hard to get it right;

to my support staff who helped me live, run a business, and write a book at the same time;

and to my friends, who thought I had deserted them.

CONTENTS

PREFACE

As interior designers, we deal with business issues every day. We engage in business development when we seek new clients. We deal with finance when we arrange to purchase furniture, figure estimates, or make up a payroll. We sign contracts and letters of agreement, handle personnel problems, and seek out new resources. We deal with masses of paperwork that include writing specifications and placing orders. Often we do it without the background and advisors available to many other kinds of professionals.

Interior design is taught in schools, but the *business* of interior design is learned by trial and error as we develop our practices. This is bad for designers because it can be discouraging and limiting, and is bad for the profession because it perpetuates the myth that interior designers cannot deal with schedules and budgets.

To stay in business, we have to understand business. We don't have to earn business degrees or be personally capable of performing every function from accounting to devising retirement plans, but we do have to be able to talk with and understand the people who are specialists in these fields. To pull our weight as members of financial planning teams and to help our firms end the year with a profit, we cannot afford to wear blinders to financial matters.

If we are to develop the interior design field to the level of professionalism that we all want it to have, we must communicate both with each other and with the world at large. Other professions have strong liaison and group activities through which they share their business practices and solutions to common problems. The interior design profession needs to do the same. We can learn from each other; and by learning from each other, we can strengthen our individual firms and create a stronger and better-understood profession.

Awareness is the key. Just as we continue to learn about design throughout our lifetimes, we have to keep current with the other issues that affect the interior design field. Everything that affects business in general affects the interior design business. When insurance rates go up, we may have to modify the way we do business. The state of the stock market, oil prices, and the value of real estate affect our clients' attitudes to buying design services; therefore, they affect our interior design businesses. It's a chain reaction: If we are not running our firms profitably, we are not doing our jobs well and we lose opportunities for other design work. This may prevent us from attracting the caliber of projects we enjoy working on and find most financially profitable.

The *Interior Design Business Handbook* is written primarily for practicing interior designers—whether working independently or within large firms. Because it covers the full range of business activities and procedures for the life of a practice—from choosing a location and running a business on a daily basis to selling it when it's time to retire—it is also useful to students and as a training manual for support-staff members. Because it delineates business procedures that work for interior design firms all over the country, it's a book to refer to just before a meeting with business advisors, and one to give your bookkeeper or accountant.

Every procedure in this book works. They are in use in daily practice in my own firm and in many successful design firms throughout the United States. You can safely use any or all of them. Interior designers with the right information can quickly adapt to new situations. This book gives you the tools to get the information you need: the right way to tell your accountant what he or she should be telling you; what to ask your legal advisor so that your firm is protected from tedious litigation; and what to tell your insurance agent to ensure that appropriate coverage is in place when you need it. The *Handbook* interprets business jargon and puts it into clear and direct language. Current business practices and procedures have been adapted specifically to the needs of interior designers, and simplified for easy use.

The *Interior Design Business Handbook* is much more comprehensive than my first book on business for interior designers, *Interior Design for Profit*, partly because the climate for doing business has become more complex in the intervening years. Unlike *Profitable Career Options for Designers*—my second book—the *Handbook* focuses directly on the main business of design and not on satellite specialties such as product design or real estate. My goal in writing such a comprehensive book on business has been to provide enough information about the design field and its very distinctive business needs and practices to enable everyone who uses it to achieve profitability. With the *Handbook*, you can evaluate your practice and pinpoint areas where you might increase profits—or make a turnaround from loss to profit. If your firm is profitable, you can progress to many exciting dimensions of design. If it is not profitable, then there are problems you must resolve before you can reach your career objectives. To give an example, shipping costs were once a minor business expense. Then they tripled in a single year, and many design firms lost money. Had these firms recognized certain indicators, however, they could have diminished their losses.

Through working with many interior design firms on business development and in problem areas such as near-bankruptcy, I have found that design firms have very specific types of business problems. *The Interior Design Business Handbook* addresses the problems brought to light by this exposure to the inner workings of design firms all over the United States. I've seen what goes wrong, and how even the most talented designers can lose money. Perhaps it's because we are inventive people that we find creative ways of trying to correct our mistakes. Left to our own devices, without adequate business guidance, we often come up with incredibly complex ways of "solving" business problems that could have been handled so much better and more efficiently—if we had only known the appropriate business formula. It is my hope that the *Interior Design Business Handbook* will free up our creative energies by making the business end of interior design not only comprehensible but also rewarding—in every sense of the word.

Chapter One

FINDING YOUR PLACE IN INTERIOR DESIGN

Interior design is a profession, a career, a vocation, and a lifestyle. It is not just a job. To practice it successfully, it is important to have a clear idea of what interior design involves and an appreciation of its demands. It is just as important to know whether you have the combination of personal attributes and interests that a professional interior designer needs.

WHAT IT TAKES TO BE AN INTERIOR DESIGNER

Design expertise comes from exposure and experience, a combination of academic study and learning on the job. Every one of your experiences contributes to your design vocabulary. Design education stresses problem-solving. The four to six years you spend in the formal study of interior design gives you the informational tools to use in your work—problem-solving skills being perhaps the most valuable tool of all. But interior design demands a tremendous amount of ongoing research. To be a responsible designer, you must study new technologies, new product specifications, new laws and regulations, and changes in building and fire codes. With each new project, there is more to study and learn. Your education never ends. Learning is part of the lifestyle.

Interior design work, by nature, requires that those who practice it learn to temper their innate idealism with the practical demands of reality. You design for real people in the real world. In every design project you undertake, you must be willing to strike a balance between what you envision as "the ideal" and what you can achieve within the project's practical constraints.

Interior design is creative work, and it attracts talented, creative people. In fact, without talent you cannot go far in this field. Your challenge is to direct and focus your creativity. There is no problem in coming up with new ideas—only in choosing which ones should be executed first, which ones have priority. Setting and acting on priorities requires mental and behavioral discipline.

The days of sitting at a drafting table and drawing pretty pictures are over—if they ever existed. Designers have to make things happen. Social contacts are important in acquiring new projects. You need to like people and you need to get along with all kinds of people and to inspire their confidence.

An interior design career depends on organization. From beginning to end, every project involves a myriad of details; keeping on top of things is absolutely critical. Even if your firm includes someone whose job is to expedite, you will always have to deal with mountains of details.

Interior design demands high energy and passion. It is almost never a nine-to-five business; on occasion, it is a twenty-four-hour-a-day profession. Interior designers need physical and emotional stamina to fuel their long hours and to cope with pressures of completing a job on schedule and to their client's satisfaction.

Most extremely successful designers—those with annual personal incomes of more than $200,000—are addicted to interior design. They live it, eat it, and sleep it. It is a passion they cannot live without. Design addiction can be destructive. But the most successful designers are people who have managed to merge good business practices with their positive addiction.

This book is about how you can integrate your love for the creative parts of interior design—and the way of life that comes with your career—with good business practice. It is about success with profitability.

A PERSONAL INVENTORY FOR PROSPECTIVE INTERIOR DESIGNERS

1. How important is interior design to me?
2. What kind of lifestyle do I want to have?
3. Do I have the innate creative abilities to become a successful designer?
4. Am I willing to spend the time and money required for the formal training?
5. How much time do I want to devote to my work?
6. In general, do I like the people in the field enough to work with them?
7. Do I have the personality to work with any kind of client?
8. Do I enjoy planning and organizing?
9. Am I self-disciplined?
10. Am I self-motivated?
11. Do I have more than average physical and emotional stamina?

FIVE TRADITIONAL DESIGNER-CLIENT RELATIONSHIPS

The designer may fill many different roles in his or her relationship with the client; the business structure established will reflect the roles accordingly. Traditional roles that designers have held in the past include pure designer, agent, merchant, employee, and contractor.

Pure Designer
In this capacity, the interior designer just provides professional design services: drawings, documents, and purchasing specifications for all interior elements and furnishings required. The scope of the work usually includes the preparation of the entire interior plan.

Agent
The designer can act as an agent on the client's behalf, placing the client's orders with manufacturers and showrooms. The monies go through the designer's firm or under his or her name. The designer is responsible for managing the project. In some cases, the contracts are written so the designer does not assume responsibility for the merchandise, materials, and the work performed.

Merchant
The designer becomes a merchant when selling merchandise. Many design firms will procure and sell merchandise. In some smaller communities, there is no choice but to act as a source of materials and to see that they are appropriately installed. The design firm may also charge a fee.

Employee

Some designers are employed by retail stores and are usually paid salary plus commission. When the client purchases items from that store, the designer services can be included or can be offered at an extra fee. More and more, firms of this type are charging some fee in addition to the retail or list price of items, depending on the individual financial structure of the company and its location.

Contractor

The designer may act as a contractor by employing the workers required to do construction, hang paper, finish surfaces, handle drapery and window treatments, and so on. In some states, the designer will have to carry a contractor's license in order to provide these services. In many instances, the craftspeople are directly employed by the design firm; in others, they work on a freelance or contracted basis.

WORKING STYLES

Many of the arts attract people who like to work alone; but interior design forces people to work together. This makes interior design almost as much a social science as an art.

Interior design touches many other disciplines. There is constant interaction with all types of construction trades, as well as with artisans from many different craft groups. A coordinated effort is of primary concern.

Working Alone

If you work as an independent designer, you can do whatever you want at whatever speed you choose. If you want to work only one day a week, you can. If your forte is specialized work that no one else wants to become involved with, perhaps you need to work alone. If you are certain that you have mastered your art to the point that you can perform every task within your specialty, and have a personality that does not require a lot of stimulation, then an independent practice is for you.

Team Work

The trend now is to work in groups, or teams. Designers who practice in groups do so because they see this as a better way to accomplish their goals. It is a growing movement. The group may not be part of a corporate structure, where a group of designers all work for the same firm, but design teams and design partnerships are working successfully now, and there will be more of them in the future.

Interior designers are also realizing that by working together, as attorneys and physicians often do, they can share a business manager, an expediter, an accountant, an insurance consultant, legal services, and other professional management personnel. This gives them a better-managed and more profitable firm, with opportunities for better retirement plans and many of the perks that are possible only in a team arrangement.

When designers work with other designers, there is a chance to test each other's designs, to determine what will work. When three other people look at a design and all say "I don't see any problems," obviously the chance of producing it successfully is much greater than if done in isolation. This kind of trial process, I have found, is important to quality design.

Increasingly clients want one firm to control the whole project, even though their project may be complex enough to require several disciplines. Therefore, they like to hire firms who have it all. Obviously, a designer can team with other design professionals. Multidiscipline design teams of architects, landscape architects, interior designers, and engineers have an advantage in bidding for larger projects. Clients usually prefer teams that have experience in working together.

Government regulations require more record keeping than ever before. The nature of the work has changed, and clients are more likely to sue if the unforeseen occurs. We need to become more professionally efficient and to develop high administrative and production standards. We need access to more sophisticated tools, such as computerized equipment. A small office cannot afford much of it. But by working together, designers can afford this kind of equipment and get the bonuses of other designers' professional knowledge and the stimulation of each other's company.

Design Associate

At one time, people became design associates because they didn't have funding or were not ready to start their own company. Today, many interior designers who have been practicing independently are associating with larger firms because the profitability is so much greater. Some interesting arrangements share profits between the management company and the associate designer. In this way the associate is responsible for writing the orders for handling all the design issues. In some instances, the designers provide their own marketing and bring in their own jobs; in other cases, the jobs are brought in by the firm.

Designers can work as hard as they want to. If the work or project is highly profitable, they profit accordingly. If they elect to do a project for little markup, perhaps as a marketing effort, this is also acceptable. Of course, certain overhead requirements must be met. If the designer decides to take time off—e.g., to study—this is his or her decision since he or she is only paid for performance.

Experienced designers have found this arrangement one of the most profitable and most pleasurable ways to work. Let someone else handle the business problems. Designers want to design. Also, the clients know there is a higher power, so they are less likely to question pricing, billing, and other contract issues. In addition to high quality management, the larger company atmosphere can also provide designers with the tools that they could not afford on their own—high-tech environment, library, consultants, support staff, communication with other designers, and so forth.

The arrangement permits the designer to work as an independent contractor. Designers cover all of their own expenses and are responsible for their own design work, but the managing company handles the actual processing of the project. The gross profits are usually split at different levels, depending on the varied responsibilities and levels of performance.

SPECIALIZATION AND SPECIALTIES

This is definitely a time for specialization. Designers with the greatest name recognition and financial success are those who have specialized. (This could lead you to wonder if being multifaceted in accomplishments and abilities does not hurt more than it helps.)

A review of design publications of the past ten years shows that less-qualified design firms can and did take the market share from "better" firms just because they were very clear in stating that they do offices, or that they do nothing but medical facilities, or that they do only restaurants.

Specialization most often leads to better profit. Specialists know their work; it is easier to do it because they did it last week. If you choose to specialize, you can vary certain facets of the work, but you do not have to relearn eighty percent of the technology to lower the risk of error and speed up design production.

Interior design has been a broad-based service profession—blanketing residential, contract, and industrial work. In the next decade, however, interior design will be more specialized than it has been and some of the best and most interesting jobs will probably be in the specialties. The following pages offer brief looks at one hundred areas of specialization.

Client demand can cause you to change your area of expertise. A designer in Ohio specialized in education interiors. In time, she found that although she had become a specialist and did some of the most up-to-date and innovative designs for education, the demand was no longer there. She was forced to change her orientation and began designing psychological/psychiatric spaces, working with many therapists to develop spaces to support their therapies. When interest in this dwindled, she found herself specializing in interiors that supported profit-making endeavors—professional services, manufacturing, general business, and spaces with a marketing and/or production component. In each instance, she was able to use some of what she had learned in the previous speciality. Still, she had to study, bring in many consultants, and do a lot of traveling to meet with other specialists in the course of mastering new specialties.

Acoustic Design
Hearing is one of the five senses; sound is an integral part of every environment. As space becomes more expensive and people live and work closer together, quiet has become a luxury. Specialists in acoustic design consult on projects ranging from concert halls, conference rooms, open offices, and restaurants to residential design. Controlling sound has become a science. In open landscape offices, there are sound-breaking panels and sound maskers. Tele-conferencing rooms need the sound to be contained. On the other hand, restaurants need a certain amount of noise in order to sell food. In any space, from residential to the most technologically demanding commercial environments, there are sounds we want to hear and sounds we don't want to hear.

Administrative Building Design
Every major company has an administration building with needs and demands that require design. The demands change as the products change, and interior designers are called in to streamline and to develop spaces supporting work flow. At one time, we just designed offices, but today social environments are also important. Sometimes, more important decisions are made over a cup of coffee than in the boardroom.

Airplane Design
This is a unique specialty. Airplanes range from a standard passenger carrier to a flying conference room or living space. Designers must consider design elements in terms of weight, fire safety, and psychological and environmental effects.

Amusement Park Design

Some designers work on theme parks, developing the visual components that enhance rides and exhibits. These can incorporate animated figures and appeal to all the senses, even that of smell. These designers may develop unique signage for the park, design the fixtures, or be involved with the service areas: food service, restrooms, souvenir shops. Park design has this in common with museums and community buildings. Safety, effectiveness, and efficiency are important. Profitability is determined to be effectiveness of the fantasy, and everything has to work so that the fantasy is unbroken. Designing traffic patterns to keep people moving is an art in itself.

Apartment/Condominium/Co-op Design

With more multiple-housing developments in every part of the country, this specialty presents major opportunities. Some interior designers do only apartment layouts; others do only lobbies and corridors. Still others are responsible for the social rooms, which include function rooms, social areas, televideo conference centers, computer rooms, office and secretarial areas, and athletic areas.

Aquarium Design

This specialty is not limited to aquatic parks. There are designers who do large aquarium design for homes, offices, and other businesses. There is a restaurant where one enters by walking over a sizable aquarium. Aquariums as a design element serve several purposes. Medical evidence suggests that gazing at an aquarium reduces blood pressure, and there is a social push toward using natural, earth-friendly materials in public spaces.

Art Consultant

Searching out existing art and contracting for the creation of art suitable to a specific interior environment is the function of the art consultant, who usually works for the client. They provide the background to support the art investment. The specialist must have an extensive knowledge of fine art disciplines as well as a practical and artistic understanding of interior design.

Art Dealing

Interior designers with an interest in fine art understand what people enjoy and will buy, they understand the space, and they also know how to place art properly. This is a major asset for an art dealer, because art sells best when it can be envisioned or placed in an interior.

Audiovisual Center Design

Television, computer, videocassette recorder, and stereo equipment provide entertainment and worldwide communication for residential and commercial use. They are often clustered in the same area or room. The technical requirements of these devices demand a knowledge of electronics, acoustics, and lighting disciplines.

Auditorium Design

This is a fascinating field, and very different from stage design. Acoustics and sight lines in theater design are vital and complex. Productions can be made or destroyed by very small design elements of the house.

Barrier-Free Design for the Physically Limited

New laws require that new commercial and public buildings and renovations to existing buildings make the space accessible to those in wheelchairs. Barrier-free design is increasingly desirable for all spaces. Probably more money has been invested in designing for the physically limited or orthopedically disabled than for any other group. Some interior designers specialize in reviewing products and buildings for this group to ensure that standards are met. This specialty is included in almost every project.

Bathroom Design

At one time a neglected and utilitarian room, the bathroom today joins the kitchen as a selling point for houses. Modern bathrooms may include spa-like environments with whirlpool baths, saunas, and hot tubs. Public restrooms and bathrooms for commercial spaces demand state-of-the-art detailing. A new consciousness of human factors has greatly improved aseptics, safety, and the adaptations needed to make the bathroom barrier-free. International bathing customs have their influence, bringing us the European fixtures, the Oriental soaking tub, saunas, and steam rooms. Environmental concerns have brought new products and codes.

Beauty and Barber Shop Design

Beauty and barber shops are often mixed-media salons. The designer may be asked to provide appropriate space for services such as waxing, facials, manicures, and cosmetology in addition to hair care. State regulations and requirements differ. Interior designers in the beauty field often work with or for suppliers, who may offer complete financing and turnkey projects.

CADD Specialist

A designer who is also expert at computer-assisted drafting and drawing is increasingly important today. Computers are instrumental in communicating with other design professionals. Designs created on CADD may be used by the client as a basis for in-house space management. CADD's accuracy and ability to make quick changes is invaluable. This former specialty is a basic tool of most design specialties.

Carpet and Rug Design

Who should know better how to design carpets and rugs than interior designers, who are responsible for a large volume of floorcovering sales. Interior designers working with textile specialists can develop the most suitable rugs for a given situation. Designing handwoven rugs is very different from designing for the technical demands of Axminster, Wilton, tufted, or woven machines. A designer must either study at a textile-intensive school, such as the Philadelphia Textile School, or work extensively in the carpet field.

Ceramic Tile Design

This field encompasses foreign and domestic sources as well as artist-made and mass-produced tiles. Ceramic tiles are used for high traffic, functional areas as well as decorative effect, including murals and sculptures.

Closet Design

Space is at a premium today, and closet space especially so. Around the country, businesses that do only closets are designing storage components and new ways to store almost every item.

Code Safety Design Law Specialist

This person keeps up-to-date information on building, fire, and safety codes in all states. The specialist designer may consult with other designers, contractors, manufacturers, and owners.

Color Consultation

Color and its effects on people is a recognized science with well-documented results. Color is the most noticed of all the design elements. This speciality is used by all the design disciplines as well as marketing firms, corporations, governments, and medical practices—anywhere encouraging specific reactions is desired.

Commercial Design

This specialty designs everything except residences. It includes retail, businesses, offices, laboratories, factories, medical facilities, and other commercial space. Most commercial designers specialize further. Within the specialty of design for medicine, there are several subspecialties.

Computer Office Design

Designing to accommodate computer use is much in demand. Office requirements of computers have changed dramatically since computers first emerged in the workplace. In some ways, the requirements are less rigorous. Specialists in designing offices to accommodate computers usually work for the computer companies, and may travel across the country explaining the requirements and conveniences of combining computer and staff functions.

Construction Supervision

Designers supervise, manage, and review the components of a project and advise on decision making. Interior designers are often hired to act as liaison between the contractor and client. Sometimes they are responsible for hiring other consultants and contractors.

Corporate Campus Design

The designer creates a total environment. The corporate campus promotes efficiency and expresses the mission of the company through design tailored to meet the specific needs of that company. Campuses can include administration buildings, training centers, manufacturing or production facilities and fitness centers. Some demand space that can be leased to support companies.

Corporate In-House Design

The staff interior designer for a corporation maintains its design identity. The designer may initiate and complete the design or hire design consultants on major design projects, as well as act as liaison between outside consultants and the firm.

Country Club Design

These spaces combine aspects of residential and commercial design. The buildings must conform to area regulations and codes for fire, safety, labor, and industry. They must encourage proprietary feelings among the membership but must also give the staff the tools to run programs with time and financial efficiency. Facilities may include indoor swimming pools, ball courts, gyms, locker rooms, restaurants, and areas for business meetings and socializing.

Dental Office Design

This is a highly engineered segment of the medical field; the design specialist must have an understanding of the mechanics as well as the antiseptic and medical aspects of the discipline. The dental profession has exerted the effort to develop business management techniques and to improve use of time to make dentistry more efficient and professional. Space design for dental offices is an integral part of the new dentistry.

Design for Children

Environment affects a child's behavior; there is a body of research indicating that what stimulates a child is not what stimulates an adult. Spaces for children must be adaptable, because children change and grow so rapidly. These spaces include every place a child might use: doctor's offices, libraries, schools, and retail spaces, not just bedrooms.

Design for In-Home Medical Care

At one time, patients with chronic, debilitating illnesses were confined to hospital wards, but the trend is toward in-home care. Not only do these patients enjoy the comforts of home, but there is also less risk of acquiring new infections while their immunities are low. This specialty means more than just installing a hospital bed. The residential space must be adapted to meet geriatric, orthopedic, or other medical requirements of both patient and caregivers.

Design for Vision and/or Hearing Impairments

Not every person sees or hears as well as the next. The number of people affected grows each year in proportion to the aging of the population. More than 60 percent of people in the workforce today have some hearing loss, and probably a much larger percentage have some vision impairment. People are becoming more aware of the problems. There is an increased knowledge of the issues and more technology available to resolve the problems. There are successful applications for every situation—from residences to theaters.

Display/Exhibit Design

Retailers, wholesalers, specialty shops, museums and all types of public spaces can use display and exhibit design to sell products as well as ideas. These displays may be permanent or built for travel. These exhibits must make an impact but also be easy to take down and set up.

Energy Conservation Design

An energy specialist advises on energy-efficient products and space planning for better use of energy. This may include solar design, adapting existing structures or developing new ones; or it may be simply finding new uses for traditional products and appropriate uses for new ones.

Ergonomic Design

Ergonomic design is the science that relates people to the way they use things. It is an engineering science based on the physical needs of the human body. Factors considered are the measurements of the human body, human sensory capacities, comfort, body functions, safety, and emotional satisfaction.

Facility Management

The person or department responsible for the physical management of the facility coordinates purchasing, repairs, and maintenance. Facility managers plan and act as liaison between the firm's executives and the consulting designers, architects, and engineers.

Factory/Production Consulting

This specialty includes traffic control and designing to improve safety and increase productivity. See Ergonomic Design.

Forensic Consulting

This specialty was created by the litigious times we live in. When a product is made or used incorrectly and results in injury or death, a forensic designer may be consulted by attorneys. In addition to expertise in ergonomics and product construction, the designer must also be familiar with court terminology and the correct way to testify. This field requires not only training but a special personality that holds up well in court.

Furniture Design
Interior design and industrial design must be blended for good product design. The interior designer knows where the furniture goes and how it is used; the industrial/furniture designer knows construction techniques.

Geriatric Design
As our society grays, design for the mature market gains in recognition as a specialty. Retirement centers, nursing homes, even condominiums are designed to meet the physical, psychological, and cultural needs of older people.

Graphic Design/Signage Graphics
These specialists can develop a corporate image or design graphics that define the space or movement of people through public-use facilities. More than standard interior design training is required. Designers with this specialty are able to not only create a corporate or institutional image but coordinate all of the elements that contribute to that image.

Greenhouse Design
At one time greenhouses were simply for plants. Now they are incorporated into residential and commercial spaces that also accommodate people. Depending on the climate, greenhouse design can involve controlling temperature, light, and humidity. Insulating elements and the design atmosphere are other factors. Manufacturers consult interior designers on the design of greenhouse components; some designers have made this their specialty.

Hard-Surface Flooring Design
Designing this flooring product demands a knowledge of color trends, as well as a working knowledge of the properties of wood, ceramics, marble, vinyl, and other appropriate materials.

Hardware Design
The work of interior and industrial designers enhances the functional and decorative effect of knobs, hinges, and handles—hardware for use in buildings and on furniture.

Health Club Design
Personal fitness became important in the eighties, and health clubs are not just places to exercise, but meeting spots for people with similar goals and interests. Athletic, aerobic, and recreational facilities of all sorts are proliferating. Keeping the facilities safe, convenient, and appropriate to their specific sports is involved enough that some designers have made it their specialty. It has some aspects in common with country club design.

Historic Preservation and Adaptive Re-use
This field demands technical and scientific knowledge. The research that determines the actual colors, materials, and wallcoverings attracts many designers. Adaptive re-use of older buildings—converting existing structures rather than razing them and building anew—can require integrating historic esthetics and modern functional requirements. Some areas offer substantial tax abatements for adaptive re-use.

Hospital Design
Today some areas in a hospital have such complex technical requirements that hospital designers with a particular specialty have international practices. Specialties proliferate. Some designers do only emergency rooms and intensive care units, others design patient and visitor areas, and some designers combine both. Insurance and legal requirements along with cost-effectiveness place demands and constraints on the design. It is highly unlikely that a specialist in hospital design would also work on a nursing home project; the demands are very different.

Hospitality Design
This field encompasses luxury spaces for community and celebration as well as functional accommodation. Designers may specialize in restaurant dining halls, training centers and convention spaces, guest rooms, lobbies, and corridors.

Interior Landscaping
Plants add a natural quality to even the most static environment. This field requires knowledge of landscaping and botany in order to place plants where they are suitable. It may include contracting to provide maintenance and design changes for seasonal updates and plant health. While greenhouses are primarily to keep plants healthy and growing, interior plantscaping is an increasingly important component of a building's atmosphere. Design factors include temperature, light, and humidity control.

Journalism
This is a way to expand the design field, making our work more understandable to people inside and outside the field. Designers can educate through columns and articles on design for newspapers and magazines, and recently, on television as well.

Kennel Design
In the competitive world of breeding pedigreed pets, space design for each species is a serious business. You must understand animals and their needs. In kennels, there are areas for grooming and training and food preparation and nutrition, as well as testing. Maintenance and health care are a prime concern.

Kitchen Design
Scientific and artistic detail go into the design and planning of components for residential and personal-use kitchens. The designer must have a complete knowledge of currently available products as well as the dietary requirements of the users.

Legal Office Design
Image, cost, and work efficiency have become important here. An environment that supports the legal professionals and the visiting clients and consultants provides visual and acoustical privacy. Law offices now incorporate highly technical equipment as well as areas for specialized personal interaction.

Library Design
Libraries are individual and specialized, catering to local needs. A library in a county seat will be different from one on Wall Street. Libraries need space planning and marketing, with special attention to lighting and acoustics. Many libraries have exhibit areas or function rooms. They are true multimedia environments, lending books, videocassettes, art, and music. Electrical demands

have increased greatly with the advent of computers, which are used for card catalogs, periodical indexes, and subject-dedicated databases.

Licensing
Many designers license their names to a product line. The designer can style or develop the product or merely endorse it.

Lighting Design
Lighting fixtures are a very important item in a room. Scale, structure, engineering, and a knowledge of the end use are critical components of good fixture design as well as the technical requirements and codes for specific projects.

Lighting Fixture Design
In any space, your eye goes to the windows and to the lighting fixtures. Scale, structure, engineering, and a knowledge of the end use are critical components of good fixture design.

Liturgical Design
Churches and synagogues are not just monuments, but living centers actively serving the community. Some offer recreation areas for children. These buildings are used for social events, theater productions, educational lectures, and community activities. Of course, each religion has its own design requirements; the designer must know and understand the liturgy.

Manufacturer In-House Design
Manufacturers have staff designers who work not on design but on merchandising. In order to promote sales many contract office furniture manufacturers offer interior design services at little or no cost to the end user. The practice grew rapidly throughout the 1980s and may eliminate design positions with local dealers.

Manufacturer Representation
This sales position is the link between manufacturer and interior designer. Some of the best manufacturers' representatives are former interior designers or dealers. They understand the product, they know how to sell it, and they appreciate what interior designers want. Within assigned territories, manufacturers' reps call on designers, providing catalogs, assisting in specification preparation, and writing purchase orders.

Marine Design
This specialty requires extensive knowledge of fire codes, marine standards and regulations, weights, and materials. Many products must be made specifically for marine use. Marine design encompasses all sizes of ships and boats, from working boats to cruise liners the size and complexity of small villages. The design demands range from stripped-down, where every inch must have more than one use, to extravagant, with swimming pools, shops, ballrooms, and health spas. The designer deals with physical, psychological, and ergonomic issues as well.

Marketing Specialist
This person develops and positions design firms with appropriate clients. Some designers are better at design work than selling, so the need for and value of this specialist is well recognized and compensated.

Medical Center Design

Hospitals, clinics, rehabilitative care centers, and nursing homes have requirements so specific and technologically complex that only a specialist could keep up with the constant changes in standards, codes, and equipment. The specialty includes emergency rooms, intensive care units, lobbies, and administrative support.

Medical Office Design

Every medical specialty requires special equipment as well as appropriate space planning, traffic patterns, and storage management. Today's specialties use such an intensive array of high-tech equipment that offices need total replanning every few years. A complete understanding of the medical procedures and equipment, legal aspects, codes, and aseptic demands is needed.

Modular Prefabricated Design

This area of the building industry is rapidly growing. It is cost effective to build standard components in a factory-controlled situation. A high level of quality, with skilled engineering, can be accomplished by prefabricated design. Understanding requirements of building and delivery is critical.

Model Home Furnishing

These firms do nothing but furnish model homes, renting or selling the components to contractors or developers for a specific period. The installations include all appointments, from table settings to towels for the bathroom—everything to create the impression that a real person lives there.

Mortuary Design

The funeral home must comfort and support people at an emotionally vulnerable time. There are presentation and financial aspects to consider as well as the appropriate physical support for heavy objects and space for behind-the-scenes management.

Mural Painting

Quite a few mural artists are interior designers with a fine arts background. They first paint a miniature for the client, then execute the full-size product on canvas or directly on the wall. This art form has become very prominent.

Museum Design

At one time only people with backgrounds in history or art history worked in museums. However, museums have many opportunities for interior designers to design exhibits, promotions, and community projects. Since preservation of artifacts is as important as the display, understanding the effects of humidity and lighting on artifacts is important. Interior designers may work directly for the museums or be employed by consulting firms that specialize in museum work.

Office Design

This ranges from the one-man at-home office to entire high-rise office buildings. This specialty requires a knowledge of high-tech equipment as well as an understanding of management and office production.

Park Design

Amusement parks, municipal, and other parks need safety, effective traffic patterns, management systems, and efficiency. Designers may be called on to develop unique signage, to design fixtures or the service areas: food service, restrooms, souvenir shops. Some designers work only on theme parks.

Passenger Train and Bus Design

This is another area where interior designers are much needed. Passenger trains and buses make up a major portion of our transportation system. These vehicles are constantly being improved so that they are safe and more comfortable and attractive. If public transportation is pleasurable, it will be used by more people.

Party and Ball Design

Designers organize and orchestrate parties and balls for corporations, charities, and other organizations. Entertainment and celebration requires appropriate atmosphere. It is not enough just to put people into a ballroom for so many hours; they want fantasies brought to life.

Photographic Set Design

This specialty works with manufacturers and advertising agencies to create settings designed to sell products. They maintain an inventory of props and backgrounds, spend weeks creating and building a set, then tear it down immediately after photographing it. Successful photographic set design requires an understanding of what photographs well and what does not, as well as what can be faked.

Plumbing Fixture Design

To design sinks, lavatories, bath tubs, and spas, the designer must have training and a special interest in sculpture. Sometimes the specialist will be asked to recolor or redesign an existing line, but more often, the project means creating new shapes.

Prison Design

State and local governments are turning to private companies for help in constructing prisons, which are then leased back to the government. Some organizations, such as Volunteers of America, actually operate the prisons. Prison design is a specialty in the midst of change. Social scientists suggest that new prisons should not just house prisoners but also rehabilitate them.

Product Design

Opportunities in the field of product design are as extensive as there are products. Designers can make vital contributions in helping manufacturers find and develop products that are wanted, function well, and suit the environments they will be used in. Many designers help develop building products. Every now and then you see a building product with style; the manufacturer probably hired an interior designer.

Product Display

Interior designers have traditionally designed store windows and product displays. Never has it been brought to so refined an art form as recently. This strong effort in merchandising often permits unlimited budgets, which encourage free range of ideas.

Product Evaluation

A large part of the income of certain designers comes from reviewing products for manufacturers to determine their practicality, design quality, and marketability. This is a sound investment for manufacturers.

Product Marketing
Interior designers are well qualified to assist in product design development, complementing the manufacturer's design staff. Consulting interior designers can help maintain a firm's position in the marketplace. Interior designers assist with marketing products by developing ways to use the product.

Professional or Promotional Organizations
Trade and professional organizations and product promotion organizations often hire interior designers as spokespersons or interpreters to build links between the product group and the designer or client. The designers' skill in organization and promotion can strengthen the organization. Designers understand the needs of the end user as well as the multitude of design disciplines involved in the manufacturing process.

Project Management
This can be as simple as handling interior design development for one's own firm or as complex as running a project under a turnkey proposition. It requires complete understanding of various crafts.

Psychiatric Care Facility Design
While many codes are the same as other medical facilities, the form of therapy determines the design response. Use, practicality, and ease of maintenance are prime concerns.

Public Relations
Interior designers with strong communications skills may choose to draw media attention to the work of other designers rather than to run a design practice of their own. Some act as liaison between manufacturer, designer, and end-user.

Purchasing
The designer may act as a purchasing agent for large companies, reviewing and testing products, then negotiating and ordering the furnishings.

Real Estate Development
A knowledge of space, its uses, and its potential for change has given many interior designers an edge in real estate sales and development. Some designers assist developers by restructuring and designing buildings for turnkey or development projects.

Real Estate Upgrading
Build a better home, please the client, and sell: These are the objectives in design upgrading for luxury development homes. Many experienced designers have moved into this specialty: There is opportunity for creative design and it pays very well.

Rendering
Rendering is a special art, requiring graphics, fine art, and design understanding. A good presentation is vital: Many design firms, even small ones, hire good renderers, either staff or freelance. Fees can run into the thousands of dollars.

Residential Design

At one time the most prevalent design specialty, residential design also can be the most lucrative. It requires a knowledge of human behavior within living spaces, an understanding of and ability to communicate with people, and the social respect of the client. Generally, people hire residential designers whose tastes and communications skills are similar to their own.

Restaurant Design

There is room for design in every restaurant, from the fast food stands in malls to local eateries to establishments for gracious dining. Knowledge of all design disciplines as well as food management is essential.

Restaurant Kitchen Design

This requires a knowledge of kitchen equipment and the know-how to adapt it to the preferences of individual restaurateurs. Kitchen specialists work as independents or for equipment suppliers. Kitchens for country clubs, educational facilities, and large commercial restaurants are typical projects.

Retail and Specialty Selling

Selling is part of every design practice. Some designers have found it more lucrative to own, manage, or work for retail and specialty stores. Designers are good salespeople, especially in design-related areas, because they understand how to use a product. The best salespeople are consultants who show clients how to use a given product. Interior designers may help develop a product mix for a specific store; this often means creating a design package to be sold by other people. It also can mean working with a group of artists to market their work.

Retail Store Design

This popular specialty requires skill in image development, marketing, traffic patterns, and security and concern for financial return on space. Custom fixturing is often part of the design. The designer may be customizing local spaces for national chains or working with individual store owners.

Security Systems Design

Everyone cares about security, either for personal safety or theft prevention. Safety and security have also become increasingly vital to all spaces, from commercial to residential.

Set Design

Many interior designers started in set design; others expanded their practices to include set design. Although it is a unionized profession, there are still some opportunities. Set design for movies, theater, dance, and opera is a different world. You build for show, not to last. You design everything to be seen from a certain perspective. The size and design of the theater—whether it is a proscenium or a theater-in-the-round—affects the placement of furniture and props. The director's vision of the production is critical to the choice of furnishings.

Shop-At-Home Services

If you can show the client a product sample in his or her space, very often you can sell it. There are extremely successful firms that specialize in shop-at-home service. Some stock a van or truck with a coordinated line of pictures, accessories, pillows and draperies. They distribute their products to representatives or franchise owners.

Shopping Mall Design

This is large-scale marketing. Each store in a mall must contribute to the total mall concept, which ranges from discount to luxury. Each mall promotes a different lifestyle or environment. Designers may work directly for the mall owners to coordinate all mall activities and designs. They work with individual retailers and also in the common areas.

Showroom Design

In Manhattan, Rome, Paris, London, and every small city in the country, showroom designs and presentations account for an amazingly high dollar figure. The primary job of the showroom is to sell a product. Whether the showroom is beautiful is a question of taste, but whether it works and produces can be measured. Specialists in this field most often work in larger cities.

Spaceship and Rocket Design

This is the ultimate challenge in ergonomic design—every inch must count. Many consumer products have been developed as a result of studies done for spaceship design.

Solar Design

Design for solar buildings is not just solar collection but a matter of coordinating solar and environmental concerns with human needs. Energy efficiency, sun control, sunlight-resistant materials, and insulation are key.

Stadium and Arena Design

While architects and engineers are most often involved with shaping the space, interior designers are consulted on public areas, service areas, and even choice of seating. It has aspects in common with theater and store design. Safety and security are also prime concerns.

Storage Design

Space is at a premium today, making planned storage an essential design element. Storage specialists catalog the clients' storables, then plan for growth. Custom storage can range from making tiny drawers to accommodate contact lenses to developing automated filing areas for offices. Good storage means placing things in convenient locations near where they will be used and putting lesser-used items in less accessible places.

Tabletop Display Design

Restaurants and department and specialty stores use tabletop display to sell food and tabletop products. Clients today expect drama and practicality.

Teleconference Center Design

Teleconference centers exist not only in large corporations but also in community centers and occasionally in apartment complexes. This discipline may specify the shape of the room, lighting, choice and placement of furnishings, and even the teleconference equipment. Sight lines, light and sound control, and audibility are prime concerns.

Tenant Development Services

Interior designers work with landlords and developers to coordinate interior spaces for homes, apartments, and commercial offices. They may devise color schemes and layouts or may only ensure that the work of other designers coordinates with what exists in the building.

Textile Design

Interior designers with special knowledge of textiles design rugs, fabrics, and textile wallcoverings. This combined discipline creates products that are appropriate, distinctive, and easy to use.

Training Center Design

Education takes place in more places than schools and colleges. Corporate training centers are found in office buildings; smaller firms use hotel meeting rooms or convention centers. Special demands include adaptable lighting, accommodating audiovisual equipment, and attention to acoustics and sight lines.

Transit Center Design

Airports and train and bus terminals have become almost total living environments for some people. Interior designers are called on to entertain people, enhance people-movement, and accommodate their needs with airport shops, small conference areas, VIP clubs, and cocktail lounges. There is not much one cannot do in transit centers these days, from banking to seeing a podiatrist to hiring a secretary. Transit centers have become like cities in the range of services offered for the daily commuter as well as the person who may have a layover of many hours. Chicago's O'Hare airport has a laser show. Some centers offer college course; others have educational displays. There is usually a church or chapel.

Turnkey Services

A turnkey design service does everything from securing the property, designing and building the facility, to installing furnishings and finishing to the finest detail. All the client needs to do is turn the key and open the door.

Underground Habitation

Because the constant temperature underground is 55 degrees Fahrenheit, underground space has become a practical and appropriate area for living and working. Computer centers, for example, are located underground. This field is relatively underdeveloped.

Vacation Home Design

Second homes are big business, but they often must be designed as turnkey projects because the clients are involved elsewhere. The vacation house requires accommodating the needs of leisure living.

Wallcovering Design

Many interior designers design wallcoverings, drawing on their expertise with color, pattern direction, and scale. The field demands production and design expertise as well as an understanding of current trends.

Wall Finishes

Marbling, fresco, and textured finishes—some of which have not been seen for centuries—are in demand. This specialty is no longer limited to historic restoration work; commercial and residential clients also request novel wall finishes.

Window Treatment Design

Draperies, shades, louver drapes, valances, cornices, and a broad spectrum of other treatments make up this specialty. Insulation, ventilation, light control, and energy conservation are all part of today's window treatment design.

FINDING YOUR PLACE

With a plan, effort, and research, anyone has a reasonable chance to find his or her career niche—whether that means general practice or specialized work, or whether it means working independently or in a firm.

Using this book, you will learn virtually everything you need to know to design your successful independent career. Personally, I have a bias about starting to work independently too soon: It can be suicidal, and for that reason I strongly discourage it.

If you want to give yourself the best chance for success in your career, find someone whose work you admire. Find yourself a mentor and learn everything you can from that person. That usually means going into an established firm. But before you invest several years of your life in a firm, invest some time in learning as much as you can about the firm and its principals. Chances are that as a new member of the company, you are not going to be able to change it to suit yourself; you will have to work their way.

Find out exactly what kind of work the firm does. Look at its work in trade and design press magazines and books. Talk to their clients, ask staff or contractors who have worked with the firm about the projects they have worked on. And approach the firm directly. You do not have to say why you are interested in the firm; you can say merely that you'd like the opportunity to see more of their work because you admire it. Most design firms are proud of their work and will be happy to show and tell you about their projects. Visiting their installations will tell you quite a lot about the quality of the firm.

Find out as much as you can about the principals within the company—especially the person you've identified as the one you'd like to have as your mentor. Know their education and business backgrounds. Be familiar with their career histories: Where did they start, and how long has it taken them to reach their present status? That information may rest with former employers, clients, and other designers.

An interior design firm works as a team. In selecting a new job relationship, as in choosing a marriage partner, it is important to have a sense of how well the team works. You're going to spend a lot of time with these people and you're going to share many different experiences and pressures. You want to learn as much as you can to ensure that you will be a complementary member of the team.

If you put the same care into planning your future that you put into your interior designs, it is possible to have what you want from your career. No one can expect to have the perfect job handed on a platter. Instead, plan for, plot, and go after the job you want and really should have. Do it in a professional manner and you will find your place. You will probably also be successful.

After one of my lectures, a senior student at the Philadelphia Textile School came to me for advice on how to get a job in textiles arts in her home state of Colorado. She had found that most of the textile design positions were in the northeastern United States around New York and Philadelphia. I asked what she meant by no jobs. Wasn't there even one company?

Yes, she admitted, there was one specializing in fabrics for men's and women's ready-to-wear clothing, but she didn't know much about them other than that they had a large factory, had been in the same location a number of years, and had said they had no openings when she asked.

Her father was in insurance and I pointed out that he would know a lot of people in the community and could find out about the major people in the firm and their educational and work backgrounds. "You want to know about their families," I counseled, "whether they live within the community or whether they commute from a distance—anything you can find out about how these people relate to this company."

I suggested she use her Saturdays and free days to visit apparel speciality stores and department stores in big cities of neighboring states to research this firm. She could talk to the buyers about how they felt about the fabrics made by that particular textile company. She should create an outline of appropriate questions for every buyer: whether they liked the quality, which colors sold better, which year the line was best. It would take about six months to accumulate the information she needed to put into a professional presentation.

After this was completed, I suggested that she test the presentation, polish it, refine it, and ask her professors to review it. Then, at my urging, she called the president of the firm when she went home for Christmas vacation. She told him she had spent six months doing research on his company, and then she asked for an appointment to review it with him. She got the appointment. He was surprised at her interest in his firm, and he was intrigued by some of the comments she brought him, which differed from what he had heard from his staff and marketing people. It is hard to know just what impressed him most, but the main thing is that he was impressed by the attention she had given his company. She told him of her textile arts training and that she intended to move back to Colorado and would like to work in his company.

Her tangible interest in his firm convinced the president that he wanted her to work with them. He didn't know what job he was going to give her, but she was hired. He told her to come back in June and he would have something for her then.

MEASURES OF SUCCESS

How is success measured in the interior design profession? Is a successful interior designer one whose name appears frequently in newspaper columns and in the popular design press? Or is a successful designer one who has achieved a reliable, steady income and some continuing creative satisfaction?

Public success and personal satisfaction go hand in hand. You do not have to be an Elsie de Wolfe or a Syrie Maugham to be successful today, because there are opportunities and alternatives open to you that could never have existed when these two grande dames of the industry started their businesses on chutzpah, contacts, and not much else.

The truth is that many designers we see as successful take success for granted. In researching *Profitable Career Options for Designers* (Kobro Publishing Company, 1985), I discovered that successful people are always looking ahead to the next project or projects and that their favorite project is the one they are working on at the moment.

Being an interior designer today means making choices, developing an area of expertise, and being receptive to change. This is the mentality of successful designers. They are always looking for ways to improve. None of us should say, "There is only one correct solution and it is mine." We should go out and find two or three or even a hundred ways of approaching a problem, and use the one we feel best answers the client's needs.

Chapter Two

STARTING A BUSINESS

Many of us enjoy expanding our present businesses or creating new businesses, putting ideas together and making them work. This compulsion to forever do something new can be a strength, but can also distract us from what should be our main focus: our interior design practice. Each year in our country there are many new businesses starting, and a number are very successful. This has become the period of the entrepreneur and small business. Still, many have failed.

INITIAL CONSIDERATIONS

Before starting your own business, look first at how it affects you. If you have been working for a company, you may have job tenure, a regular paycheck, paid holidays and vacation, sick leave, insurance plans, and the knowledge that when you are finished work each day you can leave it behind—it is ultimately someone else's responsibility. These benefits are not a part of a new business.

The idea of starting your own firm is exciting, but there is no point in starting it if you do not intend to make it a success. That takes an investment in years of time and effort. To start a business you will need to devote the first seven or eight years to the business, and running it well will probably require 80- to 120-hour work weeks. Is this a sacrifice you are willing to make? What about your personal needs? Will they mesh with the obligations entailed in starting a business? After all, you are not establishing just a job, but a lifestyle. Can you make this intense a commitment? If you are planning to start a primary personal relationship or a family, this may not be the best time in your life to start a business.

Are you prepared to accept the responsibility of managing a business? A designer I know started a wonderful art gallery because his mother-in-law wanted something to do. This worked beautifully as long as the mother-in-law stayed interested. But after about two years the fun wore off for her—and the designer was stuck with a gallery that had to be kept open eight to ten hours a day and required a minimum of two people to staff. If you are considering investing in a business venture for a child or relative, give the venture a careful review. Is the relative committed to the project on a long-term basis? If not, would you be able to hire staffing to continue it?

Personal Traits

Do you have the right personality to start a business? It takes a certain type of person to succeed in business. The following is a list of questions to ask yourself before starting your own business:

1. *Are you in good health?* You need to be in good shape to endure the physical and emotional rigors of starting a business.

2. *Do you really have all the energy that it takes to make this project succeed?* Almost all people who succeed in their own businesses have boundless physical energy. If your physical energy is limited, perhaps you should consider teaming with another professional who can carry part of the burden.

3. *Are you a self-starter?* Are you the type of person who gets things done and starts projects on your own initiative? In your own business you will have to act without anybody else pushing you or reminding you. ✓

4. *Do you enjoy other people?* Do you really like all kinds of people? You will find yourself working with a variety of professions and personality types—laborers, persons with limited education, high-level professionals, and eccentrics. ✓

5. *Are you a leader?* Your staff will be following your cues. You must be someone that people are ready to follow. ✓

6. *Are you ready for the responsibilities of a business?* Do you understand exactly what it entails? Before deciding to start your own business, investigate a number of other businesses to get a real knowledge of what you are facing.

7. *Are you a good worker?* Are you the kind of person who does not mind what it takes to get a job done, you will keep working as long and as hard as is necessary to complete a project well? Running your own business will demand your complete dedication. ✓

8. *Are you well-organized?* Interior design is a field that requires high organizational abilities. ✓

9. *Are you a good decision maker?* Do you enjoy making decisions? You will need to be ready to make decisions quickly and accurately without the fear of failure.

10. *Do people have confidence in you?* Have you built a rapport with the people who have worked with you? For people to do business with you, they must have confidence that if they give you the job, it will get done. ✓

11. *How committed are you to running your own business?* Too many designers start in business with the idea that it will be fun for a while. If that is your attitude, probably you should not consider starting in business. To develop a business always takes much longer and requires more energy than you might imagine. ✓

12. *Do you have the excitement that it takes to carry this through?* Your enthusiasm will inspire your staff to do its best. Are you turned on about the business and ready to handle whatever comes up? ✓

13. *Are you a good communicator?* You must be able to express yourself clearly and to talk with others at all levels; this is the only way to share ideas and work together. ✓

14. *Do you know what you are doing?* Do you really know the interior design field or at least the specialty that you are selecting? It is much cheaper to learn in someone else's studio than to do it yourself. You must understand the field on a professional level. You are the last word; therefore, you must know everything about the work that you are going to be doing, or where to get the answers. Know your field well before you start in business.

15. *Have you had any business training?* You have no idea how much you need to learn until you begin a business. Spend some time reading and learning about any unfamiliar business processes. Don't even consider starting your own business until you've researched the business end of it. ✓

What other problems can you foresee in starting your own business? What do you expect to get out of this business? List what you consider to be the assets and the benefits of starting the business.

PLANNING AHEAD

A successful business starts with a good plan. Too many designers enter in business impulsively, without a plan. In today's business climate, a business without a good basic plan is not likely to succeed.

First, prepare an action plan. It should cover when you expect to start; where you want your business to be located; what you expect your profit plan to be; what areas of business you expect to make money from; and how you will charge—by fees, by markup, or by hourly rates (see pages 205–10). Every step of basic business planning (see Chapter 3) also applies.

Also prepare a financial plan. Determine just how much money will be needed. Further on in the book there are details of these business requirements.

Before you start your company or venture, make sure that you have your clients lined up. There is no point in starting a design business, or any other kind of business, without a good client base.

Review your present client load to see which clients you feel would come with you to a new business. It usually takes several years to develop a good client base. There is no point starting in business without a list of clients because it is difficult and expensive to go out and find that first client. If you have your clients and sources developed ahead of time, you automatically decrease the period it takes to start turning a profit.

People are your biggest asset, if you can put together the right people. You may make a plan with a particular person in mind and then find that person may not be available. It is not realistic to expect someone to work for you unless you can offer the individual something that really holds his or her interest.

Make sure that there really is a market out there. Sometimes the fact that no one else is offering a service means that there is no market for the service. When you have a lot of other competitors, this may mean that there's a tremendous market for your service, which you can top if you can find a better way of selling to that market.

Do you know where your customers live? Are you in the correct geographic area? Interior designers work in very wide areas; however, it is most effective to work in an area that supports you. You can travel for a portion of your jobs, but it is usually too expensive to travel for every job.

Do you have the ability to produce the products or items? Many businesses in the design field start with great ideas but have inadequate staff or production capabilities. There is no point in selling something that can't be delivered. Plan in advance where your materials will come from and how your products will be manufactured. Having the ability to produce a few dozen items is not of much value if you need to sell thousands to make the business profitable.

Write a list of required resources—manufacturers, showrooms, dealers, contractors—and spend time developing a good rapport with them. Make sure that your resources get to know you and the quality of your work. Usually your resources will be sources you have used in the past—people you know think well of your design work.

All business ventures require money. Try to have more money than you need; you always will use more than you expect. Look for and find a resource for three to four times the amount of money that you think you will need. Too many businesses fail because they don't have enough capital. It is easier to find these funds before you start a business than it is when you are actually committed.

If you have more money than you need, it is easy to pay back the loan or keep the overage in a savings account or interest-bearing fund in the interim and draw from it as needed. Paying that bit of extra interest is an inexpensive insurance toward your project's success. It is very easy to borrow for building and equipment, but difficult for "soft costs" such as salaries, staffing costs, advertising, and other day-to-day expenses.

How much money have you saved? How much of your own funds are you ready to invest? Unfortunately, there are few resources for financing a small business. Usually you will need to use your own funds or have someone assisting you. Most design firms need higher levels of financing.

If you are not using your own money, you may have to take on a partner or develop other types of obligations. If you need money and have to take in a partner, discuss with your attorneys ways of accepting either stockholders or partners. When you establish which way you will be going, build into your plans ways to adjust or change the agreement. In almost every instance, as a business develops it becomes necessary to change the structure. Can yours be changed? Your attorney and your accountant can advise you on this.

Have you figured into your financial projection the amount of income you expect during these start-up years? What salary will you require? Can you live on less than what you have been making in order to permit your business to progress? Talk to your bankers and be sure that they understand where you are going. Ask them to specify what borrowing ability you can obtain. Specifically, ask them about various loans such as long-term loans, short-term loans, lines of credit, and individual project borrowing.

After determining how much money you need to start your business (which is stated in various parts of this book), you also need to consider how much credit is available from your suppliers—what terms they will offer you. Also, determine what type of credit terms you are going to be able to work out with your potential clients. Often interior designers can get retainers and deposits on items, and can carry certain portions of their business. But it is foolhardy to think that you can carry it all. Understand and outline your anticipated financial condition, both on accounts receivable and accounts payable.

How long will it take to make the venture work? Can you take that time from your other endeavors? If you acquire sufficient business to keep you busy thirty or forty hours a week, and your time sells for $75 to $100 an hour, the new venture must be very good for you to afford to pursue it. All business takes time, usually three to five times what you would estimate.

The question is not only how long it takes to get started, but also how long it takes to get established. New clients and projects don't just walk in the door; they must be cultivated, which requires continuing effort. As you do your break-even financial analysis, do an analysis of the time required and see how that compares to the time you're really willing to spend.

A break-even analysis is a valuable test to make on your business venture. It determines whether it is worth investing a stated amount of money and time in this project in order to reach a certain level of profit. For a new business, you should prepare a one-through-five-year break-even analysis (see pages 295–97). An accountant or a business consultant can help you prepare one.

Almost any new business venture or project will take three to five years to get started. The initial planning requires a considerable amount of work, but it is nothing compared to the work of actually running a business. Time spent planning now is inexpensive—and is absolutely essential in the total process of starting a business. The plan should include several test points and stop-and-go points. List certain levels at which to reevaluate your plan, deciding whether to forge ahead, stop, or veer off into a new direction.

ADVANTAGES AND DISADVANTAGES

There are a number of advantages to running your own business.

1. You have complete control. You have the right to make the decisions. Therefore you can direct the activities and the design direction of the business.

2. You have complete freedom to be as creative as you want. You can do things your own way.

3. You determine how great the profits will be. You can make as much money as you like, depending upon your ability, talents, ideas, and energies.

4. You have the ultimate job security. You can't be fired. If you do not bring in business, you are not going to have a company. Still, you cannot be forced to retire.

5. There is great satisfaction in running a successful business. Since it is your business, you can justifiably feel proud in taking all the credit.

Starting your own business also has some large disadvantages.

1. Running the business will demand long hours. Very few businesses run on a nine-to-five basis. Most independent designers work twelve, fifteen, sixteen hours per day. Often you will have to perform tasks that you would have never been asked to handle as an employee. When the job must be done, you are many times the person left to do it.

2. There is the risk you will lose your investment. If you make money it is yours, but if you lose it, all your personal assets could be in jeopardy.

3. Your income will fluctuate with the success of the business. In the first years there is often a greater fluctuation than in later years; however, this is one of the risks of a small business. Your employees get paid, your suppliers get paid—and you get what is left.

4. The responsibility for the business is all yours. If something goes wrong, you are responsible.

5. All of the pressures are basically yours to bear. You must please all your clients. You must meet all your credit obligations, tax and insurance demands, and the payroll. This has to be done on a regular basis; not just when you feel like it.

6. There are many federal, state, and local laws you must abide by, as well as all kinds of stipulations applied by your insurance companies. It is amazing how many regulations there are to restrict business activities—and many are very expensive. It is wise to review your objectives with both your attorney and your accountant before you start your business.

GETTING FEEDBACK

Find yourself several advisors who will work with you on this project and who will continue to be your advisors throughout your business career. You especially need a good accountant and a good attorney, as well as an insurance advisor and other consultants who will work on design projects when needed (see pages 98–105). Be sure that you have these people lined up before starting your new venture. Confidentiality is important in starting a new business, so you may need to look outside your community for consultants if you cannot find people with whom you have developed a long-term rapport.

Business Consultant. Once you have prepared your plans, find a good business consultant—someone who is familiar with the interior design field—and see if he or she can find anything wrong with them.

Accountant. Ask your accountant to prepare a financial projection (see Chapter 3) and a break-even analysis. His thoughts may be different than those of a business consultant, as the two view business from different perspectives. You need to compare both points of view.

Financial Advisor. The financial aspects of the venture should be reviewed by a financial advisor. This should be someone other than your accountant or your attorney. The financial advisor's job is to really look at the financial development of your project, taking into consideration the resources of money that are available to you and your overall company potential.

Lawyer. An attorney will tell you whether you are putting your existing business or personal assets in undue jeopardy.

Insurance Advisor. This person will check that you can properly cover your major risks with insurance. For example, a designer was interested in restoring downtown properties, but found she could not purchase any kind of insurance on the project during construction or until the buildings were actually occupied. Because the restoration project would take two years in an underpoliced neighborhood, she and her insurance advisor decided it was much too heavy a risk.

Designer. Try your idea out on another designer or experienced person in your field whom you can trust; someone with perhaps more experience who is in a noncompetitive situation. We test every venture we plan with a few designer advisors before going any further. It is often surprising and exciting what additions or revisions they suggest. They are usually good at helping to build and mold a project.

Consultants. Talk with other people in businesses that are similar to yours and see what you can learn from them. What can you learn from their successes or failures? Develop for yourself a list of consultants and people that you can call on and depend upon.

BUYING AN EXISTING BUSINESS

Is it worth buying a business that someone has started? Very often it is, because the business has an established clientele. If you can work in the business for a while, you can get an intimate knowledge of the condition of the firm and whether the practice is appropriate for you. Although it is more common for a design firm to be dissolved rather than sold on the retirement or death of its owners, many interior design businesses are being sold and can be valuable to the young designer.

It is a sound idea to ease into the business by working with the firm and developing a rapport with the clients as well as the sources before committing to buying an established firm. There is one strong benefit: a structure is already established.

However, do not shortchange yourself. Although the practice is established, you will need the same business plan as you would if you were starting your own business. There are certain advantages in taking over an existing business, but there are also areas where the business could be strengthened or revised to take into account your own skills and weaknesses. The firm may need updating to present-day standards. You probably will want to shift some of the priorities. Talk with your legal and financial advisors to determine the best buy-out plan for this business.

Advantages

The following are some of the advantages to buying an existing business.

1. *An established business has a greater potential for success.* The location of the business has been preselected; people know about it, and they are inclined to go there. There are years of advance marketing that you will not have to do. If the business has been profitable, it will be much easier for you to continue to make a profit.

2. *The amount of planning that would be necessary to start in business has been lessened.* Therefore you can make your first sale that much sooner.

3. *Usually the clientele is already established.* If proper introductions are made, you can continue with them and then start to build your own clientele.

4. *There may be some inventory there to get you started.* Office equipment and supplies are in place; these are items you do not have to buy and set up before making your first sale.

5. *Financing is usually easier to procure for the purchase of an existing business than for starting a new business.* Often it can be prearranged with the previous buyer. An exact figure is far easier to establish.

6. *You may be buying a business at a bargain price.* The sellers may need to sell. They may want to see their business continue and thus be willing to work with you and help set up the situation to your advantage.

7. *You can call on the experience of a prior owner.* Even if you are not in complete agreement with the previous owner, at least you have a point of reference to check against. It is easier than doing it yourself.

8. *A lot of the original hard work of setting up has been eliminated.* Not that there is no work to be done or adjustments to be made, but these can be handled gradually as you have time and money available. You do not have to do everything at once.

9. *Often there is a group of experienced employees; you do not have to train them all.* If there are people you can work with, you begin with a tremendous advantage.

10. *There are many past records available, in business and in clients, that can help you build and market for future business.* You will know what clients have used before and therefore be better able to serve them than if you moved into an area with no records or no client background.

Disadvantages

There are also some clear disadvantages.

1. *If the business was poorly managed, the management problems can carry over into your business.*

2. *If the employees who are working for the company are not good, they can get in your way.* Sometimes you are better off not to have any employees than to have badly trained employees. Consider this and your obligations to the employees before committing to purchasing this business.

3. *Many policies established by the previous owners may no longer be appropriate and may be difficult to change—both with clients and employees.* Review these standards. (One reason it is wise to work in a firm for a period of time before determining whether you should buy is to get an idea of just what exists there.)

4. *Much of the inventory might not be appropriate to current-day sales.* While you may be able to sell off some of it for instant capital, you will find that a lot of inventory that people have in stock is just not currently saleable.

5. *You may be short of money for extending and developing the business if you put all of your monies into buying the business.*

6. *The location and the image of the firm may not be appropriate for your intended practice.* If this is the case, it is probably better to start your own

business. But if the existing business has a blend of styling and background that relates to yours, then it could be very worthwhile.

How can you find out about businesses that are available?

▶ They are often listed in <u>design magazines or in classified display ads.</u>

▶ Sometimes <u>realtors</u> will know of one in a given area.

▶ <u>Brokers who deal only with businesses</u> have many of them listed.

▶ The <u>Chamber of Commerce</u> will often have listings of businesses for sale.

▶ <u>Trade sources usually are our best resource.</u> The people a business buys from and works with usually know the position of the business and its quality.

▶ Professionals—accountants, attorneys, bankers—can be of help in introducing you to businesses, but often they do not know the details or the background that trade sources and other designers would have.

▶ <u>Other designers</u> usually know of people who face a problem, who have decided to retire, or who for some reason want to get out of business. If you start here, <u>it is usually best to use other professionals to review the business before considering a purchase.</u>

Evaluating an Existing Business

Buying an existing business is not only an excellent way to start in business, it is also an excellent way to expand one's business. More and more designers are buying up other practices. <u>The most efficient way to evaluate an existing business is to work there for a time to test its health and suitability to your goals.</u>

Before making an offer, investigate whether the business is a good one to buy. First of all, find out as much as you can about it. Visit with people who work there. Talk to the owners of the firm and find out the names of their suppliers. When you learn their resources, <u>talk to the resources to learn what kind of a company the firm has been and what size volume it does.</u> Very often sales reps will give you a lot of this information, although since it is on an unofficial basis, it must be considered that way. Sometimes it does give us leads as to the direction and the success of a business.

<u>Visit some of the projects that the firm has done and consider whether you would be proud to associate your name with this type of work.</u>

<u>Have the company evaluated by other people in the field. Is the owner's asking price reasonable?</u> It is usually best to have several people review this. Although the <u>opinions of accountants, lawyers, and other professionals are worthwhile, you should get an evaluation from someone in the design field who can look at the business objectively.</u>

<u>Ask to see the books for at least the last five years</u> so that you have a basis for judgment about the firm. A design firm cannot be judged on just two years of work, because the field is much too changeable. <u>Have your accountant look at the financial statements and the general history of the company.</u> Also, find a good <u>financial consultant</u> in the interior design field to give you an interview. If possible, talk to some of the firm's <u>clients;</u> find out what kind of work they do and how they would feel about the business continuing.

There are many ways of doing this type of investigation and it has to be altered according to the status of the current business. Is it a situation where everyone knows the business is for sale, or is it more confidential? Either way, do a thorough investigation.

<u>*Determining a Firm's Dollar Value.*</u> There are many different formulas for estimating the dollar value of a company. You need to determine the floor and ceiling values so you can establish the range for negotiation.

The floor value of a design firm is the amount of cash that would be required to establish a comparable design firm, starting from scratch. To arrive at this figure, you should analyze the basic costs involved in starting and running a business.

1. *Initial Fees.* Calculate the fees you would need to pay in the start-up years (legal and accounting, for example).

2. *Physical Property.* An existing business has already paid for the facility, leasehold, and equipment. You should consider the time and money you would need to find and establish a new space.

3. *The Cost of Establishing a Business.* Try to determine what the cost of starting the business and the amount of money required to fund it up to this point might have been. This would include covering the many losses that are usually incurred in the start-up years. This final cash figure could be considerable since it generally takes a while for a design firm to become profitable. Usually when you take over a firm, it is profitable from day one.

4. *Employee Training.* Training employees to work effectively as a group is a large financial investment. You will save considerably by starting out with a trained team ready to produce.

5. *Any Promotion or Advertising Efforts Already Developed.* Generally, through promotion and advertising, the positioning of the firm has been established.

The ceiling value of a firm takes into account the firm's history and its potential for becoming more valuable than its present worth. To determine ceiling value research the following:

1. *Profits.* What is the firm's level of profits? Does the firm have the ability to continue at this level? While the financial sheet of a service organization is generally easy to analyze, it is often difficult to determine the profitability factor and the cash flow analysis.

2. *Good Will.* Good will that can be transferred from an old ownership to a new one is a major factor in establishing a high ceiling value for a firm. However, the value of good will has to be determined on an individual basis. Generally, design businesses are highly personalized and the owners are very involved in every part of the design service. If the owner is no longer there, how much of the good will of the firm will evaporate? Is the owner going to continue with the company, or is the owner willing to sign a noncompetitive agreement?

3. *The Client Base.* A firm's client base and the continuing projects you will inherit greatly influence the ceiling value. Most important is the ability of this firm to sustain its client base. Are the clients dedicated to the design firm and willing to continue using the firm through the next ownership?

4. *The Internal Self-Sustaining Structure.* Is the management structured and well designed to continue into a new ownership?

5. *Location.* A firm's location plays a major role in establishing its ceiling value. For example, if a business is located in a progressive area or one with a pleasant climate, these factors make the firm significantly more valuable than a business located in a less desirable area.

6. *Staff.* What are the general skills of the employees? In design businesses, there are not always a lot of hard assets such as buildings and equipment. In a design business which offers purely professional service, the assets are represented in the fees of services rendered. The inventory is, in essence, the staff and the price that is charged for their design services.

7. *Special Information.* Trade names, copyrights, patents, and other information including customer lists and mailing lists are assets you should consider in determining a firm's ceiling value.

The return expected from the investment of capital, taking into account changing economic conditions, is a determinant in calculating the ceiling value of a business. Buyers will normally pay a multiplier of approximately five times the firm's pretax income, which would be the firm's annual profits plus the salary of the owner. For example, if a company's profits per year are $100,000, and the owner draws a $75,000 salary, the pretax income would be $175,000. The firm's ceiling value would be $875,000, or five times $175,000. In determining the firm's pretax income, be sure to factor in any excessive travel and entertainment expenses and other fringe benefits. For example, if the owner received an additional thirty percent of his salary in the form of special perks, this would raise the value considerably.

There are three basic ways of evaluating a purchase. One is through the adjusted net worth. The second is multiplying the annual billings by a multiplier of .5. The third is multiplying the pretax income by five.

In the purchase or sale of a business, the buyer and seller usually have conflicting interests. For example, it is usually to the advantage of a seller of a corporate business to sell the stock, whereas it is usually to the advantage of the buyer to buy the assets. There are various provisions in the IRS code that, to a considerable extent, provide the seller of corporate assets with the tax advantages of a corporate stock sale and also provide the buyer of a corporation with the advantages of an asset purchase. Because the requirements of these code sections must be strictly adhered to in order to qualify for the benefits, it is imperative that you discuss the contemplated transaction with your accountant and lawyer *before* you enter into any negotiations.

SELECTING THE RIGHT FORM OF OWNERSHIP FOR YOU

There are basically three forms of business ownership: the sole proprietorship, the partnership, and the corporation. There are advantages and disadvantages to each form of ownership; you should discuss them with your accountant and attorney before deciding. Of course, the form can be changed if circumstances suggest such a move.

Sole Proprietorship

A sole proprietorship is the simplest form of ownership and the easiest to establish. An individual begins a firm and is automatically a sole proprietor. All profits earned by the business belong to the owner, who also bears all losses. The owner has total authority over the business operation. There are few legal restrictions with the sole proprietorship except for the general civil and criminal laws, which apply to all forms of businesses.

If you are a person who likes to take charge, it is a very attractive form of ownership.

Advantages. There are many advantages to a sole proprietorship. You are the boss. You have complete control over the size of the business and its direction. You can stop and start the business as you choose. You can simply make a decision and go from there. If you are looking for a situation where you have maximum control and minimal government red tape, sole proprietorship may be your best choice.

A sole proprietorship is the easiest type of business to form legally, which also makes it the least expensive. You do not have the expense of setting up a corporation, and bookkeeping to meet government regulations is less expensive.

You keep all the profits. You can withdraw them for your personal use, consistent with business requirements or contractual obligations; it is your money.

A sole proprietorship, as an entity, does not pay income taxes; rather, the owner reports the gain or loss on his or her individual income tax return (whether filed singly or jointly with a spouse).

Disadvantages. While a sole proprietorship offers enormous freedom, with that freedom comes great responsibility and risk. One of the main disadvantages of a sole proprietorship is that you are totally responsible for everything that happens. In the event that you fail, your personal assets could be claimed by creditors. This may include your home, your automobile, and your savings. Unlimited liability is probably the worst feature of this type of business.

The owner must come up with the total capital that is required for the business. The amount of capital you are able to raise is limited by what you yourself have or are able to borrow. In a partnership or a corporation you can draw on the resources of other people.

Because you have no co-owner to share the trials and tribulations of operating a business, you need to be the kind of person who is capable—and willing—to do everything.

A sole proprietorship may find it difficult to attract high-quality employees because there may not appear to be as promising a future. However, an agreement might be made to arrange for an orderly transfer of part or all of the business under specified conditions. This would provide a greater incentive for top employees to join you.

Partnership

A partnership is an association of two or more persons, formed to operate a business for profit. Although a formal agreement is not legally required for partners, I would insist that a legal document called the "Articles of Co-Partnership" be drawn up to establish the understanding between or among the partners.

Among the important items that should be in the partnership agreement are:

1. How profits and losses are to be shared.

2. How authority is to be divided.

3. Whether the partners are to be paid a salary (in addition to the sharing of profits and losses).

4. Whether interest is to be paid to partners on their investment in the firm.

5. An understanding as to what withdrawals of funds may be made by the partners.

6. How disagreements are to be settled. (Perhaps by appointment of an independent arbitrator.)

7. What happens upon death or disability of a partner.

8. How assets and liabilities are to be divided in the event the partnership is terminated.

These are only a relatively few of the items that should be included. A meeting of the partners, with their individual lawyers, should be held before a partnership is started in order to avoid misunderstandings.

Types of Partnership. There are two types of partnership: general partnerships and limited partnerships. In a general partnership, all partners have unlimited liability for partnership debts. In a limited partnership, the limited partners are liable only to the extent of their investment in the partnership. A limited partnership must have at least one general partner (who will have unlimited liability). The general partner must be active in the operations of the business. A limited partner may or may not take active part in the management of the business.

Many types of relationships can be established within a partnership. This often permits people of different talents and skills to enter a business. With designers, it can be a merging of different talents within the interior design field or a collaboration of people from various interconnected fields such as architecture, landscape architecture, engineering, lighting, and business management.

Advantages of a Partnership as Compared to a Sole Proprietorship. Usually two heads are better than one. One person may oversee the design functions, while another handles the bookkeeping or expediting. One can add tremendous strength to the other.

Partnerships are easy to start. There is very little additional expense except writing up your partnership agreements and establishing the way that you are going to work.

There are more money and resources available. Usually, all partners contribute capital to the firm. Also, they may be a source of additional capital, if necessary, or perhaps loans.

Partners can provide the business with a high-quality staff. Someone who is willing to be your partner many times would be unwilling to be your employee. Sharing in the ownership and profits brings in a high level of interest.

Advantages and Disadvantages of a Partnership as Compared to a Corporation. A partnership also has some advantages (as well as disadvantages) as compared with a corporation. A major advantage is the absence of red tape; there are fewer governmental regulations and requirements.

On the other hand, a major disadvantage is that there are fewer perks and fringe benefits available to a partnership. Also, as mentioned elsewhere, unlimited liability is a major disadvantage of a partnership.

Partnerships do not have as great an ability for acquiring capital as corporations do. An individual who may be willing to invest in a corporation may, because of the unlimited liability, refuse to become a partner.

Corporation

A corporation is a legal entity formed under the laws of one of the states. As such, a corporation is considered to be an "artificial person." Each state has its own requirements for incorporation; if you choose to incorporate, you should engage an attorney to handle the matter. A corporation is considered to be "domiciled" in the state of incorporation, but it may engage in business in any other state by registering with such state as a "foreign" corporation.

A corporation, as a legal entity, is subject to federal corporation income taxes and is also subject to various taxes in each of the states in which it registers to do business. In addition, of course, it is subject to all taxes imposed on businesses generally, such as payroll taxes and sales taxes.

There are both advantages and disadvantages to a corporate form of business as compared with a partnership or sole proprietorship. These should be discussed with your accountant while you are still in the planning stages of structuring your business, before you have started to establish a business structure. If there remains any uncertainty, but you nevertheless must proceed in getting the business started, operate as a sole proprietorship (or a partnership, if more individuals are involved). There are few problems in incorporating an established business, whereas terminating a corporation and then continuing business as a proprietorship or partnership can become complicated and costly in terms of tax implications.

So many factors enter into the tax situation of a sole proprietor, partnership, or corporation, that it cannot be said unequivocally that any one form of business operation is more tax-advantageous than another. You and your accountant must review each situation separately and make projections under each of the various assumptions before deciding on which structure is right for you. There are factors other than taxes to be considered in deciding which business structure is advisable for your situation. The tax implications, in fact, may be one of the least important considerations in this matter.

Some of the other advantages and disadvantages of a corporate form of business as compared with a proprietorship or partnership are as follows:

Advantages. The principal advantage is that a corporation has limited liability. A shareholder is liable for business debts only to the extent of his or her investment.

There are more perks and fringe benefits available to the shareholder-employee.

It is usually easier to transfer ownership. The shareholder needs only to assign his or her stock certificate(s) to the new owner. This also facilitates the settlement of an estate upon the death of a shareholder. The business continues without being interrupted by the transfer of ownership.

It is easier to raise capital for a corporation because a prospective investor may not be interested in a partnership, which would subject him or her to unlimited liability.

Disadvantages. As a creature of state law, a corporation has more red tape involved in complying with the more numerous and sometimes complex regulations and requirements.

If your firm is a large organization, business arrangements sometimes become more cumbersome because of the formalities that a corporation must observe that a proprietorship or partnership can ignore.

Other Considerations. You should keep in mind that a business operation need not be confined entirely within a single corporation, partnership, or proprietorship. Often, for tax or other purposes, it is advantageous for real estate to be held separately by the individuals involved or by a second corporation. The first corporation, which operates the business, would then pay rent to the entity owning the real estate. Such arrangements have so many advantages that it is of utmost importance to review them at the time you are planning your business structure.

When you form a corporation, it is important to have a shareholder's agreement. If one of the shareholders dies, decides that he or she is going to retire, or does not want to be in the business any longer, without a shareholder's agreement he or she can sell or bequeath his or her stock to a stranger that you might not want involved in the business.

A shareholder's agreement should require, among other things, that the withdrawing shareholder first offer his or her stock to the corporation or to the remaining shareholders for purchase at a specified or determinable price.

Most large interior design firms work under a corporate structure. Not nearly as many architectural firms do this, with the reason being that in the past it was not considered appropriate for licensed professionals, such as doctors or lawyers, to practice under any kind of a limited-liability vehicle. Professional service corporations, commonly known as "PCs," came into existence to permit professionals to utilize the corporation for business and tax benefits without reducing their professional liability. In PCs, the licensed professional remains fully liable and accountable for any negligence that would be committed by him or her or any person on his or her staff under his or her direction.

It is felt that licensing of interior designers probably would not affect their working under a standard corporation since there are many other licensed professional companies that have incorporated, such as insurance agents, stock brokers, and many types of contractors.

Stockholders in a Corporation. Each person who owns stock in your corporation is a stockholder. This does not mean that every person who holds stock needs to be active in the company, but they do have the right to vote for the corporation's board of directors and on certain corporate policies.

The board of directors represents the stockholders. The stockholders elect the members of the board annually, and their terms can vary according to the bylaws. A shareholder may vote for himself or herself to be a member of the board, but it is not necessarily a requirement that a board member also be a shareholder.

The board of directors is responsible for setting corporate policies. Any major decision affecting the corporate officers must be made by this board. The board must meet on a regular basis—at least annually—and keep records of their meetings and decisions.

Corporate Officers. The corporate officers have various carefully delineated functions.

1. *Chief Executive Officer.* The CEO is the officer of the firm responsible for the activities of the company. This position is usually held by the chairman of the board or the president.

2. *Chief Financial Officer.* The CFO is the executive officer responsible for handling the funds. This includes signing checks, keeping financial records, and supervising all financial planning. The CFO is usually a vice-president in charge of finance, a treasurer, or in some small companies, a controller. Many state laws require that a corporation have a treasurer, and therefore this person can have more than one title, such as vice-president/treasurer.

3. *Chief Operating Officer.* The COO is the officer of the firm who is responsible for the day-to-day management of the corporation. Usually it is the president or the executive vice-president. The chief operating officer reports to the chief executive officer.

4. *Chairman of the Board.* This person is the member of the corporation's board of directors who presides over board meetings and is the highest ranking officer of the corporation. The position can carry either major or minor power, depending on the term the chairman is elected for and on the policies of the corporation. The chairman of the board is often a position reserved as a prestigious term for a past president or a large stockholder or family member.

5. *President.* This person is the highest officer of the corporation after the chairman of the board. He is sometimes titled the chief executive officer, in which case the president would outrank the chairman. The president is appointed by the board of directors and reports directly to the board. In a small corporation, the president and the chief executive officer are usually one and the same, having authority over all matters in the day-to-day management and policy-making decisions of the company.

6. *Outside Director.* This person is a member of the company's board of directors who is not an employee of the company. Outside directors are usually paid a director's fee, which is a set amount for each board meeting, or a certain amount annually. They become part of the decision-making process of the design firm and are often used for business development or to increase the company's operational knowledge.

While I would not discourage a business association with a relative, I should remind you that such relationships are usually much more sensitive than associations among nonrelated parties. In the event of a major disagreement, not only is the business relationship disturbed, but the effect on family relationships may be traumatic.

Buy/Sell Agreements

In any business with another person, you need a buy-sell agreement. I cannot overemphasize the importance of such an agreement. It should be considered in the pre-planning stage of the enterprise, before the business association is effected. Your accountant should be consulted in planning the agreement and your lawyer should draft the agreement.

There is always a tendency, when people engage in a business association, to think that there could be no disagreement they would not be able to resolve amicably. Aside from the fact that such disagreements occur, a more compelling reason for having a buy-sell agreement is to assure, to the extent possible, that no unwanted parties are brought into the business. Without a buy-sell agreement, one of the owners could sell or otherwise transfer all or part of his interest to a person not acceptable to the other owners. This could happen, for example, if one of the owners dies and leaves his or her interest in the business to a spouse, child, or any person not acceptable to the remaining owner(s).

There are several ways by which a departing owner may dispose of his or her interest. The remaining owner(s) may purchase the interest, or the business itself (usually in the case of a corporation) may purchase the interest in a "stock redemption" transaction. A word of caution with respect to the latter: Some states have laws that restrict such redemptions in certain circumstances; if you are contemplating a redemption, check first to see whether your business may properly do so.

More often than not, the business itself is unable to purchase the interest without so depleting its capital that it would no longer be able to continue as a going concern. For this reason, it is important for the firm to have a means of funding the purchase. One way of providing these funds is for the firm to take out life insurance policies on the owners, with the company as the beneficiary. The insurance proceeds can then be used to fund the redemption without diminishing the firm's capital.

Life insurance policies can also be used to fund the purchase of interest by the remaining owners. In this case, each owner is beneficiary in a policy on the life of the other owners.

An agreement must be reached as to how the cost of the insurance premiums are to be shared, since the premiums may differ widely for each insured owner. Because the agreement is beneficial for the departing owner as well as for the remaining ones, an equal sharing may be equitable. Whatever the case, this question should be decided and included in the buy-sell agreement.

It is not uncommon for one or more owners to be uninsurable. In such a situation, the firm needs to provide other means of funding the buy-out. The first right to purchase is meaningless if the funds required are not available.

The amount to be paid for shares in the firm should be fixed or determinable, and the entire buy-sell agreement should be reviewed periodically in order to update or amend it as the situation suggests.

The IRS will accept for estate (death) tax purposes the value prescribed in bonafide buy-sell agreements, unless the value is clearly unrealistic. Accordingly, in a situation where estate taxes are an important factor for an owner, the IRS position may need to be considered when you are establishing the buy-out price.

Taxes

Aside from the taxes that are peculiar to corporations, all businesses, whether conventional corporations, S corporations, partnerships, or proprietorships, are subject to the regular taxes imposed on all subject taxpayers. Examples of some of the more common of these are:

- income taxes (federal and state)
- social security taxes (federal)
- unemployment taxes (federal and state)
- local wage taxes (withheld from employee)
- mercantile taxes (local)
- real estate taxes (local)
- sales taxes (collected from customer)

See pages 311–16 for additional information.

Your accountant should be fully aware of the tax implications for your business in the jurisdictions in which it is located. (This is an additional reason to engage an accountant as soon as a business enterprise is contemplated.) The accountant can then see to it that all forms and applications are properly filed. Income taxes will vary, depending on your firm's structure.

Sole Proprietorships. A sole proprietor reports the firm's profit or loss on his or her personal income tax return. It is then taken into account with the other elements in his or her return in determining his or her tax liability.

Partnerships: A partnership does not pay income taxes as an entity. Rather, a partnership files a "Partnership Return of Income," which shows, among other things, the distributive share of the profit or loss for each partner. Each partner then includes this amount in his or her individual income tax return and it is taken into account in the determination of the income taxes he or she must pay. It should be noted that a partner must report and pay income taxes on his or her entire share of the profit, even though it may not have been actually distributed to him or her that year. In other words, a partner reports his or her share of the income or loss in the year it is earned (or lost) by the partnership, regardless of when distribution is actually made. Distribution, in fact, is simply a withdrawal of capital from the partnership and there is no tax implication for the partnership by reason of the withdrawal.

A partnership must also file a "Partnership Return of Income" in all states (and some local jurisdictions) where business is conducted (in addition to filing it with the Internal Revenue Service). As with the federal government, the partnership pays no income tax as an entity to the state or locality. The individual partners must report and pay tax as individuals on their distributive shares. It is noted then that a partner may be subjected to income tax in a state or jurisdiction where he does not reside. There is little or no overlapping or double taxation, though, because the various taxing jurisdictions usually provide for a credit or offset for income taxes paid to other jurisdictions on the same reportable income.

Corporations. A corporation is a legal entity apart from the owners and, as such, is subject to corporation income taxes (not to be confused with income tax requirements of proprietorships or partnerships).

Corporations are subject to federal income taxes and also to state or local income taxes in the jurisdictions where they engage in business (provided, of course, that the particular state or local jurisdiction imposes an income tax on corporations; most states and many localities do).

S Corporations. An S corporation (formerly called Subchapter S corporation) is a conventional corporation in every aspect except for income taxes. An S corporation is one whose shareholders (as well as the corporation itself) have elected to be taxed much in the same manner as a partnership would be taxed. As with a partnership, the S corporation does not pay income taxes as an entity, but the shareholders report and pay taxes on their distributive shares.

A corporation must meet certain requirements in order to be eligible to elect S corporation status. Because these requirements have, at various times, been changed, I will not list them here. If you are considering S corporation status, consult with your accountant to see whether or not your corporation is eligible under the laws in effect.

S corporation status is particularly advantageous in a new business that anticipates several years of losses before profits are generated. In an S corporation, the owners can deduct the losses on their individual income tax returns. When the business becomes profitable, the owners can then elect to terminate the S corporation status and revert to a conventional corporation (if a conventional corporation is considered at the time to be more desirable). After a revocation or termination, a corporation must wait five years before a new S corporation election may be made. S corporation status can be elected effective with the inception of business; therefore, this is a matter to be considered in the preplanning stage of the enterprise.

In addition to income taxes, states (and some localities) impose various taxes peculiar to corporations. These taxes vary in each state and locality and no generalizations can be made. State and local corporate tax implications should be considered at the time you are planning the form of business structure for your firm. Needless to say, you should select an accountant who is knowledgeable in the various taxes as well as competent in accounting matters.

Licenses

It should not be overlooked that some states require interior designers to be licensed, and soon an increasing number will be doing so.

Other types of license or permits that may be required are:

▶ zoning

▶ building codes (including parking facilities)

▶ safety standards

Fictitious Name Registration

To use any name other than your own for your business, you must file a fictitious name registration request. Your attorney can help you with this. First, a review (or search) is done by the office with whom the application is filed to determine that no one else has the same name registered in your state or geographic area. If the name is cleared, then various forms must be filed before the formal registration certificate is furnished. In certain states this registration is only good for five years or so and must be renewed. Check with your state to determine its requirements. If your registration needs renewing, make sure to mark in your books to have this done on a regular basis. Many companies have run into problems because registrations have not been properly renewed.

DEALERSHIPS

There is a tremendous change taking place in dealerships—in both residential and office furniture lines. In the past, through arrangements with residential and office furniture resources, larger design dealerships had many lines available. About forty to sixty percent of the merchandise they sold was from the smaller lines.

As long as they were able to meet a certain yearly volume and, in some cases, if they did not carry conflicting lines, they were given special privileges by the factories they represented. These privileges, which varied according to each furniture company, were usually better discounts, advertising reimbursements, exclusivity on certain items, and priority in deliveries.

Now, however, most well-known manufacturers are asking for exclusivity. They require interested dealerships not only to carry their line exclusively, but also to meet their management standards. Moreover, companies such as Herman Miller have opened their own pavilions in the contract field, just as companies like Henredon and Drexel Heritage are requiring showrooms exclusively devoted to their lines.

This changes the role for the interior designer. If a designer works for a company-directed dealership, then the designer doesn't have the opportunity to use any other line they might select. If a designer works for a company with diversified lines, then the designer usually doesn't have access to the major lines.

The purchasing options for the independent interior designer are also being strongly affected by these dealerships. In some cases, the dealerships refuse to sell to interior designers. In other instances, when the interior designers refer jobs to dealerships for processing, the dealership attempts to cut the interior designer out of the picture by suggesting that the client use the dealership's design department the next time.

Some of these dealerships are developing great management systems. In fact several of them were on *Inc*'s list of the five hundred fastest-growing private companies. They have transformed small businesses (in some cases, family businesses) into very attractive companies for others to buy. Some have started franchising dealerships and have a large corporate buying center. These companies are very sophisticated in their methods, are completely computerized with CADDs, and have invested heavily in expensive equipment. They have hired strong marketing and image firms and play a significant role in the field. Their great advantage is that they know their line, and by working as a unit they can afford the very best talent and equipment.

If a designer chooses to become part of one of the major dealerships, obviously there are advantages, because these firms do a lot of advertising and offer special pricing and shipping and installation processes that would otherwise be unavailable to an independent design firm.

JOINT VENTURES AND ASSOCIATIONS

Joint ventures and associations are important vehicles that can help to broaden your scope as an interior designer and can be very profitable as well. A joint venture allows two firms to work together under the same contract, while each firm still remains independent and is responsible for its own professional performances, legal positioning, expenses, profits and losses. Joint ventures are similar to partnerships, both legally and financially, except that they are usually established to accomplish a single objective and then terminate, whereas a partnership is generally formed to operate indefinitely. They can provide a new avenue to markets and can often give interior designers opportunities to work on larger projects—ones they would not be able to do independently because of the architectural, engineering, and other professional services required.

Interior designers often joint venture or associate with other designers when one designer is doing a large project in a distant city and needs someone local to supervise it. This can help the management of the project considerably.

In a joint venture or association, you obviously want to associate with a firm that you know or have worked with before and that you know will take responsibility for their portion of the work. A great deal of research is needed to determine whether a firm would make a good associate. When investigating a firm, check with other professionals they have worked with, as well as with their past clients, and learn how their other joint ventureship projects worked out.

It is also important to determine the structuring of the project before developing the parameters of the venture or association. Many design firms find forming an association with another firm better than formal joint venturing because they do not require the legal paperwork needed to set up a joint venture. Clients, on the other hand, often prefer joint ventures so that they have one firm to relate to. In an association, each firm can point the finger at the other one if something goes wrong.

Before marketing for a project, it is best to have some form of a preliminary agreement that identifies the firms and the positions each will play on the project. Roles should be clearly defined and all fees and administrative structures firmly established before going after the project. Going into these ventures casually can prove disastrous.

Chapter Three

PLANNING FOR PROFIT AND GROWTH

Most of us work in the interior design field because we love it. Because we really love it means we are willing to pour energy—no holds barred—into doing everything necessary to make each project absolutely great. We don't measure the effort that goes into it, and there is no yardstick for what should be accomplished.

One Monday I asked my staff how many of them would come in to work if they were not getting paid, and most of them said they would. I asked some of my fellow interior designers the same question, and they all concurred, saying there was nothing they would rather do.

This kind of devotion can be good for our clients because they get outstanding projects. On the other hand, if it is all done for love, we may never finish or get paid. Designers need to measure their love of the design process against the time spent and money earned.

SETTING GOALS

In planning your company, deal first with your personal goals—where you want to be as a professional—and then with the financial goals of the company. Remember, all planning is based on assumptions. This is why you should bring together the best possible people that you can find to help you plan a program based on their experiences as well as your own. Chances are good that your assumptions will become realities because they have direction and planning.

Personal Goals

Each of us has personal needs and desires. You cannot deny them if you are going to be happy and fulfilled. Personal goals are often dependent on obtaining certain business objectives; it helps to correlate the two. Do your personal goals fit realistically within the interior design field?

We each know more about ourselves than anyone else in the world: what we like and dislike, what works best for us, and how we work best with other people. We know if we like to live alone or with other people. We know how much we value our profession. We also know our financial requirements—whether we want to live modestly or comfortably, whether we require a more-than-adequate income.

A good way to define your personal goals is to decide where you see yourself five years from now. Determine what lifestyle is most comfortable for you and best enhances your creativity.

Sit down and take stock of how you actually feel about the interior design field, even if you did not do so at the beginning of your career. How important is it to you now? Do you want to spend the rest of your life in design? Or do you just want to dabble in it for several years to gain experience before going into another field? It is important to put your private thoughts into perspective.

You can learn more about yourself by writing down these goals. This can be done alone or with another person. Sharing your goals and objectives with other professionals or friends is often enlightening. Other people can remind you of certain personal preferences you might not have considered.

As you list your goals, organize them in the order of their importance to you. List-making and priority-setting reinforce what you know and organize your thoughts so they are manageable. I begin each day with a list of goals, and what I expect gets done. Lists help me to accomplish more.

After listing your goals, make another list of the things that annoy you, the things that you really want to avoid. Do you feel good about your work? The people in your life? Yourself?

List at least a half dozen activities that you enjoy doing purely for fun and the last time you had an opportunity to do any of them. All outstanding creative designers need balance in their lives to be able to continue to develop in their careers. To each person this is something different. We need to create safeguards to prevent burn-out. If a designer burns out, he or she is out of a job. Our career demands that we are always up and ready with new exciting ideas.

What should you be doing differently to make yourself happier? Less frustrated and bored? Finding the answers to these questions can prove to be an adventure in self-discovery. Review your problems of the past few years so you can eliminate as many of them as possible during the coming years.

It is a good idea to review your goals every three to six months to be sure they can be accomplished. You may find that you have the wrong sets of goals. My goals have been revised many times, but at least there is a goal pattern. It makes me feel more secure to think that I am ruling and running my life, rather than letting it run me.

Business Goals

What are your goals? To make a profit? Many interior design firms with beautifully designed offices are really not in business to make a profit. They do not have to; they have income from other sources. But is that really a business? A business is an organized entity that manufactures a product or provides a service with the goal of making a profit.

Managing an interior design firm involves being a good planner and understanding the importance of setting overall business objectives. Possible goals might be growth, increased profit, increasing the rate of profit, or increasing your market share. Consider the big picture of your goals—where you want to be five years from now. At the same time be flexible. We are creative in our work of interior design, so be creative in planning your business goals.

Your goals may change from year to year, depending upon your financial situation and even different tax rulings. All business plans require testing. Often some of the best master plans and strongest strategies on paper can prove unproductive during the testing period. This compels us to restructure and reestablish our business goals.

Many companies never accomplish their goals because they have not defined what they are and have not organized their efforts to achieve the goals. Define your business goals very clearly to determine just how they fit with your personal goals, as well as those of your employees. The principals of the firm must agree on the firm's goals.

Are your goals simple? If they are too complex they will be hard for your fellow workers to understand and help achieve.

Reaching Business Goals. Procrastination can keep you from reaching any business goal. Allow time in your regular schedule for planning and effectively developing your goals. Learn to balance large, important issues against the unimportant. Do not spend all your time putting out fires, but make sure you are working toward the goals you establish.

In order to plan my company's goals, I hire the very best business consultants I can find—professionals with different orientations—to help me. Planners often offer quite different input than that of your accountant or attorney. They usually show more creative ability and foresight within the business planning. It is also helpful to work with someone in the interior design or a related field. These people can expose you to marketing objectives as well as to different trends they see developing.

Be sure to also review your business goals with your accountant, your business consultant, and your attorney. On several occasions I have had what I thought were very exciting business directions for my company, only to find after review with my accountant that some of these projects would require me to pay in taxes the money I thought I would be saving.

Review your business goals every few months. If you have not accomplished a portion of them, go back and re-evaluate them. They might be the wrong goals for your company.

Mission Statement. It is often difficult for a firm to remain focused on its goals. Creating a mission statement and using it as a constant daily reference helps keep you on the right track.

Determine your business direction—whom you expect to service and what your products will be—and put this into a mission statement. For example, our firm specializes in professional office design. This is our business direction. Our staff has a strong background in both medical and legal practices. This is what we do best. Don't let yourself flounder all over the design field trying to find the right spot. Find an area in which you excel and where there is a client demand, and service those clients.

Your mission statement needs to be constantly reviewed by you and all of your employees. I keep my mission statement inside a book I refer to daily.

FORMULATING A BUSINESS PLAN

Planning for the year is not something that is done within an hour or so. Once a year or anytime you are considering changing the structure or direction of your firm, you should take one week out to devote to the planning and goal setting for the next year.

Write down your business plan. This helps you firm up your thinking and helps ensure that you have covered all of the essential issues before making actual changes in your business. The plan is also a useful reference later on; it enables you to compare your objectives, benchmarks, and levels of accomplishment over a given time period. After you create your plan, go through it with your accountant and attorney to be sure that it fits with your company's structure from a tax viewpoint as well as from a legal one.

Your plan should consider the following:

1. *Type of Business*. The exact type of design services or design business you intend to establish or develop, as well as who your anticipated clients will be and how you will be charging, head the list of elements in your business plan.

2. *Location*. Operating costs for a design firm can vary considerably, depending upon the part of the country in which it is located. Generally, costs are highest in the larger cities in the Northeast or on the West Coast. Take location costs into account.

3. *Product*. Determine exactly what you are selling. Are you selling professional services only or are you also selling merchandise? Designers in smaller communities must often provide additional services that firms in major cities do not need to offer, such as handling installation and certain follow-up and purchasing procedures. While these services can in some instances be profitable, the expense in maintaining divisions to coordinate

them can be quite risky. Installation and purchasing services can destroy a firm's financial base.

4. *Facilities Required*. What facilities will you require in order to provide your service? Will you need a showroom? An office? Can you work out of someone else's showroom for a while? Your residence? Write out exactly how you intend to present yourself.

5. *Marketing Plans*. No matter what type of design business you enter, you will need to promote, market, and sell your product or services. How do you expect to carry this through?

6. *Your Competition*. Are there other businesses in your area that you see as offering competition? Our field at present has considerable competition, not just from other design firms, but from other professions and disciplines. Many kinds of specialists call themselves "interior designers"— plumbing supply houses, kitchen cabinet salespeople, "decorating contractors," retail furniture salespeople.

Find out how strong your competitors are, what kind of people they are, and what their business experience is. Make sure you know exactly who your competition is and what you expect. If your speciality is office design and there is already an office-equipment dealer in the area who gives away the service, you have a built-in problem. *how you differentiate yourself*

7. *Available Funds*. How much cash do you have on hand? How much more could you afford to invest in this project if necessary? You will need to have reserve funds available. Have you established credit with various resources? Do you have a line of credit at the bank? Set up a budget for your company so you know where the money is going over the next year.

8. *Revenue Expectations*. How much do you expect to take in? From what resources? What percentage of your revenue do you expect to come from professional fees, and how much from other sources?

Judging the expected revenue for an interior design firm is complex because some firms work on a professional-fee basis only, which makes all income gross income. Other firms sell merchandise, and while their volume figures could be much larger, their gross income could be lower. The majority of interior design firms that are highly profitable have mixed sources of income, which may consist of professional-service fees, extra purchasing fees, commissions, markups, and royalties, for example.

9. *Expense Projections*. Write out your expected expenses for the next six months to a year. After enumerating these expenses, make additional allowances for the many unknowns.

10. *Administrative Structure*. Good profitability comes from what you do on a daily and weekly basis, and you need administrative structure for that.

11. *Support Services and Staff*. Make a list of the support services and staffing required to run your business successfully. Do you have these people in line? Are these people who want to work with you and are able to work for you? Do you have backups available? Sometimes when you believe you have adequate personnel resources they become committed to something else. If you have backups for these situations it will make your life a lot easier.

On the whole, the most profitable design firms are quite small (under five members) or quite large (over fifty members). Firms whose personnel number between five and fifty usually are not able to hire the quality of operational and financial management personnel they must have to run effectively.

12. *Your Time Schedule.* If you are taking your firm in a new direction, consider how much time this will take and how the rest of your business will be affected.

PLANNING FOR PROFIT

Contrary to popular perception, the most profitable firms are well-run residential design firms with a high level of creative design. Specialty companies also show good profit, and firms that design very unusual work (what is described in the field as fantasy work) generally tend to show excellent profit. Commercial work can also be very profitable, but the field is extremely competitive and requires high amounts of volume and repetition in order to show profit.

Very few interior design firms that charge purely on an hourly or a per diem basis are outstandingly profitable. The most profitable firms base their charges on value, which means a certain fee base for a certain project. However, there is a certain degree of risk in this type of management. If you quote a price for a particular job, you are committed to that fee. Therefore, you need to know how to produce within a particular range. This is easier to do when you specialize.

Today, specialization is one of the most profitable ways for designers to operate. Because specialists have experience in one area, they know exactly how to handle and price their work. They know their precise profit factor.

Factors That Affect Your Profits

In the past when design firms went out of business it was usually due to poor financial management. Today businesses are forced to close far more often as a result of lawsuits against them. Win or lose, a lawsuit generally costs the firm a considerable amount of money, not just in legal fees, but in the stigma a lawsuit creates against a company. Liability insurance can reduce your cash losses, but it cannot retrieve your lost reputation.

Job processing strongly affects profitability. The faster the job can be completed, the more profitable it is. Because of internal as well as external issues, designers tend to have some jobs that drag out too long and decrease profits. You need to find some way to shorten this period.

This can also affect your profits. Most firms expect their accounts receivable to be paid within thirty days. However, investigation shows that it is far more common for firms to be paid within sixty days, and sometimes accounts go uncollected for six to nine months, or even years.

On the whole, a trait that keeps many designers from achieving high profits is that we try to make each job a bit different. While creativity is part of good design, having too broad a range of projects can make profit projections difficult. The design firms that tend to be the most profitable are those that are willing to do repetitious work.

Ways to Increase Profits

There are two primary ways of increasing profit:

1. Increase the total sales or the amount of income secured by the design firm.

2. Increase the amount of profit or mark-up. It is important not to simply increase additional sales, but to carefully and constantly keep track of the percentage of profit on each particular job. This is the basis of marketing as much as it is of any other financial program.

Growth is really the key to profits for many business endeavors. The future of a company depends on its flexibility and willingness to grow. Determine whether you should get larger or smaller or stay the same size. Decide which will be the most profitable direction for your company to go.

Many people feel that doubling or tripling a firm's size overnight is the way growth is accomplished. This is simply not so. Growth is a gradual process reached by improving the company's services by increasing its opportunities to acquire more qualified personnel and additional technical knowledge. Management needs to anticipate the requirements necessary for growth.

Management consultants can show you many sophisticated formulas for projecting your company's growth, but this is usually a quite involved and costly process. A designer can utilize a simple formula for business development by assessing the needs of clients he or she expects to service against the qualifications and background of the design firm. By matching the needs of clients to the firm's capabilities, a designer can determine a profitable direction for his or her firm.

Analyzing Your Firm and Its Direction

In planning your firm's development, you will want to analyze the firm's experience by carefully looking at each of its activities and projects from the past five to ten years. (Projects that were performed more than ten years ago will have little relevance to today's market unless they were particularly outstanding. Even then, their usefulness in marketing is limited.) Determine which areas have been the most profitable for you during the last five years and which jobs can help you acquire the jobs that you want to do over the next five years. A marketing structure must be based on work to be done, building on the experience of work that has been done in the past.

For each project that the design firm has done, you will need to list the following:

1. *Name of the Project*. The name of the project should be what you commonly call it, such as the particular name of the building, the name of the corporation, or the name of the residential client.

2. *Name of the Client*. The name of the client is the name of the person for whom you worked on this particular job, whether it is a board of directors or the managing director of a project.

3. *Location of the Project*. List the exact address. Also note whether the project was located in the same town in which you are (or were) located, or whether it was a distance from you. Include any information regarding difficulties in reaching the project or communication problems.

4. *Type of Construction*. Identify whether the project was new construction or remodeling. Also outline your involvement in the construction of this particular project—whether you, as the interior designer, were involved in part of the architectural planning or whether you came into the project at a later date and were merely responsible for the furnishings.

5. *Size of the Project*. Break this down as far as you think necessary. Depending upon the size of your design firm, you may want to define specific areas of carpeting, wall surface materials, drapery and window coverings, and so forth.

6. *Type of Services the Firm Provided*. Outline all of the services you provided, from the basic design to follow-through with construction inspections and feasibility studies to presenting various types of drawings.

7. *Design Accomplishments*. List what the objective of the job was and whether it was accomplished from the owner's viewpoint as well as from the interior design firm's viewpoint. Include both the negative and positive aspects of the job, and determine whether the project is one you are pleased to have on your list of accomplishments.

8. *Size of the Fee.* List the size of the fee the firm received and the charging method that was used. Include details on how you were actually paid for the project—whether you were paid directly by the client or through an independent contractor or other source.

9. *Profit of the Project.* List the firm's net profit on the job. This is calculated by computing all the costs—the expense of personnel time, the cost of materials, the fees for supplying furnishings—and subtracting from that figure the overall income from the project.

10. *Percentage of Profit on the Total Project.* The percentage of profit on the total project is the net profit divided by the total contract value for your services.

11. *Source of the Job.* It is important to identify the source of the job so that additional marketing information can evolve. Under this category, list the components that you feel contributed to your getting the job. List all the sources that you feel were involved, whether the job was a referral from an individual who had used you on a previous project, or whether advertising, newsletters, or any other media helped you get the job.

12. *Expected Referrals.* After completing each job, review it from a marketing viewpoint to see just how this job can be used to secure future projects (see page 108).

13. *Publicity Potential.* After completion you may want to interview the client and discuss with him or her other projects he or she might want to do with you. You might ask whether the client would enjoy or consider magazine

Design project analysis sheet. This sheet will help you plan your firm's development by determining which areas have been the most profitable for you during the last five years and which jobs may result in your acquiring future jobs.

DESIGN PROJECT ANALYSIS		
Client:	Project:	Staff:
Address:	Contact:	Date: Started:
	Phone:	Completed:
Type of Construction:(new, renovations, etc.)	Size of Project: Construction Budget: Furnishings Budget:	
Type of Services the Firm Provided:	Design Accomplishments:	
Size of the Fee:	Source of the Job:	
Method of Charging:	Expected Referrals:	
Profit of the Project:	Percentage of Profit on Total Project:	

© Design Business Monthly

or publication exposure. It is important to review the client's attitudes before going further in this issue. Also, you might want the job to be considered for design competitions. Many designers have learned to take a single project and capitalize on it.

After you have made up a sheet like this for each of your projects, file the sheets by year so that you are able to judge how many projects you undertook during a particular year, what types of projects they were, and how successful they were. When the year is over, go through the file and summarize:

▶ the types of jobs done

▶ the number of jobs done

▶ the amount of costs for each job

▶ the percentage of profit for each job

This sheet will help you understand the trends of your company as well as the trends of the marketing area around you.

Evaluating Your Staff

Once you have defined your firm's direction, you must determine whether the staff that you have now is properly oriented to handle your objectives. Evaluate the ability of each and every staff member. You may have to replace certain staff members in order to achieve your goals.

Have every member of your staff complete the design staff questionnaire on pages 82–84. Analyzing the information on the forms will help you clarify your direction. The form should be updated annually by all staff employees. Then, when you are considering a new project, the staff's experience may help you sell your firm to a new client.

What makes successful projects? Winston Churchill once said: "It's going from failure to failure, without the loss of enthusiasm, that counts." I think that this is part of what makes a person successful—how he or she handles failure. If we concentrate exclusively on our failures, however, we diminish our self-confidence and lose much of the excitement that exists in any successful designer. I've heard everyone say—and I've heard it quoted many times—that failure can teach us a lot. But I don't believe failure can teach us as much as success can.

When you review design work and see something you like, be sure to accentuate the pluses. Of course, if there are problems they should be acknowledged so they are not repeated. But promoting what is good within a staff, and within yourself, is the most important thing. At the end of every day, look at what you've done that you did well, and invest some time in examining the best parts of that activity. Ask yourself, How can I do it again? Can I make it even more polished?

Reexamine your design projects from time to time to see what you did best on each one. Do the same for each of your staff members to pinpoint their strengths. If their strengths are in areas that they enjoy, try to let them concentrate on those areas. People are usually more successful in the areas that they really like.

SELLING YOUR BUSINESS

If you plan to sell your business in the next few years, there are things you can do now to get the best possible price and to establish the best situation for the sale. First of all, try to show as many profits on your books as possible. Interior designers tend to enjoy the perks their business can bring, rather than leaving them in the firm. Because you plan to sell the business, you want to increase the perceived value and to leave as much in the company as possible.

Spend time developing your clients and try to establish as many contracts as possible for continuing projects. This is valuable to any prospective purchaser.

Organize any copyrights or patents you might have. If you plan to sell them with the business, present them in a professional manner.

Update your mailing lists and all of your contracts.

Reexamine inventory with an eye toward eliminating what is not up-to-date. Can out-of-date items be turned into cash? If not, get rid of them. Make your studio appear as organized and attractive as possible.

Hire a good appraiser to evaluate your building and the various advantages of your property location.

Organize your business management system so that it can be easily taken over by someone else the day they walk in. Established procedures are very valuable to the next owner.

Review your work force and try to have the best people possible. Employment contracts and noncompetitive agreements are also assets when selling a business.

Take stock of your financial position. Determine what capital is required to run the business and what capital is excess. Consult your accountant as to the best position on this. You may have $400,000 in working capital, but the business could be run well with $200,000.

The price of a business is often based on the amount of business it generates. The last ten years of a business are the most pertinent in determining its value. Projected sales over the next five years could help contribute to the firm's value, which is why contracts or any other potential work could be a tremendous asset.

Chapter Four

SETTING UP A DESIGN STUDIO

The success of an interior design practice is very much affected by the physical space out of which it operates. Not only the building, but its furnishings, equipment, and location are important to both clients and staff.

THE RIGHT LOCATION

How much does location affect your business? It may not affect it at all. If you are going into a speciality and expect your range of clients to come from a wide geographic area, or if clients don't visit your office, you need not invest heavily in location. If, on the other hand, your design practice is dependent upon the surrounding community, you must look at the location in those terms.

Market Proximity and Client Base

Is the area a practical base for you? If you specialize in computer-center design, for example, will you be accessible to your market? The location of a business can affect whether it succeeds or fails.

Are there clients in the area? Before you select an area in which to establish your design practice, determine whether the community is accustomed to purchasing, or would like to purchase, interior design services. It may be an area where people really are not interested in design. They may feel that if their furniture hasn't fallen apart yet, there is no need for them to buy anything new. Some people are just not stimulated by the design fashions of today. There are also certain areas where the financially elite do not buy new things. These areas obviously are not good markets for interior design, where business is based on change. If the community you are considering is this staid and/or established, it is probably not a good location for an interior design business.

Find an area with a broad customer base. It is better to be where there are a large number of clients, not just three or four. Very few interior designers can make a living from the projects of the same few clients.

Is there a high enough income base? If most of the people in the area earn a top salary of $20,000 a year, they probably do not have money to spend on interior design services. Most interior design clients have income levels that start in the $75,000 to $100,000 a year range.

If the community is prosperous, moving, and changing, it usually is a good environment for an interior designer. Any growing community has tremendous potential. On the other hand, if the community is very quiet and retiring, it probably will not have the client base you need.

What is the median age of the people living in the area? In general, most very young people feel they cannot afford interior design services. The age variables of design clients are changing, however, and with the great surge in retirement homes and new condominium units, older clients have now become strong consumers of design services. Some senior citizens are ready to do things very differently from the ways they had done them in the past. Take a look at the attitudes as well as the ages of the people that you are looking to as your clients.

Sizing Up the Competition

How much competition is there? And how does what the competition offers differ from what you offer in terms of design services? In any community you are considering, it is important to be aware of what the competition is doing and how strong they are. Is the community economically strong enough to support your competition and you?

Residential Suitability

Is this an area where you want to live? Where your employees will want to live? Can they afford to live in the area? It is very difficult to put an interior design practice in an area where no one wants to be. You must consider your labor force.

Staff Availability

Affordability of support staff has become a major issue in selecting locations. Many firms in the affluent, elite northeastern communities are moving into other areas because they cannot get affordable support staff. If you are going to have to pay four times as much for a secretary in one community as in another, it might be worth considering life in the cheaper community to make your design practice succeed, particularly if your practice requires a large support staff.

The Business Climate

Is the location one in which you can do business? Investigate the zoning restrictions or any community restrictions in the area. Zoning restrictions are often a major source of aggravation for a firm. Some areas are more heavily zoned than others. Find an area where you are wanted; it is less expensive and

QUESTIONS FOR EVALUATING A LOCATION

1. Is it close to my market?

2. Are there sufficient potential clients with adequate income levels to support a design firm?

3. How much competition is there?

4. How do I feel about making this area my home for the next ten years?

5. What is the quality of the area's schools and cultural community?

6. Is there good police and fire protection?

7. Is there affordable housing available for both management and working staff?

8. What is the quality of the available staffing?

9. What will be the cost of employees?

10. What is the quality of the business climate?

11. Does my business conform to the zoning within this area?

12. What are the taxes?

13. Are merchandise and materials readily available?

14. Can I get the contractors I need to perform the tasks required?

15. Am I able to get the warehousing I need or can I supply it for myself?

16. How will I be able to process the jobs in this location?

17. Do I have the appropriate traffic flow?

18. Is this a good neighborhood in which to be seen?

time-consuming than fighting zoning regulations; I know this from bitter experience. My firm survived, but I can easily imagine a new firm being destroyed by the battles we endured.

Can you have deliveries made or do retail business there? Some areas prohibit interior designers from doing business in typical office centers. Review the licensing requirements of the area before you select your location.

Location can also make a difference in your taxation rates. Sometimes being just outside of a city's border can change your taxation rates. Carefully review what your taxes will be in any location you are considering.

You need easy access to suppliers and warehousing. While not every interior design firm sells merchandise, they all have to make sure that any merchandise they specify is in good condition. If you have to travel fifty or sixty miles to check merchandise every time you make a delivery, or if you are not checking it, then you are in trouble. Interior designers must be responsible for their work and therefore do need to have these services conveniently located.

Correct Visibility

In the early years of a design firm, it is usually best to be located somewhere where you can be seen. In most cases, however, heavily trafficked areas, such as shopping centers or very busy streets, are not ideal. These locations require additional staff to handle the many people who will just stop in to visit. At first, select a slightly less trafficked area so that people entering your offices have to intentionally come to see you. The right type of traffic is far more important than the volume. However, try to select a safe, desirable area; the condition of the buildings surrounding yours can reflect on you. Be sure you are attracting the right type of client.

A BUILDING FOR YOUR BUSINESS

Some design firms need space that projects an image. Others could be located above a garage and it would not matter. Knowing your customers, your needs, and your budget will guide you in determining what space is right for you. There are times when it is valuable to put together a good real estate package, but there are other times when one must keep major funds for the day-to-day business management.

Your firm's quarters must look professional. They must look like an interior designer's firm. However, you should not put so much money into a building that it leaves you without working capital.

If you expect clients to come to your office, it must be reasonably convenient for them. Whether your office is located in a rural or urban area, it must be accessible. If you expect your clients to arrive by car, make sure there is adequate parking for them. Too many firms allow only enough parking space for the design staff and leave nothing for clients. Think of the clients first; if there are not enough spaces for both clients and staff, arrange for your staff to park elsewhere.

Fortunately, interior designers tend to have a good sense about location. When I found my building, I asked several designer friends from other communities to come and look at it with me. This helped immeasurably because they pointed out certain major drawbacks and some positive factors that I might have missed. All of us have developed friends in other communities; this is a good time to use them as consultants.

What your interior space should look like is largely determined by the type of services you offer. If you are going to bring clients there, however, it must look like an organized working space. Interior designers are selling organization through design. If our offices are not organized, how can we recommend organization to our clients? My personal belief is that an interior design studio must be very well organized to conform to clients' expectations if nothing else. Still, they also like to see action, so do not worry about showing that you are busy.

QUESTIONS FOR EVALUATING A BUILDING

1. Is the building physically suitable for a design business?

2. Does the exterior of the building reflect my design image? If not, can it be adjusted within a reasonable range to suit?

3. Is there an opportunity for any type of display or image-attracting area?

4. What is the cost of purchase or lease?

5. Can I design the space to fit the value, or am I paying for a lot of real estate that I will never be able to use?

6. How will the building hold up over the next ten years?

7. Is there room for future expansion? Can it be done here or will I have to move?

8. What kind of history does the building have? What kind of business was there before? Did it do well?

9. Is it a pleasant place to be?

10. Is it a safe environment for both my employees and my customers? Am I going to have to worry about safety or provide a lot of extra security measures?

11. Is it in a stable neighborhood?

12. Is the building easily accessible to my clients? Can they find the location? If they will be driving, do they have parking?

13. Does the interior layout of the building correlate with the objectives of my design firm? Will it be easy to adapt into a productive area?

14. Is the lighting good?

15. What is the condition of the HVAC?

Leasing Versus Buying

With both property and equipment, leasing should always be considered as an alternative to purchasing because leasing does not require a large capital outlay. This can be a real advantage for small businesses, which are generally under-capitalized. Leasing provides them with the freedom to use their money in more profitable areas. Leasing property or equipment also allows you to try it out to determine whether you really want to invest in it.

Types of Leases. The terms leasing and renting are often used interchangeably, but there are differences. Usually renting refers to a short-term lease and leasing to a long-term agreement. Leasing also often offers many additional financing benefits, sometimes permitting 100 percent financing. In other instances, leasing may also have considerable tax advantages.

There are many different leasing arrangements; each needs to be carefully reviewed in order to determine its appropriateness for your situation.

Most leases fall into one of two categories: gross lease or net lease. Under a gross lease, the lessor is responsible for all the expenses, including maintenance, taxes, and insurance. Under a net lease agreement, the lessee (the person leasing the property), is responsible for these overhead expenses. This is becoming a more common type of lease.

Advantages and Disadvantages of Leasing. Some of the <u>advantages</u> of leasing are the following:

1. You have the use of the building or equipment <u>without a large initial cash outlay.</u>

2. If you are taking a loan or mortgaging a property, you often need to pay twenty, twenty-five, or thirty percent of the value as a down payment; with <u>many types of leasing no down payment is required.</u>

3. Your payments are spread out over a <u>long period of time.</u>

4. <u>You are protected against being stuck with a building or equipment you do not want.</u> If you determine that a location is not right for you, you can move on. If equipment you have leased becomes obsolete, you can simply arrange to lease another type of equipment.

5. <u>There are many tax benefits in leasing.</u> In most instances, lease payments are totally deductible as operating expenses. Today the government carefully reviews leases to determine if they are a disguised purchase rather than a true lease. Have your accountant review details of the contract.

6. <u>The people who lease equipment to you are generally experts</u> on it, so if you have any problems there is always someone to call.

7. Usually, <u>flexible payments schedules can be arranged as required for your business situation.</u> For example, if your cash flow is weaker at certain times of the year, due to certain contracts, normally you can arrange to make payments at times when you are in a better cash flow position.

There are certain <u>disadvantages</u> to leasing.

1. There are certain <u>tax advantages in owning property or equipment</u> that are not available to the person who leases them. However, you should check with your accountant to see whether leasing or owning is best in your particular tax situation.

2. At the end of the lease, the property or equipment still belongs to the lessor. <u>If you had purchased it, you would have an asset.</u>

3. Sometimes tax benefits can make <u>purchasing a property or piece of equipment considerably more affordable.</u> You need to do a cash analysis to determine whether it pays for you to purchase rather than lease.

4. Usually a lease is for a specific term, and <u>you must pay for the full term of the lease whether you need the space or equipment for the entire time or not.</u> If you own property or equipment, you have the <u>option of selling it when you no longer want it.</u>

Before deciding to purchase a sizable item, whether it be real estate or an expensive piece of equipment, <u>have your accountant do a cash-flow evaluation of the cost of the lease.</u>

Home Studios

If clients never see your studio, home offices can be practical. Some very profitable businesses are run out of designers' basements; <u>but they also use the rest of the house—the living room and the dining room—as a showcase.</u> The actual work with samples and plans is done in the basement and is not seen by clients. Many interior designers have adapted their apartments, turning the dining room or a second bedroom into a very effective design studio. Whether this would work for you depends completely upon the type of practice you have and how much you use your studio for client interaction.

If you work out of a home studio, you must be very careful to continue to maintain a professional appearance. Many doctors and dentists have worked from home offices for years; but then, there is no question in anyone's mind as to whether medicine is a profession. An overly casual environment can cause clients to doubt the professional creditability of the interior designer. If you have children and/or pets running around all day, your home might not provide the right atmosphere in which to meet with sales reps or clients.

Another common practice that some designers find practical is to combine a design studio with living quarters for the designer. My design studio in Harrisburg occupies a very large, thirty-three-room house. In part of the house there is a small apartment, which I use as my home when I am in Harrisburg. This setup is both practical and convenient for me because I usually work extended hours. I am often up and at my desk before the sun rises and sometimes work until very late at night. This had become a safety and security concern when I used to travel between my residence and my studio. In fact, the police suggested that I avoid coming and going at these hours because I had created a pattern that criminals could exploit.

Working and living in the same building can be convenient. However, there is no privacy. When you live above the studio, you are, in a sense, working twenty-four hours a day. Everyone knows that if you are home you are available if they need you. Weigh your lifestyle, your practice, and your preferences carefully when considering whether a design studio at home is appropriate. Generally, we all need to be able to get away from our work, at least at some point of our lives.

Many designers who have home studios are also associated with larger firms under an associate or partnership arrangement. This allows their project management to be handled off of the firm's premises.

The IRS has become less lenient than it was about offices at home. Under current laws, home office expenses are deductible only if that space is used exclusively for your business. If the IRS has reason to believe that the main part of your business is at another location, and your office at home is supplementary, the expense of maintaining it is not deductible.

EQUIPPING YOUR OFFICE

Business equipment and supplies do not sell design, so keep your stock of these as minimal as possible. Your investment needs to be in producing the design project. It's wonderful to have a CADD, but can you really make it cost-effective at this point? If you must have one, can you share one for a while? For every piece of equipment that you consider buying, do a break-even analysis on it first. Ask yourself if it is really appropriate for your practice right now, not two years from now. Remember, you are planning a growing business. Therefore not everything needs to be done immediately.

Drafting Equipment

Until recently drafting equipment has been very simple. Now interior design firms are being forced to acquire more state-of-the-art equipment for drafting and graphics. Usually, instruction on how to use the equipment properly comes as part of the equipment package. Regardless, interior designers and their staffs often enroll in classes on new graphics and drafting techniques because they want to know fast ways of creating beautiful drawings.

When starting up a design studio, you will need to purchase or lease certain basic equipment. The average design studio needs a small blueprint machine at least, as well as some basic equipment to keep day-to-day work on schedule.

The quality of drafting equipment you need depends upon the amount of money you have to spend and the amount of drafting you anticipate doing. Many designers already have certain drafting equipment from school. An average draftsperson can look exceptional if he or she has the right equipment and the right resources.

Blueprint Machine. In general you should acquire the highest quality equipment you can afford. However, in the small office an average quality print machine is usually sufficient. Should the need arise for a large quantity of prints or excellent quality prints, you can send the printing out to a printing source that offers a wide variety of services. Blueprint machines can range from just under $1,000 to five times that amount. The reason for buying the more expensive model is that it is faster.

Drafting Table. Drafting tables come in many sizes; 30″ × 42″ and 37½″ × 60″ are most commonly used in interior design studios. They also range in cost from several hundred dollars to over $1,000. The size of your firm will determine how many tables you will need.

Drafting Machine. A drafting machine is a piece of equipment that goes right on the drafting table to draw the lines and calculate the different degrees. It eliminates the need for a parallel straight edge and triangle. It is also about ten times as expensive.

Supplies. You will need to stock your studio with triangles, scales, templates, drafting tape, lead holders, lead pointers, erasers, paper, and other supplies. When purchasing paper, keep in mind that the color of your printing depends upon the paper you use. Duplicate prints can be made directly from sepia paper. When giving a print to another design professional, you will want to duplicate the original and furnish sepias.

CADD System. CADD is becoming a fairly standard tool for interior designers. CADDs range in price from around $10,000 per designer station for computer, software, and drafting equipment (plotter) to over $100,000 for systems with full architectural capacity. Even a small CADD system will save you a great deal of time. If you want to change an interior plan or try something different, you can do it in a matter of seconds, rather than redrafting a whole plan. See page 67 for more detailed information.

Optical Scanner. An optical scanner makes an exact replica of a picture or photograph. Designers use this device to trace an object, either from a freehand picture in a book or from a floor plan. Then it can be translated directly onto their own drawing. This is a fast, inexpensive way of doing freehand sketches.

DRAFTING EQUIPMENT FOR A SMALL DESIGN OFFICE

1. Drafting table, 30″ × 42″ to 37½″ × 60″ (one for each designer)

2. Parallel straight edge or drafting machine

3. Blueprint machine

4. Drafting stool

5. Supplies: triangles, scales, templates, drafting tape, lead holders, lead pointers, erasers

6. Paper: custom-printed vellum drafting paper with firm's logo, 18″ × 24″ sheets and 24″ × 36″ sheets; print paper for machine, 18″ × 24″ and 24″ × 36″ sheets; sepia paper, 18″ × 24″ sheets

7. Basic starter CADD system

Computers

For interior designers it is no longer a question of whether or not to computerize. The questions are how many computers to buy and for which functions. Computers expand a design business's range and permit the firm to handle a larger workload without adding staff or greatly increasing overhead. To survive and to get the competitive edge, interior designers need to work with present-day tools.

The role of the computer in interior design has changed radically over the past few years. The biggest difference is that the computer is no longer simply a tool for the support staff. At one time, only bookkeepers or secretaries worked with computers. Today, almost every executive not only has a computer, but uses it as a tool to run the business. With computers, information such as a graphical representation of profits or of time expenditures is at an executive's fingertips.

The best reasons for using a computer are:

1. Accuracy. It is not possible to do as exacting work manually. The computer checks mathematics and prevents errors.

2. Easy to compare your work with that of other consultants, such as architects and electrical engineers.

3. Fast and easy changes. Changes that would have taken hours or days to redraw can be done in a matter of minutes.

Computers are replacing secretaries and/or bookkeepers in small offices. Much or all of this work can now be done accurately by designers themselves. Also your accountant can review your books each month by modem for a very low fee, saving you money.

You also need to look at how long it takes to learn to use a system. A number of software packages on the market are very hard to learn. They take anywhere from several weeks to six months to really understand, and that is a major investment. Other packages that are equally capable, but geared for computer novices, can be learned in several days or a week—a significant savings.

If your firm already has some computer equipment, you may be able to reduce your costs by adding onto the existing system.

What does a one-person design firm need in setting up a computer system? If you are starting a new company, don't spend one or two thousand dollars on a typewriter that only types. Instead, buy a word processor or a computer, both of which have a far greater range of functions. If you don't need graphic print capability, you can produce letter-quality printing with a printer costing a few hundred dollars or more, depending on its speed. This will give you the look of an IBM Selectric typewriter. For several thousand dollars you can purchase a laser printer. The resulting documents look as if they are originals, but you have the added benefits of different type sizes and faces and the ability to do graphics.

Areas to Computerize. Routine management procedures such as bookkeeping and financial management are usually the best areas to computerize first, followed by information resources. The next area would be drafting, where programs such as the CADD drafting system can greatly increase your business capacity.

In the typical design office, the bookkeeping and order-processing information is stored on one computer in the business office. However, the design office also needs access to information on delivery schedules and products. Your system could be networked to the design office. The idea is to be able to get the necessary information to as many sources as possible. If you need access to accounting functions, you should be able to get the information without having to go to the accounting room by using the computer at your workstation.

The CADD System. Many offices in the past had a CADD specialist. Today, designers usually have their own CADD workstations but share the output devices such as printers and plotters. CADD is great for conceptual designing. Using CADD, designers can play with options to be sure they will work, rather than having to do roughs and then having them drawn up by a draftsperson. Decisions can be made much faster when using CADD. However, most design offices are keeping a drafting table for doing quick drawings.

Smaller CADD systems suitable for routine work are available for about ten percent of the cost of the large-frame CADD systems. A small system would include a computer, the software programs to run it, and the necessary plotters. Prices vary, depending upon the maintenance agreement, the system's speed, and the geographical area of purchase.

The larger, more expensive systems have a place, but they really are not necessary for the type of work most interior designers do and, in fact, may not even be necessary for many architectural procedures. They have many more features in them than are really necessary.

Software: When setting up a computer system, find the software program most suitable to your firm before you buy a computer (the hardware). Too many firms have bought computer hardware and then have not been able to find compatible software packages. Both IBM-compatible and MacIntosh equipment are standard in the architectural and design fields. Because architectural specifications and programs are available on the IBM-compatible equipment, it is likely that most interior design software will be IBM compatible as well.

Interior design is a specialized field, so it is usually best to buy software from a firm whose programs are designed primarily for interior designers. That way you don't have to purchase capabilities you'll never use. Training on how to run and use these programs is usually part of the package.

There are software packages that eliminate a lot of the manual time that designers used to have to take to specify furniture, fixtures, and equipment. Such software helps you to identify items on a floorplan and allows you to describe the item in as much detail as you need. It takes care of counting every item and introducing them into the budget. The software also produces several types of documents that can be used for bidding or internal use. This software also identifies what you may have omitted. If one hundred types of furniture are identified and only ninety-nine are specified, a person might never notice; but the computer quickly alerts you to the discrepancy.

Computer graphics packages sold for desktop publishing systems can give your proposals a more polished look. Besides the obvious advantages of formatting and error-free typing with these programs, you can also include illustrations and photographs in your proposals.

The design industry is still in its infancy as far as computer use is concerned, but the technology is changing quickly. Every year there is an even broader range of software packages to choose from.

Telephone Systems

Telephone systems today offer so many options that there are many considerations in determining which system to buy or lease. Most of us are learning that some of the new technology is convenient for our design business programs. However, a lot of the offerings are in excess—items that we don't use or don't really need.

When determining what system to buy, work out and list your needs first. Determine how telephone-intensive your practice is. This will then help you to decide just how many phones you need and what kind of services you will require. In some design firms, every person needs a phone. If staff persons are doing marketing or a great deal of customer-relations work, they will be on the phone most of the time and will therefore need their own independent lines.

Define which type of equipment and features you need and review the systems available to determine which best meets your demands.

If you use a modem or telefacsimile ("fax") system, keep these lines separate. They should not tie into your phone system. See below for information on fax and modem technology.

Require that your business or office manager, as well as one or two of your design staff, review the different systems to determine whether they really supply the services that are appropriate for your firm. Very often a management person will review the system from one viewpoint and the marketing department from another. These points of view need to be considered before purchasing.

When considering a new phone system, get at least three quotations and then compare them, both in terms of price and features.

Check the service records of the individual companies you are considering. Consult other people who have used the company's system to determine whether the company has provided appropriate service.

Also review the teaching methods of the company. Does the company train the firms that purchase its system to manage the system and get the most out of it?

Whether you choose to purchase or lease your telephone system is a matter that should be reviewed by your accountant. The decision is generally determined by the cash-flow position of your company.

To purchase or lease a system requires a long-term contract, which makes it very difficult to change systems or alter the one you have. So take time and be sure that you have the appropriate system installed. Try to buy or lease a system with an approximately thirty percent growth potential so that as you need additional phones the system will be able to accommodate them. The life of a system is anticipated to be from twelve to fifteen years. However, technology today is changing rapidly and you may find yourself changing your telephone system more frequently to obtain new features.

Fax (Telefacsimile) Machine. This is a computer system similar to a photocopier, used for transmitting words or images through a telephone system. For example, a designer can send drawings or details over the telephone to a factory to determine feasibility of design or for pricing. The receiver must also have a compatible system.

Modem. This instrument is a modulator-demodulator that codes information into audible frequencies for transmission through telephone lines. For example, a design studio can be connected by modem with a fabricating firm. The design firm can then transmit drawings directly from its CADD to the factory. Drawings are usually clearer when sent by modem than by fax machine since transmission is from one computer to another. Again, the receiver needs compatible equipment.

Voice Mail. This machine is an advanced type of answering machine. It lets the caller leave a message when he or she gets a busy signal or no answer at the extension he or she is calling.

The Design Library

In your practice, you will constantly be needing information for efficient management of resources, to specify products, to control business operations, and to meet government regulations. Your design library will need to contain directories, catalogs, and an unwieldy collection of samples for carpets, fabrics, wallcoverings, laminates, paints, yarns, and wood finishes. Reference books, professional journals, new product brochures, tear sheets, and articles clipped from magazines and showhouse guides add to the incipient chaos.

In a design studio, it is important to allow space for a good working library.

Because there is no convenient resource for the samples, product catalogs and directories, or even the specialized publications interior designers need, designers have to supply most of their own reference materials. The quality of your library strongly affects how well you are able to perform your services.

The first rule in establishing a design library is to define your studio's needs and then to research the companies and sources to secure the appropriate products to fill those needs. Don't keep anything that is not useful.

Every collection that goes into your library needs an assigned position. Catalogs should be kept together, as should samples. You need open shelving for books, magazines and catalogs, and standard drawer files for smaller catalogs not kept in binders and articles and pages torn from magazines. Product samples come in all shapes and sizes and should be filed according to their physical properties. Lucite trays and drawers are invaluable for some carpet samples; so are standard metal file drawers. Within your catalog section, furniture for contract office space should be kept together, apart from lighting fixtures or upholstered furniture.

A cross-referenced card file is necessary for easy retrieval of information. Many product lines are apt to be classified in more than one category. An office-furniture catalog might include desks and seating as well as some accessories and wallcoverings. Most companies supply more than one type of product, so the card file should be organized both by company and by product type. It is a simple matter to also note on the card whether you have samples, if these are purchased or complimentary, and where they are kept.

Professional assistance in setting up an organized and easy-to-use library is available. Susan Noel has designed interior-design and architectural libraries for both small and large firms based on traditional library standards and coded according to the Construction Specifications Institute's system. She goes into a firm and physically sets up the system, taking six to ten months. Her library system offers complete documentation of every item used in the field, and cross-references and documents the position of each item and catalog.

AN INTERIOR DESIGN LIBRARY COLLECTION

1. Catalogs

2. Price lists

3. Textbooks and reference books

4. Directories and bibliographies

5. Professional journals and periodicals

6. Research and reference reports

7. Clippings and tear sheets

8. Fabric samples

9. Carpets

10. Wood and finish sample chips

11. Paint chips and wallcovering samples

12. Lighting samples

13. Other sample items, depending upon the type of practice

Although a design library is highly individual, there are basic categories we all handle.

1. *Catalogs from Vendors.* These are a designer's primary source of specification information on all design projects. They are expensive to produce and space is increasingly valuable, so you should only keep catalogs for the product lines you use, which means you must make a constant review of product lines. Catalogs are easiest to handle when placed on open shelves alphabetically by the manufacturer's name within product categories.

2. *Price Lists.* Before filing these, you must carefully label them as to whether they are at-cost or at-list prices. Some are easy to identify, but others need careful scrutiny. Price lists are often filed directly with the catalogs. If the price list is at cost and this file is directly referenced by clients, studios occasionally will file these price lists individually. Price lists for different categories should be kept separate; i.e., fabric lines should be kept from furniture lines. Keep discount information either in the master file or with the price list. Some design firms code this information so that if the customer sees the price list, he or she will not be able to easily discern the information.

3. *Textbooks and Reference Books.* These are invaluable for every designer.

4. *Directories and Bibliographies.* These are important reference tools and should be grouped together because they are constantly used for specification requirements. Duplicate directories are useful for those most often used.

5. *Professional Journals and Periodicals.* These magazines are easiest to keep track of when one person is responsible for them and a distribution schedule is designated (see pages 265–67). You should be able to manage with a single subscription of each magazine, with an appropriate circulation schedule and filing system. A special section of the library should be devoted to their storage. Periodical storage boxes can be used, but storing magazines on open shelves is more practical since these publications are usually used as reference materials for their first year or so.

6. *Research or Reference Reports.* These need to be indexed for easy retrieval. This type of material is often used with individual proposals. They should be filed in manila folders and labeled according to the subject and date.

7. *Clippings and Tear Sheets from Catalogs or Magazines.* These should also be filed in folders. Some of the newest products and best photographs of products appear in magazines, and your clippings can be good selling tools.

8. *Fabric Samples.* These may take up minimal space if your design firm is in a major market city when there is easy access to showrooms. In this case, samples are borrowed at no charge for one week to thirty days. These are called memo samples, and there is no charge unless the designer fails to return the sample. Outside of these market cities, design studios usually purchase samples at the beginning of each season because the mailing time for memo samples would drastically increase the time of developing a project.

    The samples themselves have a life of two to four years. Many studios tag and code these so the resources are not identifiable to the customer. Upholstery fabric samples are generally twenty-seven by twenty-seven inches, and other fabrics are a yard and a half or one full repeat. Designers need some fabric samples that can be cut and worked into presentation boards, so even a city practice has some outlay for samples.

Firms that do not maintain a physical selection of fabrics use catalogs defining types of fabrics available from each supplier, and have an appropriate collection of price lists.

9. *Carpets*. Carpet samples are normally presented in folders and are best filed on shelves alphabetically by company name and type of carpet. Additional three-by-five-inch samples are useful and should be filed according to color as an effective cross reference; this size is also good to use on presentation boards. Larger carpet samples—usually eighteen by twenty-seven inches or larger—are kept on open shelves. Some design firms buy samples of the carpets they use frequently, but companies that do purely contract work quite commonly receive these samples on a complimentary basis.

Anything unusual—the rare fabric or unusual catalog—is ordinarily purchased. Companies you work with in volume will give you samples, but in residential work and specialty fields, purchasing samples is the norm.

Storing samples of oddly shaped items is best done in shelves and drawers, according to size. These may be wood chips or larger items used for construction, depending on the type of projects you do. Keeping a room organized for these samples can be the most difficult part of maintaining a design studio.

The use of computers may decrease the physical space needed for catalogs. Some of the larger manufacturers have developed a modem that check specification information for their direct dealerships, and there is hope that this practice will spread to general use.

Reference checks via computer allow a design to get information on an unfamiliar source on a per-inquiry basis, and many reference materials are now available in software packages easily accessed by the computer.

Even when specification checks and catalog resources are completely computerized, however, design studios will still need product libraries. Clients want to feel a fabric, and designers want to test and see the quality of a carpet, wallcovering, fixture, or other product.

Chapter Five

DEVELOPING A TEAM OF STAFF AND CONSULTANTS

*Form for fore-
casting labor
requirements. This
form will make it
easy for you to
determine what
kind of personnel
you will need in
the future and
which jobs you
can accomplish in
a given period of
time.*

Aside from you, the most valuable asset of your design firm is the staff. So much emphasis is put on building, properties, dealerships, or lines, that it is sometimes forgotten that the quality of your support staff contributes to your success or holds you back. When you begin your business, or consider any growth or restructuring, carefully review what part you plan to play in that growth and what kind of staffing you need to accomplish your goals. Staffing your business with the best quality of people should be your design firm's highest priority.

FORECASTING REQUIREMENTS

The nature of the projects you have scheduled determines what kind of person- nel you will need in the future. This forecasting is easy when you keep an ongoing list of each project you have, the type of staffing required for each project, and the

Project:	Type of Staff Required:	Hours of Work Required:											
		JAN.	FEB.	MAR.	APR.	MAY	JUNE	JULY	AUG.	SEP.	OCT.	NOV.	DEC.

FORECASTING LABOR REQUIREMENTS   Year:

© Design Business Monthly

hours of work that you anticipate will be needed from your staff during the next twelve months. Keep this information on a form and use a separate form for your staff to list their individual projects; their estimated hours of work for the next month and the months to come; and any other job responsibilities that they have, such as marketing. Keeping these two forms up-to-date will help you analyze which jobs you can accomplish in a given period of time.

In day-to-day business it is easy to assign projects and then to forget what a given person is doing and how much time it ought to take. Fortunately, business is not static; but in taking on additional priorities you can sometimes forget about your staff's previous commitments. These forecasting sheets on the staff members and their projects tell you where they are going and how frantic their schedule is. You can see, at a glance, whether a project needs additional support or whether you can handle it in-house by reapportioning the work loads.

These sheets are effective for firms of all sizes, even a single-person firm. Employee scheduling sheets can also be valuable aids in forecasting the income from current projects. They indicate which projects should be completed in a certain time and what the compensation from them should be.

Before considering hiring anyone, do an analysis of the project. Outline the direction in which you see your company going and determine what is financially practical for you to do. In analyzing the job, you should check the following:

▶ What is the work to be accomplished?

▶ Do I need additional help to do it or can I use the staff that I have, working overtime or extra at some point?

Monthly staff work plan. On this form staff members list their individual projects and responsibilities for the month and the estimated time they will need to perform them. This form can help remind you what a given person is doing so that you can utilize your staff most effectively.

MONTHLY STAFF WORK PLAN		Month:			
Person:	Project:	Estimated Time Required:			
		Week 1	Week 2	Week 3	Week 4
Other Responsibilities:		Time Required:			

© Design Business Monthly

- Is there any temporary staffing available?

- Could I hire a consultant or someone out-of-house to help us for this period of time?

- Am I going to need the kind of person who can do this work on a continuing basis?

- What kind of experience should the person I hire have?

- What type of skills are necessary to do this job?

- What is the labor market today?

- Can I get the type of person I want, and if not, can I modify this job to fit the kind of person I am able to get?

- What am I able to pay?

- Will this job remain attractive for the person I hire in the future?

- Will the person I hire be able to develop his or her career here and perhaps still fit into other parts of my design firm?

STAFF POSITIONS

When planning your business, you need to consider not only how many staff members you should have, but also what types of employees are necessary for your firm's size and goals.

Chief Executive Officer (CEO) Principal

The performance of the chief executive officer or the designer who starts the company and/or runs the firm plays a major role in the success of a design company. A chief executive officer of a highly successful, rapidly growing firm usually works at least 65 to 100 hours a week. The CEO has a heavy investment in the firm emotionally, physically, and financially. In design firms that do not have a great degree of growth, investigation shows that their principal people usually work fewer than 65 hours per week or are not as excited or as stimulated as the higher performers.

Because the performance of the firm as a whole is so dependent on the CEO, there need to be some safeguards in place to keep that CEO stimulated and excited about the work. It is all too easy for a CEO to burn out because of the stress of various administrative problems. Therefore efforts must be taken to keep that person enthusiastic if everyone else in the firm is to continue at a high performance level.

In *In Search of Excellence*, Thomas Peters and Robert Waterman clearly state that the chief executive officer has a lot to do with the performance level of the corporation. I find this even more so in design firms. So does Stuart Rose, whose *Achieving Excellence in Your Design Practice* (Whitney Library of Design, 1987) concentrates on design-firm management.

It is not just the CEO's design talent and design excitement, but his or her excitement for business and ability to use the tools of business that generate success.

Some of the most successful design firms do not have a formal structure within the group. In these firms, CEOs have hands-on involvement with all of their key people. These design firms work as a team, and the chief executive officer usually refers to the firm as "we." These designers have a vision that they are able to share with their staff and their clients. This intimate involvement and excitement are what makes these companies successful.

Managing Director or Business Manager

The managing director or business manager is responsible for the management of the company, whether the firm has three or four people or as many as seventy-five. The business manager is responsible for coordinating schedules, processing and expediting orders, managing finances, and handling any business management problem that arises. This person usually has the authority to fire and to hire. He or she deals with most of a company's consultants, such as accountants, attorneys, and other business professionals.

Although a business manager usually has very little to do with the design end of a business, he or she can assist in setting standards for markups.

Usually the business manager should be a person with a business-management background rather than one in interior design. If we want to make a firm financially successful, we need different outlooks on a job.

It is important for this person to be familiar with current business vocabulary because most interior designers are short on business education.

Marketing Director or Manager of Business Development

Most design firms find it necessary to have a director in charge of developing business. Most design firms that are successful (running close to their total potential productivity) have one or more people doing marketing or business promotion for them.

Marketing and sales are usually part of every staff member's responsibilities. However, a good marketing program requires a primary person on the staff devoting his or her complete attention to this area. The marketing director has a great deal of control over the general direction of the company and therefore the authority endowed in this person is considerable.

A marketing director should be a person who enjoys developing and creating business—a person who likes to sell. This kind of personality is of great profit to any firm. Finding a good marketing director can be difficult. Most firms hire a person who has design experience but prefers to be out there selling and developing business. The salary or income of a marketing director is usually very high, which is why this position often attracts other staff members.

Human Resource Manager

The human resource manager was formerly known as the personnel administrator. In a small firm, the human resource manager job may be handled by the principal, but in a firm with twelve designers or more, this job requires a specific employee. This may be either a staff member or a consultant.

Today, the position of human resource manager goes far beyond what was the typical personnel manager's job of hiring and firing and establishing a personnel structure. The human resource manager is now asked to build a unified, productive work force that is motivated to achieve the company's objectives. This person needs to be a results-oriented individual, willing and able to develop a work force to fit the diversified needs of a design firm. Both small and large firms are realizing that staffing can greatly increase or inhibit the quality of a company's growth.

The functions of this position are basically staffing, personnel-program administration, and planning for future staffing needs.

Human resource managers are involved in many different areas, including the following:

▸ *Staffing*. They ensure that positions are filled with qualified individuals who are trained appropriately and are able to meet the company's objectives.

▶ *Training and Organizational Development.* They can devise programs, procedures, and methodology to improve the performance of individual staff members. They can develop training programs, bring in consultants, and introduce new equipment that will elevate the staff's productive capabilities so the company can grow and be more profitable. The staff will have the opportunity to do better work, advance, and gain better income.

▶ *Salary and Benefits Program Administration.* They organize the total compensation programs of the company as a whole, as well as individual salary situations.

▶ *Employee Relations and Communication.* They create an environment that helps the company and the individual workers be more productive. They help with overall structuring and decision making to develop a feeling of teamwork among the staff. They develop communication programs that are necessary for employees.

Receptionist

In most design firms, the receptionist and the person who answers the phone are the same person. This person represents you more than any other person in your firm, and the quality of his or her interaction with clients is very important to the clients' attitude towards your company.

To be a good receptionist requires knowledge, control, grace, and courtesy. Find someone who knows all the people in your firm, what their strengths are, and how the firm operates. Then place that person in this key position and pay him or her well. Make sure that you have someone who is a "greeter"—someone who has courtesy and charm. It makes for very happy clients, and also helps keep your day's schedule workable.

Other Staff Positions

Depending on the size of your design firm, you may want to hire various other types of staff members, including the following:

▶ *Assistant Designer.* This is a trained designer who works with a more advanced design professional. While this person has a formal education in design, he or she may lack the necessary experience, creativity, or drive to be in a position with more responsibility.

▶ *Bookkeeper.* This person records business transactions in an orderly fashion. (See pages 239–40 for additional information about this important position.)

▶ *Draftsperson.* This person draws plans or sketches. He or she usually has special training in architecture and design.

▶ *Installation Specialist.* This person is responsible for all the details of actual installations. His or her skill and ability to handle problems on site keep the work moving. An installation specialist also knows how to present a project with great showmanship. The closest analogy is "magician."

▶ *Librarian.* This specialist manages a design firm's library. He or she may have a formal design education, or simply a long-term experience with the firm. A secretary or member of your design support staff could be trained to handle this function.

▶ *Project Manager.* This person manages the resources and activities used to achieve a set of objectives on a project within a specified time schedule.

▶ *Renderer.* This is an interior designer or illustrator who creates drawings called renderings of interior design or architectural work, usually while the work is still in the conceptual stages.

- *Salesperson*. This person sells design services or products.

- *Secretary*. This person handles correspondence and manages routine office work.

- *Staff Designer*. This is a person with a design education who works for a design firm or department. The necessary qualifications and responsibilities for this position vary according to the designer's abilities and the firm's administrative structure.

Short-Term Staff

If you have a special project that you know is only going to last two or three months, you should see if you can either hire a freelancer or borrow a staff person from another firm.

Freelancers. The interior design field is full of freelancers who are available and willing to work with you on specialized projects. In hiring a freelancer it is important to define the parameters of the relationship. When your project is confidential, for example, you need to be careful in hiring freelancers. The person you hire should be asked to sign a statement to the effect that he or she understands that this project requires confidentiality. Freelancers are a very good resource, and if you use these people regularly, you can hire them as independent contractors, which relieves your firm of some overhead expenses.

Borrowing a Staff Person. We all know designers working in other communities. It is often possible to borrow a worker from another firm for a week or two to get you through a special project. This is a good way of bringing an expert into your firm. You have the benefit of knowing the standards of the design studio that they come from, and they can often gain new perspectives from being in your studio for a while. Design firms that work closely together can easily borrow and exchange staff members, which gives them the flexibility of being able to do large projects without the encumbrance of a larger staff.

Independent Contractors

Today the majority of design firms use as many independent contractors as possible. By hiring independent contractors, firms pay for services as they are rendered, saving on staffing costs. With the heavy fluctuation in design work most firms experience, using independent contractors helps them keep overhead down.

Among the independent contractors a design firm might use are the following:

- *Artisan*. A skilled mechanic in a manual occupation. This person is more highly skilled than a tradesman or craftsperson.

- *Craftsperson*. One who practices a trade or manual occupation with a certain degree of skill that separates him or her from tradesmen.

- *Contractor*. A person or company who undertakes to perform work, usually for a specific project at a specified price within a certain time limit.

- *Tradesman (or Tradesperson)*. A worker in a skilled trade such as plumbing, carpentry, or electrical wiring. This person is generally not as highly skilled as a craftsperson or artisan.

What are the differences between an independent contractor and an employee? The IRS scrutinizes this grey area carefully. One must take care in maintaining the records which prove the legitimacy of these independent contractors in the case of a tax examination. Here are a few guidelines from tax experts that will classify whether someone is an independent contractor or an employee.

Acknowledgment of Independent Contractor. If you are taking on an independent contractor and want to be sure that you will not be responsible for taxes and other liability issues, it is important to acknowledge the independent contractor's status. Either use an agreement similar to the following example or have your attorney write up one for your specific situation. You will also want to document the types of insurance that your contractor will have, noting any liability issues relating to your company. It is advisable to list the type of policy, the liability limits, and the company with which he or she is insured; show this list to your insurance agent to be sure that the coverage is appropriate.

FINDING THE RIGHT EMPLOYEES

The ability to attract and to keep good workers is an extremely valuable asset. It is not easy to do. People work together for many reasons. In the design field, financial considerations are not always the major ones.

How do design firms acquire new staff members? Two of the most common ways are through working together on a project and by learning about someone from a resource or individual who knows your firm. Other sources of recruitment for new staffers include design schools, other designers, ASID, and any professional groups where one has the chance to meet design professionals. Many firms find the most successful employees are students right out of school whom they can train in their own work methods.

Writing a Job Description

Before hiring a new person, prepare a job description. This should include the approximate duties that will be performed; the responsibilities; and the specific

ACKNOWLEDGMENT OF INDEPENDENT CONTRACTOR

This acknowledges that _____ has been retained

for services (describe services here)

These services as stated above will be paid for in the following manner:

Amount:

Method of Payment:

It is acknowledged that:

A. The undersigned shall be deemed an independent contractor and is not

    an employee, partner, agent, or engaged in a joint venture with

    Company.

B. Consistent with the foregoing, the Company shall not deduct

    withholding taxes, FICA, or any other taxes required to be deducted

    by an employee as I acknowledge my responsibility to pay same as an

    independent contractor.

C. I further acknowledge that I shall not be entitled to any fringe

    benefits, pension, retirement, profit sharing, or any other benefits

    accruing to employees.

D. I further state that I have the following insurance covering my

    work:

    Type of Policy:

    Limit:

    Company:

                                        _____

skills, necessary education, and experience required. For some jobs, we can train the new staff member, but for others we need a competent individual who can perform the job immediately. Review your work objectives so that they properly mesh with your staff selection.

A job description should include the following information:

▶ *Job Title.*

▶ *Start Date.* The date you will need this person.

▶ *Immediate Supervisor.* To whom will the employee report? Is the new person to be an assistant to another designer or an assistant to your expediter? Whatever the position is, clearly spell out the chain of command.

▶ *Required Background.* For example, "This person needs a degree in interior design and three years of experience working in the commercial office-related field."

▶ *Job Responsibilities.* List specifics, such as design layout work, or assisting with the presentation.

▶ *Desired Experience.* What experience would be ideal? Perhaps you would like the person to have worked with certain types of landscape panels. Or maybe he or she should be familiar with all the components required in building and putting together a state-of-the-art office.

▶ *Special Problems.* Are there special problems associated with this particular job? Will the job require working with other people with whom the new employee must be compatible?

▶ *Travel Requirements.* Write down whether the employee will be handling some out-of-town projects which will require him or her to travel to other cities. List the percentage of time you anticipate he or she will spend out of town.

▶ *Salary Range.*

▶ *Benefits.* Other compensation, such as health insurance, paid vacation days, and merchandise discounts.

▶ *Opportunities.* Does the job offer a chance for professional growth?

▶ *Limitations.* What are the negative features of the job? In our firm we have three people in line for promotion ahead of any newcomer. A new employee cannot expect rapid promotion.

Trying a Person Out

If you can, it is good to try out a prospective employee on a special project. If the person is unemployed, he or she can come into your studio and work for a few weeks; otherwise he or she can work on a weekend basis or after hours. Trying a job is a great way for both the employee and the employer to test the situation.

INTERVIEWING A PROSPECTIVE EMPLOYEE

Every firm has a different interviewing procedure. I need an outline with me when I am interviewing a prospective employee, or I forget what I need to cover.

Interview Techniques

In the interview, compare the job requirements with the stated abilities and experience of the applicant. Discuss the requirements with the applicant, and discuss what you understand his or her background to be. You should usually ask to see a résumé and a portfolio. And it doesn't hurt to have the person fill out a standard application form on the spot; it gives you some basis for your evaluation. If the person is applying to be on your design team, you should have him or her fill out the design staff questionnaire on pages 82–84.

Because most design firms are small, if a new person doesn't fit in it can cause a lot of problems. Try to get the applicant to talk about his or her background. Take notes, and when you are finishing the interview, review these with your candidate. Try to find out what the applicant's career goals are so that you can determine whether the job you can offer will fit with his or her objectives. If you are seriously interested in the person, you may want to mention the fringe benefits and extra duties of the job.

Equal Opportunity Laws. There are a number of laws that prevent an employer from discriminating against an applicant on the basis of race, religion, sex, national origin, or age. According to the Small Business Administration, you may not ask the following questions without risking being considered discriminatory against an employee or a prospective employee. Be warned.

QUESTIONS NOT TO ASK

Employers have often asked questions about the following topics in the past, but today they are considered discriminatory.

▶ Marital status

▶ Birthplace

▶ Age

▶ Religion

▶ How or when citizenship was obtained

▶ Extracurricular or nonprofessional affiliations or memberships in organizations

▶ The applicant's wife's maiden name

▶ The applicant's maiden name

▶ Relatives. (However, after people are employed, you can ask them for the name and address of their next of kin in case of an emergency.)

▶ How skill in a foreign language was acquired

▶ Any arrests for crimes. You may ask, however, if a person was ever convicted of a crime. (Note: It is illegal to refuse to hire an employee for falsely answering a question about his or her arrest record.)

▶ Whether there are children

▶ Physical characteristics. It is illegal to ask questions about an applicant's weight or height or to request a photograph of the applicant.

▶ If the applicant was ever refused bonding

▶ Possessions; whether the applicant owns a car or a home

▶ Whether the applicant's spouse works or parents work or any information about their jobs

▶ Previous wages or salaries and any extras that the applicant has received

---

Design staff questionnaire. This questionnaire should be filled out by design staff applicants, and it should be updated annually by each member of your design team. These forms will help you in planning your company's objectives, evaluating your staff, and matching projects with appropriate staff members.

DESIGN STAFF QUESTIONNAIRE

| Name: | Address: | Phone No.: |
| | | Date: |

Education:

Design School or College:

Degree Received:

| Courses Studied: | From: | To: |

Awards Received:

Other Education: (workshops, seminars, etc.)

Subject:	Dates Attended:

© Design Business Monthly

Employment Experience:

Company: From: To:

Your Title:

Job Experience:

Company: From: To:

Your Title:

Job Experience:

Company: From: To:

Your Title:

Job Experience:

Company: From: To:

Your Title:

Job Experience:

Professional organizations to which you belong and offices, committees,
or posts that you have held in these organizations:

Any special abilities or knowledge that you feel would be of benefit to
the firm, i.e., certain social acquaintances, fluency in foreign
languages, knowledge within other disciplines, list of prospective
clients with whom you are familiar or have had experience:

© Design Business Monthly

Design Project Experience:

Type: Date:

Client or Owner:

Cost of Total Project:

Cost of Work Done by Design Firm:

Services Rendered by Design Firm:

Your Responsibilities:

Accomplishments on this Project:

Type: Date:

Client or Owner:

Cost of Total Project:

Cost of Work Done by Design Firm:

Services Rendered by Design Firm:

Your Responsibilities:

Accomplishments on this Project:

Other Relative Information:

© Design Business Monthly

Obviously firms have preferences in design styles and qualifications, but you must be very cautious not to allow personal prejudice to enter into your selection criteria. It is too easy to be sued for discrimination. A firm can still select people that it would like; however, it must be cautious that the applicants are judged for their professional merit and suitability.

Legal Commitments. Be careful what you promise new employees. On paper their qualifications may be excellent, but on the job they may not perform to expectations. Yet, in many instances, you can be held liable for commitments made to employees. Employees can also be held liable for their commitments to their employers. You must be cautious in the way you outline a project to a new employee. If you can, give a person a test period to evaluate his or her capabilities before you make definite commitments.

Getting References

When a prospective employee interviews with your firm, you may want to obtain information from his or her previous employer. For legal reasons, it is best to get written permission from the applicant authorizing the previous employer to release information about the applicant's work so the previous employer will not be put in jeopardy. This will help you get a better quality of information. At the time of the interview, you ask the prospective employee to sign a release form. Then send the release with your questions or the form that you want filled out by the previous employer.

It is advisable to have an attorney prepare a release form to ensure that the statements are legally stated and that the proper release of liability is included.

When sending an applicant's previous employer a request for information about the prospective employee, you should try to include the authorization-to-release-information letter signed by that person, so that the firm knows that they have their former employee's permission to give out this information. A letter similar to the one found on page 86 could be used.

Hiring an Employee

When you decide to hire a person to be an employee, send him or her a letter defining the position and the conditions of the employment to prevent this from becoming an issue later on. A special notation should be made that the association will be an at-will relationship; this means that either the employer or the employee may determine to end the relationship at any time. Again, for legal purposes, it is well to have this documented.

Noncompetitive Agreements. It is becoming common in the design field to ask employees to sign noncompetitive agreements when you hire them. In signing this, an employee agrees that if he or she leaves your employment he or she cannot work at the same type of business in that same community for a period of time, which could be six months, a year, or longer. These agreements are very common, but our attorneys have advised us that they are difficult to support and expensive to fight. I have seen agreements restricting a designer from working in the field for as long as ten years. Such an agreement would never stand up in court because it is denying a person his or her livelihood.

If you are considering moving from a job where you have a noncompetitive agreement, review it with your attorney first. Clarify your position before negotiating a future job.

If you are considering hiring someone who has an agreement with another company within your city, it would be best for you to run the agreement by your attorney. He or she can prepare a document to absolve your company of any responsibility, leaving all the liability with the prospective employee. However, you may be recommended to delay the hiring until the situation is legally clear.

Request for employment reference. A letter such as this should be sent to a prospective employee's former employer.

DATE:

RE:

Dear (former employer):

We have received an application for employment from _____,
seeking a position with our firm in the above capacity. We understand
the applicant was previously employed by your firm. We would appreciate
a reference on the individual, including confirmation of the dates of
employment with you, a performance evaluation, and the reasons for
termination. We have enclosed a release signed by the above-named
person.

Please advise whether your reference should be held confidential.

Thank you for your anticipated cooperation.

Very truly,

_____

*Employment letter.
This letter should
be sent to a person
when you decide
to hire him or her
to be an employee.
It defines the
position and the
conditions of the
employment for
future reference.*

DATE:

TO: (employee)

Dear (employee):

We are pleased to confirm your being employed by our design firm in
the position of _____. You will report directly to
_____, to start employment on _____, 19___.

Your salary shall be $_____ per _____. You will also be
covered by Blue Cross and Blue Shield plans and receive fringe benefits,
as explained. For the first year, vacation time shall be prorated and
you will be entitled to _____ day's vacation this year.

It is understood and accepted that the employment relationship we have
agreed to is an at-will relationship, and that it may be ended by either
party, at any time, and for any reason.

If you agree this letter sets forth our understanding, please sign the
enclosed copy and return it for our files.

We look forward to your joining the company.

Very truly,

_____

Agreed and accepted:

_____

(Employee)

Noncompetitive agreements are not legal in all states; but if they are legal within your state, you may find them helpful. It has been my experience that very few of these agreements hold up in court, but they sometimes encourage an employee to be more focused during the time of his or her employment.

Notifying Other Applicants

When you decide not to hire a person you interviewed, send that person a letter or call him or her promptly. Tell the person frankly that the position has been filled so he or she can continue job hunting. It is kind, and can create good will, to give applicants some idea why they were not selected. However, be careful what you say to avoid your words' being construed as a form of discrimination. It doesn't hurt to keep on good terms with these people; at some time they might fit in for another type of job with your firm. The design world is a small one; it usually pays to be friendly towards as many people as possible.

SALARIES AND BENEFITS

The salaries and compensations of interior design firms vary considerably from firm to firm and from town to town. Interior designers earn from very minimal to very high rates. The high rates are based almost completely upon performance. Normally designers begin at a starting rate and receive raises according to their productivity or the amount of work that they are able to bring into a firm. In today's market, the designers who are able to bring in the work, or become part of that sales team, are generally the best paid. There are some high performers in different, unusual situations, but it is usually the designer who has proven ability to make things happen who gets the highest compensation.

A designer's performance can be easily measured. Designers' charges are usually based either on an hourly rate, for productivity, or on a flat rate, for value. When designers are paid in terms of value, this can bring in higher revenues to the firm and therefore reap larger profits. In addition to salaries, many designers earn either a percentage of the firm's year-end profits or a percentage of the profits on the jobs that they handled.

Designers who work in sales are usually given a direct percentage compensation of the business that they bring to the firm.

The higher a job is within a firm, the less fixed the salary or compensation tends to be. With higher jobs, the income is more apt to vary based on individual productivity or the profits of the firm. Designers who are holding the highest paying jobs in firms may have as high a ratio as ten percent fixed salary and ninety percent variable income. Designers in lower positions will receive either fixed salaries or salaries supplemented with small percentages of income based on productivity or profits.

Designers' income levels are not what they could be. In order for the level of income to be raised, higher levels of productivity need to be established. In almost every company that I have reviewed, I have found that if the firm were able to get an additional twenty or thirty percent more new business, or were able to enlarge its projects to get an additional twenty or thirty percent profit margin, the firm would be able to pay its employees considerably more. Today's interior designers need to review just what makes them productive to determine how they might develop their salary potential.

Design Firm Benefits

Many of us work in the design field because we enjoy meeting people and like the work we do. But emotional benefits don't pay the rent. Today everyone needs some form of financial benefits. The majority of design firms do not have as large a benefit package as is offered by other, larger businesses. But most are attempting to remedy this as best they can.

```
DATE:


TO:



We appreciate your interest in employment by our firm.


We regret to inform you that the available position has been filled, and
we cannot consider your application at the present time.


We will keep your application on file for future reference should an
opening arise.


Very truly,




_____
```

Health Benefits. Standard Blue Cross/Blue Shield, or any other health insurance program that can give employees standard health benefits, is generally one of the primary benefits an employee expects. Whether the company or the employee pays the premiums depends upon the individual's contract. You should look for a package with the appropriate flexibility to meet your individual employees' needs. Pat Choate, in his book *The High-Flex Society,* suggests that insurance plans should be designed so that the coverage can remain with the employee should he or she leave your firm.

Vacations. Traditionally, design firms are not outstanding in terms of vacation benefits offered. Although larger firms will sometimes have different vacation schedules, most firms give employees one to two weeks. Many design firms require the entire staff to take vacations at the same time because they feel they cannot work with a short staff. Other companies do not permit more than one person to be gone from any department at a time. Obviously, your individual production schedule must be considered, but it is the rule that designers do not take vacations at prime contract periods, such as when a big contract is due or when there is a large installation. Since most design firms are of moderate size, work schedules have to take priority over personal ones, and vacation and off-time are arranged around contracts.

Insurance. A design firm is required by law to provide workmen's compensation insurance to its employees. Some firms also offer insurance coverage in case of illness or death.

Discounts. Usually interior design firms try to make available to their staff any interior furnishings that they have access to at reasonable or moderate terms. Sometimes employees will be given a discount on the retail price; in other instances they will be charged a small percentage over cost. It is usually appropriate for the firm to get some compensation for order-processing and delivery. Great buying privileges are one of the perks of working for a design firm.

Retirement Plans. In many situations, affording a proper retirement plan is difficult for small firms because the actuarial costs are so high. It costs a minimum of $1,200 per year plus $200 per employee to meet the government requirements for a deferred benefit plan. If you do not have a large enough group to have a retirement plan within your company, you might offer to match your employee's contribution to his or her existing retirement accounts. For example, you might offer to contribute up to 5 percent of their income, not to exceed $1,000. In this way your employees are getting some contribution, although not as much as they might be receiving from a more accelerated plan. Retirement plans must be set up according to government regulations, and they require constant updating. Check with your accountant and financial advisor regarding retirement plans, as the new tax laws are not yet clearly defined and revisions are being made almost daily. There are many companies that have been forced to change their plans due to the new regulations. Bringing in special consultants to help you set up your firm's retirement planning is almost a must.

Tax-Deferred Qualified Retirement Plans. Today most profitable design firms are exerting much effort to develop and maintain a well-trained team. In order to do this, appropriate compensation programs need to be in place. Fortunately, there have been many changes in the last few years that make it practical and cost effective for smaller companies to have good tax-deferred savings plans. The administration costs for managing a program according to government regulations by a qualified plan administrator can vary, based on the complexity of the plan, from as low as $300 to as high as $2,000 per year.

There are many advantages to these types of plans. Since they are tax deferred, a person is permitted to accrue a larger amount of savings than would be possible if taxes were paid at the time the monies were earned. Most often we are in a higher tax bracket during these high-income years than when we retire.

This is an area where it is best to consult your financial advisor. Plans are usually required for all employees, but many exclusions are permitted. There are ways to design plans to dedicate greater funding to long-term, more valuable, or higher paid staff members. There have been, and will be, considerable changes in the ruling of qualified employee pension plans. In most cases, it is best to have a professional administer your plan.

There is a limit to the income on which these plans are based: $200,000 + CPI (Consumer Price Index), which is the government's standard for cost of living increases. The two plans can be used in combination if the person is making less than $200,000 per year and would like to maximize his contributions and maintain discretionary flexibility.

Defined Contribution Pension Plan. A nondiscretionary plan for deposits to a tax-deferred account. This plan allows 1% to 25% of payroll with a maximum limit of $30,000 to an individual's account.

Profit-Sharing Plan. A way of allowing an employer to create tax-deferred deposits on a discretionary basis. There is a limit of 15% of payroll, with a maximum of $30,000 to an individual account balance.

401K Plan. This provision of a profit-sharing plan allows for employee contributions on a tax-deferred basis. This plan can stand alone or be used with a profit-sharing plan.

Defined Benefit Plans. This plan first establishes a defined benefit. If you are an older person and want to put away a lot of tax-deferred money, this plan can be used to create larger deposits. The funding for a pension or profit-sharing plan may be developed through many vehicles. These consist of Exchange-listed stocks, mutual funds, guaranteed profits from insurance companies, savings bonds, corporate bonds, and any paper issued by the agencies of the government.

Stock Ownership Plans. Many design firms offer ownership opportunities, often the key to maintaining a high-level staff. A recent study by the National Center for Employment Ownership confirms that

▶ Employee-owner companies enjoy increased rates of growth after installing a plan.

▶ Companies offering ownership to most or all of their employees have a median annual sales growth twice that of other companies.

▶ Employee-owned companies have greater operating margins and returns on equity than similar companies not sharing ownership.

▶ Over a ten-year period, most design firms provide substantial financial benefits to employees.

Key Person Insurance. The death or disability of a primary person within a firm must be expected to cause major losses or heavy financial obligations to a company. This insurance not only protects the firm against such possible losses, but can also assure that an appropriate person (beneficiary) will have funds to purchase the company from the heirs. This type of insurance can make a major contribution to the successful management of a company at this time of crisis by providing indemnification for the loss of services. This insurance can

▶ Pay for the recruitment and training of a suitable replacement

▶ Aid the company in maintaining its credit standing

▶ Secure the business so it can continue by providing working capital

- Provide funds to redeem the key person's stock so the remaining staff can control the firm rather than the deceased person's family or relatives
- Provide benefits for the key person's family
- Fund a deferred compensation plan for the key person's retirement

EMPLOYEE EVALUATIONS

It is traditional for a firm to have year-end evaluations of employees. In a small design firm, however, it is better to evaluate staff performances as you finish a project. When the job is fresh in everyone's minds, the evaluation is more valuable and effective. You talk over the job with your staff. You might say, "This is what we did that we feel is great, and this is the part you played. Perhaps next time you would like to take on more responsibility or to carry out certain tasks that you did not do on this project."

As a firm grows larger, the evaluation process must become more formalized. In large firms, regular written employee evaluations are a good practice.

Reviewing Goals

When you evaluate your staff, you should also review their initial design staff questionnaires (see pages 82–84). The information on the questionnaire is useful in determining the value of an employee to the firm, both for reviewing his or her salary and in marketing future projects.

In order for you to properly place and develop new and existing design staff members, you should have them update their design staff questionnaires every year. While some of the information will remain the same, education and employment experiences often change. Their changes and additions should be recorded with a summary of their goals and objectives, so that when new opportunities arise within the firm you can try to match them with the personal objectives of your staff.

HOW MUCH DO YOU COST?

Do you know how much you and your employees cost? Figure out exactly what each employee costs your company, and then determine whether the employee is really earning what he or she is being paid. A person's cost is not just the salary he or she takes home. It includes all of the fringe benefits he or she receives—vacation, health insurance, sick leave, extra time off, business lunches, trips to conventions or shows, a car, and all the other expenses and benefits that this person enjoys, such as extra travel and meetings that he or she is able to enjoy on company expense. You find that you are paying for a lot of extras. Health insurance, vacations, and sick time are just part of it. Many corporations say that a staff person costs them approximately thirty to forty percent more than the salary. Within the design field, the cost is very similar.

You may discover, as I did, that your present staff is not really what you need. It is nice to have a well-known person who enhances the reputation of your studio—but is he or she producing, or is the person there just for cosmetic purposes? How much is having this person worth? Is he or she part of your image? Your advertising? You must evaluate your staff on a regular basis to be sure that your employees continue to fit the business objectives of your company.

Understanding the goals of each individual in your firm can help you in planning company objectives. When a staff member's objectives vary from the direction the design firm is taking, it is time to have a discussion with that employee. For instance, you might say, "This is where we see our company going . . . how would you feel about this direction?" or, "I realize that you would like to learn more about computer technology, but I see your abilities as stronger in marketing. How would you feel about moving into the marketing area? I'd like it if you would try relating to some clients directly to see if you enjoy it." This ongoing, yet documented, interaction is important in long-term relationships. Once a person writes down his or her objectives, you have a more reliable statement than you would receive in casual conversation. It's a good point of reference to be able to say, "Last year you felt the best thing you did was this particular job; now I see you going in a completely different direction. How do you feel this compares with what you had planned back then?"

Write down what is expected of your employees. Describe their jobs. Define each employee's position within the company; list his or her wages, promotion opportunities, and responsibilities. Outline his or her benefits, working hours, pay schedule, and any overtime payment.

It is helpful to be able to consult a personnel manual when you are reviewing salaries. Often, when someone wants additional salary, you can adjust other benefits in order to be able to afford a salary increase.

Sometimes employees are given benefits which they may not consider of value, although the benefits cost the company money. Small companies should ask the employees which benefits they feel are worthwhile and which they feel have no value to them.

Before adding a new employee, do a break-even analysis on the person and all of his or her costs to be sure you can really afford him or her.

Notice of Unsatisfactory Performance

When you are considering terminating an employee, first give him or her a memorandum verifying that there are certain unsatisfactory elements in his or her performance. This memorandum can be followed up at a later date with appropriate resignation forms. The purpose of issuing this notice of unsatisfactory performance is simply to protect the firm against any claims of discriminatory termination. It is an excellent policy to have this memorandum for use as a support for any dismissal.

TERMINATION OR RESIGNATION OF AN EMPLOYEE

When you terminate an employee, it is a good idea to inform him or her in writing, citing the specific reasons for termination. This will formally state the issues just in case the employee should question the reason. On receiving the notice of termination of employment, the employee should acknowledge receipt and return the acknowledged notice to the company; severance and other benefits should not be paid until the acknowledged notice is received. When you are terminating a corporate officer or director, you need to receive from him or her a formal resignation, which you must formally acknowledge. Samples of these letters are on pages 95 and 96.

Resignation with Formal Acknowledgment

When a corporate officer or director leaves the company, he or she must submit a formal resignation stating his or her position as a corporate officer and also the fact that he or she has officially resigned from the corporation. In that way the person ensures that he or she will no longer be responsible for actions of the corporation or involved in the corporation in any fashion. This resignation is then acknowledged by the board of directors.

Notice of unsatisfactory performance. This memorandum should be issued to employees whose work is a problem and whom you are considering terminating. It can help support any dismissal and protect your firm against claims of discriminatory termination.

DATE:

TO: (employee)

This memorandum confirms our meeting of _____, 19___, during which you were advised that your job performance has been unsatisfactory in the following respect(s):

You were advised that the deficiencies must be corrected if you are to remain an employee in good standing and that you should take the following actions to correct the problem(s) described above:

We have every confidence the problem(s) will be corrected, and that you will become a valued employee.

Sincerely,

_____

(Employer)

Receipt of the above notice is acknowledged:

_____

(Employee)

```
DATE:


TO:  (employee)



We regret to inform you that on _____, 19___, your

employment with the firm shall be terminated for the following

reason(s):



Your severance pay and any fringe benefits due shall be according to

company policy.


Please call for an appointment so that we may review with you the

termination and arrange for the return of any company property in your

possession.


Again, we regret this action is necessary.


Very truly,



_____

(Employer)



Receipt of the above notice is acknowledged:



_____

(Employee)
```

Acknowledged resignation. When a corporate officer or director leaves the firm, he or she must submit a formal resignation such as this, which you must formally acknowledge.

DATE:

TO:

Management:

Please be advised that the undersigned hereby resigns as

_____ of the corporation effective upon acceptance.

Please acknowledge acceptance of said resignation on behalf of the

corporation.

Very truly,

_____

(Corporate Member)

The foregoing has been accepted pursuant to vote of the directors/

stockholders of the corporation effective _____, 19___.

_____

(For the Corporation)

```
DATE:


TO:  (employer)



I hereby tender my resignation from the firm effective _____,
19___.


At that time I shall deliver all property of the firm in my possession.


Very truly,



_____

(Employee)
```

Exit Interview

When employees resign, it is a good idea to have an interview with them to learn the reasons why they are leaving. This will help you evaluate what sort of person you need to hire as a replacement. You may find that the job is not appropriately structured, in which case, you will want to revise the job before hiring another person. Or you may find that the qualifications of the departing employee did not fit the job.

It is a good idea to write a report on each exit interview and add it to the employee's design staff questionnaire. I state the name of the employee; the date of the exit interview; the date the employee was hired; and the employee's address, sex, marital status, age, and educational background. Generally we use our regular staff evaluation form, but we add the reason for leaving and the type of separation.

After the exit interview, you should determine what action to take: to hire another person, to ask another staff person to take on the additional work, or to fill the void in some other way.

While you may wish the employee were staying, you can make the most of his or her departure by using the occasion to learn information about your company that can help you with your future direction.

HIRING CONSULTANTS

Every year American businesses spend billions of dollars on consultants to address specific problems that their in-house staff may not have the expertise or time to handle. Smaller companies in particular find that consultants can make the difference between success and failure, profit and loss.

Appropriate consultants can help solve many types of problems for the design firm; they can also become part of a team on a design project. A good reference and directory of consultants is valuable to the management structure of a firm. We need many types of consultants for many reasons.

When to Hire

You should hire consultants for the following reasons:

1. *To bring in additional expertise.* If you do not have a specialist on a particular subject within your staff, it is economical to hire a consultant with expertise in that area. This is the case whether the subject is accounting, law, computers, or design specialities such as lighting and hospitality.

2. *To make a design team stronger.* You can hire consultants to suit particular projects. In this way you can assemble a team of experts that are seldom found on any one person's staff. Consultants make a firm stronger.

3. *To review management or processing.* It is a good idea to bring in a consultant to determine whether your management is up-to-date or whether there are other processes more appropriate for managing your operation.

4. *To resolve conflict.* Design firms often have conflicts regarding employees or staffing. Sometimes these can more easily be resolved by bringing in another party to act as an impartial observer or a mediator.

5. *To act as advisors to your staff.* You might hire consultants to train staff, to act as their mentors, and to help them develop their individual potentials.

6. *To broaden the spectrum of information available to everyone within the company.* This can help you compete with the very large specialized firms.

You should not hire a consultant under the following conditions:

1. *When your need is not defined*. There is no point in hiring a consultant unless you know exactly which areas you want him or her to address.

2. *If your need will be very long-term*. For a long-term need you would be best off finding a person who would become part of your company.

3. *If the consultant is not experienced with situations similar to yours*. If the consultant is extremely overqualified or has been dealing with very large companies, he or she may not understand your individual small issues.

4. *If the timing is not appropriate*. A consultant should be brought in to your firm only when there is time for him or her to digest the information that is going to be reviewed. There is no point in bringing a consultant in during a crisis if his or her interaction will take a considerable amount of time to comprehend and use. Unless the consultant can become directly involved in the crisis management, you should see the crisis through before bringing him or her in.

When I was younger, I thought that for anything I wanted to learn, I could take some courses, or enroll in college. As I developed my business I found myself wanting additional knowledge in business and other specialized areas. I discussed this with a number of my business consultants, and they told me that the best way I could get the most appropriate, clearly defined, and up-to-date information for my subject was to hire a group of consultants. In essence, I was advised to look at my individual needs and to find the best possible consultant available.

I have been using consultants extensively now for over thirty years. There is barely a week that passes in which my firm does not use a consultant for some reason. Some of their fees have been startling, but usually the consultants are more than worth it. When I have had a properly defined project and been able to clearly state it to my consultants, their response has been amazingly quick and direct.

Consultants are part of our everyday vocabulary. We could not run our small firm without them. If you were within a very large corporate structure, perhaps you would not need as many consultants. But for us it is one of the most rewarding methods of learning I've experienced. Consultants have also pointed me toward other specialists they believed I should know about or meet. They have recommended lectures, people, courses, and books. When a consultant recommends I review information, I know the time I am spending will not be wasted, but very worthwhile.

Whom to Hire

There are two consultants every firm will need: an accountant and an attorney. At my firm, we also call on a number of other advisors for a variety of reasons. Whenever I see a problem, I contact some outside consultants for their review and opinion. They bring us an objective review and management expertise that we could in no way have ourselves. Hiring a consultant gives us strength in areas outside our major interest.

Your Accountant. You need the services of an accountant from the time you begin planning your office until the day you sell it. Too often, accountants are treated as post-mortem people. To get maximum value, you must learn to use accountants in your planning stages as well as for your annual review. If he or she becomes part of your company, you will get more from the relationship.

Your accountant can help you with your cash management systems and day-to-day operating techniques so that you can use your money to your best advantage. I don't like any accounting system that leaves room for question. I want to know ahead of time what we've done, where we stand, how our projects are developing financially, and how our time management is being handled. Any good accountant can set this up for you.

Invite your accountant to look over all your future business plans. Subtle flaws can result in unbelievable tax consequences or can greatly affect your cash flow.

Your accountant should also review your leases, loan agreements, contracts, and any long-term commitments before you are inextricably involved. You may want him or her to review your insurance as well and to comment on the policies you have purchased. Because your accountant knows your financial needs, he or she is able to spot quickly whether your coverage is adequate. If it is not, he or she can recommend what else you should have. This can be exceptionally helpful.

The more your accountant is told about your operation, and the less he or she has to discover by searching and probing, the more quickly he or she can start helping your firm. Accountants bill by the hour, so it pays you to make their job easy. I recommend inviting your accountant and your attorney to regular meetings where you and they discuss the advancement and structure of your company. Be sure they know each other and are familiar with what the other does on your behalf. Meet with your accountant several times a year, and pick his or her brain about every financial aspect of your business.

When it is time for your accountant to review your books, be sure the records are up-to-date and all the numbers are ready. For the lowest accounting prices possible, use your own bookkeeping staff to prepare the records. It is difficult and expensive for an outside person to come in and update your records. Have your books ready for your accountant, on time, and in clean, readable condition, and you won't be paying accountants' prices for clerical work.

Don't be afraid to ask your accountant questions, but remember that the orientation of accountants is to be conservative. If you have stated a plan of action and your accountant suggests it is not financially feasible, or does not recommend it, don't be afraid to ask for alternatives. It may be that only one phase of the project is inappropriate and that you can easily adjust the plan.

Our accountant here has worked with me since 1956. Mr. Samuel Ledger became our accountant because he was very easy for me to understand. He taught CPAs locally and was used to explaining financial matters in elementary language. Every time I consider an addition, a subtraction, opening another business, closing one, a move or a change, Mr. Ledger is one of the first people I call in to see if my idea is economical. There have been times when I have had projects I thought were extremely exciting until he showed me how the taxes and additional accounting records required would make them impractical.

Before I met Mr. Ledger, I worked with a firm of many accountants who insisted on doing it "their way," who really didn't care what my company wanted—only that it was done according to proper accounting principles. These accountants could not communicate. It was important to me, when I started, to have someone who was able to relate to me in terms I understood. The first accounting Mr. Ledger did for me was to prepare my annual taxes. I would take him my little red book every year and he would do my accounting and charge me $25.00. The account has grown considerably, and he has taken on a number of other accounts we referred to him. He has become a part of our company over the last thirty years, and I think he has learned to enjoy us as we have learned to enjoy him.

Learn to talk with your accountant. You should understand every form report your accountant gives you. If you don't understand one, ask your ac tant to explain it to you. If he or she can't explain it to your satisfactic someone who can explain it to you in terms you understand. State your a... Start him or her thinking as to how they can be accomplished from a financial viewpoint.

Your Attorney. You need an attorney when you are starting your business to determine the form it should take. Should it be a sole proprietorship, a partnership, a limited partnership, or a corporation? These and other types of ownership are explained in Chapter 2 (see pages 40–45). You, your attorney, and your accountant should work together to tailor your business structure.

Other times to use attorneys would be for contract interpretation, drafting, and review; for working out problems with clients who file suits; and for negotiating with employees.

Your attorney can also help you maintain your business structure. He might assist in preparing corporate minutes, corporate resolutions, and the documents required for tax and legal purposes.

I asked a number of attorneys how large a part they felt an attorney should play in a company structure. The answer was, in essence, "As large a part as the client requires." Some people need a person to talk to when they are testing ideas. An attorney is a good person for this, but an expensive one. Other people talk to an attorney only when they have a definite problem—a lawsuit or a contract dispute, for instance.

I think there is a middle ground. For an attorney to give you the best service, you should bring him in before the final die is cast so he can mold the manner in which the issues are handled. Consult with an attorney if you think there is going to be a suit; don't wait until someone sues you. Your attorney can help with the negotiations or preparations for a possible legal suit.

Selecting an attorney is difficult. I think the best way to go about it is compare notes with other businesses. Ask for recommendations from people who have used an attorney's services. Some attorneys do not want small business accounts. It is important to deal with an attorney who is interested in and handles small businesses.

You can find an attorney by consulting recognized law listings. Probably the best-known directory is the *Martindale-Hubbell Legal Directory*, available in most public libraries. It lists attorneys by representative clients and gives financial references. It also rates the attorneys for general ability and overall reputation.

The *Martindale-Hubbell Legal Directory* has three ratings—"A," "B," and "C"—for general ability. To be classified under any of these categories, an attorney must have been in practice for a particular period of time, and must be rated by fellow attorneys. While "A" is the highest rating, many good attorneys do not have an "A" rating simply because they have not been in practice long enough.

The directory also has three ratings for overall reputation: "V," "AV," and "BV." The "V" rating stands for a very high reputation. However, an attorney with an "AV" rating is well above average in reputation, and a person with a "BV" rating may be just as good. Reputation ratings tend to reflect an attorney's years of experience, rather than his or her level of integrity. They do not reflect on ability.

When you meet with the attorney you have chosen, discuss your business objectives and your interests. Do not be put off if the attorney is not particularly enthusiastic. We hire attorneys for their skills and experience, not to have the same enthusiasms we have. From experience, an attorney knows that everything that crosses his or her desk is not necessarily going to succeed.

The attorney will try to diminish your enthusiasm to see if you have both feet on the ground and are aware of the realities. It is part of his orientation.

Ask the attorney whether he or she will actually do your work or farm it out to another lawyer. Very few lawyers today practice in a one-person office; most are in partnership or are part of a large company. If you expect your attorney to do all the work, make that clear at the outset; he or she will price accordingly. If your work would be farmed out, get some idea from the attorney of who will perform the legal services and how they will be handled, so that you are not disappointed with the outcome.

Judging the quality of an attorney's work can be just as difficult as selecting the attorney in the first place. Results are your best guide. Has using this attorney reduced or eliminated your firm's disputes and litigations? Are you in trouble with tax authorities or in other areas where he represents you?

The lawyer-client privilege means your lawyer cannot be forced to reveal anything you told him in preparation of your case. However, you should be aware that this privilege does not apply to your accountant, your corporate treasurer, other employees, professional advisors, or board members.

Your Financial Planner. At one point the financial planning of a firm was handled by its banker and accountant. Today, however, the financial world is much more complex, and many firms find that using a financial consultant can be valuable in planning their financial structure.

The financial planner will review all of your assets and liabilities, including your income tax returns, your wills, and any settlements, contracts, deeds, mortgages, insurance policies, and other papers relating to your financial position. With this information he or she will calculate your net worth, give you a monthly cash-flow statement (if your accountant has not already given you those), and recommend a plan for you which takes advantage of your best financial opportunities.

A financial planner will review everything from your types of mortgages to your kinds of investments, retirement plans, and company structures. He or she will look at your total financial position, not just your company's—a different viewpoint than that of your accountant.

Financial planners can come from many different backgrounds. Anyone can say he or she is a financial planner, so you must use caution in selecting a planner. Look at the person's credentials. He or she should belong to either the International Association for Financial Planners or the Institute of Certified Financial Planners. Many colleges and business schools also offer programs in financial planning, and while people who have attended these classes may have certificates or a degree, this in no way guarantees their expertise.

I have found that the best way to find a financial planner is through a reference from a personal friend, your banker, your accountant, your lawyer, or someone else who normally works with planners. When interviewing a financial planner, ask to see the kinds of plans he or she has done for other people. Also ask what types of firms have used him or her. Some planners will only take very large accounts; others will take reasonably small ones.

Planners usually cost anywhere from $1,000 and up, depending on the area they are in and the type of services they offer. They usually charge a fee; and this is the only type of planner I would recommend. I feel that someone who earns a commission on whatever he or she sells you cannot have an objective viewpoint. It is usually worthwhile to review your program every year with a financial planner.

Each consultant brings his or her own knowledge and experience to a situation. Consultants you should consider hiring include the following:

▶ *Accountants.*

▶ *Advertising and Promotion Consultants.*

▸ *Architects.* If a designer initiates the project, it is common for the designer to hire an architect as a consultant.

▸ *Attorneys.*

▸ *Business Development Consultants.*

▸ *Business Service Consultants.* These would be consultants in areas such as computer programs, special reports, and different office procedures.

▸ *Collection Agencies.*

▸ *Compensation Specialists.* These firms organize compensation performance schedules that relate to the performance of the company.

▸ *Design Consultants.* In my firm we use a number of design colleagues as consultants to review our ongoing projects. Without the input of other designers, I am sure that I would have made many more mistakes than I have. When something we're concerned about comes up on a project, we have another designer review it. When I purchased the building that I am in, I asked two other designers to review my plans for the building to see if they could find any ways of improving on them. It was amazing how much they found.

   Design consultants can help guide you in determining which issues must be handled now to avoid later cost increases. In this way they can help improve your profits.

   You must find designers who are not in your locale. They need to be from another city or in a noncompetitive position.

▸ *Engineers.*

▸ *Educational Consultants.* These consultants recommend the different kinds of educational programs that might be appropriate for your staff, either on an in-house basis or on a special basis.

▸ *Employee Benefits Consultants.* There are a lot of recently formed companies who review your benefit-package plan. They can also create a package for you, show you how to manage it, and present it to your employees. Most of these consultants cater to larger firms; however, some are available to small design firms.

▸ *Financial Planners.*

▸ *Human Resources Consultants.* There are firms solely dedicated to the development and implementation of employee-relations strategies. These firms specialize in compensation training, development, communication, and management effectiveness. They will create policy manuals, handbooks, and supervisory training procedures. These firms usually work with larger firms of a hundred or more.

▸ *Import and Export Specialists.* If you plan to do work abroad, you should consult this kind of specialist. He or she will determine how you should handle your work abroad, addressing such issues as government regulations, legal permits, representatives, shipping, joint venture involvement, and anything else related to working in a specific foreign country.

▸ *Insurance Specialists.* Although you can often use your insurance agent as your consultant, there are specialists who will review your insurance and determine whether you can consider other options for your program. These specialists are usually available to associations and larger midsized firms, where bidding for policy coverage is appropriate.

▸ *Leadership Consultants.* There are many consultants who train and consult on leadership. Every chief executive officer and manager understands that there are many problems in leadership. These consultants can help train you in some techniques that will be helpful to you in leading your specific firm.

▶ *Management Consultants*. These consultants are available through accounting firms or as individual consultants. They will review your management procedures and determine just what can be done to improve the individual management of your firm. Almost every design firm uses some management consulting because an outsider has the necessary distance from the day-to-day operations to provide an overview of a management system.

▶ *Marketing Consultants*. Marketing consultants specialize in setting up marketing programs and in showing firms how to develop these programs.

▶ *Mergers and Acquisitions Consultants*. These consultants are very useful if you are considering merging with or acquiring another company. They will help you explore and evaluate the different options available to your company and provide assistance in staff evaluation.

▶ *Productive Systems Analysts*. Any firm that has production scheduling or any kind of production system can use productivity systems analysts. These specialists review manufacturing and professional service organizations to determine their individual productivity.

▶ *Record and Information Managers*. Certified record managers provide systems for handling all forms of documents, from the initial stages through the final disposition. They will review any kind of base form. Usually you should hire those with backgrounds in records and management systems within the design field.

▶ *Recruitment Specialists*. Customarily only large firms use recruiters, but small firms can benefit from their use, too. It is often difficult to know how to locate and attract the particular person that you need. Professional recruiters can help set up the structure and procedures for you.

▶ *Software and Computer Consultants*. There are specialists in almost every field who can determine what software packages would best suit your needs. You give them the details of what you would like to produce and they, in turn, will put you in touch with the best software packaging. Usually it is best to meet first with a software consultant to determine what software is required, then meet later with a computer consultant. It is too expensive to make a mistake.

▶ *Telemarketing Consultants*. For telephone communications, both inbound and outbound, there are many training programs and consulting services available. These companies will review your individual demands and come up with a program that is appropriate. They will also provide training for the program.

▶ *Training Consultants*. There are consultants who can be brought in to train your staff, depending upon your needs. They can also be hired on a per-assignment or per-project basis to help bring your staffing up to date. Using training consultants is often less expensive than sending your employees to school.

Consultant Contracts

The contract with your consultants can be an ongoing contract or a specific one, depending upon your requirements. Before you hire a consultant, it is a good idea to draft a contract or a letter of agreement. (Your consultant may give you a letter of agreement.) But first define your service requirements so that your goals will be based on reality. Your goal may be being able to train a designer in the use of a CADD. If so, explain to the consultant the type of work that you expect the designer to be doing so that the consultant can set priorities on what is taught. It may be more important to teach space planning than other types of drafting to this designer. By carefully defining your goals you will save a tremendous amount of your consultant's time—and your money.

Your agreement should also state the starting and completion dates of the project. Every project has time assignments; you need to know how many hours the consultant will be working—and the consultant needs to know how many hours will be required—in order to plan your schedule and estimate your costs for the project.

Add a requirement, or clause, in your agreement to cover any additional work or modifications that might be needed. For example, if the consultants are going to continue to consult on a weekly or monthly basis or be available for telephone consulting, what will your costs be?

Outline in your agreement what support the consultant will require. If the consultant is in your space, will he or she need an individual office? A secretary? Determine just what kind of time, personnel, and physical requirements are necessary for him to do his job.

Include a definition of termination. If you find that you are not happy with the contractor's handling of the project, you need to know how you can terminate the relationship. This should be defined before you start working together.

Spell out financial arrangements: the fee per hour or day, the set fee for the assignment, or the reward in the case of your negotiating a contract. If the consultants help get a contract for you, they might be paid on a percentage basis. Outline the payment schedule, listing exactly when the fee will be paid and what your obligations are so that you can be prepared. Spell out which expenses and other items you will cover. These might include travel expenses and other expenses incurred in relation to the job.

Be sure that you have a confidentiality clause in your document. You are hiring a consultant because you want top-quality, up-to-date information and the best caliber work. The product of your cooperative effort should be used only for your firm and not by competitors.

Determine up front the right of ownership of information or any products or sales that are developed from your relationship with a consultant. I make it understood from the beginning that when I use a consultant, this is *my* project, done for *my* client. I do the billing, and my consultant has no right to work for the client independently of my corporation.

Your agreement should include a right-to-advertise clause to prevent the consultant from using your company's name for promotional purposes without written approval. The consultant can usually list your name on a résumé without consent, but this should be clearly documented in your agreement.

You need a statement in your agreement regarding the legal process. It should be clearly stated that in the case of any litigation, the consultant is required to cooperate with your company.

A consultant will usually want to put some kind of stop-work clause into the agreement, which means that if you do not pay at a given prescribed time, he or she has the right to stop working.

An appropriate up-front agreement is crucial with consultants. It makes for a better working relationship and helps eliminates problems later on. Even though you expect never to disagree, formulating the process by which to disagree in advance is always advisable.

Chapter Six

MARKETING AND SELLING

Marketing is the process of getting goods and services to the customer. It can be divided into three major areas: market development, advertising and public relations, and sales.

Just as McDonald's has learned to sell hamburgers and hospitals have learned to sell medicine, interior designers need to learn to market and sell design services. We need to develop the techniques of communication that work with the particular client group we seek, because it is the person who knows how to market and how to sell who gets the business.

A designer's business is to solve problems that the client cannot or does not want to solve alone. It is the designer's job to identify the problem and then, by technical skill and experience, show the client how to solve and how to expedite the situation. To sell their services, interior designers must show that they are businesspeople who understand construction and appropriate schedules and budgets.

Only an informed consumer can differentiate between partial service and full service, unqualified and qualified designers; and it is up to us to educate the consumer through marketing. The longstanding method of obtaining new clients through word of mouth is no longer adequate, even for firms who have been in business for decades.

The majority of design firms rely on referrals as their major marketing tool. This is no longer enough, as many newcomers to the field have spent as much time developing their marketing techniques as other firms have spent developing design skills.

MARKET DEVELOPMENT

To maintain your business activity and required growth three years in the future, you have to seek new business now. The business practice of marketing is an effective tool for controlling short-, middle-, and long-term development.

The first and most important part of marketing is to establish your company's overall goals and to define the design firm's strengths and abilities. You can then identify which strategies you need to achieve your objectives.

Before beginning your marketing program, answer the following questions:

1. What is the size of your firm and what is its general organization?

2. What types of employees do you have and what are their areas of expertise?

3. Who is the person in your firm responsible for your marketing efforts?

4. What are your firm's strengths?

5. What are your firm's weaknesses?

6. How do you expect to overcome these weaknesses?

7. Who will carry out your firm's marketing efforts? List what is to be done and who will handle it.

8. What selling tools are available to you and what ones will you need to acquire?

The most costly mistake marketers can make is to place their entire emphasis on existing or prospective clients and to overlook in-house capabilities.

Finally, for market development to be effective, it must be a highly systemized, structured process, with exact schedules and reviews of each part of the client interaction—from the first contact on through to proposal writing and the follow-up.

Market Research

Your market is your actual and potential clients. Today most interior designers need to develop business, and a prime tool for doing this is market research.

The purpose of market research is to identify additional business areas and to evaluate ways that might be effective in securing business in these areas. The effectiveness of basic market research can be quite large in proportion to the time and effort put into it. The business activities that make up market research include analyzing and understanding consumer circumstances, economics, and attitudes; it is also knowing the competition and being aware of relevant government regulations. The ability to recognize early trends is fully as important as knowing the current situation.

All marketing is guesswork. However, the more information you can acquire in your research, the more scientific and profitable your marketing becomes. It is possible to hire someone to do all or part of your market research, but very few interior design forms are large enough to afford this luxury. Those that are large enough may wish to consult *Bradford's Directory of Marketing Research Agencies,* which lists market research firms, their principals, number of employees, and the type of market research they do.

Investigating the Competition. To exist in the marketplace, you need to know your competition. It is relatively easy to find out what your competition is doing just by being observant. As interior designers we have the ability to know what was done on a project and how, just by looking at it. In addition, many times clients, friends, and other people will give you information.

Competition for the interior design dollar has become increasingly aggressive. Published surveys rate interior design as the highest paying of the design professions, over architecture, landscape architecture, and engineering.

The competition comes from all directions—from large architectural firms with small interior design departments to the spouse of the CEO and the office-supply distributor who suddenly announces that he or she has a design department. Even the manufacturers themselves offer competition. Some are qualified, and others are not.

Often designers are not competing with their peers, but with people who may have minimal, if any, design training. Many of these newcomers are unaware of the scope of interior design, do not provide full service, and can undercut professional interior designers' prices as a result.

We need to maintain rapport with our design competition and to work with them if possible. It is usually best not to talk down a competitor; instead show a potential client how your design services are exceptional.

Identifying the Client. At one time, it was thought that marketing was selling a product to a client. Today, marketing is determining who needs what you have to sell. Is it saleable? Is the client ready for this product or service at this particular time? A professional designer should pinpoint his or her marketing area. It is quite costly to blanket the field; even a large design firm cannot afford to do this.

Set geographic limits for your marketing efforts. Ask yourself the same questions you would ask yourself in deciding on a location for a new business (see pages 59–61). Being where you are visible and where there is work makes marketing easier.

Identify the kind of person you want to attract as your potential client. If your focus is hospitals, it would be foolish for you to allocate research funds or marketing energy in their residential area.

Sources for Jobs
Every interior designer has many sources for potential clients. The following list of prospects should always be considered.

Referrals. The best source for new clients is referrals. Because design is a sizeable investment, prospective clients are wary of hiring an interior designer without knowing something about him or her.

One of the best prospecting methods is to review your present work to see if there are contacts from these jobs who can help you to get more work. No job stands alone. There are always other jobs that come from each particular job. The clients for whom you have done satisfactory work are excellent referral sources if you keep in touch with them. Ask them if they would be willing to write testimonials or case studies on their projects. These can often be published or mailed to a prospective client. Call a client and ask him or her to give you an overview, either through an interview or a written comment, of just what he or she thought of your job.

Anyone who uses an interior designer creates a demand among his or her friends and acquaintances for design work. These people probably don't want exactly what the others have; these are potential clients.

1. *Friends.* Some people work well with friends and others prefer an arms'-length relationship. You alone can determine whether you wish to work with friends, but many designers begin their careers this way.

2. *Interprofessionals.* Engineers, architects, and other professionals in design-related fields are excellent sources for clients. They often have jobs that need interior design services.

3. *Contractors.* You should interview both general contractors and sub-contractors to find out what type of projects they are working on and whether there are any opportunities for a design professional.

4. *Manufacturers, Representatives, Wholesalers, Suppliers, Distributors.* All have salespeople in the field and are aware of future projects. These groups can be excellent sources for the interior designer to develop.

5. *Business Development Organizations.* Every region has several organizations dedicated to business development. The Chamber of Commerce is a traditional one, but there are many more. Some only handle business development for special groups, such as minority-owned firms.

6. *Government.* A major purchaser of design services and products today, the government is a special type of client with specific communication requirements, both in qualifying for a project and in documenting the job. In order to formulate the appropriate approach, you may want to attend one of the courses given on this subject by the Small Business Administration and/or other localized business development organizations. These organizations have prepared up-to-date guides and contact lists.

7. *Government Officials.* Often the officials within a community are aware of new building projects and new industries that are coming into the area.

8. *Owners.* Owners of any large project, such as an apartment building or an office building, are an excellent source for learning about new tenants. Normally the owners are interested in maintaining a good standard within their building, and so are happy to share this information.

Networking. It is often said in business that it is not what you know, but who you know and how you use those contacts that counts. The process of developing and using your contacts for informal advice and moral support as you pursue your career is called networking. It is a popular and valuable tool for interior designers because through networking you can learn about jobs, people, and situations that credit reports cannot cover. With a good networking system, it's easier to find the right type of client.

Some networking relationships may be quite profitable, but not all are effective. Time spent networking is an investment. Is the return adequate? If it isn't, perhaps you have the wrong networking group.

People tend to label almost any interaction as networking. However, effective networking must have a goal, a strategy, and a direction. Set as your goal that in the next month you will meet a certain number of people: prospective clients, suppliers, contractors, competitors, and perhaps a few masters in the field. Allow yourself a specific amount of time to make these contacts and then make use of mealtimes, or even exercise periods, to interact with these people. Then write out a networking program for the next twelve months.

The basis for a good networking system is your list of friends, your telephone book, your correspondence files, and even your address book. This is your current group for normal interaction. If you can, separate these lists into personal and business acquaintances.

For networking to be successful, you should follow these guidelines:

1. *Meet business contacts on a regular basis.* To do so, plan events and situations to occur on an average of every four to six weeks throughout the year. In addition, go to events, either alone or with someone from your group. Go to seminars, workshops, meetings—any kind of an organized program. You'll find that at almost any community meeting you end up speaking with new people or renewing an acquaintance. Exchanging updates on what each of you has been doing paves the way for more useful conversation.

2. *Make the first contact.* Do not be afraid to say hello to someone, or to call a person about a situation. People are usually flattered that you have taken the time to call them.

3. *Ask the right questions.* You can probably acquire *some* information about anything just by contacting four or five people. Just ask: "Who do you know that could do this particular craft?" or "Where can I find this item?" People like to be asked questions. They enjoy being considered authorities.

4. *Network with your competitors.* Many designers see other designers solely as competitors. I don't. Other designers help us get jobs because they create an audience of people who want design services. No one's services are appropriate in all situations. Talk to your competitors. There are many ways to share information without jeopardizing your business. Good relationships with your fellow designers can save you a lot of aggravation and money, just in the tips that are shared.

5. *Stay in touch.* You must keep in regular contact with anyone with whom you want to build a networking system. Sometimes it is better *not* to start a relationship if you cannot keep it up. Keep in contact with people on a four-to-six-week basis. Often a short note or a phone call is all that is needed. If they are not available, leave a message. Just make sure there is some kind of contact on a regular basis so that when you do need special information from these people, they remember who you are. Then they are usually happy to respond.

6. *Send birthday and anniversary cards.* If you can, learn the dates of your contacts' birthdays and anniversaries and send them cards. A number of professionals organize these mailings on a yearly basis, with all the cards addressed and ready to go on January 1. Their secretary then puts the cards in the mail on specific dates to assure that they reach their destination at the proper time. If you cannot organize these mailings on an annual basis, do it at least on a monthly basis. Keep a book with these special dates and names in it. Many well-known businessmen seldom get a birthday card, so when they do get a special card, a few flowers, or a small gift beautifully wrapped, this makes a great impression. They will remember you sometimes years later.

7. *Send "thank you" notes.* When someone does a favor for you, send a note thanking him or her. Saying "thank you" is important, but you will make more of an impact if you also send a handwritten card. All it has to say is something like "thank you for the favor you did for me last Tuesday."

8. *Promote others.* In introducing people to other people and recommending them for projects, you accumulate good will. It is always good to be owed a favor. When I meet people who are good in specific disciplines, I make a point of trying to help them progress as far as possible within their given field. I try to have them meet the right people in the right situations—and I expect them to recommend me in return.

    Reciprocity is expected when you give a person a reference. A designer I know in Arizona recommended a landscape architectural firm to the point where the firm had twenty jobs at one time from his recommendations, but he got no client referrals from the firm. He mentioned the lack of reciprocity to the principal of the firm and, although the principal was supportive, no jobs resulted. The firm did not understand enough about interior design to be able to sell any designer. So the designer started looking for a more reciprocal situation. Sometimes it's not that the firm doesn't recommend you; it's that they are not able to *sell* you.

9. *Try to enlarge your networking system.* Usually everyone that you can introduce to your network makes the system a stronger and more valuable marketing tool.

Getting the Right Jobs

You must determine which clients are worth approaching and how much is appropriate to invest in each individual project.

Larger projects and continuing commissions are the most financially desirable projects, but remember that many firms are going after those jobs. Sometimes the most lucrative projects are from smaller clients, with whom the principal of your firm has taken the time to develop a rapport. These clients appreciate the attention and are often willing to reward the designer, both financially and with good design opportunities.

Review your success in getting jobs. If you are trying for jobs in a certain area, and you've lost the last six or eight of those jobs, you're either going after the wrong jobs or your whole marketing presentation needs to be reviewed.

Taking the wrong job can destroy your firm. There is no faster way to ruin a project and to diminish your reputation than by taking on a project that is beyond the ability of your firm, or that is inappropriate for your firm. It is exciting to move into a new area, but you shouldn't jump into an area before you are ready to handle it.

QUALIFYING THE JOB AND THE CLIENT

There are several key items that you should look at in qualifying a job from a potential client.

1. Is it the right type of job for you?

2. Is it the right size job?

3. Is there opportunity for professional growth? Does the job offer new challenges?

4. Is the prospective client used to making decisions?

5. Is he or she reasonable—or overly demanding? Check with a number of other designers and/or contractors who have worked with this person to get a feel for what he or she is like. If the person has a great ego problem and needs boundless support, the job may get to be too time-consuming and difficult to handle.

6. Is the timing right or will you have to rush to prepare your proposal? Usually a poor proposal is worse than no proposal.

7. Does the client pay his or her bills properly? Does he or she have a good credit rating and is he or she willing to meet the requirements?

8. Is this particular prospective client connected with any special competitor of yours? If the prospect has a relative or friend in the design business whom he or she has given previous business, it is probably not worth pursuing this client to any great extent.

9. What will it cost you to develop this particular client? Is it worth it in relation to the payoff of the potential project?

Sources of Market Information. A lot of market research can be done from the materials available from the government. Look in "Government Publications and Their Use," available from Brookings Institute, Washington, D.C. 20003. Another source is the popular "Guide to the U.S. Publications." To get government publications, write to the Superintendent of Documents, U.S. Government Printing Office, Washington, D.C. 20402, or contact the Small Business Administration Office or Department of Commerce Field Office.

For the most specific information, define your market group. If your specialty is residential design for the highly affluent, you should read the social columns and announcements in many publications to watch the social movement of your potential clients. Designers who specialize in space planning for large offices might want to add *Commerce Business Daily* to their reading lists. This publication lists government jobs being put out for bid.

It is important for the interior designer to be aware of general economic trends, as well as specific developments planned by different organizations for which design services could be required. Publications that are helpful include:

- *Wall Street Journal*
- *Barron's*
- *Business Week*
- *Forbes*

▶ *Time*

▶ *New York Times*

▶ *National Observer*

▶ Other local papers published by statewide business organizations, such as *Business Magazine* and *Banking Magazine*, and magazines related to each individual discipline in which you are working can also be valuable. Newspapers and magazines should not be underestimated as information sources as they are media to which our clients are constantly exposed.

Read what your prospective clients read. If you are to work in a specialty, you must have an understanding of the current issues and changes within that specialty.

Two other publications you should read are *Standard & Poor's Industrial Surveys* and the *Dodge Reports*. *Standard & Poor's Industrial Surveys* analyzes trends in construction, utilities, retailing, and transportation.

McGraw-Hill publishes the *Dodge Reports*, available for specific geographic areas. This is an excellent outline of the buildings under construction within a given area, the firms that are designing them, the details of the contracts, and the other professionals involved in the projects.

Your Marketing Staff

Traditionally, most market development was done by the principals of the firm; however, today the client development process has become so extensive that it is impossible for the principals to be active in the design process and also handle all the market development. They are really two completely different functions. It is better to have someone specifically devoted to this function. The person handling the marketing division must have both a good knowledge of the design field and excellent interpersonal skills. This combination is very difficult to find. The person responsible for marketing often influences the design decisions because of his or her liaison with the client.

PUBLIC RELATIONS

Public relations are those business functions concerned with informing the public of your abilities, activities, and policies; and attempting to create a favorable public opinion. Public relations can include hiring a publicist, but for most interior designers it consists of personal interaction such as attending community functions and inviting the public to see their work.

Public relations has three purposes:

1. to make you known to your resources;

2. to make you known to your peers;

3. to make you known to potential clients.

You tell people about your firm with your studio, your personal appearance, your business card, your stationery, the community meetings you choose to attend, your portfolio, and in many other ways. Public relations is not orchestrated for you; you engage in public relations with each client contact—even with the way your telephone is answered. The goal is to present yourself in a favorable light. Research shows it takes a minimum of seven to ten contacts to build enough rapport with a prospective client to be able to sell to him or her.

A professional publicist directs a public relations campaign from a palette of resources and techniques, choosing those which best suit the client. Public relations is labor-intensive. Choose activities that suit your skills and personality, and they will become part of the way you do business.

Fundamental Public Relations

You can contribute tremendously toward improving your firm's public relations by the following activities—which demand only time.

1. *Provide the best service possible.* Clients will usually return to you and will give you good recommendations.

2. *Call on potential clients.* Visit developers and other people that you know may have contracts available.

3. *Talk to current clients.* See if they will introduce you to other people who could be good prospective clients.

4. *Attend every event possible within your community.* Try to be very visible within the community where you want to develop business. Be seen at places where you feel your clients will be. If you are interested in a sport or cultural activity, be a regular supporter and meet everyone there.

   Taking part in community affairs is an excellent way to show your future clients that you are interested in their lifestyle—that you not only approve of it, but are a part of it. Many designers have acquired their total client list by being active in community affairs. It is important, however, to become active in an area in which you are really interested, as well as one that offers a good source of clients.

   Watch your position on controversial issues. As a general rule, it is not good marketing for an interior designer to take sides in public. Some people are very active in political and highly controversial social issues, and they will judge you by your position on these issues.

5. *Go to various conferences or seminars and sit with your prospective clients.* Do not sit with other designers or professional people; you want to appear accessible to your clients, not exclusive.

6. *Meet people.* Schedule lunch meetings. Some designers have breakfast, lunch, or dinner with a different prospective client every day. Getting out there and meeting clients is very important.

7. *Be aware of your personal appearance.* People may make judgments as to whether or not they will retain you as a professional designer merely because of your personal appearance. You should try to develop a personal style that will be attractive to the type of clients for whom you will be working.

8. *Learn to advertise yourself.* It is easy to forget how important it is to be visible. Become an authority on something. A number of designers I know have developed a personal interest and become world experts. One expanded her expertise in Art Deco at a time when few people shared this interest. Through her lectures on this subject she was able to get jobs in other parts of the United States, as well as in other parts of the world. Without that special interest, those exposures and opportunities would never have been available to her.

Many designers donate their services to charitable organizations. I think it is important to submit a bill with your donation for one principle reason: to let the client realize the value of the services that you are donating. Very often, designers will donate many hours or weeks of their time to a community organization, and the organization will feel that they are getting something that took no effort or was of no financial value. If these organizations get a bill and perhaps even a quotation ahead of time stating, in effect, that you are donating so many thousands of dollars worth of your services, you will receive proper recognition for your contribution to the project.

The Tools of Public Relations

Good public relations requires you to spend at least a modest amount for certain promotional tools. Your public-relations budget should be a predetermined amount. The figure generally budgeted for promotion is three to five percent of gross income (not gross sales), although some consultants suggest five to ten percent. I suggest you put this amount of money aside specifically for promotion to assure that you have future jobs. New businesses usually need the largest budgets.

Your Business Card. One of the first things each client sees is your business or calling card. This should be regular in size and include the basics of all business cards: name and title; telephone number (with area code); company name; type of business; and logo (if you have established one). To eliminate any one of these items may cause problems at a later date. Your business card is your insurance that you are represented properly when you or your staff cannot be there in person. Great care should be taken to make sure it is accurate.

Your Stationery. Your stationery should be of a standard quality and color to accept a type of correction fluid. Do not use erasable bond; the typing can smudge. Use reasonably well-designed stationery and business cards, it is attractive if the two coordinate. Note: It is important to use someone who is qualified in graphic design for designing both your stationery and your business card.

Letters of Interest. Sales letters are an important medium for everyone. Since every firm has stationery, these letters are a personal way of directing your particular business to the attention of good prospective clients. Your letter should

1. suggest that you understand the client's problem;

2. state your standard practice of working;

3. set a date for a follow-up call. Be sure to then follow up on the letter; otherwise there is no point in sending it out.

Your Portfolio. Whether you are a beginning designer or an established professional, your portfolio is an important part of your professional presentation and must be updated constantly. This does not mean that some of your older designs cannot be included; it means that you must have the portfolio in readiness at all times and it must be reasonably representative of your work. Initially, it might be the portfolio you created in art school.

Your portfolio or design presentation may include slides, photographs, and brochures. Its style and presentation will vary according to your design specialty. Ideally, you should be able to adapt your presentation to your client's needs.

Mailings. Mailings are valuable to keep your name in front of the client. Anytime you have good information, send it out—let your clients hear from you. Send out a report and perhaps some photographs of the work you are doing.

Brochures. Folders or brochures are good advertisements. A brochure can be done very simply or very elaborately.

Whether it is expensive or inexpensive is not the main factor; it is important that it be well designed. You might want to use a graphic designer on this project. The brochure should state what an interior designer is—what you do—and perhaps provide a list of questions and answers. It can also have a plain side on which notes can be written when discussing a particular issue with a client. The key here is good design (and be sure it is current) stating something that will be of appeal to your prospective client.

Use care in distributing your brochures; mass marketing usually produces less than a three percent return. Like your portfolio, your brochure should be reviewed as your business changes; evaluate it at least every two years.

Dear Mr. Cross,

We understand that you will be interviewing design firms to help you renovate your health care facility. We are most interested in being retained for this project.

We have had a general interior design and space planning practice in Home City since 1958. During this time we have been responsible for a number of projects similar to yours, including the space planning of and specification of furnishings for over 200 patient rooms and adjacent lobbies in two area hospitals, dental and optometric offices, and dormitories for 2,000 students at a residential college.

On most of these projects, in addition to providing the traditional design services, we also analyzed the space, developed the project jointly with the client, and supervised the contractors as well as the installations.

You will be particularly interested to know that on the hospital projects we worked with Stevenson Bros., a highly skilled general contracting firm with an excellent record in this state. We and Stevenson Bros. are prepared to collaborate again on your project.

Our staff includes specialists in planning and design, both of spaces and of furniture. In addition, we also have long-standing working relationships with several local structural and electrical engineering firms and the well-known architectural firm of Tower & Stone.

To tell you more about our firm we have enclosed a brochure, project fact sheets, and a magazine article about one of our past projects.

We look forward to meeting with you to discuss our qualifications in more detail.

Sincerely,

James Doe
President
Doe Design, Inc.

Letters of Commendation. When you receive a letter of commendation from an outstanding client, ask him or her for permission to copy it and send it to other prospective clients.

Some designers and architects send out letters of commendation as a regular mailing to prospective clients and past clients. See pages 117–18 for sample letters.

Public Relations as an Investment

There are certain public-relations activities that can help bring your firm to the attention of potential clients.

Entertaining. Business entertaining is a very valuable marketing tool for designers. It is important to have a space to entertain in that represents your design style. If you cannot entertain in a space that is yours, you should consider using your client's space. I know several designers who make a point of entertaining in their client's spaces as soon as they complete a project. They feel that this both compliments their client and shows pride in the project; it also shows potential clients the type of quality of work that they do. It has brought them a gratifying number of new projects.

When selecting the place for your entertaining, determine whether this is the image you want to present. We are in the image business. Make sure that your space makes a positive statement for you.

Most entertainment expenses are deductible when the goal of the entertaining is to make a sale or to achieve a definite business objective. You do not need to get the job in order to take the tax deduction, but you must prove you are working toward a specific job.

Entertaining has many advantages. Very often you and your guests feel more at ease. There is time to discuss design ideas and develop concepts. Telephone interruptions and other day-to-day problems can be put aside.

For a profit-oriented evening, keep your party down to eight to ten people. If it gets to be too large, you will not have the opportunity to interact with your clients.

Some designers entertain in a client's space before beginning a project. Other designers have gained permission to give a party in completed client space. Use your creativity in entertaining, but document what you spend so that you have no problems with the IRS. Estimates are no longer accepted; you must have receipts and your program for the evening must be clearly defined.

Entertaining in your studio can bring positive results. Most interior designers have reasonably attractive studios; even small studios usually have one or two nice spaces or a conference room where people can gather. Try to bring clients and prospective clients into your space.

Having groups of people in for lunch or an early cocktail party is a low-stress way of marketing yourself and your firm. Invite people who might enjoy seeing what you are doing. While you cannot expect people to take three hours to see everything you are doing or have done, usually anyone can take an hour for lunch. Plan to keep your presentation or program short and to the point.

I try to have different groups of people in at least once a month. At times we'll ask an old client to come as a catalyst, or to bring along anyone else who might be interested in the kinds of projects we've developed.

When these groups are visiting, you should invite them to see any items you think might be of interest to them—a special book you have in your library, your new CADD system, some new products you are trying.

Make sure they pass by a few samples of your work, either photographs or drawings, as they walk into the conference room; this stimulates curiosity. These informal gatherings introduce design services in almost a museumlike atmosphere—there is no perceived pressure to buy, only an effort to acquaint potential clients with a range of design services.

```
Professional Administrative Service

123 North Broadway

Stamford, CT  06900



Prospective Clients:


We chose the architectural and interior design firm of I. B. Designer

and Associates for our office space and all public areas, as well as for

the entrance to our new corporate storage facilities in Connecticut.


We feel that we made an excellent choice.  Mr. Designer's unique

solutions to the almost overwhelmingly large spaces are pleasing to

everyone who is working in these areas--a factor most important to me

and my firm.


We are all very proud of our various new facilities, as is Mr. Designer.

We would definitely recommend this firm to anyone for any project

whatsoever.


Sincerely,



J. A. Smith

President
```

Major Storage and Shipping Concern
999 Warehouse Street
Philadelphia, PA 99999

To whom it may concern:

When we decided to replace our entire facilities with newer, more modern areas, the interior design and architectural firm of Professional Design of Paoli, Pennsylvania, was hired to handle the entire project.

Not only was the firm involved in every aspect of the job, but the firm also kept the project within the allotted budgets while maintaining the original scheduling. The firm also displayed a continuance of integrity, pride, and professionalism throughout this entire project.

We were impressed by Professional Design Company and recommend this firm as the finest we have ever used.

Sincerely yours,

I. M. Jones
President

Show Houses. Show houses give you an opportunity to present your talents. They are a good way to expose your work to the many people who are interested in seeing quality furnishings or in retaining a good designer.

Before you commit your firm to participating in a show house, find out what rules and regulations apply. Also check on the coordinators. Have they run a show house before? What are their responsibilities? Some show houses allow you to staff the rooms. Others insist your work speak for itself.

Show houses are expensive, which can be a major drawback to using this method of advertising. If you elect to participate in a show house, take the time to do it well in order to properly represent your design talent.

In metropolitan areas, many wholesale sources will supply designers with products to use in show house displays. This reduces the cost of doing the show house. The show house staff will have a list available of sources that are willing to supply paint, carpeting, furnishings, electrical fixtures, as well as many services such as paperhanging and carpentry. This list should be made available to you when you are negotiating to design a room within a show house. In small towns, these arrangements are not generally available, which makes the cost of participating in show houses considerably higher.

Show house projects should be designed so that they can be favorably photographed. When selecting your room, consider both the exposure to visitors and the photographic qualities of the space.

Contests. One of the easiest, least expensive public relations efforts is to enter the contests sponsored by design resources. Very often you are competing with fewer people than you are on the average design bid.

Most contests want photographs and drawings of actual installations as opposed to conceptual drawings. In a competition, the quality of your photography can be as important as the quality of your design; you may want to take new photographs of a job. Even if you do not win, your work will have been exposed to magazine and newspaper editors and may be published.

Publication. Get your work published, if at all possible, in local papers and consumer-oriented magazines. Publication in professional journals and magazines is not usually as worthwhile; these are read primarily by your peers, and they do not bring you work. Publication is only useful when your work is seen by prospective clients.

If you can, try to write articles for magazines; again, consumer-oriented magazines are the most valuable. Send your clients and prospective clients reprints of your articles or press releases that feature your studio.

Publicists

Is it worthwhile to hire a professional publicist? Yes, if you can afford to support a long-term campaign. Most publications have anywhere from a week to a nine-month lead time, and people rarely act immediately on what they read. They may carry a clipping around for years before they can afford to hire a designer. Public relations is an investment in time as well as money.

Publicists are most useful when you consistently do spectacular work and/or have new products and ideas to sell throughout the year. When the requests for information and photography that you receive from magazines and newspapers become so numerous that they interfere with your ability to run your studio, then you need a publicist to sort out which requests deserve your personal attention.

Most interior designers need a publicist on a one-shot basis, but publicists rarely work this way. They need a consistent flow of information to maintain credibility with their editorial contacts. Interior designers can rarely supply this, but their resources can.

Any large or national product manufacturer normally has a public relations program, for which they need examples of products in use. Carpeting, laminate, wallcovering, and tile manufacturers usually have their own programs. Sometimes the manufacturer of a fiber used in carpeting has the publicist. There are also associations of manufacturers who have public relations programs, such as the National Association of Mirror Manufacturers, the Marble Institute of America, the International Linen Promotion Commission, and the Wool Bureau.

When a product manufacturer photographs a design project, it is usually because his product is predominant, if not used exclusively. Some designers even specify their projects with this in mind. If your project meets the product manufacturers' standards, and fills a need, they may offer photographs of it to a magazine or include it in publicity packets going to newspapers and news syndicates. These publications will often then contact you for more information.

Designer friends of mine have seen photographs of their work appear on full pages in ten or twelve magazines in a single month—and the publicity has cost them nothing except their time and effort. By working with your resources, it is possible to get the kind of exposure no interior design firm could afford.

If specific product manufacturers do not choose to publicize your work, and if it does not fit any of the categories of available design competitions, this does not mean that your work can't be publicized. However, you may have to hire the photographer and place the work with a magazine yourself.

Find out which magazines are appropriate for your special project and what their requirements are for publication. ASID's pamphlet "How to Get Your Work Published" includes a list of magazines that publish design work, their addresses, their editors' names, and their requirements. In all cases, it helps to double-check the editor's name with a phone call. A correctly addressed, well-photographed project will prejudice an editor in your favor.

Some magazines prefer to be approached by a designer rather than by his or her publicist. The editor can then contact the designer directly with questions and get specific answers in the designer's own words. This avoids having both questions and answers filtered through a third party.

ADVERTISING

At one point it was considered unprofessional for interior designers and other professionals to advertise. Now that lawyers and doctors advertise, the stigma is gone and some designers do place ads for their firms.

Advertising is most valuable in announcing the formation of a new firm or any change of direction for an existing firm. It is also useful for keeping your name before the public.

Many designers place courtesy ads in art programs. However, this is not advertising as much as it is a public relations effort to support local art activities. When you integrate these courtesy ads into a planned advertising effort that is part of your marketing program, they can be more effective in bringing in new business inquiries.

Choosing the Right Publications

The market research you did for your business development plan (see pages 52–54) has defined what services you provide, your geographic area, and the type of customer you wish to attract. You will need this information to determine in which publications you should advertise.

Although we see some very expensive and opulent ads for design firms in *Architectural Digest*, the *New York Times Magazine*, and professional design publications that are also available to outsiders, these are not appropriate for all firms. Unless you have an international or national clientele, national advertising is not advisable. Your advertising should reach the customers you want and can service. For most interior designers, advertising in regional and local publications is more effective.

Repeating a full-page ad three or four times a year will usually give you sufficient exposure. A quarter-page (or smaller) ad should be run more often. If your business is largely residential, a national full-color ad in *Architectural Digest* will undoubtedly give you prestige; but unless you can afford to repeat the ad several times during the year, it's a long shot.

The Design of Advertisements

Because a successful advertising campaign is built on continuity, regional and local publications will often help you design an ad at little or no cost above the cost of typesetting. They will often incorporate elements from your stationery or brochure design.

While line drawings dress up an ad, photography can be tricky. Only high quality or professional photography will serve your purposes. With photography, small imperfections can become major ones when the publication has a high print run.

An advertising agency can usually create the best looking and most effective ad for you. This is important because interior design is a visual profession. Ad agencies are skilled in creating ads to meet the individual requirements of magazines and other publications. They keep information on file regarding ad sizes, type sizes, screen requirements for black and white photography, and separation requirements for color photography. They also keep track of the circulation, demographics, and prices for ads in specific publications.

Don't go to anyone until you have worked out your marketing plan and determined what you want to accomplish. The more specific you can be, the better your advertising can be directed to meet this market.

A 1987 survey* of interior designers from six midwestern chapters of ASID stated that the majority of respondents agreed that marketing is an effective way to create new business activity, and that there is a need for advertising by interior designers. Of the respondents, the firms who advertised operated closer to their capacity level of business than those who did not advertise. More firms in communities with less than 100,000 in population budget for advertising than those in large communities; and those who advertise indicated that their advertising budgets had increased in the past five years.

Photography

Why should you photograph your work? If all you need is a visual record of contents to accompany an inventory for insurance purposes, a competent amateur can do the work for you, even with a point-and-shoot camera and a flash cube. However, if you are using photographs to show prospective customers a record of your work, you should hire the best photographer you can afford. Record shots are usually taken using a 35-mm camera, slow film, a wide-angle lens, and a tripod. Slow film will give definition and clarity to the photo; the tripod is a must with slow film.

The better the quality of the photography, the better your work appears to be. Take the time to analyze the quality of the work shown in national and regional magazines.

Excellent photography has an arresting quality. It takes hold of you and elicits a reaction on an elemental level. Good photography can manipulate the way you feel about a subject by changing the way you perceive it. The magic of photography is achieved with angles, lights, and the photographer's skill. An excellent

*Partially funded by the Iowa State University Achievement Foundation, and reported in the *Journal of Interior Design Education and Research*, vol. 13, no. 3, Spring 1987, pp. 21–30.

source of information on the photography of interiors is Norman McGrath's book, *Photographing Buildings Inside and Out*, published in 1987 by the Whitney Library of Design.

Cost. Photography of the type found in national shelter magazines and advertising is an investment of several thousand dollars. Not all of your work merits, or even requires, this elaborate and precise a visual record.

You might try to get your client to agree to pay half of your photography fee. Clients may be interested in having these photographs for many reasons: for their personal records, for insurance purposes, or, if the clients are a business or professional account, for use in their own marketing program.

Publication Requirements. Be sure to consider the final use of your photographs in determining whether you need transparencies, black and white shots, or color prints.

If you plan to submit photographs to a magazine for editorial use or advertising, you should first check with the publication in which you hope to be published to find out their particular requirements and standards for photography. Don't invest in a form of photography that the particular publication you want cannot use.

Creativity in photography is exceptionally important. If you are using a photograph for a magazine or publication, be sure it is properly laid out and well designed. Magazines want something that is attractive. Even if you are forced to move furniture or alter your design, be adaptable when working with the photographer.

Photographers. I recommend that you use professional photographers who are familiar with interior design work. These special photographers are available in most areas and their costs vary according to the locale.

Interior photography is an art form, an area of photography so specialized that books on photography rarely devote more than two pages to it.

How good a photo is depends on the photographer's eye for composition and his or her knowledge of films, cameras, and lighting. An error in choosing film, lighting, or filters for a job can result in colors that are not true. Almost as important is the skill of the film lab. Sloppy processing in the film lab can also give your colors unwanted casts.

The interiors photographer must compensate for unique problems. What you see when you look into a room is not what the camera sees. A camera's distortion of small spaces is so extreme that what is seen through the viewfinder as perfectly centered is, in fact, off to one side. This distortion can vary in degree from camera to camera (it is worst with point-and-shoot cameras) and depending on the distance between the subject and the camera. The skilled photographer knows his or her camera and has learned to compensate.

You don't have to be a photographer yourself to get good results from a photographer, but you must provide some basic information. No matter how brilliant the photographer is, he or she is not a mind reader. If you don't tell him or her what you expect, don't be surprised when you don't get it. On rare occasions a photographer is so experienced that he or she will be able to tell you what is important about your space. Don't take the photographer's knowledge for granted; discuss what you need by answering the following questions.

1. What spaces are the most important?

2. Does the room have a focal point?

3. What qualities do you wish to capture? Is there a mood you feel your work evokes? The photography can enhance or diminish this mood.

4. Do you need a photograph of the whole room, or will shots of certain areas be more effective? If you designed a table specifically to enhance a sculpture, for example, tell the photographer. If what you are selling is efficient use of space, tell the photographer. Otherwise, you may get photographs that do not help sell your work.

Interiors are not static works of art. They change with use; they weather and acquire marks of wear. A carefully placed display of collectibles may be shoved aside to make room for a stack of work brought home from the office.

Interiors are at their best during the first month after installation. Be sure that your work is photographed correctly the first time; you are probably not going to get a second chance. If the work is being photographed for possible publication in a national magazine, bear in mind that it may take several days for the photographer to fine tune the lighting and the angles.

Videotaping

Videotaping is an excellent tool. It is the most effective way to document projects from beginning to end. With the help of a reasonably good photographer you can prepare a great presentation; people like to see the before-and-after shots. Although some design firms have produced quite costly videotapes, there are also reasonably inexpensive ways to produce them.

Videos make a dramatic and enjoyable presentation because they show action. They can be particularly exciting if they include color and music.

Most clients are now accustomed to seeing design videotapes and really prefer video presentations to slide shows. Almost every household in the United States now owns a VCR, so sending your videotape home with someone to review or passing it around among a group of potential clients can save you time in your initial sales efforts.

A collection of slides can also be worked into a video presentation. As with any brochure or marketing presentation, videotapes must be kept up-to-date. Videotape presentations are useful for approximately two years, after which time they need to be reshot to incorporate newer work. Because videotapes become out-of-date so quickly, you should not put so much money into one that you can't afford to change it with reasonable, minimal effort.

Designers have also been bringing their videocameras into showrooms and markets to photograph demonstrations of products being used. These videotapes can then be shown to the designers' clients. However, this is a very expensive way to retain information gathered at the market.

SELLING

Selling interior design services requires finding a prospect with a problem, convincing the prospect that you have the ability and experience to solve that problem, and converting that prospect into a client.

Although your portfolio and your photographs can support your sales effort, what sells a job is your skill at communicating to the client the abilities of your firm to do the project.

How to Sell

Some interior designers are excellent salespeople. In the past, they might have been called hucksters, but now we realize that marketing and professional sales abilities are needed to get the right projects. A salesperson has to be very positive, enthusiastic, and proud to work for his or her firm. He or she knows and respects the competition, but believes that his or her firm will do a better job for the client.

Most good salespeople are able to see a situation as the client sees it. They can understand and respect the client's opinions and can work with a client without necessarily having to agree with him or her. Salespeople help develop rapport between a firm and a client. Because of their sensitivity to the client, they create an atmosphere in which good decisions can be made.

Good salespeople have a lot of drive. They must be willing to do whatever it takes to get a job. They have to be able to keep their enthusiasm high; they can't allow themselves to be discouraged. Even after they've lost a job, they have to keep right on going after the next job.

A number of salespeople operate along the K.I.S.S. principle, which means: Keep It Short and Simple. Good presentations are prepared with precision, but they are delivered in a very short, simple, and direct fashion.

There should be no surprises when you are trying to sell to a client. Make it easy and comfortable for your client. Encourage him or her to ask questions. The more the client talks, and the less you talk, the better it is. In a sales conversation the client should talk seventy to eighty percent of the time and the salesperson twenty to thirty percent of the time; this is the perfect balance. Try to encourage your clients to give you information, to tell you what they think is important. During a sales conversation, your ability and willingness to listen is crucial. So are your skills of observation. You can often pick up visual cues from the surroundings, what the client wears, and body language.

Cold Calls. For many people, the idea of making cold calls is off-putting. That may be because they don't know how to do it. Cold calling is a specialized sales technique that has highly developed procedures and steps. If you are familiar with them and understand them, cold calling can be very successful. Among the top 100 design firms, many get a majority of new business through cold calls.

Successful cold calls begin with research to determine which clients are worth pursuing with expensive one-to-one visits or formal presentations. The cold calling "division" of a design firm can be as small as a single person or as large as a whole department of telephone operators. One firm claims that it has sixty people constantly working the telephone. Small firms may do cold calls on an individual basis.

One Florida design firm specializing in banks has a remarkably high cold-call success rate. When the chief designer completes a bank in a given town, he makes a point of visiting every other bank in the region and introducing himself. He will tell them about the bank he has just completed and suggest that they stop by and visit it. He will also ask them when they will be ready to update. While visiting these other banks he is usually able to tell, just by looking around, what could be done in their spaces and what styles would be most suitable. For those banks he feels are his most likely prospects, he actually does the design preparation and budgeting without further contact or expressions of interest. He then returns with the completed design and the contract, and generally sells the project in the same visit.

The Emissary Method. When the principals are not able to do all of the market development, it can be effective to hire a person to act as an emissary. This person will pre-interview prospective clients. He or she will size up the project and its general qualifications. He or she will describe the design firm in glowing detail, telling the potential client about the principals in charge, the design staff, and the management group. Then this person sets up a time for a formal presentation, at which he or she is present. By the time of the presentation, the emissary will have developed a friendship with the prospective client. An emissary will assist in the communication between the client and the design team and will bring business to a firm. But he or she will continue to look out for the interests of the prospective clients he or she has developed.

Client Attitudes in Buying Design. Some design jobs are sold purely on emotion, but the majority are sold to management-oriented decision makers.

What clients wanted in an interior designer fifteen or twenty years ago is different from what they are looking for today. In 1970 most clients were looking for a total service organization with a lot of design know-how and high creativity. They looked at past projects, your availability to do the job, and lastly, your prestige.

Today clients look first at your experience with their type of project; then at your experience with their firm. They next evaluate your ability to complete the project on time and within budget, and your accuracy in making estimates and specifications. On down the list of their considerations is the kind of design work your firm does, the firm's quality of management, your enthusiasm, the size of the firm, and the 'in-house capabilities of your firm.

The Initial Interview

The initial interview is your client's first opportunity to see you as a person. Sometimes it can even be his or her first real contact with the interior design profession. It is also your first chance to evaluate the client. Ask yourself if you think it will be possible to establish the rapport needed for the duration of the project. Or does this person have personality traits that spell trouble?

Advance Research. Before the initial interview, try to find out as much about the prospective client as possible. If the client was referred to you, check with the person who referred him or her.

Defining the experience level of a client is helpful. You may want to call a designer who has worked with the client before to find out how that collaboration went. A designer can tell you a lot with just a few sentences.

One of the most difficult things to do is to qualify clients. Too many designers continue to solicit business from clients who are impossible—either they don't pay or they're too demanding. Why not leave those clients for your competitors, and spend your time and effort in finding clients who are the type of people for whom you want to work?

Whether a project is a residential or a contract one, do a credit check on the client (see pages 308–10). You will also want to learn what the client firm's objectives are and who the other professionals involved in the project are. Who are the principals of the firm? Who will be in charge, and what are his or her accomplishments and interests? Sources for this information include Dun & Bradstreet reports (see pages 309–10), conversations with contractors, and building reports (these list the contracts let on a building for construction, electrical wiring, and plumbing, and the budget for each). From this information you can get a working idea of the possible design budget.

Planning the Interview. The next step is to write out your objectives for this meeting. In an initial interview, you need to determine the scope of the project, the client's needs, the scheduling, the financial expectations, and any restraints. Before this meeting you should consult and the design service outline and the meetings forms on pages 197 and 255.

The location of the initial interview is a matter of personal preference. I hold my initial interviews on the job site so I can see some of the particulars and assess the client's experience. Seeing where and how the client lives or works helps me to determine his or her design standards. I gather all the visual clues possible. If a client says he or she wants to redo an office inexpensively, I have no idea what he or she means until I see the space. If the room is done in one-of-a-kind pieces, and the client says he or she wants to scale down, I know I still have a workable budget.

Plan what you will wear to the interview. The way you look and dress is critical. If you appear to come from a different world, your clients may find it difficult to relate to you. You are there to create a liaison, and the way you look is part of your presentation. Some of us are more comfortable in simple fashions; others prefer flamboyance. Your appearance must fit your personality and design tastes.

Leave nothing to chance. Make a checklist of topics you need to discuss and take notes during the meeting. Some designers take notes directly on their design service outlines (see pages 197–202). Not only does this save time, but it also reinforces the client's belief that he or she is dealing with a professional.

Your topic checklist must include carefully researched written cost estimates and a time schedule. If costs are revised later because of a substantial design change, put your financial expectations in writing. Most money problems between client and designer occur because the designer has not carefully presented his or her financial expectations.

The Prospective Client Report. When you are interviewing a new prospective client, there is some basic information you need to document. The prospective client report on page 127 is an outline for your initial interview. It includes a space to record the necessary general information, such as name, address, and contact person. It also provides a space to list a definition of the project, the client's objective, and the results of the meeting. At the end of the form is a section in which to note the research or information you will need for the next meeting, the date of the next contact, and the general financial arrangements. Usually it is best to fill out this sheet immediately upon leaving the client's. (Do not do it while you are there; it will be distracting.)

Interview Techniques. The initial interview can tell you a great deal. Ask questions about the client as well as what he or she needs, wants, and can afford. Listen carefully to the answers; note the client's body language. At first, it is usually best not to offer an opinion or make a judgment; try to be neutral. Smile or nod, and use short answers such as "yes," "sure," "right," and "of course."

Has the prospective client ever used an interior designer before or is he or she acquainted with someone who has?

Where did he or she hear of your firm, and what does he or she know about you?

Has the client seen a space you designed or spoken to a former client? If not, arrange for him or her to speak to a former client in the same business the new client is in. Each profession has its own jargon and interests. It is important for a client to understand something about the design business and the scope of services available, and they will understand better if it is put in terms they use every day.

Observe. Question. Probe. Use state-of-mind probes, questions such as "How do you feel?" and "What do you think about this?" to draw out the prospective client.

Use echo probes. Repeat what the client says to encourage him or her to expand on a theme. Or return to an issue you have already discussed, and ask a reflective question.

Does your language say what you mean, or is it open to interpretation? A single comment can influence or color the whole job. You should aim for simplicity and clarity in everything you do and say in an initial interview. Many clients do not understand the design field or its vocabulary. When discussing sizes, always relate them to an item the potential client has in his or her home or office, something familiar that he or she can visualize.

If, during the interview, it becomes apparent that the prospective client is not appropriate for your firm, bow out as gracefully as possible. No amount of money can compensate for the emotional strain and physical upsets some people seem to generate.

Prospective client report. This form is useful for documenting basic information when you are interviewing a prospective client.

PROSPECTIVE CLIENT REPORT	Referred By:
Client:	Contact Person: Position:
Address:	Phone No.:
New Address: (if moving)	Directions:

Project:

Objective:

Result of Meeting:

Research or Information Needed for Next Meeting:

Date of Next Contact:

Financial Arrangements:

© Design Business Monthly

The following interviewing techniques can help you to determine the acceptability of a client.

1. *Trust your gut reaction.* It's not always easy to spot the potential problem client, but the first rule of interviewing is to trust your gut reaction. Our initial responses to people are based on nonverbal clues. You can often sense a problem without being aware of the source or reasons.

2. *Probe the humor index.* What amuses us or not taps our deepest prejudices and values. Arm yourself with a few quips and funny stories. If your prospective client reacts blandly, the prognosis for a good rapport between the two of you is not good. If he or she responds negatively, it is definitely not good.

3. *Assess the empathy level.* Every designer has a story or two about something that went wrong on a job, whether through an "act of god," a personal miscalculation, or a factory error. Test the potential client's reaction to one of these stories. A person who says, "That had better not happen on my job!" or is overly critical of the event is probably a client you would want to send to a competitor of whom you are not too fond. Look for some expressions of sympathy or understanding—a viewpoint that reflects tolerance.

4. *Use the "what if" probe.* This strategy is intended to determine the potential client's reactions to frustrations and disappointments. You might believe you can meet your client's expressed deadline, but you also know that things can go wrong. Using the "what if" probe, you might say, "I'm pretty sure everything will be finished by Christmas, but I don't have control of every link in the chain. All sorts of things can go wrong—strikes, floods, factory errors—and these could delay completion. Being optimistic, I don't think they will. But what if they do?" Assess your client's reaction to predict how he or she might behave if a problem does arise.

5. *Listen to the prospective client's words.* The words you need to be most aware of are "should," "ought," "must," and "have to." The "must" and "should" types betray a lack of flexibility and a penchant for rage and unreasonable demands. Quite often inflexible people have learned to mask their aggressive feelings with a facade of cordiality and superficial responsibility. But they cannot hide the manner in which their underlying hostilities slip out in their conversation. For example, "You must be sure that the project is completed by the fourteenth." The sentence may be said pleasantly, with a warm, friendly smile, but it contains the giveaway "must." Take notice.

There are many, many individual interview techniques. No matter which you use, it helps to keep a list of the ones that work for you on your interviewing sheet with the outline of the questions you want answered.

Another designer described a dream job he had turned down. The potential client lived in a well-appointed residence that was to be remodeled in a way that perfectly fit that designer's particular style. However, his initial interview at the prospect's home was interrupted by two phone calls, which she took in the kitchen. He overheard her saying, "Sue him!" and "Don't take anything from him!" After he heard "Take him to court!" two times, the designer knew he had to tread carefully because he was obviously dealing with a very litigious person. There was no guarantee that he would not be the next person she sued that month. He learned later that the designer who *had* accepted the work wound up embroiled in a lawsuit.

Charging for the Initial Interview. Should you charge for the initial interview? There are designers who say they wouldn't walk out of the studio without being paid for their time, but my policy is usually not to charge for the first interview. This interview gives me an opportunity to look over the space and the situation and to determine whether I want the job. I've walked into a number of situations that I felt were inappropriate to my practice. Because I did not charge, I have felt free to walk out.

If you are going to charge, notify the client before you go out to the site of a potential project and clarify exactly what the charge will be. Some designers regard the initial interview as part of their marketing effort and do not charge or charge a very small fee. If someone just wants a simple answer, you may be providing more of an on-site consultation. Make your policy clear before the interview. One way is to send out a written agreement stating, for example, "We will review your reception room for the change of wall color. Our consultation fee for that interview will be $200." Have the prospect sign the agreement and return it to you before you meet with him or her.

As a consultant to design firms, I receive many phone calls on the question of charging for initial interviews. Designers are saying: "What do I do? I sent my assistant out there and the clients were very nice. But then when I sent them the bill, they didn't want to pay it. Is my assistant not handling it properly?" I find that these problems more likely stem from the fact that the management has not structured this situation properly. If getting paid for initial interviews is a problem, and you do not want to consider them part of your marketing efforts, then state your fee in advance over the phone and in a written letter of agreement. This will save you a lot of aggravation. Remember that many of our clients have never purchased design services of any kind before and don't really know the customary procedures. Help them by giving them the price tag in advance.

The Presentation

When you are presenting at a large, formal interview, who should attend the interview? The principal of the firm usually needs to attend, as well as the person who will be responsible for the project itself—the project manager or the person who will be dealing with the client on a day-to-day basis. You might also consider including several expert consultants or other in-house staff members. If the presentation is for a small job, take two or three people. If it is for a larger job, you may take four or more people. However, be careful not to take along too many people; it is a general rule that you do not ever want to have more people on your team than the client has on his or her selection committee.

For formal presentations, usually the client establishes the time and duration of the interview, allotting each presenter a half hour, an hour, or two hours, depending upon the issues to be covered. Then the client introduces the first design firm's chief executive officer or the principal in charge, who then introduces the team and outlines the presentation.

Sometimes you will be given an opportunity to choose the order in which you fall in the presentation scheduling. The last position is ordinarily the best, and the next best would be the first position. The middle presentation position is usually the weakest spot.

At a team presentation, the principal generally makes the introduction and then immediately turns over the presentation of the project to the person who will be in charge of the project—the project manager—because this person has the strongest and most direct relationship with the client. After that presentation, both the project manager and the principal answer questions. If the presentation is held in the design office, the principal might then give a tour of the offices, or the principal and the project manager might take the clients on a tour of other similar projects.

The Agenda. Make enough copies of the agenda so that each member of the client firm who attends can have one. The copies of your proposal save them from having to write down every detail; they will have the names and the positions of each of the presenters, and some of the main items will be listed on the agenda as well. Leave space on the copies in case they want to write notes.

The agenda usually should be bound or presented in a formal, attractive way. Make sure that it has your company's name prominently displayed. The clients usually see many people during a bidding period; you don't want them to confuse you with some other design firm.

With your agenda, or after your presentation, you may want to pass out additional information on your group, such as magazine articles, newspaper articles, or brochures.

Should visual aids be used and, if so, what kind? A lot of people feel that the most deadly presentation is a slide show in a dark room. If you are going to use slides in presentations to very large groups, make sure that any text on the slides is readable from at least twenty feet away.

Where should the interview be held? It can be held in the client's space, in your office, on the site of the potential project, or, if you can arrange it, at a completed project of yours that is similar to the one you hope to design. This can be an excellent way of showing off your work.

Presentation Techniques. Clients basically want to know who you are, what your firm does, how long you have been in business, where your office is located, what kind of services you are able to provide, and what types of consultants and other professionals you would be bringing to the project. They will want to know about recent jobs you have done that are similar to their project—and how those projects were particularly successful. There are three basic client concerns: quality, schedule, and budget.

When making a presentation, you should try to relate whatever you present to the client's project. Clients don't want to hear you talk about your old projects; they are interested in their own. In some of the most outstanding presentations I have seen, the designers have said, "Here is your problem, and this is our solution."

Clients like a designer who is on their team, who shows understanding for their viewpoint. Designers who have a similar background to that of their clients can do this more easily. Clients need encouragement from their designers. And often they need help to understand just how products work and how they will fit into their lifestyle, whether it be at their business, factory, or residence.

When you use new technology—be it tungsten lighting or ergonomic seating—you need to reduce the complexity of technical data in your presentation so that it is easier for your clients to understand.

It is not enough just to show clients how products work and how simply they can be operated; you must relate a product to the client's problem. Don't just tell a client that a low-voltage lighting system is the solution; go through the system with the client: explain how it works, and then show it in actual use on a job site. Letting a client see the real-life applications of a product allows him or her to become comfortable with the new technology.

As designers we often become so involved with new products and new design ideas that we think everyone understands what we do. This is not true. Take your cue from the client's spaces as to how much background and understanding he or she has about what you are presenting. The find an easy way to present it. Use words your clients will understand; do not feel you need to use a professional design vocabulary.

DON'T EMBARRASS YOUR CLIENTS

This is something I learned early in my career. I was working on a large corporate project and one of my client liaisons asked me to make a private presentation to him several days before I was scheduled to give my presentation to the board of directors. The project was a historic restoration and my presentation showed I had done my homework. I described certain types of credenzas and cornices, and made liberal use of other design terms. After I used one such term my client liaison stopped me and asked, "What does that mean?" So I explained. He gave this valuable advice: "Don't embarrass your clients. Don't make them have to ask you what you mean." I later read that only the smartest people explain things in the simplest terms. People who lack confidence are the ones who are most apt to use words others might not understand.

You never endear yourself to a person by embarrassing him or her, nor do you develop clients by embarrassing them. Make it easy for them to understand what you are doing. Make them feel comfortable and you will never want for clients.

Should you show enthusiasm? There is a saying that enthusiasm indicates you will accept a low fee. Show that you are interested in doing the job, and that you want the job, but not that you do need the work. Generally if you are too enthusiastic, they will worry that you haven't been getting business, and they will wonder why.

Here are some tips that will help you sell the project.

1. Make sure your presentation is completely thorough, very organized, and exciting. You put the client to sleep with a dull professional presentation. You should appear intelligent, aggressive, and talented. Let the potential client realize that you are accustomed to winning jobs.

2. Check with the client in advance as to how much time is available for your presentation and structure it accordingly. There is nothing worse than preparing a presentation that takes three hours and then finding you only have thirty minutes in which to give it. Such a situation can cause you to lose your orientation and give a poor presentation.

3. In making your presentation, say why a client's project is of interest to you, and show how many elements of the project are similar to ones you have handled before. Describe the expertise and knowledge of your staff and explain how they will interact on the project. If other staff members are going to occupy a primary position on the project, it is important for you to have those people take part in your presentation. When the principal makes the presentation and then vanishes, leaving the job to be handled by his staff, clients feel neglected. They want to feel that their project is important and is in the hands of the best people possible.

   If you, as the principal, are going to be involved personally in the project, say so and explain what your dedication will mean to the project.

4. Provide references to previous clients who have used you for similar jobs. Before going to an interview, I will often send my prospective client a list of previous clients and suggest that he or she speak to those clients before we come for our presentation.

5. Explain how your design firm is different from the others in competition. What are your strong points? What can you offer the client that other studios cannot?

6. Put your most important information on the first page of your agenda and make it very easy to read and understand. Remember that what you write will be read by every person on the selection committee. Is it clearly stated? Have you presented your company as you had intended? Have a capable person review your proposal to make sure that it is stated in an appropriate fashion and that there is nothing that can be misunderstood.

7. When making a presentation, speak up so that everyone in the room can hear you.

8. Dress in businesslike clothing. Generally it is better to be a bit on the professionally neutral side than to seem too artistic. However, it depends on the type of design that you are presenting as to what is appropriate. Not everyone expects to see you in a banker's suit.

9. Go over your presentation; rehearse it and try it out on everyone you can before the actual presentation day. Practice until you feel very comfortable with the presentation. If you have the opportunity, videotape yourself and see how you are coming across.

10. Be aware that there is almost always someone in the selection group who does not want to hire you, someone who really has it in for you. All you can do is present your team in the best way possible.

11. Give the client something in advance. Prepare an analysis, build a model, draw some sketches, or take some photographs. Try to give the client something that shows that you have put in effort already. In many states in this country, as well as in Europe, architects and designers often completely design a space before being awarded the job. I am not sure how they can afford to do this, but it happens. Even if you are not doing a full presentation, try to make the client feel that you have taken time on the project.

Presentation Costs. Generally, interior designers will spend about four to ten percent of their fee to get a job. This figure includes money spent on general promotion plus the direct marketing expense for special projects. Established firms usually spend approximately four percent of their fee. However, with new firms, this percentage is often as high as ten, fifteen, and even twenty percent. The newer the firm, the more it costs to get projects.

Negotiating

When situations come up that require special negotiating—such as a client wanting special handling with a project, or a better price, or an adjustment in a quotation—it is best to turn the negotiation over to someone else within your company. Should a situation arise that cannot be amicably handled, it is a good idea not to have a salesperson in a position to be blamed. It is best to let the salesperson continue to be the good guy. Do not let him or her deal with the problems of the client he is attempting to sell.

Sharing these responsibilities, even within a small firm, works to your advantage. The client realizes that there is another administrative person handling decisions, which makes your design firm appear to be much more professional. Even if you are making the decision yourself, and you are one of the chief executive officers, it is best to turn this kind of interaction over to someone else in the firm.

Closing the Sale

One of the most difficult parts of selling is to know when and how to close. Have a list of leading questions ready. Prepare questions that cannot be answered with a yes or no; this will require the client to give an extended answer.

You might say: "Now that we've reviewed your plans, what other questions do you need answered before you are prepared to make a decision on the project?" Or: "If we are the selected designers, when would you like us to start work?" Other good questions are: "What are your scheduling plans so that we can alert our studio to reserve time for the appropriate people required for this job?"; "When will you need your plans and specifications?;" and "Shall we start working on the final designs for you?"

If you don't get a positive response to these questions, go back over the preliminary portion of your presentation to make sure you understand your position. Attempt to reorient or resell the project.

It is important to keep an itemized list of every point you have discussed on a project, as well as what results you achieved. File this list so you can refer to it during future contacts.

Sometimes designers lose a project because they oversell. The client is ready to buy, and the designer talks him or her out of it. Losing a sale can sometimes happen simply because the designer neglected to ask for the job.

It takes an average of seven to ten calls to develop a client, and some designers stop too soon. You should try to establish a date for calling a client before you leave his or her office. You might say: "I will call you at the end of the month and I will have these other details ready for you at that time". On the prospective client report (see page 127) there is space for information or research to be done before you see a potential client again. You may want to use a tickler system to help make sure you call these people at the appropriate times.

Debriefing

One of the best ways that you can develop your firm's standards is to understand why you lost a job. This review is probably one of the most effective learning methods there is. If you've made a presentation on a project, and you suspect or know that someone else got the project, follow up. Call the client and find out why your firm wasn't chosen. Before you call or speak with the client, however, prepare a list of questions that you want answered, so that you can make the conversation only a few minutes long. Reading from a predetermined list also lets the client know that the call is a standard procedural one used to evaluate your position in the field.

First of all, ask how the client made his or her decision and who was selected for the project. Then ask how your presentation compared to the others, and what the client thought of your presentation. Finally, ask the client whether your firm could be considered for any other projects he or she has planned.

It creates good will to talk to the prospective client who decided against using your firm and let him or her know that you are pleased that he or she made a decision. You congratulate the client, and add that you would like to work with him or her in the future should he or she ever become disappointed with the design firm that was chosen. Your goal is to leave the client with a pleasant and positive impression of you and your firm. You are professionally disappointed, but not angry that you didn't get the project. You will not let losing this project stand in the way of your being considered for another project.

CONTRACTS AND LETTERS OF AGREEMENT

An interior design firm's contract is one of the most critical documents that it has. A contract can either make or break a project. It must be written in legal terms, although most designers prefer to see it written as simply as possible. To see that your contract is appropriately designed for both your firm and your client requires a cooperative effort between the management of your firm and your legal consultant.

When accepting contracts with large corporations, where the client writes the contract, your attorney needs to review both the client's contract and your contract to assure they are in harmony.

At least once a year you should review your projected design ambitions and your legal positioning to be sure that your contracts reflect where you stand.

When you are determining the services that your firm will offer a client, you should review your contract carefully to be sure that your firm is able—both practically and legally—to provide the services for which you are negotiating. It is more prudent for a design firm to offer fewer services—but ones that it can securely perform—than for it to offer services that may put the firm in jeopardy.

ARE LETTERS OF AGREEMENT REALLY BINDING?

Do we really need to use contracts like those of AIA and ASID, or is there another more valid form? Several attorneys have said that there is no contract written that guarantees against dispute and misunderstanding. However, contracts are valuable because they spell out some of the areas of possible dispute and litigation. They define, and make the client aware of, potential problems. They acquaint clients with trade terms and familiarize them with the ways interior designers charge and calculate their fees. So I feel a contract is valuable in clarifying your communications and diminishing misunderstanding.

It is not necessary to use a contract, but if you choose not to use one, and if anything wrong happens, you are the person who did not take the initiative or the time to clarify to your client your position and services.

General Provisions

When preparing a contract or letter of agreement, you should be sure to include the methods for completing the project—how it is going to be contracted. Make it clear in your contract whether you will be responsible only for the design and the specification writing, the supervision of the project, or the coordination of the complete turnkey project. The financial formats also need to be included.

Also, review and define exactly which areas are to be designed. If you have agreed to do three offices, and the client has decided to add three more, you will need to prepare a different contract or proposal.

When preparing a contract you should carefully review with the client the exact scope of the project to determine what your responsibilities are when there are other design professionals involved. Define their precise responsibilities and clarify how any overlapping responsibilities will be handled.

A contract that is going to involve other architects or contractors should clarify exactly which items are included in your fee. For example, a phrase in your contract could state that since you are involved with the selection and the detailing of items involving lighting fixtures, wall coverings and paints, floor coverings and finishes, custom hardware (whether it be plumbing or other decorative hardware), all cabinetwork that is included for any areas, built-in or other custom woodworking or doors, will be covered under the fee for interior design services; and, although these items may be purchased by the contractor, the percentage-of-fee billing does apply to them.

State your firm's position regarding purchasing and fee schedules. For example, if a client of ours purchases items involved in the implementation of the interior design, which is part of the design, our office will assist in any way possible with these purchases. But it is understood that our standard design fee will apply to these purchases as well as to the items that are purchased through our studio. This includes items purchased through other contractors or individually, as they are specified, and would include items purchased for the room at a later date.

Ways to Prevent Lawsuits

Major disagreements between client and designer usually arise from a breakdown of communication; unfortunately, they can lead to lawsuits. To prevent lawsuits, assume nothing and document everything in contracts or letters of agreement. Here are a few suggestions:

1. A design contract should clearly describe the services to be rendered and the extent of the designer's responsibility. Generally when a contract document that is ambiguous or incomplete goes to court, the ruling is against the author of the document. Declare exactly what you will do—and then live up to your contract.

2. List the amount of compensation you expect and explain exactly how this will be computed. State how billing is to be done—on an hourly basis, on a specified total-project-cost basis, on a daily basis, or on a percentage basis—and include a payment schedule. Make reference to all of your billing and collection requirements. Many contracts state that work will not continue if these conditions are not met.

3. Watch your time commitments. If you commit your firm to a schedule where the project will take six months for design ordering and installation, it is safer to say that your firm will finish the project three months after the completion of the construction program, when the building is available for interior work. If the construction is delayed, your project will then be delayed, too. Committing to a date over which you have no control can be disastrous. Do not assume responsibility for anything you cannot control.

4. Stipulate who owns the drawings and specifications. You may be liable for design or material failures if a client uses your documents for a different project subject to different requirements. Copyright your drawings and your specifications. If you own the copyright, then it is nontransferable to another owner. If your client needs to own your specifications or documents, you should retain ownership of the copyright.

5. Retain the right to use your designs and your documents as you choose. You should be free to adapt the details to other projects, publish them, or use them in any way.

6. Consider the possibility of licensing the documents. You may want to negotiate for the client to have the nonexclusive rights to copy and reproduce the documents for a specific project; however, make sure this license is not transferable to any other project.

7. Thoroughly delineate the duties and obligations of each party involved in the project. When using consultants, be sure that they provide documentation of their responsibilities and positions in respect to the project so that you are not liable for their responsibilities. Make it clear when you require support documents on the project, without which you cannot continue. For example, you might need the engineering documents, the architectural documents, and specifications that affect your design. Make delivery of these documents part of the contract, since the absence of such documents could delay the project or add to your liabilities.

8. Be careful how your contract lists the prices that are to be charged. You cannot be responsible for your suppliers' price increases. Unless you have total control of the project, don't let your contract in any way tie in with these financial obligations.

9. Note that your design detailing relies upon the work of other people. Specify that you are using information from particular data and document its source, whether it is the architectural prints, for example, or the client's specifications. If a problem arises from an error based on faulty information, this documentation can give you a legal out.

10. If the project requires certifications, such as for flameproofing, fire retardants, and so on, have these prepared by the appropriate agencies and have them addressed directly to the client's project so that the organization doing the documentation is responsible, not you. Also, any guarantees that are appropriate to the project should be sent directly to the client so that if anything should occur, the guarantors are responsible.

11. Spell out exactly how changes will be handled. In the precontract phase, determine how additions or deletions will reflect on your fee or charges. It is important to document this early in the job when it is easy to negotiate; after you have started a project, it becomes far more difficult.

12. Disclaim responsibility for changes made by anyone but yourself. This way, the minute the owner makes any changes in the design, you automatically are no longer responsible for the total project. Even if the change the client makes is small, you must relieve yourself of responsibilities. Small changes can affect the quality and safety of the design.

13. Try to put all documents in clear, simple, and plain language. Avoid words that suggest excellence or any form of perfection. These are not clearly defined and can create unreal expectations, which may lead to lawsuits.

Types of Contracts and Letters of Agreement

Designers work with many types of contracts. Many designers prefer to use ASID documents or a preprinted contract because they feel these are more easily accepted by the client. These forms are very adaptable.

Many firms have their own standard printed contract that merely requires filling in several blank spaces. Each interior design studio has it own preferences.

ASID Documents. ASID has prepared contract documents suitable for the various design services. A careful review of these will assist a design firm in both defining services to be rendered and understanding the appropriate legal terms for presenting them. Many firms' legal advisors suggest the firms use these ASID documents, because they are generally accepted documents and stand a better chance of holding up in court. Other firms find them forbidding and have their legal counsel prepare special documents suitable to their practice. Whether your firm elects to use a formal contract or a simple letter of agreement, these contracts represent the best source of information for reference in preparing your documents.

Some of the issues included on your contract are specific to your locale and your type of practice. There are very large jobs done with simple letters of agreement. In some more litigious areas doing even a small project without an extensive contract could be risky. Contracts or letters of agreement must be authored to suit you, your firm, and your client.

ASID Standard Form of Agreement for Interior Design Services (B171).

American Society of Interior Designers

ASID Document B171

Standard Form of Agreement
For Interior Design Services

*THIS DOCUMENT HAS IMPORTANT LEGAL CONSEQUENCES; CONSULTATION WITH
AN ATTORNEY IS ENCOURAGED WITH RESPECT TO ITS COMPLETION OR MODIFICATION*

AGREEMENT

made as of the   day of   in the year of Nineteen
Hundred and

BETWEEN:

(hereinafter referred to as the Owner)

AND:

(hereinafter referred to as the Designer)
For the following Project:
(Include detailed description of Project location and scope, and identify other professional consultants to the Owner below and overleaf, if necessary.)

The Owner and the Designer agree as set forth below.

ARTICLE 1

DESIGNER'S SERVICES

BASIC SERVICES

The Designer's Basic Services consist of the five phases described in Paragraphs 1.1 through 1.5 and any other services included in Article 17 as part of Basic Services.

1.1 PROGRAMMING PHASE

1.1.1 The Designer shall consult with the Owner and other parties designated in this Agreement to ascertain the applicable requirements of the Project and shall review the understanding of such requirements with the Owner.

1.1.2 The Designer shall document the applicable requirements necessary for the various Project functions or operations, such as those for existing and projected personnel, space, furniture, furnishings and equipment, operating procedures, security criteria and communications relationships.

1.1.3 The Designer shall ascertain the feasibility of achieving the Owner's requirements identified under Subparagraphs 1.1.1 and 1.1.2 within the limitations of the building or buildings within which the Project is to be located.

1.1.4 Based on a review, analysis and evaluation of the functional and organizational relationships, requirements and objectives for the Project, the Designer shall provide a written program of requirements for the Owner's approval.

1.2 SCHEMATIC DESIGN PHASE

1.21 Based on the approved written program, the Designer shall prepare for the Owner's approval preliminary diagrams showing the general functional relationships for both personnel and operations.

1.2.2 The Designer shall review with the Owner alternative approaches to designing and carrying out the Work.

1.2.3 Based on the approved relationship diagrams, the Designer shall prepare space allocation and utilization plans indicating partition and furnishings locations and preliminary furniture and equipment layouts. The Designer shall provide an evaluation of the program and the Project budget, if one has been established by the Owner, each in terms of the other, subject to the limitations set forth in Subparagraph 4.2.1.

1.2.4 The Designer shall prepare studies to establish the design concept of the Project indicating the types and quality of finishes and materials and furniture, furnishings and equipment.

1.2.5 The Designer shall submit to the Owner a preliminary Statement of Probable Project Cost, based on the recommended design concept and on current costs for projects of similar scope and quality.

1.3 DESIGN DEVELOPMENT PHASE

1.3.1 Based on the approved schematic design and any adjustments authorized by the Owner in the program or Project budget, the Designer shall prepare, for approval by the Owner, Design Development drawings and other documents to fix and describe the size and character of the interior construction of the Project including special design features to be incorporated into floors, walls, partitions or ceilings.

1.3.2 The Designer shall prepare such data and illustrations for furniture, furnishings and equipment as may be appropriate for the Project, including specially designed items or elements, to indicate finished appearance and functional operation.

1.3.3 The Designer shall recommend colors, materials and finishes not otherwise specified for the Project.

1.3.4 The Designer shall prepare such other Design Development data, illustrations and documents as may be appropriate for the Project, as described in Article 17.

1.3.5 The Designer shall submit for the Owner's approval a further Statement of Probable Project Cost, based on anticipated unit costs and prices.

1.4 CONTRACT DOCUMENTS PHASE

1.4.1 Based on the approved Design Development submissions and further adjustments in the scope or quality of the Project or in the Project budget authorized by the Owner, the Designer shall be responsible for the preparation of, for approval by the Owner, Construction Documents consisting of Drawings, Specifications and other documents setting forth in detail the requirements for the interior construction work necessary for the Project. The Work described by such interior construction documents is intended to be performed by the Owner or under one or more Contracts between the Owner and Contractor for construction.

1.4.2 Based on the approved Design Development submissions, the Designer shall prepare, for approval by the Owner, Drawings, Schedules, Specifications and other documents, setting forth in detail the requirements for the fabrication, procurement, shipment, delivery and installation of furniture, furnishings and equipment necessary for the Project. Such Work is intended to be performed under one or more Contracts or Purchase Orders between the Owner and Contractor or supplier for furniture, furnishings and equipment.

1.4.3 The Designer shall advise the Owner of any adjustments to previous Statements of Probable Project Cost indicated by changes in requirements or general market conditions.

1.4.4 The Designer shall assist in the preparation of the necessary bidding and procurement information, bidding and procurement forms, the Conditions of the Contracts for Construction and for Furniture, Furnishings and Equipment, Purchase Orders, and the forms of Agreement between the Owner and the Contractors or suppliers.

ASID DOCUMENT B171 • INTERIOR DESIGN SERVICES AGREEMENT • ASID® • ©1977
THE AMERICAN SOCIETY OF INTERIOR DESIGNERS, 1430 BROADWAY, NEW YORK, N.Y. 10018
©1972, ©1977 • AIA® • THE AMERICAN INSTITUTE OF ARCHITECTS, 1735 NEW YORK AVE., N.W., WASHINGTON, D.C. 20006

1.4.5 The Designer shall assist the Owner in connection with the Owner's responsibility for filing documents required for the approval of governmental authorities having jurisdiction over the Project.

1.4.6 The Designer following the Owner's approval of the Contract Documents and of the most recent Statement of Probable Project Cost shall assist the Owner in obtaining bids or negotiated proposals, and assist in awarding and preparing contracts for interior construction and for furniture, furnishings and equipment. All bidding and negotiating activities shall be coordinated by the Designer.

1.5 CONTRACT ADMINISTRATION PHASE

1.5.1 The Contract Administration Phase will commence with the award of one or more Contracts or the issuance of one or more purchase orders and, together with the Designer's obligation to provide Basic Services under this Agreement, will terminate when final payment to Contractors or suppliers is due, and in the absence of a final Certificate for Payment or of such due date, sixty days after the Date of Substantial Completion of the Work, whichever occurs first.

1.5.2 The term Contractor as used herein shall mean each person or entity awarded a Contract by the Owner or supplier to whom a purchase order is issued by the Owner or the Owner's agent in connection with interior construction, procurement or installation for the Work. Each such Contractor shall be referred to throughout the Contract Documents as if singular in number and masculine in gender. The term Contractor means the Contractor or the Contractor's authorized representative.

1.5.3 Unless otherwise provided in this Agreement and incorporated in the Contract Documents: the Designer shall provide administration of the Contracts for Furniture, Furnishings and Equipment only as set forth below and in the edition of ASID Document A271, General Conditions of the Contract for Furniture, Furnishings and Equipment, current as of the date of this Agreement.

1.5.4 The Designer shall be a representative of the Owner during the Contract Administration Phase, and shall advise and consult with the Owner. Instructions to the Contractors shall be forwarded through the Designer. The Designer shall have authority to act on behalf of the Owner only to the extent provided in the Contract Documents unless otherwise modified by written instrument in accordance with Subparagraph 1.5.20.

1.5.5 The Designer shall assist the Owner in coordinating the schedules for delivery and installation of the Work, but shall not be responsible for any malfeasance, neglect or failure of any Contractors or suppliers to meet their schedules for completion or to perform their respective duties and responsibilities.

1.5.6 The Designer shall visit the Project premises as deemed necessary by the Designer, or as otherwise agreed by the Designer in writing, to become generally familiar with the progress and quality of the Work and to determine in general if the Work is proceeding in accordance with the Contract Documents. However, the Designer shall not be required to make exhaustive or continuous inspections at the Project premises to check the quality or quantity of the Work. On the basis of such on-site observations, the Designer shall keep the Owner informed of the progress and quality of the Work, and shall endeavor to guard the Owner against defects and deficiencies in the Work of the Contractors.

1.5.7 The Designer shall not have control or charge of and shall not be responsible for the means, methods, techniques, sequences or procedures of construction, fabrication, procurement, shipment, delivery or installation, or for safety precautions and programs in connection with the Work, for the acts or omissions of the Contractors, Sub-contractors, suppliers, or any other persons performing any of the Work, or for the failure of any of them to carry out the Work in accordance with the Contract Documents.

1.5.8 The Designer shall at all times have access to the Work wherever it is in preparation or progress.

1.5.9 The Designer shall determine the amounts owing to the Contractors based on observations at the Project premises and on evaluations of the Contractors' Applications for Payment, and shall issue Certificates for Payment in such amounts, as provided in the Contract Documents.

1.5.10 The issuance of a Certificate for Payment shall constitute a representation by the Designer to the Owner, based on the Designer's observations at the Project premises as provided in Subparagraph 1.5.6 and on the data comprising the Contractor's Application for Payment, that the Work has progressed to the point indicated; that to the best of the Designer's knowledge, information and belief, the quality of the Work is in accordance with the Contract Documents (subject to an evaluation of the Work for conformance with the Contract Documents upon Substantial Completion, to the results of any subsequent tests required by or performed under the Contract Documents, to minor deviations from the Contract Documents correctable prior to final completion, and to any specific qualifications stated in the Certificate of Payment); and that the Contractor is entitled to payment in the amount certified. However, the issuance of a Certificate for Payment shall not be a representation that the Work is without latent defects, or that the Designer has made any examination to ascertain how and for what purposes the Contractor has used the moneys paid on account of the Contract Sum.

1.5.11 Unless otherwise provided, the Designer's duties shall not extend to the receipt, inspection and acceptance on behalf of the Owner of furniture, furnishings and equipment at the time of their delivery to the premises and installation. The Designer is not authorized to reject nonconforming Work, sign Change Orders on behalf of the Owner, stop the Work, or terminate the Contract on behalf of the Owner.

1.5.12 The Designer shall be the interpreter of the requirements of the Contract Documents and the impartial judge of performance thereunder by both the Owner and the Contractors. The Designer shall render interpretations necessary for the proper execution or progress of the Work with reasonable promptness on written request of either the Owner or a Contractor, and shall render written decisions, within a reasonable time, on all claims, disputes and other matters in question between the Owner and the Contractor relating to the execution or progress of the Work or the interpretation of the Contract Documents.

1.5.13 Interpretations and decisions of the Designer shall be consistent with the intent of and reasonably inferable from the Contract Documents and shall be in written or graphic form. In the capacity of interpreter and judge, the Designer shall endeavor to secure faithful performance by both the Owner and the Contractors, shall not show partiality to either, and shall not be liable for the result of any interpretation or decision rendered in good faith in such capacity.

1.5.14 The Designer's decisions in matters relating to aesthetics shall be final if consistent with the intent of the Contract Documents. The Designer's decisions on any other claims, disputes or other matters, including those in question between the Owner and the Contractors, shall be subject to arbitration as provided in this Agreement and in the Contract Documents.

1.5.15 The Designer shall review the final placement of all items and inspect for damage, quality, assembly and function in order to determine that all furniture, furnishings and equipment are delivered and installed in accordance with the Contract Documents.

1.5.16 The Designer shall recommend to the Owner rejection of Work which does not conform to the Contract Documents. Whenever, in the Designer's opinion, it is necessary or advisable for the implementation of the intent of the Contract Documents, the Designer will have authority to require special inspection or testing of the Work in accordance with the provisions of the Contract Documents whether or not such Work be then fabricated, installed or completed.

1.5.17 The Designer shall review and approve or take other appropriate action upon Contractors' submittals such as Shop Drawings, Product Data and Samples, but only for conformance with the design concept of the Work and with the information given in the Contract Documents. Such action shall be taken with reasonable promptness so as to cause no delay. The Designer's approval of a specific item shall not constitute approval of an assembly of which the item is a component, and the Designer's approval of a Sample or Samples shall not constitute an approval of that item as delivered and installed if not in conformance with such approved Sample.

1.5.18 The Designer shall prepare Change Orders for the Owner's approval and execution in accordance with the Contract Documents, and shall have authority to order minor changes in the Work not involving an adjustment in the Contract Sum or an extension of the Contract Time which are not inconsistent with the intent of the Contract Documents.

1.5.19 The Designer shall conduct inspections to determine the Dates of Substantial Completion and final completion, shall receive and forward to the Owner for the Owner's review written warranties and related documents required by the Contract Documents and assembled by the Contractors, and shall issue final Certificates for Payment.

1.5.20 The extent of the duties, responsibilities and limitations of authority of the Designer during the performance of the Work shall not be modified or extended without written consent of the Owner, the Contractors and the Designer.

1.6 PROJECT REPRESENTATION BEYOND BASIC SERVICES

1.6.1 If the Owner and the Designer agree that more extensive representation at the Project premises than is described in Paragraph 1.5 shall be provided, the Designer shall provide one or more Project Representatives to assist the Designer in carrying out such responsibilities at the Project premises.

1.6.2 Such Project Representatives shall be selected, employed and directed by the Designer and the Designer shall be compensated therefor as mutually agreed between the Owner and the Designer as set forth in an exhibit appended to this Agreement, which shall describe the duties, responsibilities and limitations of authority of such Project Representatives.

1.6.3 Through the observations by such Project Representatives, the Designer shall endeavor to provide further protection for the Owner against defects and deficiencies in the Work, but the furnishing of such project representation shall not modify the rights, responsibilities or obligations of the Designer as described in Paragraph 1.5.

1.7 ADDITIONAL SERVICES
The following Services are not included in Basic Services unless so identified in Article 17. They shall be provided if authorized or confirmed in writing by the Owner, and they shall be paid for by the Owner as provided in this Agreement, in addition to the compensation for Basic Services.

1.7.1 Providing financial feasibility or other special studies.

1.7.2 Providing planning surveys, site evaluations, environmental studies or comparative studies of prospective sites, and preparing special surveys, studies, and submissions required for approvals of governmental authorities or others having jurisdiction over the Project.

1.7.3 Providing services relative to future facilities, systems, furniture, furnishings and equipment which are not intended to be completed or procured during the Contract Administration Phase.

1.7.4 Providing services to investigate existing conditions or facilities or to make measured drawings thereof, or to verify the accuracy of drawings or other information furnished by the Owner.

1.7.5 Preparing documents for alternate, separate or sequential bids or providing out-of-sequence services requested by the Owner.

1.7.6 Providing services in connection with the work of a construction manager or separate consultants retained by the Owner.

1.7.7 Providing Detailed Estimates of Project Cost, analyses of owning and operating costs, or detailed quantity surveys or inventories of material, equipment and labor.

1.7.8 Providing services for planning tenant or rental spaces.

1.7.9 Making revisions in Drawings, Schedules, Specifications or other documents when such revisions are inconsistent with written approvals or instructions previously given, are required by the enactment or revision of codes, laws or regulations subsequent to the preparation of such documents or are due to other causes not solely within the control of the Designer.

1.7.10 Preparing Drawings, Schedules, Specifications and supporting data and providing other services in connection with Change Orders to the extent that the adjustment in the Basic Compensation resulting from the adjusted Project Cost is not commensurate with the services required of the Designer, provided such Change Orders are required by causes not solely within the control of the Designer.

1.7.11 Making investigations, surveys, valuations, inventories or detailed appraisals of existing facilities, furniture, furnishings and equipment, and the relocation thereof, and other services required in connection with work performed or furnished by the Owner.

1.7.12 Receipt, inspection and acceptance on behalf of the Owner of furniture, furnishings and equipment at the time of their delivery to the premises and installation.

1.7.13 Providing consultation concerning replacement of any Work damaged by fire or other cause, and furnishing services as may be required in connection with the replacement of such Work.

1.7.14 Providing services made necessary by the default of any Contractor or supplier, by major defects or deficiencies in their Work, or by failure of performance of either the Owner or the Contractor under any Contract for the Work.

1.7.15 Preparing a set of reproducible record drawings, schedules or specifications showing significant changes in the Work made during the performance thereof based on mark-up prints, drawings and other data furnished by the Contractors to the Designer.

1.7.16 Providing extensive assistance in the utilization of any equipment or system such as initial start-up or testing, adjusting and balancing, preparation of operation and maintenance manuals, training personnel for operation and maintenance, and consultation during operation.

1.7.17 Providing services relating to the Work of any Contractor after issuance to the Owner of the final Certificate for Payment for such Contractor's Work, or in the absence of a final Certificate for Payment, more than thirty days after the Date of Substantial Completion of the Work.

1.7.18 Preparing to serve or serving as an expert witness in connection with any public hearing, arbitration proceeding or legal proceeding.

1.7.19 Providing services of consultants for architectural or structural, mechanical and electrical engineering services for the Project.

1.7.20 Special studies for the Project such as analyzing acoustical requirements, record retention, communications, and security systems.

1.7.21 The purchasing of furniture, furnishings, or equipment by the Designer with funds provided by the Owner.

1.7.22 Providing services for the design or selection of graphics and signage.

1.7.23 Providing services in connection with the procurement of works of art.

1.7.24 Providing any other services not otherwise included in this Agreement or not customarily furnished in accordance with generally accepted interior design practice.

1.8 TIME

1.8.1 The Designer shall perform Basic and Additional Services as expeditiously as is consistent with professional skill and care and the orderly progress of the Work. Upon request of the Owner, the Designer shall submit for the Owner's approval, a schedule for the performance of the Designer's services which shall be adjusted as required as the Project proceeds, and shall include allowances for periods of time required for the Owner's review and approval of submissions and for approvals of authorities having jurisdiction over the Project. This schedule, when approved by the Owner, shall not, except for reasonable cause, be exceeded by the Designer.

ARTICLE 2

DESIGNER'S SPECIAL RESPONSIBILITIES WITH RESPECT TO INTERIOR DESIGN

2.1 Neither the Designer's authority to act under Subparagraphs 1.5.12 and 1.5.16, nor any decision made by the Designer in good faith either to exercise or not to exercise such authority, shall give rise to any liability on the part of the Designer to the Owner, the Contractor, any Subcontractor or supplier, any of their agents or employees, or any other person.

2.2 Except with the Owner's knowledge and consent, the Designer shall not (1) accept any trade discounts or (2) undertake any activity or employment, have any significant financial or other interest, or accept any contribution, if it would reasonably appear that such activity, employment, interest or contribution could compromise the Designer's professional judgment or prevent the Designer from serving the best interests of the Owner.

2.3 The Designer accepts the relationship of trust and confidence established with the Owner by this Agreement, and covenants with the Owner to provide professional skill and judgment and to cooperate with other design professionals retained by the Owner in furthering the interests of the Owner.

2.4 The Designer represents to the Owner that the Designer's services shall be performed in accordance with recognized professional standards, and that to the best of the Designer's knowledge, information and belief, the Contract Documents prepared by the Designer shall comply with the requirements of the applicable codes and regulations in effect at the location of the Project at the time of issuance of such documents.

ARTICLE 3

THE OWNER'S RESPONSIBILITIES

3.1 The Owner shall provide full information regarding requirements for the Project.

3.2 If the Owner provides a budget for the Project it shall include contingencies for bidding, changes in the Work, and other costs which are the responsibility of the Owner, including those described in this Article 3 and in Subparagraph 4.1.2. The Owner shall, at the request of the Designer, provide a statement of funds available for the Project, and their source.

3.3 The Owner shall designate, when necessary, a representative authorized to act in the Owner's behalf with respect to the Project. The Owner or such authorized representative shall examine the documents submitted by the Designer and shall render decisions pertaining thereto promptly, to avoid unreasonable delay in the progress of the Designer's services.

3.4 If services are required under Subparagraph 1.7.21, the Owner shall provide and maintain working funds with the Designer if required, to pay invoices charged to the Project for materials and furnishings, to secure cash discounts and for required deposits.

3.5 The Owner shall furnish structural, mechanical, chemical and other laboratory tests, inspections and reports as required by law or the Contract Documents.

3.6 The Owner shall furnish all legal, accounting, and insurance counseling services as may be necessary at any time for the Project, including such auditing services as the Owner may require to verify the Contractors' Applications for Payment or to ascertain how and for what purposes any Contractor uses the moneys paid by or on behalf of the Owner.

3.7 The drawings, specifications, services, information, surveys and reports provided by the Owner pertaining to the Project shall be furnished at the Owner's expense, and the Designer shall be entitled to rely on the accuracy and completeness thereof.

3.8 If the Owner observes or otherwise becomes aware of any fault or defect in the Project or nonconformance with the Contract Documents, prompt written notice thereof shall be given by the Owner to the Designer.

3.9 The Owner shall furnish the required information and services and shall render decisions as expeditiously as necessary for the orderly progress of the Designer's services and of the Work.

3.10 The Owner shall provide suitable space for the receipt, inspection and storage of materials and equipment.

3.11 The Owner shall contract for all temporary and permanent telephone, communications and security systems required for the Project so as not to delay the performance of the Designer's services.

3.12 The Owner shall be responsible for the relocation or removal of existing facilities, furniture, furnishings and equipment, and the contents thereof, unless otherwise provided by this Agreement.

ARTICLE 4

PROJECT COST

4.1 DEFINITION

4.1.1 The Project Cost shall be the total cost or estimated cost to the Owner of all elements of the Project designed or specified by the Designer, including the costs of managing or supervising construction or installation.

4.1.2 The Project Cost shall include at current market rates, including a reasonable allowance for overhead and profit, the cost of labor and materials furnished by the Owner, together with any equipment so furnished, whether fixed or movable, and any furniture or furnishings so furnished, providing said equipment, furniture or furnishings have been designed, selected, or specially provided for by the Designer, including the costs of managing or supervising construction or installation. The cost of used materials and equipment shall be determined as if purchased new for the Project.

4.1.3 Project Cost does not include the compensation of the Designer and the Designer's consultants, or other costs which are the responsibility of the Owner as provided in Article 3.

4.2 RESPONSIBILITY FOR PROJECT COST

4.2.1 Evaluations of the Owner's Project budget, Statements of Probable Project Cost and Detailed Estimates of Project Cost, if any, prepared by the Designer represent the Designer's best judgment as a design professional familiar with interior design. It is recognized, however, that neither the Designer nor the Owner has any control over the cost of labor, materials, furniture, furnishings or equipment, over the Contractors' methods of determining bid prices, or over competitive bidding, market or negotiating conditions. Accordingly, the Designer cannot and does not warrant or represent that bids or negotiated prices will not vary from the Project budget proposed, established or approved by the Owner, if any, or from any Statement of Probable Project Cost or other cost estimate or evaluation prepared by the Designer.

4.2.2 No fixed limit of Project Cost shall be established as a condition of this Agreement by the furnishing, proposal or establishment of a Project Budget under Subparagraph 1.2.3 or Paragraph 3.2 or otherwise, unless such fixed limit has been agreed upon in writing and signed by the parties hereto. If such a fixed limit has been established, the Designer shall be permitted to include contingencies for design, bidding and price escalation, to determine what materials, furniture, furnishings and equipment, finishes, component systems and types of construction are to be included in the Contract Documents, to make reasonable adjustments in the scope of the Project and to include in the Contract Documents alternate bids to adjust the Project Cost to the fixed limit. Any such fixed limit shall be increased in the amount of any increase in the Contract Sum occurring after execution of the Contracts.

4.2.3 If Bidding or Negotiating has not commenced within three months after the Designer submits the proposed Contract Documents to the Owner, any Project budget or fixed limit of Project Cost shall be adjusted to reflect any change in the general level of prices which may have occurred in the interiors industry between the date of submission of the Contract Documents to the Owner and the date on which proposals are sought.

4.2.4 If a Project budget or fixed limit of Project Cost (adjusted as provided in Subparagraph 4.2.3) is exceeded by the lowest bona fide bids or negotiated proposals, the Owner shall (1) give written approval of an increase in such fixed limit, (2) authorize rebidding or renegotiating of the Project within a reasonable time, (3) if the Project is abandoned, terminate in accordance with Paragraph

12.2, or (4) cooperate in revising the Project scope and quality as required to reduce the Project Cost. In the case of (4), provided a fixed limit of Project Cost has been established as a condition of this Agreement, the Designer without additional charge, shall modify the Drawings, Schedules and Specifications as necessary to comply with the fixed limit. The providing of such service shall be the limit of the Designer's responsibility arising from the establishment of such fixed limit, and having done so, the Designer shall be entitled to compensation for all services performed, in accordance with this Agreement, whether or not the Contract Administration Phase is commenced.

ARTICLE 5

PROJECT AREA

5.1 If the net or gross floor area of spaces for which interior design services are to be performed, defined as the Project Area, is used as a basis for the Designer's Basic Compensation, it shall be computed as set forth in an exhibit appended to this Agreement.

ARTICLE 6

DIRECT PERSONNEL EXPENSE

6.1 Direct Personnel Expense is defined as the direct salaries of all the Designer's personnel engaged on the Project, and the portion of the cost of their mandatory and customary contributions and benefits related thereto, such as employment taxes and other statutory employee benefits, insurance, sick leave, holidays, vacations, pensions and similar contributions and benefits.

ARTICLE 7

REIMBURSABLE EXPENSES

7.1 Reimbursable Expenses are in addition to the Compensation for Basic and Additional Services and include actual expenditures made by the Designer and the Designer's employees and consultants in the interest of the Project for the expenses listed in the following Subparagraphs:

7.1.1 Expense of transportation in connection with the Project; living expenses in connection with out-of-town travel; long distance communications, and fees paid for securing approval of authorities having jurisdiction over the Project.

7.1.2 Expense of reproductions, postage and handling of Drawings, Schedules, Specifications and other documents, excluding reproductions for the office use of the Designer and the Designer's consultants.

7.1.3 Expense of data processing and photographic production techniques when used in connection with Additional Services.

7.1.4 If authorized in advance by the Owner, expense of overtime work requiring higher than regular rates.

7.1.5 Expense of renderings, models and mock-ups requested by the Owner.

7.1.6 Expense of any additional insurance coverage or limits, including professional liability insurance, requested by the Owner in excess of that normally carried by the Designer and the Designer's consultants.

ARTICLE 8

PAYMENTS TO THE DESIGNER

8.1 PAYMENTS ON ACCOUNT OF BASIC SERVICES

8.1.1 An initial payment as set forth in Paragraph 16.1 is the minimum payment under this Agreement.

8.1.2 Subsequent payments for Basic Services shall be made monthly and shall be in proportion to services performed within each Phase of services, on the basis set forth in Article 16.

8.1.3 If and to the extent that the Contract Time initially established in any Contract is exceeded or extended through no fault of the Designer, compensation for any Basic Services required for such extended period of Administration of the Contract shall be computed as set forth in Paragraph 16.4 for Additional Services.

8.1.4 When compensation is based on a percentage of Project Cost, and any portions of the Project are deleted or otherwise not completed, compensation for such portions of the Project shall be payable to the extent services are performed on such portions, in accordance with the schedule set forth in Subparagraph 16.2.2, based on (1) the lowest bona fide bid or negotiated proposal or, (2) if no such bid or proposal is received, the most recent Statement of Probable Construction Cost or Detailed Estimate of Project Cost, for such portions of the Project.

8.2 PAYMENTS ON ACCOUNT OF ADDITIONAL SERVICES

8.2.1 Payments on account of the Designer's Additional Services as defined in Paragraph 1.7 and for Reimbursable Expenses as defined in Article 7 shall be made monthly upon presentation of the Designer's statement of services rendered or expenses incurred.

8.3 PAYMENTS WITHHELD

8.3.1 No deductions shall be made from the Designer's compensation on account of penalty, liquidated damages or other sums withheld from payments to Contractors, or on account of the cost of changes in the Work, other than those for which the Designer is held legally liable.

8.4 PROJECT SUSPENSION OR TERMINATION

8.4.1 If the Project is suspended or abandoned in whole or in part for more than three months, the Designer shall be compensated for all services performed prior to receipt of written notice from the Owner of such suspension or abandonment, together with Reimbursable Expenses then due and all Termination Expenses as defined in Paragraph 12.4. If the Project is resumed after being suspended for more than three months, the Designer's compensation shall be equitably adjusted.

ARTICLE 9

DESIGNER'S ACCOUNTING RECORDS

9.1 Records of Reimbursable Expenses and expenses pertaining to Additional Services and services performed on the basis of a Multiple of Direct Personnel Expense shall be kept on the basis of generally accepted accounting principles and shall be available to the Owner or the Owner's authorized representative at mutually convenient times.

ARTICLE 10

OWNERSHIP AND USE OF DOCUMENTS

10.1 Drawings, Schedules and Specifications as instruments of service are and shall remain the property of the Designer whether the Project for which they are prepared is executed or not. The Owner shall be permitted to retain copies, including reproducible copies, of Drawings, Schedules and Specifications for information and reference in connection with the Owner's use and occupancy of the Project. The Drawings, Schedules and Specifications shall not be used by the Owner on other projects, for additions to this Project, or for completion of this Project by others provided the Designer is not in default under this Agreement, except by agreement in writing and with appropriate compensation to the Designer.

10.2 Submission or distribution to meet official regulatory requirements or for other purposes in connection with the Project is not to be construed as publication in derogation of the Designer's rights.

ARTICLE 11

ARBITRATION

11.1 All claims, disputes, and other matters in question between the parties to this Agreement, arising out of or relating to this Agreement or the breach thereof, shall be decided by arbitration in accordance with the Construction Industry Arbitration Rules of the American Arbitration Association then obtaining unless the parties mutually agree otherwise. No arbitration, arising out of or relating to this Agreement, shall include, by consolidation, joinder or in any other manner, any additional person not a party to this Agreement except by written consent containing a specific reference to this Agreement and signed by the Designer, the Owner and any other person sought to be joined. Any consent to arbitration involving an additional person or persons shall not constitute consent to arbitration of any dispute not described therein or with any person not named or described therein. This Agreement to arbitrate and any agreement to arbitrate with an additional person or persons duly consented to by the parties hereto shall be specifically enforceable under the prevailing arbitration law.

11.2 Notice of demand for arbitration shall be filed in writing with the other party to this Agreement and with the American Arbitration Association. The demand shall be made within a reasonable time after the claim, dispute or other matter in question has arisen. In no event shall the demand for arbitration be made after the date when institution of legal or equitable proceedings based on such claim, dispute or other matter in question would be barred by the applicable statute of limitations.

11.3 The award rendered by the arbitrators shall be final, and judgment may be entered upon it in accordance with applicable law in any court having jurisdiction thereof.

ARTICLE 12

TERMINATION OF AGREEMENT

12.1 This Agreement may be terminated by either party upon seven days' written notice should the other party fail substantially to perform in accordance with its terms through no fault of the party initiating the termination.

12.2 This Agreement may be terminated by the Owner on seven days' written notice to the Designer in the event that the Project is permanently abandoned.

12.3 In the event of termination not the fault of the Designer, the Designer shall be compensated for all services performed to termination date, together with Reimbursable Expenses then due and all Termination Expenses as defined in Paragraph 12.4.

12.4 Termination Expenses include expenses directly attributable to termination for which the Designer is not otherwise compensated, plus an amount computed as a percentage of the total Basic and Additional Compensation earned to the time of termination, as follows:

- **.1** 20 percent if termination occurs prior to or during the Schematic Design Phase; or
- **.2** 10 percent if termination occurs during the Design Development Phase, or
- **.3** 5 percent if termination occurs during any subsequent phase.

ARTICLE 13

MISCELLANEOUS PROVISIONS

13.1 Unless otherwise specified, this Agreement shall be governed by the law of the principal place of business of the Designer.

13.2 Terms in this Agreement shall have the same meaning as those in AIA Document A201, General Conditions of the Contract for Construction, and in ASID Document A271, General Conditions of the Contract for Furniture, Furnishings and Equipment, as appropriate, current as of the date of this Agreement.

13.3 As between the parties to this Agreement: as to all acts or failures to act by either party to this Agreement, any applicable statute of limitations shall commence to run and any alleged cause of action shall be deemed to have accrued in any and all events not later than the relevant Date of Substantial Completion of the Work, and as to all acts or failures to act occurring after the relevant Date of Substantial Completion, not later than the date of issuance of the final Certificate for Payment.

ARTICLE 14

SUCCESSORS AND ASSIGNS

14.1 The Owner and the Designer, respectively, bind themselves, their partners, successors, assigns and legal representatives to the other party to this Agreement and to the partners, successors, assigns and legal representatives of such other party with respect to all covenants of this Agreement. Neither the Owner nor the Designer shall assign, sublet or transfer any interest in this Agreement without the written consent of the other.

ARTICLE 15

EXTENT OF AGREEMENT

15.1 This Agreement represents the entire and integrated agreement between the Owner and the Designer and supersedes all prior negotiations, representations or agreements, either written or oral. This Agreement may be amended only by written instrument signed by both Owner and Designer.

ARTICLE 16

BASIS OF COMPENSATION—MULTIPLE OF DIRECT PERSONNEL EXPENSE

The Owner shall compensate the Designer for the Scope of Services provided, in accordance with Article 8, Payments to the Designer, and the other Terms and Conditions of this Agreement, as follows:

16.1 AN INITIAL PAYMENT of   dollars ($)
shall be made upon execution of this Agreement and credited to the Owner's account as follows:

16.2 BASIC COMPENSATION

16.2.1 FOR BASIC SERVICES, as described in Paragraphs 1.1 through 1.5, and any other services included in Article 17 as part of Basic Services, compensation shall be computed on the basis of a MULTIPLE OF DIRECT PERSON-NEL EXPENSE as defined in Article 6, as follows:

(Here insert basis of compensation, including rates and/or multiples of Direct Personnel Expense for Principals and employees, and identify Principals and classify employees, if required. Identify specific Phases or services to which particular methods of compensation apply, if necessary.)

16.3 FOR PROJECT REPRESENTATION BEYOND BASIC SERVICES, as described in Paragraph 1.6, compensation shall be computed separately in accordance with Subparagraph 1.6.2, as follows:

(Here insert basis of compensation, including fixed amounts, rates or multiples and identify extent of on-site Project Representation, if required.)

16.4   COMPENSATION FOR ADDITIONAL SERVICES

16.4.1 FOR ADDITIONAL SERVICES OF THE DESIGNER, as described in Paragraph 1.7, and any other services included in Article 17 as part of Additional Services, but excluding Additional Services of consultants, Compensation shall be computed as provided in Paragraph 16.2 for Basic Services.

16.4.2 FOR SERVICES OF CONSULTANTS, including architectural, structural, mechanical and electrical engineering services and those provided under Subparagraph 1.7.19 or identified in Article 17, a multiple of
(   ) times the amount billed to the Designer for such services.

(Identify specific types of consultants in Article 17, if required.)

16.5 FOR REIMBURSABLE EXPENSE, as described in Article 7, and any other items included in Article 17 as Reimbursable Expenses, a multiple of   (   ) times the amounts expended by the Designer, the Designer's employees and consultants in the interest of the Project.

16.6 Payments due the Designer and unpaid under this Agreement shall bear interest from the date payment is due at the rate entered below, or in the absence thereof, at the legal rate prevailing at the principal place of business of the Designer.

(Here insert any rate of interest agreed upon.)

(Usury laws and requirements under the Federal Truth in Lending Act, similar state and local consumer credit laws and other regulations at the Owner's and Designer's principal places of business, the location of the Project and elsewhere may affect the validity of this provision. Specific legal advice should be obtained with respect to deletion, modification, or other requirements such as written disclosures or waivers.)

16.7 The Owner and the Designer agree in accordance with the Terms and Conditions of this Agreement that:

16.7.1 IF THE SCOPE of the Project or of the Designer's Services is changed materially, the amounts of compensation shall be equitably adjusted.

16.7.2 IF THE SERVICES covered by this Agreement have not been completed within
(   ) months of the date hereof, through no fault of the Designer, the amounts of compensation, rates and multiples set forth herein shall be equitably adjusted.

ASID DOCUMENT B171 • INTERIOR DESIGN SERVICES AGREEMENT • ASID® • ©1977
THE AMERICAN SOCIETY OF INTERIOR DESIGNERS, 1430 BROADWAY, NEW YORK, N.Y. 10018
©1972, ©1977 • AIA® • THE AMERICAN INSTITUTE OF ARCHITECTS, 1735 NEW YORK AVE., N.W., WASHINGTON, D.C. 20006

ARTICLE 16

BASIS OF COMPENSATION — FIXED FEE

The Owner shall compensate the Designer for the Scope of Services provided, in accordance with Article 8, Payments to the Designer, and the other Terms and Conditions of this Agreement, as follows:

16.1   AN INITIAL PAYMENT of   dollars ($)
shall be made upon execution of this Agreement and credited to the Owner's accounts as follows:

16.2   BASIC COMPENSATION

16.2.1   FOR BASIC SERVICES, as described in Paragraphs 1.1 through 1.5, and any other services included in Article 17 as part of Basic Services, Basic Compensation shall be computed on the basis of a FIXED FEE of
dollars ($).

16.2.2   PAYMENTS for Basic Services shall be made as provided in Paragraph 8.1 monthly, in proportion to the services performed, so that the Basic Compensation for each Phase shall equal the following percentages of the total Basic Compensation payable:

(Include any additional phases as appropriate.)

Programming Phase: percent (%)
Schematic Design Phase: percent (%)
Design Development Phase: percent (%)
Contract Documents Phase: percent (%)
Contract Administration Phase: percent (%)

16.3   FOR PROJECT REPRESENTATION BEYOND BASIC SERVICES, as described in Paragraph 1.6, compensation shall be computed separately in accordance with Subparagraph 1.6.2, as follows:

(Here insert basis of compensation, including fixed amounts, rates or multiples and identify extent of on-site Project Representation, if required.)

16.4 COMPENSATION FOR ADDITIONAL SERVICES

16.4.1 FOR ADDITIONAL SERVICES OF THE DESIGNER, as described in Paragraph 1.7, and any other services included in Article 17 as part of Additional Services, but excluding Additional Services of consultants, Compensation shall be computed as follows:

(Here insert basis of compensation, including rates and/or multiples of Direct Personnel Expense for Principals and employees, and identify Principals and classify employees, if required. Identify specific services to which particular methods of compensation apply, if necessary.)

16.4.2 FOR SERVICES OF CONSULTANTS, including architectural, structural, mechanical and electrical engineering services and those provided under Subparagraph 1.7.19 or identified in Article 17, a multiple of ( ) times the amount billed to the Designer for such services.

(Identify specific types of consultants in Article 17, if required.)

16.5 FOR REIMBURSABLE EXPENSES, as described in Article 7, and any other items included in Article 17 as Reimbursable Expenses, a multiple of ( ) times the amounts expended by the Designer, the Designer's employees and consultants in the interest of the Project.

16.6 Payments due the Designer and unpaid under this Agreement shall bear interest from the date payment is due at the rate entered below, or in the absence thereof, at the legal rate prevailing at the prinicipal place of business of the Designer.

(Here insert any rate of interest agreed upon.)

(Usury laws and requirements under the Federal Truth in Lending Act, similar state and local consumer credit laws and other regulations at the Owner's and Designer's principal places of business, the location of the Project and elsewhere may affect the validity of this provision. Specific legal advice should be obtained with respect to deletion, modification, or other requirements such as written disclosures or waivers.)

16.7 The Owner and the Designer agree in accordance with the Terms and Conditions of this Agreement that:

16.7.1 IF THE SCOPE of the Project or of the Designer's Services is changed materially, the amounts of compensation shall be equitably adjusted.

16.7.2 IF THE SERVICES covered by this Agreement have not been completed within ( ) months of the date hereof, through no fault of the Designer, the amounts of compensation, rates and multiples set forth herein shall be equitably adjusted.

  ASID DOCUMENT B171 • INTERIOR DESIGN SERVICES AGREEMENT • ASID® • © 1977
THE AMERICAN SOCIETY OF INTERIOR DESIGNERS, 1430 BROADWAY, NEW YORK, N.Y. 10018
© 1972, © 1977 • AIA® • THE AMERICAN INSTITUTE OF ARCHITECTS, 1735 NEW YORK AVE., N.W., WASHINGTON, D.C. 20006

ARTICLE 16

BASIS OF COMPENSATION — PERCENTAGE OF PROJECT COST

The Owner shall compensate the Designer for the Scope of Services provided, in accordance with Article 8, Payments to the Designer, and the other Terms and Conditions of this Agreement, as follows:

16.1 AN INITIAL PAYMENT of   dollars ($)
shall be made upon execution of this Agreement and credited to the Owner's account as follows:

16.2 BASIC COMPENSATION

16.2.1 FOR BASIC SERVICES, as described in Paragraphs 1.1 through 1.5, and any other services included in Article 17 as part of Basic Services, Basic Compensation shall be based on a PERCENTAGE OF PROJECT COST and computed at   percent (%) of the cost of construction, procurement and installation which is the Project Cost, as defined in Article 4.

16.2.2 PAYMENTS for Basic Services shall be made as provided in Paragraph 8.1 monthly, in proportion to the services performed, so that the Basic Compensation for each Phase shall equal the following percentages of the total Basic Compensation payable:

(Include any additional phases as appropriate.)

Programming Phase:	percent (%)
Schematic Design Phase:	percent (%)
Design Development Phase:	percent (%)
Contract Documents Phase:	percent (%)
Contract Administration Phase:	percent (%)

16.3 FOR PROJECT REPRESENTATION BEYOND BASIC SERVICES, as described in Paragraph 1.6, compensation shall be computed separately in accordance with Subparagraph 1.6.2, as follows:

(Here insert basis of compensation, including fixed amounts, rates or multiples and identify extent of on-site Project Representation, if required.)

16.4   COMPENSATION FOR ADDITIONAL SERVICES

16.4.1   FOR ADDITIONAL SERVICES OF THE DESIGNER, as described in Paragraph 1.7, and any other services included in Article 17 as part of Additional Services, but excluding Additional Services of consultants, Compensation shall be computed as follows:

(Here insert basis of compensation, including rates and/or multiples of Direct Personnel Expense for Principals and employees, and identify Principals and classify employees, if required. Identify specific services to which particular methods of compensation apply, if necessary.)

16.4.2   FOR SERVICES OF CONSULTANTS, including architectural, structural, mechanical and electrical engineering services and those provided under Subparagraph 1.7.19 or identified in Article 17, a multiple of
(   ) times the amount billed to the Designer for such services.

(Identify specific types of consultants in Article 17, if required.)

16.5   FOR REIMBURSABLE EXPENSES, as described in Article 7, and any other items included in Article 17 as Reimbursable Expenses, a multiple of   (   ) times the amounts expended by the Designer, the Designer's employees and consultants in the interest of the Project.

16.6   Payments due the Designer and unpaid under this Agreement shall bear interest from the date payment is due at the rate entered below, or in the absence thereof, at the legal rate prevailing at the prinicipal place of business of the Designer.

(Here insert any rate of interest agreed upon.)

(Usury laws and requirements under the Federal Truth in Lending Act, similar state and local consumer credit laws and other regulations at the Owner's and Designer's principal places of business, the location of the Project and elsewhere may affect the validity of this provision. Specific legal advice should be obtained with respect to deletion, modification, or other requirements such as written disclosures or waivers.)

16.7   The Owner and the Designer agree in accordance with the Terms and Conditions of this Agreement that:

16.7.1   IF THE SCOPE of the Project or of the Designer's Services is changed materially, the amounts of compensation shall be equitably adjusted.

16.7.2   IF THE SERVICES covered by this Agreement have not been completed within
(   ) months of the date hereof, through no fault of the Designer, the amounts of compensation, rates and multiples set forth herein shall be equitably adjusted.

ASID DOCUMENT B171 • INTERIOR DESIGN SERVICES AGREEMENT • ASID® • ©1977
THE AMERICAN SOCIETY OF INTERIOR DESIGNERS, 1430 BROADWAY, NEW YORK, N.Y. 10018
©1972, ©1977 • AIA® • THE AMERICAN INSTITUTE OF ARCHITECTS, 1735 NEW YORK AVE., N.W., WASHINGTON, D.C. 20006

ARTICLE 16

BASIS OF COMPENSATION — AREA FEE

The Owner shall compensate the Designer for the Scope of Services provided, in accordance with Article 8, Payments to the Designer., and the other Terms and Conditions of this Agreement, as follows:

16.1   AN INITIAL PAYMENT of   dollars ($)
shall be made upon execution of this Agreement and credited to the Owner's account as follows:

16.2   BASIC COMPENSATION

16.2.1   FOR BASIC SERVICES, as described in Paragraphs 1.1 through 1.5, and any other services included in Article 17 as part of Basic Services, Basic Compensation shall be based on an AREA FEE and computed at
                                                 dollars ($) per square foot of the Project Area, as defined in Article 5, for which services are performed.

(Insert above the term describing the basis of the Project Area, such as "gross," "net" or "rentable.")

16.2.2   PAYMENTS for Basic Services shall be made as provided in Paragraph 8.1 monthly, in proportion to the services performed, so that the Basic Compensation for each Phase shall equal the following percentages of the total Basic Compensation payable:

(Include any additional phases as appropriate.)

Programming Phase:	percent (%)
Schematic Design Phase:	percent (%)
Design Development Phase:	percent (%)
Contract Documents Phase:	percent (%)
Contract Administration Phase:	percent (%)

16.3   FOR PROJECT REPRESENTATION BEYOND BASIC SERVICES, as described in Paragraph 1.6, compensation shall be computed separately in accordance with Subparagraph 1.6.2, as follows:

(Here insert basis of compensation, including fixed amounts, rates or multiples and identify extent of on-site Project Representation, if required.)

16.4 COMPENSATION FOR ADDITIONAL SERVICES

16.4.1 FOR ADDITIONAL SERVICES OF THE DESIGNER, as described in Paragraph 1.7, and any other services included in Article 17 as part of Additional Services, but excluding Additional Services of consultants, Compensation shall be computed as follows:

(Here insert basis of compensation, including rates and/or multiples of Direct Personnel Expense for Principals and employees, and identify Principals and classify employees, if required. Identify specific services to which particular methods of compensation apply, if necessary.)

16.4.2 FOR SERVICES OF CONSULTANTS, including architectural, structural, mechanical and electrical engineering services and those provided under Subparagraph 1.7.19 or identified in Article 17, a multiple of ( ) times the amount billed to the Designer for such services.

(Identify specific types of consultants in Article 17, if required.)

16.5 FOR REIMBURSABLE EXPENSES, as described in Article 7, and any other items included in Article 17 as Reimbursable Expenses, a multiple of ( ) times the amounts expended by the Designer, the Designer's employees and consultants in the interest of the Project.

16.6 Payments due the Designer and unpaid under this Agreement shall bear interest from the date payment is due at the rate entered below, or in the absence thereof, at the legal rate prevailing at the prinicipal place of business of the Designer.

(Here insert any rate of interest agreed upon.)

(Usury laws and requirements under the Federal Truth in Lending Act, similar state and local consumer credit laws and other regulations at the Owner's and Designer's principal places of business, the location of the Project and elsewhere may affect the validity of this provision. Specific legal advice should be obtained with respect to deletion, modification, or other requirements such as written disclosures or waivers.)

16.7 The Owner and the Designer agree in accordance with the Terms and Conditions of this Agreement that:

16.7.1 IF THE SCOPE of the Project or of the Designer's Services is changed materially, the amounts of compensation shall be equitably adjusted.

16.7.2 IF THE SERVICES covered by this Agreement have not been completed within ( ) months of the date hereof, through no fault of the Designer, the amounts of compensation, rates and multiples set forth herein shall be equitably adjusted.

ASID DOCUMENT B171 • INTERIOR DESIGN SERVICES AGREEMENT • ASID® • ©1977
THE AMERICAN SOCIETY OF INTERIOR DESIGNERS, 1430 BROADWAY, NEW YORK, N.Y. 10018
©1972, ©1977 • AIA® • THE AMERICAN INSTITUTE OF ARCHITECTS, 1735 NEW YORK AVE., N.W., WASHINGTON, D.C. 20006

ARTICLE 16

BASIS OF COMPENSATION — COMPOSITE FEE

The Owner shall compensate the Designer for the Scope of Services provided, in accordance with Article 8, Payments to the Designer, and the other Terms and Conditions of this Agreement, as follows:

16.1   AN INITIAL PAYMENT of   dollars ($)
shall be made upon execution of this Agreement and credited to the Owner's account as follows:

16.2   BASIC COMPENSATION

16.2.1   FOR BASIC SERVICES, as described in Paragraphs 1.1 through 1.5, and any other services included in Article 17 as part of Basic Services, Basic Compensation shall be a COMPOSITE FEE computed as follows:

(Here insert basis of compensation, including fixed amounts, rates or multiples, and identify Principals and classify employees, if required. Identify specific Phases or services to which particular methods of compensation apply, if necessary.)

16.3   FOR PROJECT REPRESENTATION BEYOND BASIC SERVICES, as described in Paragraph 1.6, compensation shall be computed separately in accordance with Subparagraph 1.6.2, as follows:

(Here insert basis of compensation, including fixed amounts, rates or multiples and identify extent of on-site Project Representation, if required.)

16.4 COMPENSATION FOR ADDITIONAL SERVICES

16.4.1 FOR ADDITIONAL SERVICES OF THE DESIGNER, as described in Paragraph 1.7, and any other services included in Article 17 as part of Additional Services, but excluding Additional Services of consultants, Compensation shall be computed as follows:

(Here insert basis of compensation, including rates and/or multiples of Direct Personnel Expense for Principals and employees, and identify Principals and classify employees, if required. Identify specific services to which particular methods of compensation apply, if necessary.)

16.4.2 FOR SERVICES OF CONSULTANTS, including architectural, structural, mechanical and electrical engineering services and those provided under Subparagraph 1.7.19 or identified in Article 17, a multiple of ( ) times the amount billed to the Designer for such services.

(Identify specific types of consultants in Article 17, if required.)

16.5 FOR REIMBURSABLE EXPENSES, as described in Article 7, and any other items included in Article 17 as Reimbursable Expenses, a multiple of ( ) times the amounts expended by the Designer, the Designer's employees and consultants in the interest of the Project.

16.6 Payments due the Designer and unpaid under this Agreement shall bear interest from the date payment is due at the rate entered below, or in the absence thereof, at the legal rate prevailing at the prinicipal place of business of the Designer.

(Here insert any rate of interest agreed upon.)

(Usury laws and requirements under the Federal Truth in Lending Act, similar state and local consumer credit laws and other regulations at the Owner's and Designer's principal places of business, the location of the Project and elsewhere may affect the validity of this provision. Specific legal advice should be obtained with respect to deletion, modification, or other requirements such as written disclosures or waivers.)

16.7 The Owner and the Designer agree in accordance with the Terms and Conditions of this Agreement that:

16.7.1 IF THE SCOPE of the Project or of the Designer's Services is changed materially, the amounts of compensation shall be equitably adjusted.

16.7.2 IF THE SERVICES covered by this Agreement have not been completed within ( ) months of the date hereof, through no fault of the Designer, the amounts of compensation, rates and multiples set forth herein shall be equitably adjusted.

ASID DOCUMENT B171 • INTERIOR DESIGN SERVICES AGREEMENT • ASID® • © 1977
THE AMERICAN SOCIETY OF INTERIOR DESIGNERS, 1430 BROADWAY, NEW YORK, N.Y. 10018
© 1972, © 1977 • AIA® • THE AMERICAN INSTITUTE OF ARCHITECTS, 1735 NEW YORK AVE., N.W., WASHINGTON, D.C. 20006

ARTICLE 17

OTHER CONDITIONS OR SERVICES

B171—1977 19
Revised 1983

This Agreement executed as of the day and year first written above.

OWNER   DESIGNER

_____   _____

_____   _____

_____   _____

_____   _____

20 B171—1977
Revised 1983

ASID DOCUMENTS

B171	STANDARD FORM OF AGREEMENT FOR INTERIOR DESIGN SERVICE
B177	ABBREVIATED FORM OF AGREEMENT FOR INTERIOR DESIGN SERVICES
A171	STANDARD FORM OF AGREEMENT BETWEEN OWNER AND CONTRACTOR FOR FURNITURE, FURNISHINGS, AND EQUIPMENT
A177	ABBREVIATED FORM OF AGREEMENT BETWEEN OWNER AND CONTRACTOR FOR FURNITURE, FURNISHINGS, AND EQUIPMENT
A271	GENERAL CONDITIONS OF THE CONTRACT FOR FURNITURE, FURNISHINGS, AND EQUIPMENT
A771	INSTRUCTIONS TO INTERIORS BIDDERS
#403	CONTRACT FOR PROFESSIONAL SERVICES (Residential Long Form)
#404	CONTRACT FOR PROFESSIONAL SERVICES (Residential Short Form)
#001	COMPENSATION AGREEMENT—Presented Price
#002	COMPENSATION AGREEMENT—Hourly Rate
#003	COMPENSATION AGREEMENT—Fixed Rate
#004	COMPENSATION AGREEMENT—Percentage of Project Cost

These documents are available from ASID Contract Order Request,
608 Massachusetts Avenue, Washington, D.C. 20002

Letters of Agreement. Some design firms prefer to work with a simple letter of agreement. However, these are often more difficult to write than a ten- or twelve-page contract. Since your attorney determines your legal positioning, he or she needs to write or approve these documents. Each state and each individual area has some certain restrictions that may require a change in these documents.

As you move from one specialty to another, you will need to alter these documents to fit your new needs.

In reviewing various letters of agreement from the past twenty years, I have noticed that, recently, the quantity of disclaimers is increasing at an unbelievable rate. Obviously, designers have had many problems or they would not be so cautious in their legal documentation.

Unfortunately, when there is a problem during a project, it not only affects the financial and legal aspects of a project, but very often affects your opportunity to complete a quality design project.

The following are examples of nine letters of agreement that design firms have been using. You may be able to adapt them to your firm and situation; review them first with your legal consultants.

When to Present a Letter of Agreement or Contract?

In some situations, it is to your advantage to have a simple letter of agreement or contract that can be filled in very quickly. This can be used on those occasions when you approach a client with a small project; the agreement can be presented on the spot. Often it will be signed and you will be given your retainer right then. There is a sample of a form that might be used in this manner on page 169.

In most cases, you should see and review the project before presenting a letter of agreement or a contract. Talk with the clients and investigate the situation carefully by doing some of the recommended precontract checks (see pages 125–29). The more you know about the project, the better contract you will be able to write. If you have properly outlined the contract, it can serve as an outline of the work to be done, making it very easy to coordinate the schedule and process the plan. Before presenting a contract you usually will have had an initial interview, and then spent time doing research and preparation. Often you will not present your contract until after a second or third interview. The second interview is many times used by designers to review their outline of what is to be included and to check other details that they feel should be worked into the contract proposal. The proposal should then be mailed or given to the client at the next meeting.

Don't become so excited about starting a new project that you forget about some of the legal ramifications. In today's business climate, you must be extremely cautious. Take extra time to define each project; be sure that you and your client understand the services to be rendered and the accompanying responsibilities. The obligations of the client need to be as carefully defined as those of the design firm.

Sample letter of agreement. This letter of agreement would be used with a cover page describing the project (or a space could be left above "Design Fee" for the project definition). It is suitable for either small contract or residential use.

This agreement made this _____ day of _____, 19___

between ___(firm's name)___ (hereafter called ___(firm's name)___

and _____(client's name)_____ (hereafter called CLIENT).

1. _____(Firm's name)_____ agrees to perform the following services

for CLIENT in connection with Premises at _____:

(a) DESIGN FEE

Please sign and return copy.

2. In consideration for the services to be performed by _(firm's name)_,

CLIENT agrees to pay ____(firm's name)____ AS FOLLOWS:

    (a) One-third of design fee when signing of contract.

    (b) One-third at first presentation of Design.

    (c) Balance upon completion of contract.

3. In the event CLIENT should cancel this contract then all funds paid

hereunder shall be retained by ___(firm's name)___ and in addition

CLIENT shall pay any costs incurred by ____(firm's name)___.

4. Sales tax or any other taxes are not included in contract.

5. Prices subject to change 30 days after the above date.

IN WITNESS WHEREOF the parties hereto have set their hand and seal the

day and year above written.

                                   _____

                                   _____

                                              CLIENT

Sample letter of agreement. This proposal was for a small office project. A similar proposal could be used for a simple residential project where a more formal contract might seem inappropriate.

PROPOSAL FOR PROFESSIONAL DESIGN SERVICES

TO:

RE:

This proposal for interior design planning of the first floor of the newly purchased building at this address will consist generally of the following:

1. Review of existing furnishings and equipment in present office.

2. Review of space and task requirements for the new facilities.

3. Space Planning: Review of the existing building conditions and preparation of a plan to accommodate the needs as specified; i.e., partitioning, general layout, etc.

4. Specifications for types of materials that would be required to implement the study, as well as furnishings.

5. Preparation of a master color scheme.

Specific services during the study include:

1. Presentation of the design plan to the client for review, with changes as needed to accommodate the client's preferences.

2. Preparation of the final budget estimate and design plan for client approval.

The fee to provide the services described in this proposal will be in the range of $1,500 to $2,500 with a deposit of $750 required to begin this project.

The client will provide floor plans, measurements, and prints as needed.

Designer submitting proposal and responsible for this project:

_____   _____

(date)   (signature)

I agree to the services outlined in this proposal and authorize the designer named above to proceed upon receipt of this signed agreement and my check in the amount of $750.

_____   _____

(date)   (signature)

This Letter of Agreement will serve as our agreement in outlining the services to be rendered by _____ in connection with the interiors of _____.

As Designer, I agree to do the following: consult, evaluate, plan, design, shop, budget, and supervise all contract and subcontract work that comes under my direction. For all Designing Services rendered by my firm, the following fee schedule will be used:

> Forty-five dollars per hour for my services, not to exceed two hundred dollars per day. My assistant designer and draftsman will be billed at fifteen dollars per hour. Charges will be made for all out-of-pocket expenses such as travel (other than normal commuting expenses), telephone calls, and any necessary blueprinting or professional rendering made at your request.

A time sheet and record of all out-of-pocket expenses will be kept by my office. These records will be available for your inspection. All purchases will be billed to you at prices quoted.

All purchases, design plans, or work to be ordered by my firm will be submitted for your approval in the form of estimates. Each estimate will require your signature and a fifty percent deposit to authorize the placement of any orders or the execution of any design plans. An additional twenty-five percent will be due at the end of three months if merchandise is ready but cannot be installed. The final payment will be due upon delivery.

There are no sales taxes added to the Design Fee; only to purchases. All freight charges or extra insurance ordered by you will be payable by you. I can assume no responsibility for delays occasioned by failure of others to meet commitments beyond my control. You shall have the benefit of all guarantees and warranties possessed by me against any manufacturer. Any items purchased that have been approved by you on the signed estimate cannot be canceled or returned without additional expense to you.

At this tme, I am requesting a retainer fee of $_____. This
retainer fee will be deducted from your final statement at the
completion of this assignment. The signing of this Letter of Agreement
and the receipt of the retainer fee authorizes me to proceed with this
project. In the event this project is terminated before completion, the
retainer fee will be applied as compensation for services rendered based
upon my hourly Design Fee.

If you consent to this Letter of Agreement, please sign and return one
copy of the letter to me together with the retainer fee.

I am looking forward to being of service to you.

CLIENT_____

Date_____

_____

Sample letter of agreement. This is a simple contract for professional services from design through completion, including supervision.

CONTRACT FOR PROFESSIONAL SERVICES

This contract is made between the Designer:

and the Client:

for the following project:

1. The Designer's professional services shall consist of consulting
    with the Client to determine the scope of the work; preparing the
    necessary preliminary studies; making preliminary estimates;
    preparing working drawings and specifications; and consulting with
    architects, engineers, or other special consultants.

2. The Designer will perform or procure such periodic inspections as
    the Designer may consider appropriate. The Designer will endeavor
    to warn the Client against defects and deficiencies in the work of
    the contractor(s) but shall not have responsibility for the failure
    of the contractor to comply with drawings or specification or any
    latent defect in the work of the contractor(s).

3. The Client has the assurances of the Designer that the Designer's
    service shall be rendered in good faith and in a professional
    manner; but the Designer cannot be responsible for the performance,
    quality, or timely completion of work by the contractor(s). Nor can
    the Designer be responsible for the guarantee of any fabric,
    material, or product against wearing, fading, soiling, or latent
    defect.

4. All drawings, specifications, and documents prepared by the Designer
    are instruments of service for the execution of the work on the
    project and are the exclusive property of the Designer, whether the
    work on the project is executed or note; and the Designer reserves

the plan copyright, whether the work on the project is executed or not, and said plan shall not be used on any other project without the Designer's prior written consent.

5. The Client shall pay the Designer for his services, a fee based upon time dedicated by the Designer at the following rates:

> Principle
>
> Designer
>
> Design Assistant
>
> Administrative

In addition, extensive travel expenses, long-distance telephone costs, extensive blueprinting or reproduction charges, or other out-of-pocket expenses will be billed at the Designer's cost. The Designer will bill the Client following the fifteenth and last day of each month for the fees payable to that point. The amount is due and payable within ten days following receipt of statement.

6. Additional terms:

The parties agree to the foregoing conditions.

_____   _____

Date: _____

Sample letter of agreement. This letter of agreement is used for a straight-fee or lump-sum professional service contract. It is suitable for residential or contract use.

AGREEMENT FOR PROFESSIONAL DESIGN SERVICES

BETWEEN: (designer)

AND: (client name and address)

FOR: (project)

A. PROFESSIONAL SERVICES

The designer's professional services during the course of the project consist generally of the following:

1. Consulting with the client to determine the scope of the work and preparation of cost estimates.

2. Preparing the necessary preliminary studies.

3. Planning room layouts and selecting necessary wall and floor coverings, draperies, furniture, and accessories for client approval.

4. Making preliminary estimates.

5. Consulting with architects, engineers, or other special advisors.

6. Preparing working drawings and specifications as needed.

7. Securing contractors needed to provide services for the completion of the design project, including specification of work to be done and appropriate supervision of those contractors.

B. FEES AND PAYMENT PROVISIONS

The client agrees to pay a fee of $(fee or fee range) to the designer for the services outlined above. In addition, the following expenses by or on behalf of the designer for this project will be paid by the client at the designer's cost.

1. Extensive travel (more than _____ miles monthly at a rate of 18¢/mile) above _____ miles.

2. Long-distance telephone expenses.

3. Blueprinting or reproduction charges.

4. Renderings.

If the designer arranges for other contractors to perform specific services as part of the project, the client will pay a supervision fee to the designer of 25% of each contractor's billed cost.

Payment of the fee will be as follows:

1. Initial retainer of 50% of the fee as authorization to proceed.
2. Supervision fees upon completion of contractor's work and billing.
3. Balance of fee and other expenses upon completion of project.

Invoices are payable within 10 days of receipt. Balances unpaid after 30 days are subject to an interest charge of 1.25% per month. Interest will continue to be charged on unpaid balances after 30 days even though a partial payment has been received.

C. TERMS AND CONDITIONS

1. Designs, drawings, and scale models will remain in the property of the designer unless a written agreement has been issued to the contrary.
2. Periodic inspections and observations of work on a project will be made as we consider appropriate. We do not have responsibility for the failure of contractors to comply with drawings or specifications prepared by us, nor for latent defects in their work.
3. If, after a definite scheme has been approved, the client makes a decision which, for its proper execution, involves extra services or expenses for changes in or additions to the studies, drawings, specifications, etc., the client will pay the designer for such extra services on a design time fee basis of $50/hour.

We agree to the services as outlined, the fees and payment provisions, and the terms and conditions.

Designer:_____   Date_____

Client:_____   Date_____

This letter will confirm that you are retaining our firm to assist you in the interior design of your home in _____.

Our services include the following: preparing furniture plans; shopping for and selecting all furnishings to be purchased from our sources and workrooms; assisting in paint selection and overseeing painting; and placing furniture, accessories, and art.

All merchandise purchased by you, including custom designed furniture and cabinetry, will be sold on a showroom list basis. Miscellaneous charges for freight, delivery, packing and sales tax will be additional. A written estimate reflecting the specified price will be sent to you after selection of merchandise.

A signed estimate and 50 percent initial payment are necessary before merchandise is ordered. However, proforma merchandise, inventory items, and immediately deliverable items must be paid in advance of delivery. We have been advised by our suppliers that all prices are subject to change without notice. Should this happen, we will obtain your approval before proceeding with the order,

Contracts for the work of carpenters, electricians, plumbing contractors, and similar tradespeople will be entered into directly between you and the contractor. We will be available for consulting with regard to architectural changes and additions, and for the review of the work of the above-mentioned tradespeople to ensure adherence to plans and specifications.

You will be involved for this consultation or review at the rates of $130.00 per hour for my time, $90.00 per hour for any architect engaged by our firm, $50.00 per hour for project designers and senior draftsmen, and $40.00 per hour for junior draftsmen and staff.

We request that clients sign working drawings as a confirmation of their agreement with the designs. Should you decide not to proceed with any custom furniture or cabinetry that we design for you, you will be billed at our hourly consultation rates for design time. Blueprinting charges will be additional.

Should you decide not to proceed with interior design selections that we have made in consultation with you and that you purchase directly from others, you will be billed at our hourly consultation rates for design time.

Should you terminate our business relationship, all time spent by me or my personnel (including preparation of furniture plans, selection of furnishings, and all other services described in the second paragraph of this letter) will be billed at the appropriate hourly charges. Should there be any cancellation charges, they will be billed in addition. The balance in your account will be refunded to you after the above charges have been deducted.

An authorized signature on a copy of this letter, along with a $_____ retainer, will constitute authority for us to begin the project. This retainer will be applied to final billing.

If you have any questions concerning this letter, please share them with me. I look forward to working with you.

Very truly yours,

Mary V. Knackstedt

APPROVED_____

DATE_____

We request your permission to photograph and publish our design work. Your signature below is our authorization.

APPROVED _____

Sample letter of agreement. This letter of agreement is for designers working on a percentage- or commission-compensation method where no hourly rate or other design fee is charged.

Dear :

This letter will confirm our method of operation in connection with the work we have discussed for the project at the above address.

All furniture and furnishings as well as services provided through this office will be sold to you at our net cost plus a 20 percent commission. There will be no additional charge for our design services. Travel expenses, toll telephone calls, sales taxes, shipping charges, and other such out-of-pocket expenses directly applicable to the project will be rebilled to you at our net costs on a monthly basis.

We request a $1,000.00 deposit, which will be credited to your account at the time of the final billing. Each purchase will be covered by an invoice describing the item and requesting a 50 percent deposit and your signed approval. The balance is due upon delivery. For antiques, we request payment in full when the invoice is approved. This schedule is for each invoice submitted.

If the above meets with your approval, please sign at the bottom of the letter and return one copy to us along with the initial deposit requested.

Cordially,

_____

Accepted and approved_____

Date_____

Sample letter of agreement. This letter of agreement is for a firm requiring a design fee by the hour and a percentage fee on items purchased for the project (both contracted items and furniture).

Mr. and Mrs. John Newhouse

12 Shady Lane

Tuckedaway Village, Pennsylvania

Dear Mr. and Mrs. Newhouse:

After meeting with you and discussing the design and space planning of your residence, we are ready to begin making definite plans.

This proposal outlines our firm's financial requirements and defines our services and responsibilities, as well as our role in relation to any other design professionals you may involve in this project. If you approve this proposal, by signing it and returning it to us with the initial payment, our firm will send a comprehensive letter of agreement.

<u>Design Areas</u>: The scope of the project encompasses your entire residence.

<u>Design Services</u>: For the design work of your residence, our firm will perform the following services:

1. Initial design study. The initial floorplans you provided will probably undergo some revision based on your needs and desires. Further consultation with you will clarify the extent of these revisions before we prepare the preliminary architectural and interior design concept.

2. Preliminary architectural and interior design concept. A complete design presentation shall be prepared for your approval, and will include:

    a. Architectural drawings and documents. We will detail all interior and exterior architectural changes for your project.

    b. Preparation of complete floor plans. These will be drawn to scale and will include a proposed furniture layout.

c. Finalization of all architectural and working drawings. All working drawings shall be submitted to you for your approval and for consultation with other design professionals involved with the project. Any necessary revisions will be made and final approval will be acknowledged by you in writing.

d. Preliminary design concept. After you have approved our layout drawings, we will make a complete presentation including furniture selection, material selection (fabrics, wallcoverings, curtain design, floor design, color selections, lighting, etc.), and other visual aids we deem necessary to illustrate our design plan.

<u>Purchases</u>: All purchases will be made available to you at wholesale, or "net," cost. Our firm will act as your purchasing agent and all bills from vendors will be forwarded to our office for payment. We will prepare all specifications and purchase orders, which specify payment terms with which you must comply; however, our firm will deal with all vendors on a financial basis.

<u>Compensation</u>: Our firm will bill on an hourly basis for our design and planning services as specified by the description of design services. The rates are:

    Firm principal--$110 per hour
    Senior designer--$70 per hour
    Drafting--$45 per hour

Furthermore, the fees for selecting and specifying all purchases of furniture and furnishings shall be based on certain percentages of the furniture and furnishings budget, which are:

    Thirty-five percent on the initial $100,000 of the "F&F" budget
    Thirty percent on the "F&F" budget above $100,000

If the above meets with your approval, your signature below will
indicate your acceptance of the basic terms of our agreement. Please
return one signed copy and a retainer of $2,000. We will present a more
detailed agreement for your acceptance within several weeks. Of course,
please call if you have any questions.

                                        Sincerely,

                                        Interior Design Firm

                                        By:_____
                                            President

Accepted and approved:

_____

John Newhouse

_____

Bernice Newhouse

Chapter Seven

SUCCEEDING IN PROJECT MANAGEMENT

Project management has separate and distinct stages: the programming phase; the schematic design phase; the design development phase; the contract documents phase; and the installation or contract administration phase.

The size and type of work will determine the client-designer relationship for each of these stages; however, the basic purpose of each step of the process remains the same. The programming phase will define the project and a beginning contractual agreement between the client and designer.

The schematic design phase is for preliminary design of space allocation and locations for partitions, furnishings, and equipment; establishing concepts of types and qualities of finishes and materials; and preparing a budget and estimated schedule for project completion. This phase is meant to define for the client all major decisions concerning the parameters of space, layout, quality of products, and probable costs of the project, as well as the relationships and scope of work/products to be provided by the designer or other professional disciplines prior to the next step of finalizing and detailing all aspects of the project. Client review and approval is essential prior to proceeding to the next phase.

The design development phase includes finalizing all design layouts; details of all interior construction; specifications for all products, materials, and equipment; work methods and standards, plus any other document preparation needed prior to the owners' review and approval of this stage.

The contract documents phase is the point at which decisions must be finalized for the execution or installation of the project. How the work will be managed by the design firm and/or the client, whether by one or more contracts or purchase orders between the owner and contractor or supplier for products, must be determined and mutually agreed upon. It is a time of preparing and executing the bidding, contracting, and procurement documents in preparation for the next step of the process.

The contract administration, or installation, phase commences with the award of one or more contracts or the issuance of purchase orders and formally terminates when the final payments to the contractors or suppliers have been certified. It is the step in the process which includes the actual procurement, the construction, the installation, and final finishing and placement of all elements of the total project.

THE PROGRAMMING PHASE

Your initial discussions with the client establish the parameters of the job. You will learn what type of work is required; the client's preferences and direction; the budgets; the contract terms; and the availability of other plans or blueprints. You will also discover which other professional people and/or design consultants will be involved in the project. (See pages 125–29 for a more detailed discussion of the initial interview.)

You next obtain credit information on the client from a credit bureau, his or her banks, and other resources (see pages 308–10). When you have decided to proceed with this client, you prepare a letter of agreement based on a review, analysis, and evaluation of the client's objectives, the site requirements, and the needed services of the designer—all of which are included in a written program. The letter also includes the proposed contract terms for work and schedule of payments and is presented in a form which, when signed by the client, becomes the initial contract between the client and the designer. This contract usually is for all services to be performed by the designer's firm through the schematic design phase, or preliminary design phase and the design development phase.

THE SCHEMATIC DESIGN PHASE

Existing conditions sheet. After the client has signed your contract or letter of agreement, you can begin the preliminary design phase with an examination of the existing conditions. A sheet such as this will help document these conditions.

After the client has signed your contract or letter of agreement, you can proceed into the preliminary design phase. This starts with an examination of the client's plans or premises to determine existing conditions and materials, and to evaluate aspects of the facilities that would affect delivery or accessibility to the site.

You will also review the requirements for protection of property and/or any removal of existing furniture, fixtures, and equipment. The existing conditions of the site are spelled out. Your design firm should make an inventory of the client's existing furniture to describe its condition, dimensions, sizes, details, and history. Next, you will prepare evaluations.

This is the concept stage of the design. You will cover all details affecting the interior space, including furniture, layouts, traffic patterns, existing interiors, any built-in cabinetry, lighting, special HVAC requirements, doors, and windows. At

EXISTING CONDITIONS:

| Client: | Room: | Photo No. | Date: | Page ____ of ____ |

Floor:

Walls:	N	S	E	W	Color:
Block					
Brick					
Glass					
Plaster/Drywall					
Wood/Paneling					
Paint					
Accent Paint					
Vinyl					
Ceramic Tile					
Wainscot/Chair Rail					
Thermostat					
Telephone					
Other					

Ceiling:

Lighting:

Cabinetwork:

Other:

© Design Business Monthly

this stage, you should meet with the architect and other design professionals associated with the job to exchange any special technical data as well as to establish the position and responsibilities of your design firm in relation to them.

During this stage you will do your product research, which involves finding furnishings, equipment, fabrics, and materials appropriate to the specifications and requirements of the project. You will also prepare preliminary drawings, sketches, displays, and estimates of probable project costs for presentation to the client for his or her review and approval.

THE DESIGN DEVELOPMENT PHASE

Once your preliminary work has been approved by the client, you can move it into the final design development phase. In this phase, you prepare detailed drawings and specifications based on all decisions and data collected in earlier phases and work out the detailed drawings. You also write detailed specifications for all items to be purchased, and prepare workroom or subcontractor specs.

You prepare a detailed statement of probable project cost. This includes the cost of furnishings, finishes, contracting, and materials, and review their availability. At this point, you may want to establish an allowance for accessories and any other items required to complete the project. You will also prepare a review of shipping and other installation expenses and terms. In this statement you will also review and update your payment terms. Before continuing on to the next process, you must receive and document formal approval of the proposal by the client.

Work station summary. This sheet is very helpful for reviewing the various needs and locations of different staff members, which will aid you in your design analysis.

WORK STATION SUMMARY				Client:
				Date:
Position:	Name:	Location:	Needs:	Notes:

© Design Business Monthly

Design master sheet. A sheet such as this enables you to keep the details for each room you are designing in one place. This is prepared at the design development phase, after the preliminary work has been approved by the client. You may wish to write the details in pencil in case changes are made.

```
DESIGN MASTER SHEET

Client:                    Room:                    Date:

Floor:


Wall:


Woodwork:


Ceiling:

Window Treatment:



Feature:



Lighting:

Furniture:







Accessory Items:




© Design Business Monthly
```

Room specification sheet. In the concept stage of the design, you prepare detailed descriptions. A sheet such as this will facilitate review and approval of your room specifications by the client and contractor.

```
┌─────────────────────────────────────────────────────────────┐
│  ROOM SPECIFICATION                                           │
├──────────────────┬──────────────┬──────────────┬─────────────┤
│  Client:         │  Room No.:   │  Name:       │  Date:      │
├──────────────────┴──────────────┴──────────────┴─────────────┤
│  Carpet:                                                      │
│                                                              │
│  Walls:                                                       │
│                                                              │
│  Ceiling:                                                     │
│                                                              │
│  Window Treatment:                                           │
│                                                              │
│  Built-ins:                                                   │
│                                                              │
│  Furniture:                                                   │
│                                                              │
├──────────────────────────────────┬───────────────────────────┤
│  Room Layout:                     │                           │
│                                   │                           │
│                                   ├───────────┬───────────────┤
│                                   │ Approval: │ Moving Schedule:│
│                                   ├───────────┼───────────────┤
│                                   │ Contr.:   │ From:         │
│                                   ├───────────┼───────────────┤
│                                   │ Owner:    │ To:           │
│                                   ├───────────┼───────────────┤
│                                   │           │ To:           │
├───────────────────────────────────┴───────────┴───────────────┤
│  ©  Design Business Monthly                                   │
└─────────────────────────────────────────────────────────────┘
```

THE CONTRACT DOCUMENTS PHASE

After the approvals of the design development phase, the design firm makes any further adjustments required. It then prepares construction documents and the specifications required for the construction work on the project. The design firm also may recommend contractors appropriate for the project and prepare request, receive, and review bids.

Appropriate purchase documents with detailed specifications are also prepared, including detailed requirements for fabrication procurement, shipment, delivery and installation of all furniture, furnishings, and equipment required for the project. The design firm may assume the responsibility for purchasing and project management of the installation or may merely supervise or assist, depending upon the contract.

Placing Orders

After the client accepts the proposals, your firm places all orders and finalizes subcontracts. You will meet with contractors to determine scheduling and organize delivery installations. Any additional necessary detail drawings will be prepared and reviewed. You will also review your insurance coverage to determine that all items are covered appropriately.

If the client requests any revisions at this stage, you should determine how they will affect the schedule and budget. Before making any changes in your orders, get approval from both the client and the contractor to determine the correct costs and whether the change affects the schedule.

Project master sheet. This sheet makes it easy to see at a glance everything that has been ordered for the client.

PROJECT MASTER SHEET						Date:			
Client:			Contact:			Designer:			
Address:			Phone No.: Home:			Start Date:			
			Work:			Completion Date:			
Date:	Order No.:	Supplier:	Item:	Area:	Quoted:	Exp. Ship. Week of:	Rec'd.:	Del'd.:	Billed:

© Design Business Monthly

Reupholstery checklist. This checklist outlines all project details involving re-upholstery. It is useful to include a photograph of the existing furniture for appropriate documentation (a second photograph should go to the workroom).

REUPHOLSTERY CHECKLIST

Client:	Purchase Order No.:	Date:
Workroom Time Required:	Pick-up Date:	Expected Completion:

Description of Furniture:	Fabric:
	Source:
	Number:
	Color:
Style and Approximate Size:	Description:
	Width:
	Repeat:

Instructions to Workroom:		Sample:
Changes in Construction:		
Frame to be Tightened:		
Wood to be Refinished:		Sketch or Photo:
Cushion Fill:		
Arm Hoods:		
Others:		
Special Instructions:		

© Design Business Monthly

Window treatment checklist. This is a good checklist to use when preparing specifications for any type of window treatment, including draperies, shades, and shutters. It also provides space for a sketch or photograph of the existing window or treatment.

WINDOW TREATMENT CHECKLIST		
Client:	Purchase Order No.:	Date:
Room Location:	Workroom Time Required:	Expected Installation:

Type of Treatment:	Fabric or Product Used:
	Source:
	Number:
	Color:
	Description:
	Width:
Type of Valance:	Repeat:
	Sample:

Measurements and Specifications:	Sketch or Photo:
Hardware/Rod Location:	
Length:	
Width:	
Extension:	
Overlap:	
Other:	
Accessories: (tie-backs, finials)	

© *Design Business Monthly*

Furniture, furnishings, and equipment specifications sheet. This type of specification sheet is appropriate for you to use when you are sending a project out for bids. These sheets, which normally have the design firm's name on them, can become part of a large purchasing document.

FURNITURE, FURNISHINGS, AND EQUIPMENT SPECIFICATIONS				
Project:			Date:	
Spec. #:	Quan.:	Description: (manufacturer, catalog no., finish)	Unit Cost:	Ext. Cost:

© Design Business Monthly

Letter of transmittal. Transmittal sheets are used for all correspondence between the designer, other consultants, and contractors. A transmittal sheet such as this should be attached to shop drawings, letters, prints, change orders, plans, and samples—anything that would require a comment, approval, or request.

YOUR FIRM NAME HERE
123 Main Street
YOUR TOWN, STATE and ZIP

Phone 123-4567

LETTER OF TRANSMITTAL

| DATE | JOB NO |

ATTENTION

RE

TO

WE ARE SENDING YOU ☐ Attached ☐ Under separate cover via_____the following items:

☐ Shop drawings ☐ Prints ☐ Plans ☐ Samples ☐ Specifications

☐ Copy of letter ☐ Change order ☐ _____

COPIES	DATE	NO	DESCRIPTION

THESE ARE TRANSMITTED as checked below:

☐ For approval ☐ Approved as submitted ☐ Resubmit_____copies for approval

☐ For your use ☐ Approved as noted ☐ Submit_____copies for distribution

☐ As requested ☐ Returned for corrections ☐ Return_____corrected prints

☐ For review and comment ☐ _____

☐ FOR BIDS DUE_____19____ ☐ PRINTS RETURNED AFTER LOAN TO US

REMARKS

COPY TO _____ SIGNED: _____
If enclosures are not as noted, kindly notify us at once.

CONTRACT ADMINISTRATION PHASE

After the contract development phase has been completed, the contract administration phase begins. This phase encompasses the follow-through period, the installation, and the post-occupancy evaluation.

The "Twilight Zone"

The follow-through period is known as "twilight zone." The twilight zone begins the moment a client signs a contract or places an order and ends when the merchandise is delivered or an installation is completed. During this period, all of a client's worries and insecurities about his or her project come into full flower, and if left unchecked, cause difficulty on installation day. Maintaining communication with the client for the duration of the project is the way to avoid problems.

Client Updates. Establish a regular day and time with the client for a weekly update call from your office on the stage of completion of the project. Early in the job there is often not much to report. The report may consist of saying: "We are working on your preliminary design, have completed all the data collection, and are doing research on some of the materials required."

When the client knows that once a week, on a given day, he or she will hear from you, many calls throughout the week are avoided. It also permits you to be prepared. Before speaking to your client you can consult his or her file for up-to-date information; you will be able to speak intelligently about his or her job.

In our studio each project has a master sheet (see page 178). On it we outline the components of the job and where each stands at a particular time. We call our client with the master sheet in front of us. On the back of the master sheet we keep simple records. Our managing director notes any comments the client may have during the telephone conversation. This means that in addition to having a master file with all the original specifications for a job, we have a complete rundown on exactly what is being done, with a record of all conversations and important data. If the designer wants to know what the managing director has said to a client, he or she picks up the master sheet.

When we make a presentation, we give the client a copy of the project schedule. It states when the materials are expected, as well as when the different craftspeople will be working in the client's space. If revisions are required or a final date is set, we tell the client during our weekly report. We will also send the client an updated outline of the schedule so that he or she will have the space ready for the craftspeople when they arrive on the job.

You should talk weekly to the other professionals involved on the job, such as architects, engineers, or job coordinators. Neglecting this communication destroys cooperation and can undermine the project. This regular interaction not only serves to support professionalism but is an excellent marketing tool. If clients know that you are on top of their job they feel they are receiving very special, personal care and are quick to recommend you to their friends.

This weekly communication can also spur clients to enlarge their project. Knowing that the original work is moving along smoothly and is not causing any major discomfort or interference in their lives seems to make clients feel secure about buying design services.

Tell the truth; don't keep problems from the clients. But try to have solutions. Give the client the options you have worked out and ask for his or her input. Unless you are sure of the client, don't offer more than two possible solutions. Offering more tends only to confuse the issue.

Purchasing and Follow-up. What happens to an order from the time it is placed until the product is delivered? During this period, small developments can either make or destroy an order as well as a client relationship. Regular communication with your suppliers and your client is essential.

The ability to get the job completed depends upon the designer's ability to design a project that is practical to produce within the budget and medium in which he or she is working. It must be within the abilities of your staff and craftspeople.

In addition to placing a written order for merchandise, you should also phone in the order to see if any items have been discontinued or if there is anything incorrect or incomplete about your purchase order. This follow-up phone call assures that changes can be handled immediately and not three weeks down the road, when they could affect a greater body of work. After making this call you should tell your client that the orders have been placed with no problem, or that one fabric is discontinued and, therefore, will require another selection. Ask your client when he or she can arrange an appointment to make that selection.

You must carefully consider the project schedule when you choose which materials to specify. Determine whether you can afford to specify materials from all parts of the world when you have only ninety days to complete a job.

When an order is submitted to the person processing the job (the expeditor), the design has been completed and there is an expected delivery date on the project. This date has been established by the designer and the client. The expeditor knows by seeing this date that the client is expecting this order in a set period of time, ranging from two weeks to a year or longer. Few orders are done in a period of two weeks.

Everything you consider on a project is based on the date of completion. One item may have twenty to thirty parts. For example, fabric, finish, trimmings, and several different crafts may be part of a chair. Your expediter places the orders for each and every process or material you specify.

He or she attaches one copy of the purchase order, which is marked with the date the order is required, to the initial work order. Another copy of the purchase order is placed in your "On Order" file—an alphabetical file of each and every company with whom you have orders. When you get an invoice in from Fabric Company A, for example, you can go to your "On Order" file and match the invoice with the order.

On your purchase order, you should have the name of the client and a purchase-order number. In our firm, the work-order number that we start out with follows through on all the subsequent purchase orders. This means that if a work-order number is 9046, all the purchase-order numbers would be 9046A, 9046B, and so forth.

After an order has been placed with a company, you should have an acknowledgement or some confirmation from them in approximately a week to ten days. This will tell you if the product is available, in which case you may receive an invoice for it. If it is not available, the company will let you know how long it will be before it is available, or if the product has been discontinued.

You should immediately compare all acknowledgments with your delivery expectations. If you have a year in which to deliver a sofa, for example, and there is a three-month delay in the fabric shipment, it really won't matter since you know that it only takes another thirty to sixty days to produce the sofa after you have the fabric. But if the acknowledgment says that the delivery of this fabric will be in sixty days, and the client is expecting delivery in ninety days, you know you have to do some checking. Even though you have a thirty-day cushion, you really can't count on that. This means that the fabric is expected from the mill on that date. That is not the date on which it will be delivered to you. The fabric may be coming from England or Italy. This could cause additional shipping delays before it is shipped from the factory to you.

At this point, it is important to bring the delay to the attention of the designer in charge. The designer may say: "There is a fabric almost identical to that from another firm. Let's consider using the fabric from Fabric Company B instead of the fabric from Fabric Company A." The designer will then compare the two fabrics and decide whether this is a reasonable choice. Your firm will then check with Fabric Company B to assure availability of this fabric and then put a reserve on the fabric. At that point you check with the client for approval. If the client approves the change, you call both fabric companies to change the fabric to be used from Fabric Company A's to Fabric Company B's.

When you change an order, you must notify all affected vendors. In the case of a sofa, which is to be made by an upholsterer, the upholsterer is expecting a fabric from Fabric Company A with a certain identifying number. You must write to the upholsterer to tell him or her that that particular fabric is not available, so he or she will be receiving a fabric from Fabric Company B instead.

Suppose your client decides there is no substitute for his or her fabric selection and you, as the designer, agree. If a major change of fabric must be made, adjustments on deliveries of all the other items will have to be made to coordinate deliveries. It may not be a matter of just changing sofa fabrics; it may mean changing the draperies, accent pillows, or three or four other items that go with the different fabric.

Understanding the situation, your client may be prepared to wait and to adjust the job completion date accordingly. When the client is given a choice, it makes for much better rapport.

Weekly Merchandise Checks. Another important follow-up procedure is to check, on a weekly basis, every client order and every merchandise order to see if there are any acknowledgments pending and if anything has not arrived by your expected delivery dates. When there's a discrepancy, contact the involved suppliers by telephone, fax, or letter to determine why that item is delayed or what the problem is. They may never have received your order. These weekly checks allow you to catch problems quickly, not three weeks later, when you are expecting an item on your loading dock.

A record of all the activities is kept on the master sheet for easy reference. Today there are several computer programs which can handle your design firm's source communications and documentation (see page 66).

Merchandise Inspection. Always inspect merchandise before it arrives on site. If you have an installation scheduled, check with the warehouse to be sure that the merchandise has arrived and that it is the proper color, size, and shape. Regardless of the supplier, it is advisable visit the warehouse and see the merchandise yourself. There are ways you can open and repack cartons without adversely affecting your scheduling. It is easier to check merchandise when it is in a warehouse facility than it is to do later.

By inspecting the items you can also determine in advance how complex assembling the pieces will be. If you have installers who are not familiar with assembling an intricate item, a trip to the factory for training or requesting a factory person to assist with the installation can save time in the long run. Don't get involved in an installation unless you have experts available.

Assemble any item that can be pre-assembled in your own warehouse or workroom so that you spend as little time as possible at the client's space. Also, if there is a problem during assembly, pre-assembly allows you to know about it before you reach the client's. Even if you must take the product apart again and repack it, be sure that it fits together and you have all of the pieces.

If you are unfamiliar with the installation assembly process, ask the product manufacturer if you can visit another installation site so that you can see just how this assembly is performed. It is unprofessional to deliver a product your staff cannot professionally assemble.

Organizing the Workers. Depending upon the craft, the designer should review with the project contractors and craftspeople and their management. Explain a bit about the project. Show them the completed design so that they understand why their part of it is being done in a certain fashion. If the plumber realizes what the next three steps in a job are, for example, he will better understand his limitations and know why he can't take three feet when only one foot has been allotted.

Explaining the overall project to the craftspeople involved serves two functions. First, it helps them understand how they fit into the total process. Second, it gives them a sense of pride—they understand what they are working on and that you respect them enough to make them a part of this outstanding project.

During the installation you will have a great number of different contractors and craftspeople to coordinate. To make sure that they work well together, you should understand the exact processes that are required for them to do their jobs, and program exactly how they are to work together. Go over the project with each craftsperson or delivery person approximately three weeks before the installation, and again within about four days of the installation to be sure that everything is ready. If everything is not complete and ready, it is better to change the installation date.

When scheduling an installation by any contractor or craftsperson, visit his or her warehouse and go over with him or her the list of plumbing fixtures, lighting fixtures, and other items required for the project. Often contractors will start a project thinking that they have everything they need when they only have ninety percent of it. The last ten percent will hold up the job.

You must determine whether they should go into the client's space without all the equipment, or whether they really need to collect the rest of the materials— and make any substitutions—before they start.

Plan the job so that each craftsperson or contractor can perform his or installation easily and with the least likelihood of damaging other parts of the project. When you do a project on a tight schedule, even though it requires a lot of give-and-take from the subcontractors, efficient coordination makes the project appear perfectly orchestrated. The client can usually afford to have a highly paid project manager on site for such a short period of time. If a project is done over a long, spread-out period, supervision by a top quality person is often cost-prohibitive.

Installation Supervision

Installations require supervision. Larger firms have specialists who do only installation work. In smaller firms, the project manager will supervise the project throughout the process. The art of installation is becoming quite respected as a specialty, since the quality of the project is at great risk. Whether this person is an installation specialist or a project manager, he or she should be involved with the project from the concept phase throughout the job. If a design passes this person's approval, you know it will work and can be installed without extreme difficulty.

The person who supervises the complete installation should understand the job and its composition. He or she should review the design concept in the initial stages to determine any areas where the project might be adjusted to save money or to make the installation go smoother.

An on-site project manager has to make many decisions and adjustments on the design project. It is seldom that the existing facility is identical to what is expected.

The project manager should be included in the overall design program so that he or she understands exactly which adjustments are negotiable and which are not.

Ideally, if the installation manager is familiar with the project and has checked all items that are delivered to warehouses, he or she is going to be prepared for anything that comes up. A well-prepared project manager, often one of the best-paid people on a design team, can make an installation look professional—and the design team look great.

Whoever supervises the installation must not only know the project, but must also be willing to make the adjustments necessary to keep other people working. If a supply item is required, and is not on site, the supervisor takes care of getting what is needed so that nothing stops the workers from continuing their job. The supervisor must be willing to be inconvenienced if necessary to keep the rest of the job running.

Preparing the Site. Before the day of the installation, the building management needs to be informed of the requirements of the installation team. Parking allowances, street closings, and other preparations may need to be arranged. This is all part of your preparation. Going to the extra effort of clearing a parking lot and hiring a person to direct traffic into the lot is often one of the cheapest and best expenditures you can make. The traffic coordinator can control the arrivals of various pieces so that one person doesn't arrive a half-hour early and install his or her part before its base arrives.

Although previous scheduling and planning has been done, always check the job site the day before the installation. Be sure that the space is clean and ready for you. Make sure proper temperatures have been maintained for carpet and other types of installation. Check that the HVAC system is under proper control and that it is clean and properly functioning so that dust does not become a contaminant.

It is usually wise to ask the client to be away from the site during the day of installation. If the client feels he or she must be part of the installation, you should select the appropriate times in the day for him or her to come for comments and approval. Typically, when clients are on site they become concerned with inappropriate details and the continuity of the installation is affected.

Taking Charge. Sometimes a client will say that his or her office can handle the installations; however, this should be discouraged. It is a rare client who understands installation procedures, and it only takes one careless installer to mar a project that took months or perhaps years of careful design and development.

If at all possible, designate a member of your staff to be on site throughout the installation or at least to make periodic checks to ensure that your standards are met by the craftsmen.

Typically, an unsupervised delivery team will drop dirty cartons in the middle of the space. You can end up with grease on the carpet, or worse. Make sure this never happens. What the client remembers most is his last impression of your installation process.

Installation of Furnishings

The installation is one of the strongest selling parts of a job. You constantly resell a project to the client by the way you handle the job—not just in the initial interview or in the presentation, but the whole way through the "twilight zone" and on into the installation itself. Your performance and the way your craftspeople work in a person's facility often determines both the quality of the design work and the client's opinion of your firm.

The question of whether to install a project all at one time or piecemeal is sometimes not the designer's decision. But if you can arrange to install a project all at one time—to coordinate the craftspeople tightly with the installation of furniture—do it. This definitely makes a difference in the impact of the design on the client. Most clients cannot visualize what a room will look like, even though they have seen the plans and chosen the merchandise from the options you presented. Piecemeal installation is nerve-wracking for the client, and his or her resulting insecurities can cost you time.

The way you handle an installation affects not just that project, but your future relationship with that client and his or her associates.

Planning for Problems. In order to orchestrate a polished installation, you must be prepared in advance for any problems. Have on hand the tools and equipment you need to take care of problems. Planning for problems prevents them.

With advance planning, a great deal of difficulty and expense can be avoided at the end of the project. We've all heard about the ten-foot sofa that couldn't be delivered to the thirty-fourth-floor penthouse, or the boardroom table that wouldn't fit up the elevator shaft. When considering a design project, obviously the access to the space has to be considered. Many corridors and entrances in buildings are much narrower and smaller than one would expect; these are limitations you must take into account in the planning stages.

If you are having several sofas made, order sufficient fabric to replace the back or the seat (normally two or three yards). If you are ordering a chair, one yard of extra fabric should be ordered to replace the back or the seat cushion. By ordering extra fabric in advance, if there is a problem during the course of delivery, you are ready to take care of it immediately. If there is no problem, you can give the extra fabric to the client and say: "We are including this piece of matching fabric as insurance against a cigarette burn or a small tear. Put it away and keep it just in case". Or if you have storage space, you can keep the fabric in your warehouse with your client's name on it. It's amazing how often this extra material gets used. If it doesn't get used, it has still been a great back-up. It is always better to have an extra yard of material on hand than it is to call and try to match a yard or two of fabric at the time of the installation.

When ordering carpeting, order a few extra feet. This lets you cut around an unexpected flaw or finish a closet which the carpenter created from hidden space. It gives you the chance to make your installations what they should be. A little extra carpeting can later be used to repair minor damage without requiring the whole carpet to be replaced.

Always be prepared to handle touch-ups and minor repairs. If your installation people don't have a trained repair staff, schedule a standby for that particular project to take care of any little repairs so that they are handled immediately, not three months later.

A stain-removal kit and cleaning supplies should be part of your equipment for all installations. Insist that every delivery truck that is to service you has the equipment to vacuum, dust, and clean every interior item. Any cleaning supplies needed for new textiles or other items that will be handled should be included.

It is unusual for every item to arrive at an installation in perfect condition and in perfect sequence. There are usually some adjustments required during installation. Today there are specialists who know how to touch up finishes and make minor repairs or adjustments to make an installation seem perfect. These specialists can eliminate a lot of problems and complaints.

Installer's Records. On any project that requires working at a client's premises, whether it involves installation, delivery, or another type of work, a job-assignment sheet with the client's name at the top helps control each phase. It lists the various items ready to be delivered or work to be done at that particular site, whether it is a residence or a contract space. The number of assignment sheets you will need depends on the number of stages that the project has. For example, the first phase may include removing the old furnishings and preparing the space for painting, wallcovering, and/or carpet installation.

An installation may be done at one time or in three or four different phases. It is important that everything that is to be accomplished in each phase be listed. You must verify that all the necessary materials are on hand and ready for the installation. With an installation sheet (see page 189), you will avoid forgetting items or having three parts of an item but not the other two.

When the installer arrives at the client's property, even if a designer or assigned supervisor is there, the installer calls the designer's office to confirm that he or she is on location. (Later, the time marked on the installer's time sheet is verified at the office against the master phone schedule.) In addition, when the installer arrives he or she gives the office a status report on the site. The office must be

Installation sheet. When an installer is at your client's project, he or she needs to have a list of the items that are to be completed on that day. This sheet should be prepared by the project manager or managing director; it is later returned to that person after the installer has noted the amount of time spent, the items completed, and their history and results. This simple form helps tremendously both with billing and with scheduling any follow-up work.

INSTALLATION

Client:	Staff:	Date:	From: To:

Items to be Completed Today:

Items to be Done for Next Appointment:

© Design Business Monthly

made aware of any difficulties. The installer might say, for example, "The paper hanger is not finished with the wallcovering and we can only do a little more work until this is completed. He should be finished by this afternoon. What do you want us to do?" The person who manages the time scheduling in the office will then know the movement of each person on staff. If a client has a question regarding additional scheduling, or an adjustment to the schedule, this is handled in the main office—not by the installers, who may not understand the full planning process.

When the installer is finished for the day, he or she will call the office again to say, for example, "I have completed this project and am returning to the studio," or "I am going on to the next client's job." At the end of the day, the installer will return the master sheets to the office, marking off everything he or she has completed, the time that was spent, and any additional work that would require extra charges. On the bottom of this sheet the installer or the project supervisor notes any comments made by the client, such as, "I like the way we have done the office, but I would really like to add three extra chairs to the conference room."

These notes are important reference tools that can alert the designer to additional sales opportunities on that project. These records are kept in the client's master file and are used for billing purposes. Whether the billing is done through a computer system or manually, the process is similar.

Every project needs to be managed by the office, and a firm always appears more professional when control is centered there. An installer shouldn't say to a client, "I'll be back tomorrow with these items" if he or she doesn't know where the items are. He or she should say instead, for example, "I'll go back to the office to get the three or four items I need to complete your project. As soon as I have them, our staff person will call you and arrange for me to come out again and finish up." This helps the installer by not putting him or her in the position of having to answer questions such as, "Will you be here tomorrow to finish this?" Sometimes the installer doesn't know the answer, and this gets him or her off the hook.

Installation Day. You need a script and choreography for a well-planned, professional installation day. It is more than just showmanship; time equals money. There may be clauses in the contract that require a penalty be paid for each day the project is late. If you can shorten the installation time, your profits will be better. If you spend too much time on one project, when you should be working on others, it costs you business.

When installation people arrive in a space, the designer or the project manager must impress upon them that this is a new, finely finished space. It must be treated with the utmost care, as if it were a fine piece of crystal or a lovely coutourier garment.

How the installers are dressed and how they treat the site are critical. Clients feel that their furniture deserves special handling. Insist that anyone who touches or goes near it in any fashion understands that furniture is expensive and must be handled carefully. The best people working for you *should* be the people doing the installation, but so often firms use their lowest-paid and newest person. This person should be kept in house; do your training where clients can't see it.

Inform your installation people that playing loud music, eating, drinking, and smoking in the installation area are completely out of the question. On a large installation project, you should create a break area for the workers where they may go to drink sodas and smoke; but be sure they realize they may not drink or smoke in any other part of the space. See that the break area is cleaned up when you leave, even if the installation supervisor has to do it.

You can save time and money by having coffee or sodas on hand and arranging for lunches to be delivered. It is usually a good investment to pay for and bring in the installers' lunches, just to keep the installers working and on the job.

When making a delivery it is advisable to put walk-off mats down from the truck into the space. You should also cover carpeting as appropriate; brown carpenter's paper is usually better to use than plastic runners because it is less slippery. The paper also gives the area the appearance of work in progress.

The "white glove and bootie treatment" requires installation people to wear clean white gloves and those who are walking into a clean space with clean carpets to put on fabric booties over their shoes so that they do not get any outside soil on the carpet. This obsessive concern for a project is greatly appreciated by clients, who usually have made a heavy investment in the space and want it perfect. Great care should be taken on installation day to encourage the client to feel that everything about his or her project is special. With this kind of emphasis, you can build lasting rapport with clients.

The way furniture is wrapped when it goes into a space is also important. If it is covered with clean brown paper and nicely taped, that's fine. If the paper is soiled, or in any way torn, do something about it. In the past, furniture was delivered blanket-covered and well protected. When you arrived in a client's space, the blankets were lifted off and the client got to see his or her special piece of furniture. This was good showmanship. Today plastic has replaced blankets (and it is great because it keeps items clean and dry); the showmanship is still important.

If you are merchandising or selling products, your company will make the deliveries. Again, the way your trucking and delivery processes are handled strongly reflects the quality of your overall product. Designers deliver their furnishings in many different ways. One firm, in California, uses women to do the deliveries in attractive, nicely painted vans. The women wear black slacks and white ruffled blouses, and they deliver almost all of the furniture that the firm supplies. It's showmanship. Everyone talks about the way their deliveries are made.

Never leave a job until it is presenting the very best effect it can for this stage of the project. If you have not yet completed the project when you leave, be sure that the area is thoroughly vacuumed and cleaned. Pay attention to details so that the area looks organized; many times the client will sneak a peek.

Check your insurance coverage regarding your liability position while supervising or installing a project. In Chapter 11, care, custody and control are discussed (see page 322). Obviously the responsibilities of the design firm need to be defined and addressed prior to an installation.

At the completion of the installation, go through the project and prepare a punch list of problems, then make an appointment with the client several days later to go through his or her list. Point out to the client any flaws or imperfections and explain which are going to be corrected. Show the client before he or she shows you.

Design Review. A design review should not be done just at the end of a project, but throughout the project. This is when staff members meet, not just to review the design, but also to review the scheduling, the budget, and the client's expectations. A regular ongoing review throughout the project will strengthen it and keep everyone on target. Firms often wait too long before the first design review and concern themselves more with design quality than with other issues that are perhaps more pertinent to the project's success, such as whether they are really accomplishing their communication objectives with the client.

The Maintenance Manual. You should supply a maintenance manual to the client at installation time or immediately thereafter. This manual lists each and every piece of furniture, equipment, furnishings, and/or material that is incorporated into their project—including carpeting, wallcoverings, draperies, window treatments, furnishings, textiles, lamps—and explains everything needed to keep this installation in as fine a condition as possible. It lists handling precautions, cleaning and maintenance instructions, as well as simply the right wattage for the lamping. It includes the addresses and phone numbers of other companies that should be called for various services or additional instructions for adequate maintenance.

A maintenance manual is supplied to both residential and contract clients and is part of every design package. This manual also includes all of the guarantees, warranties, and any special instructions for the products you have supplied. These warranties are automatically passed on to the client. Any certificates for flame proofing or special finishes are also supplied with this maintenance manual.

Post-Occupancy Evaluation

After the installation is complete, evaluate your performance. Discuss the project with the client and see if his or her expectations have been met. Can you expect referrals?

A post-occupancy evaluation should be made at certain periods after the job is completed; usually at three months, six months, and a year. This is a good way for you to keep in touch with your client and also to evaluate your own work. It also gives you an understanding of how the client sees the performance of your design organization. The past client follow-up summary on page 193 will help you organize these evaluations.

If there are problems, a post-occupancy evaluation positions you as a part of the problem-solving team rather than as the enemy. You are usually able to determine just what needs to be done, which makes the client appreciate you. Taking care of problems is a normal and a required part of every design project. If possible, try to find a problem that the client has not noticed and see that it is corrected. This shows your service ability.

Evaluations of this sort will help you define your future market. If the project moved ahead smoothly, meeting your profit objectives and design expectations as well as the client's needs, then your firm is capable of handling more of this type of work and should continue to market for this type of project.

Handling Complaints. How you handle complaints can be an important part of marketing and sales development because it strongly affects the way the clients relate to your firm in the future.

The fact that the client called you at all is positive. It means that he or she is interested in your firm and may plan to use you again. If this weren't so, the client wouldn't bother to call; he or she would simply go to someone else. Look at a complaint as a positive response.

In most complaints, emotion and facts get mixed. To get the facts, acknowledge the emotion, but do not respond to it. This is discussed more fully in the section on telephone communication (see page 274).

Mainly, give the client attention. Let him or her know that you are concerned, that you are on his or her side, and that you will find a way to solve the problem. Try to make the client a part of your team in solving the problem, but let him or her know the problem is a priority issue with your firm.

Past client follow-up summary. After you have completed a job, you need to stay in contact with the client. This summary sheet works very well for post-occupancy review and additional follow-ups. Normally, it is advisable to talk with clients every three to six months. This type of reference sheet appropriately filled out will help manage that process.

PAST CLIENT FOLLOW-UP SUMMARY

Client:

Contact Person:

Position:

Address:

Phone No.:

Finish Date:	Job:	Type: (room or building)	Size:

Last Contact Date:	Client's Comments:	Follow-through:

© Design Business Monthly

It is best to have scheduled programs for handling complaints. Many firms require complaints to be handled within twenty-four hours of receipt, and sooner if possible. The faster you can get back to the client, the less time he or she has to worry about the issue. Prompt handling of complaints is a very important strategy. There are some clients you can never please. But if you have gone through the whole project with the client, and he or she is generally pleased with it, usually complaints can be easily managed.

Give complaints priority handling, and try to leave the client with a positive impression of your firm. It takes too long to develop a client to let some small item become a major issue. The better your management of a project, and the more you know about the contractors, various installation people, and other people who are interacting with the client, the easier it is to avoid complaints.

Client Retention

On any residential or contract project, the designer and the client develop an intense relationship that was built on daily contact. When the project is finished, the intensity must diminish so the designer can go on to the next assignment. The client must be weaned away form the constant support and affirmation of the designer in a way that does not decrease his or her regard for the designer.

This takes special handling. If the project was an office building with 800 rooms, the designer and the project liaison worked together daily and the designer may have practically lived at the job site. In residential work, the designer has often been privy to the client's innermost thoughts and feelings. Either way, the relationship is very close and intense. The closest comparison is the relationship between patient and psychiatrist. To be abruptly dropped in this relationship can be devastating, and dropping a client cold is asking for a lot of problems.

If the client feels rejected, the designer loses him or her as a potential source for referrals and loses all chance of designing new projects for that client. A planned withdrawal is strategic.

After the installation assist the client in adjusting to the new space. Contact him or her weekly, at the same time of day as your previous call, for the first one to three months, depending upon the extent of the project. Don't wait for the client to complain; call him or her first and ask if there is any way your firm can offer help. Later, call once a month for three to six months, and then try to call again three and six months later, so that you have checked for possible problems during the entire year after the installation.

Continued rapport with someone with whom you have worked closely has the best potential of any marketing effort. After all, referrals from past clients make up the majority of new business in most firms. They know what you do and can explain it to appropriate potential clients. So spend some time on client reten-tion. Too many design firms have this great untapped reservoir of past clients that they no longer contact, and this can work against them.

Client Loyalty

Earning a client's loyalty is one of the most sought-after and emotionally reward-ing accomplishments that any design practice can achieve. Look through your list of successful jobs. You will find that many of the outstanding ones have been jobs that have developed out of other successful projects. The original project may have been one or two rooms, or one building; then you ended up doing the client's next four or five, or thirty or forty, buildings. This is a loyal client. Still, a client must be happy with every project you do or will not hire you for the next project.

One of the best things to do is to maintain quality interaction with your client throughout the project. This will ensure that every movement on the job is helping to develop the next phase of that job or the next project with that client or his or her friends or associates.

Chapter Eight

CHARGING FOR YOUR SERVICES

Before you even think about estimating a project, make sure you understand exactly what the project involves. Many designers send out estimates or proposals too soon, before they have completely evaluated a project. The more time that you take up front to get to know the client and the project, the better opportunity you will have to succeed at presentation time.

JOB PRICING

Some very successful designers refuse to give a quotation or a presentation unless the client agrees to first spend several hours with the designer to review the overall design requirements.

The design service outline form is set up for this purpose (see pages 197–202). A detailed project evaluation, documented at the precontract phase, can often help clients understand just what your design services encompass and what the costs involved entail. This form also clearly defines the job outline, the services to be rendered, and the scheduling. You should process and complete this form before turning a job over to the project manager. It is important to have the project manager assist in the preparation of this outline and the costing-out of the project. This enables him or her to understand both the project and the project goals.

Another excellent way of defining a project is to do an up-front analysis for the client for a small fee. This will permit you to carefully examine the total project. You will then know how to quote on it and also whether it is an appropriate job for you.

JOB PRICING

When pricing a job, there are four things to be considered:

1. the scope of the job;

2. the services to be rendered;

3. the staff required; their time and cost;

4. the schedule.

Obviously, the time scheduled can affect the cost of the project. The way your proposal is written strongly dictates the management style for the project. If your proposal states all of the processes to be done, then your project management list is almost complete. You know exactly who is going to do what and approximately the time and outline of the project.

Without the project plan in place, it is almost impossible to make an appropriate estimate. As you do your estimates and your proposal, try to write them in a fashion that makes it easy for later programming.

Design service outline. This outline can often help clients understand what your design services encompass and what the costs entail. You should process and complete this form before turning a job over to the project manager.

DESIGN SERVICE OUTLINE	Date:

Client:	Contact Person: Position:
Address:	Phone No.:

Project:

Decision-making Process:

Presentation Form: Floorplans:
Boards:
Renderings:
Models:

Stages of Decisions:

Client's Representatives:

Staff Involved:

Consultants:

Contractors:

Scheduled Contact Time:

© Design Business Monthly

Determining Requirements: (functional and organizational)
Space Analysis:
Traffic Flow:
Work Flow:
Personnel - Expected Growth:
Individual Space:
Visitors: Flow:
Equipment:

Storage: Records:
 	
           Supplies:
 	
           Other:

Lighting:
Acoustical:
Audiovisual:
Security:
Handicapped:

© Design Business Monthly

Scheduling:

Owner's Projected Goals:

Design Schedule:

Work Schedule:

Other Issues:

Notes:
_____
_____
_____
_____
_____
_____
_____
_____
_____
_____
_____
_____
_____
_____
_____
_____
_____
_____
_____
_____
_____
_____
_____
_____
_____
_____
_____
_____
_____
_____
_____
_____
_____
_____
_____

Design Concept:	
Architectural:	Changes:
	Details:
	Finishes:
Floor Plans:	
Wall Elevations:	
Special Details:	
Cabinet/Built-in Work:	
Furniture:	
Special Equipment:	
Window Treatments:	
Lighting:	
Acoustical:	
Security:	
Audiovisual:	

© Design Business Monthly

Project Documentation:
Floor Plans: (areas or rooms involved)
Furniture Plans:
Lighting Plan:
Elevations: (areas or rooms involved)
Finish Schedule: (special notes to be included)
Hardware Schedule:
Window Treatments:
Special Conditions:
Specification:
Bidding:
Purchase Orders:
Maintenance Manual: (companies or products involved)
Moving Plan:
Schedule:

© Design Business Monthly

Project Management:	
Coordination: Client:	
Consultants:	
Contractors:	
Scheduling:	
Shop Drawing Approval:	
Supervision:	
Revisions:	
Change Orders:	
Negotiations: Prebid Quotes:	
Contractors:	
Payment Authorization:	
Occupancy Evaluation:	
Post-occupancy Review:	
Others:	

© Design Business Monthly

Carefully defining and qualifying a project is the best way to determine the appropriate charging methods. Design firms usually invest large amounts of time in these efforts; a week or more is not unusual for a larger project. It is much better to invest a week's labor to be sure that the job is right for the firm and priced correctly than it is to take the wrong job and risk losing six months of unpaid fees.

Before beginning estimations on any project you need to:

1. *Define the scope of the work.* Exactly what is going to be done on this project and what position will you play? What kind of project is it? Is there a high-liability issue involved? Is the project one that will require a lot of research, or is it a job you can manage comfortably? How prepared is your firm for this project? If it is a bank project and you have just designed fourteen other banks, there are going to be certain procedures that will go much faster within your firm. If you have not designed a bank for a year or more, the project is going to be a bit more difficult.

   Check out a job. See if it is a project you really want to handle. If it is your type of job, it is worth putting effort into the proposal and into the presentation. If it is not the type of job you want, then do not waste your time writing a proposal.

2. *Determine the expected quality of the project.* Just how well does the client want the job done? What kind of quality has he or she received on other projects?

3. *Evaluate the design team.* Who are the other people working on the project? The architect, the design professionals, the contractors, and other professionals that have been selected will affect you and your team.

4. *Consider the schedule.* Is it a fast-track job or is it one that will be done over several years? Review your proposal with the different design people that are going to work on the project to get their feedback and time estimates. This way they are committed to the project and they will feel a much higher responsibility to complete it within the time period they specify.

   Estimating is probably the most difficult thing we do. Being able to put together good proposals and estimates is quite an art, but the only way it can be done is with very good up-front review and coordination.

   As the staff people who will work on the job estimate their time requirements, compare their estimates with past records. Some staff members tend to underestimate, while others are more accurate.

5. *Investigate the regulations and codes that apply to the project.* Are there a lot of requirements necessary to meet either city or state codes or corporate standards?

6. *Assess your competition.* How does your firm compare to other firms bidding for the job?

7. *Predict what you will gain from the project.* What is your chance of making a profit on this project? How much risk is there? Will the time commitments or other restrictions on this project jeopardize your firm's profit opportunities on other projects?

As you consider each job, look at it in terms of the benefits you can expect to accrue from it. Balance your financial expectations and the amount of time you expect to invest in the job. Also consider the marketing value of the job. We have all done jobs that were not overly profitable, but that brought us several jobs that were profitable.

Determine just what this job means to your studio. Every now and then it is worth taking a job without much profit if it offers other benefits. It may offer an introduction to a specialty, give you an opportunity to test the waters. When considering going into this type of situation, go into it with your eyes open.

If you want to change your specialty, you may find that you have to do a few projects to gain credentials within that field. This may mean taking a project at a lower fee or even without fee in order to get background and experience within this specialty.

8. *Evaluate the client.* Is he or she accustomed to working with an interior designer? Has he or she had experience either with your firm or with other firms? What kind of decision maker is the client? How many meetings do you expect to have? How many alternations are going to be required? What kind of rapport do you have with the client? Are you going to get along very easily or will it be difficult for you?

JOBS THAT USUALLY LOSE MONEY

There are certain jobs on which you usually lose money because they take too much time. Generally, they are with clients who are overly interested in the project but don't know a lot about interior design services. These clients often want to become totally consumed with the project, which requires you to spend considerable extra time with them and can cause a great deal of unexpected expense.

Community buildings can lose money for your firm. These projects require you to make multiple presentations to get the approval of the segment of the community that is involved. This can become very expensive to handle. Country clubs and other buildings where there is an overwhelming feeling of ownership by a large group of people can also be losers. Even if you restrict the project, too many people generally want to have a say in the project, which can make handling the phone calls and other interactions difficult.

HOW TO CHARGE

Determining the appropriate fee structure for a job is of primary importance for your firm's reputation and profitability. The standard set by the proposal either gives the firm an opportunity for quality design work and profit or creates a losing situation. If the project is not priced and structured properly, it can turn out to be a disaster, both from the design and profit viewpoints. Everyone loses. The firm and the staff lose because it is not exciting and interesting working on a job that is not a winner, the job loses them money, and the job could cost the firm future jobs. And obviously, the client is the big loser, as he or she misses out on getting a first-rate design.

Your client should be made aware of the way you charge and the way you handle finances. When you present a fee schedule or a quotation to a client, it is important to have an outline of all the services that you are going to include. Then, if the client says the quotation is too high, you can simply point to the areas that can be eliminated.

At this time, there are no official sources for standard fee scales for design work. Magazines occasionally publish lists of what has been charged, but these lists are not always accurate.

When estimating or creating a quotation, you should work out several different quotations and then compare them. Use different methods to arrive at these figures: a square-foot price: a dollar volume price of the estimated furnishings and finishing costs, plus a percentage; and an hourly estimate of the professional time that will take to handle the project.

Asking for a retainer, or a deposit, is important; it is part of the professional contract. In several states, designers have been discouraged from using the word "deposit" because, legally, a deposit must be placed in a separate escrow account for that client and cannot be mixed with funds of other projects. It is safer to call the advance a "retainer."

BASIC METHODS OF COMPENSATION

There are many ways of charging, and the interior design field varies considerably from the architectural field in the methods that are profitable. Normally, architectural projects have a higher dollar volume than interior design projects, while labor and detailing on interior design projects are far more extensive. In my experience, the most profitable projects are generally those that have a mixed method of charging.

Many interior designers charge a straight hourly rate. Others charge an additional percentage on each item purchased or keep a percentage of the cost of the total purchases. Some discount the retail price; others add to it. There are so many equations for how to charge that it is almost impossible to give anyone a guideline without reviewing his or her own requirements and expenses.

My solution is to have my accountant determine exactly what it will cost to run the company for the next year. I figure out our per-employee cost and our general production costs, and have my accountant review these figures. He comes up with an overall budget and suggested mark-up procedures.

Overhead Expenses

Today, overhead expenses generally equal at least 1½ to 2 times an employee's expenses. When calculating hourly fees, this expense is usually billed at 2½ to 3½ times the salary costs. This is separate from any direct expenses, which are also billed to the client. Direct expenses normally include blueprints; reproductions; illustrated drawings; models; all of your travel expenses; shipping, freight, and handling costs; and any expenses incurred during procurement and installation of the furnishings. It is always wise to keep management's overhead expenses as low as possible without sacrificing future business opportunities or quality of work produced.

Calculating Hourly Rates

Hourly rates in the interior design field in 1991 ranged between $45 and $350, and some designers in large cities earned even more. I find that interior designers very often cannot successfully charge more than psychiatrists do in a city. I do not know why this is, but it seems a good rule of thumb to follow in setting hourly rates.

The way you charge can limit your profits. If your rates cover only time and expenses, and you are paid by the hour, you have not risked much because you know that your profit is built into your multiplier and you will be reimbursed for all expenses. This is an up-front agreement. While it is safe, it offers no chance for a great profit. Unless you have your multiplier and your firm structured appropriately, this can be a difficult way to make good money.

ESTABLISHING YOUR OVERHEAD COSTS

Review all overhead costs, or fixed expenses, such as:

▶ rent

▶ taxes and licenses

▶ insurance

▶ utilities

▶ telephone

▶ advertising

▶ marketing

▶ office expense

▶ automobiles

▶ dues and subscriptions

▶ loan payments

▶ management personnel whose time is devoted to business development or management

▶ nonbillable support staff

ESTABLISHING THE DESIGNER'S HOURLY BILLING RATE

Example:

Salary per year	$24,000
*Fringe benefits (30% of salary)	7,200
DPE (direct personnel expense)	$31,200 ÷ 49 weeks = $636.73 per week

If a designer works an average of 40 hours per week, the usual number of chargeable hours is 30.

$$\$636.73 \div 30 \text{ hours} = \$21.22 \text{ per hour}$$

Using a 2½ to 3½ percent multiplier you can establish an appropriate billing rate.

2½	=	$53.05 per hour
3	=	63.66 per hour
3½	=	74.66 per hour

*When calculating fringe benefits, include holidays, sick leave, vacation, unemployment taxes, FICA, Workmen's Compensation, insurance, and pension plan.

FEE BASES

Today, most clients are aware of what standard designer fees are. Fees vary from area to area, but generally clients in any one area know what to expect. There are some basic methods of compensation.

The Design Concept Fee

This is a fee paid for ideas or for the development of the conceptual objectives. Compensation can be on a lump sum, an hourly, or a per diem basis. It may also be done on a contracted, or retail sale, basis; most designers do not work on a full retail markup. Depending on the extent and type of services rendered, markups vary.

After one of my seminars on design professionalism, a woman confided to me that a number of her fellow designers had criticized her for not charging a design fee. "I've never done it and I don't think my clients would be comfortable with it." This woman worked out of her house from 10:00 A.M. to 3:00 P.M. with only a part-time secretary to help her. Her overhead for telephone, postage, and supplies was about $7,000 annually. Her clients paid all freight and delivery expenses, and her husband paid the rent. She did $140,000 in business each year—$70,000 in gross profit. No matter how you looked at it, she had to be making between $50,000 to $60,000 a year, which is rather good for five hours of work a day. Her method worked for her. Therefore I suggested she continue doing it.

The Straight Design Fee

Compensation for doing design is on an hourly, per diem, or fixed fee basis. When the design fee is calculated on an hourly basis, the rate is usually 2½ to 3½ times the cost of the employee (see page 206). You should quote a fixed fee only after you have had enough experience with certain types of jobs to have a solid basis for estimating their costs. I charge a design fee, which is payable in advance, on every project I do. My minimum fee in 1987 was $1,000; at that time we could not introduce a project into our studio for less than that. I require larger fees for larger projects. But I always talk this over with my client during the initial interview.

Time and Expense

Many designers bill their time and expenses. If you use this method, you would bill either on a per diem basis or on an hourly basis. You build your profit into your multiplier. Generally, the multiplier is from 3 to 3½ times the cost of the designer; expenses are added. Some firms increase the multiplier to cover the expenses.

Time and Expenses with Upset Limit. Charging for your time and expenses with a "not to exceed" price limit is a very difficult billing method. It is based on time and expenses with an upset limit, or a guaranteed maximum. This is really the worst of all formats because it offers no room for extra profit and a tremendous potential for loss. Only very experienced firms can be confident of making a profit using this method of charging. The firm must be very familiar with all of the demands and details.

Time and Expenses: Estimated Amount. A safer way to charge is for your time and expenses within an estimate. This would be based on a scheduled estimate of time. This method can work well and be more profitable because there is flexibility. If the job ends up being more complex than you had anticipated, there is a basis for covering your extra charges.

Fee Plus Percentage of Savings. This billing method is based on hourly fees, plus a percentage of what you might save the client on the amount of the project. For example, if the project cost is estimated at $500,000, and you are able to bring it in for $240,000, the owner may agree to split the difference with you on a 50/50 basis. More of these types of incentive programs are being developed because clients can see and understand their value. This method makes it worthwhile for the interior designer to try to plan the project in a price-effective way.

Time-Based Fee: Open Ended. My recommendation is that if you are estimating your fee for a project based on time and expenses, you should leave it open ended if at all possible. This is among the safest and most profitable ways of quoting.

Value-Oriented Fee

The best way of charging is on the basis of value-oriented fees. This has a high risk, but it also offers excellent opportunities for profit. If you understand the project and you run an efficient design firm, this method can be controllable and profitable. If the project is in an area with which you are unfamiliar, however, it can prove to be a loss.

A value-oriented fee is based on a lump sum for a particular project. Lump-sum fees are usually profitable and often the best way of charging when the firm has done a lot of similar projects, knows the client, and has a good idea of their anticipated time expenditures. Designers who deal in specialties generally work on this basis because they have certain parts predesigned and can therefore complete a job very cost-effectively.

Per-Square-Foot Charge

A dollars-per-square-foot charge can be profitable if you understand how to charge and are experienced within this specialty. Otherwise, you can either make or lose a lot of money depending upon how well you have defined the project.

Retail Sales Basis Methods

Many clients want to buy a product, and retail organizations respond to that need. Today many traditional furniture stores have closed and are gradually being replaced by specialty companies or design gallery operations. But it takes good design service to make these businesses outstanding. Some designers use a retail shop as a marketing tool; it is a comfortable way for a new client to get to know the designer and still feel in control. The retail method enables a client to think he or she knows exactly what the whole thing is going to cost, and many residential clients understand product costs rather than fees. To the client who wants to have fun buying, this method will always remain attractive.

Retail or specialty companies usually have better buying methods and therefore can produce an item with their specifications at a better price, faster, and with fewer delivery problems than a typical design firm would be able to do. They have chosen their preferred vendors, given them a large quantity of business, and therefore can expect certain considerations.

Earlier in my career, I thought the only professional way to work was on an hourly basis. At that time, some designers earned a living by working for furniture stores and receiving a percentage of the sales. I was told that being a professional interior designer and selling furniture were poles apart. Now I see the advantages of these methods. Many design firms have found it difficult to maintain the expenses of their firms on just an hourly fee. Either they need a very high rate and a consistently busy office or they need additional forms of income, such as a percentage of the items contracted by the client. Markup and pricing methods vary according to the format of the business. This method of operation has many advantages and opportunities for profitability.

Design-Concept Fee Plus Percentage. On residential work and small contract jobs, many designers work for a design-concept fee plus a percentage of cost of the items that are to be purchased or to be supervised. This percentage applies to both construction items and furniture and accessories. The percentage varies, depending upon the location and experience of the design firm.

Hourly Fee Plus Percentage. Another method of pricing that is popular today is the time-based or hourly fee plus a percentage of the merchandise that is specified. On smaller jobs, this is necessary and possible. As jobs develop into high-level, large-quantity projects (such as large contract projects), then the fee-plus-percentage method is not normally possible.

Percentage of Cost. An interior designer can also provide his or her complete services, including furnishings and labor, at cost, adding a fee based on a percentage of the total cost. With this method, the design firm makes all purchases and passes on to the client all discounts, commissions, and savings. The client thus obtains merchandise at wholesale price plus the designer's fee. This fee will vary considerably depending on the type of work that is being performed. Obviously the larger the job, the smaller the percentage of the fee must be. When firms charge an hourly fee plus a percentage of cost, the client needs to be clearly informed that project management and follow-up on problems usually represent a large portion of the fee—from one-third to one-half of the total.

Another billing method is to charge for the cost plus a percentage of profit on the furnishings that you are handling.

PERCENTAGE OF COSTS	
Cost of items	$1,000.00
Freight	100.00
Receiving, warehousing, and delivery	120.00
+ 25% fee	305.00
Subtotal:	$1,525.00
+ State sales tax @ 6%	91.50
TOTAL:	$1,616.50

Percentage off List Price. If you act as a buying agent, you can often receive from your suppliers a percentage of the cost of items purchased by your client.

PERCENTAGE OFF LIST PRICE	
List price	$2,000.00
Less 20%	400.00
Subtotal:	$1,600.00
+ State sales tax @ 6%	96.00
TOTAL:	$1,696.00

Many firms will include the freight, warehousing, and delivery charges in their estimate. Others will make an additional charge in their billing.

The Designer as Retail Employee. Designers who are employed by retail or specialty stores are usually paid either salary plus commission or straight commission. When a client purchases items from that store, the design services are either included in the cost of the item or can be featured at an extra fee. Today an increasing number of these stores are charging professional fees in addition to their typical retail or list price; however, this will vary according to the type of store, the location, and the sales structure of the company.

The Designer as Agent. The designer, as the agent for the client, will prepare specifications, orders, and contracts, and place orders on the client's behalf, using funds that are either advanced by the client or have been paid directly by the client to the resources.

When working in this kind of arrangement, it is important that the designer makes all resources aware if the purchasing agreements and the payments will be made by the client. The designer is acting as an agent only; the client has all financial responsibilities. On some larger projects this is often preferred by the manufacturers; on others it can present complications. This must be made known up front on the original purchase orders.

In these situations, the design firm needs to clearly specify the financial and management responsibilities. If the client is purchasing directly, then the client is also responsible for dealing with the manufacturers directly on follow-up issues. If the design firm is handling the purchasing, the client is charged a fee for management.

Sales Tax

Usually designers must charge sales tax on anything that is "movable," which would include all furniture or any movable unit that goes into a project. However, if an item is "attached" to the building, and the firm is responsible for installing it, then you are required to charge use tax instead.

For example, if you sell wallcovering to a client and he or she has a paperhanger install it, you must charge the client sales tax. But if you have a paperhanger do the installation of this same wallcovering, then you must pay the use tax.

In most states, any item that is sold is subject to sales tax. This means that if you are responsible for the sale of any furniture, you must have a tax identification number and pay tax.

In most states, when you bill your client for blueprints, these also need to be taxed. However, if you include the print and drawing costs as part of your design fee, you would then be responsible for paying a use tax on the paper, art supplies, and other items used.

Taxes vary considerably from state to state. However, most interior designers, whether practicing on a professional service basis or acting as a selling agent or retailer, are responsible for some form of tax. This needs to be reviewed on a regular basis with your accountant since the laws change often.

In most states, designers do not charge sales tax on their design fee. Designers who break down their charges, and charge a set amount for a product plus a percentage, only charge sales tax on the base price of the material. If charges are invoiced as a total price, then sales tax is charged on the complete item.

Usually a firm is not responsible for charging taxes on items shipped out of state. The client receiving the merchandise is responsible for paying the tax. This issue should be reviewed with your accountant according to the specific project or installation.

CHARGING METHODS THAT IMPROVE PROFITS

If you are not satisfied with your firm's earnings at the year's end, perhaps you should study some techniques to improve your profits.

Reducing Bookkeeping

Additional expenses are an issue that has become very cumbersome. For example, if you quote charges for prints and supplies at cost plus fifteen or twenty percent, this means that all of these items must be documented. This can be very time-consuming and expensive. It is easier to quote costs for supplies for a fixed figure or for ten percent of the fee. This eliminates that extensive bookkeeping process.

Factoring in a Margin for Cost Increases

One year our accountant brought to our attention that the cost of merchandise had increased eleven percent during that year. We had been used to very few increases on the prices of merchandise and had always given our clients a firm quotation on all merchandise they were purchasing from us. We found that we had quoted *below* our normal mark-up procedures while our cost of merchandise and delivery had *increased* eleven percent. This, coupled with some additional increases in our office and overhead expenses, caused us to lose money.

When you buy merchandise you do not pay the listed price, but the price for the item on the day it is shipped to you. This can vary considerably from the amount you originally estimated. You should try to allow a ten percent variance in your estimates. For example, when you expect something to cost $4,600, you should quote $4,600 to $5,200 so that you have some cushion in case there is an increase in price.

DETERMINING THE FEE STRUCTURE

No matter how you estimate your projects, the only way of being accurate is to make a comparison to your own past work. If you don't have a similar project for comparison purposes, then you need to speak with several other designers who have done similar jobs. For comparison, it is a good idea to figure the job several different ways and compare them; for example, per square foot versus hourly rate. This can often pick up an error in your calculations.

Getting Higher Fees

Can you ask for a higher fee? You can if your office is very busy or if you are the leader in your specialty at the time. If you are very busy, it is a good time to raise your fees. Often design firms get high fees and great jobs when they are most busy and don't need the work. This is because people like to follow the person who is successful. If you are successful within a given area it is usually easier to get additional jobs.

Relating to the Client. Some people are just able to ask for higher fees—and know how to get them. The range of fees in the interior design field is extremely broad and many times the fee can depend upon the client and on the designer's presentation. Most clients know what fees are being charged within their particular area. They have a pretty good basis for comparison when you make your proposal.

In order to demand, and get, top fees, you must have a good relationship with your client. The client must feel that the design team understands his or her needs. It is the talented designer who makes clients feel that they are getting exactly what they want who is really successful.

Repackaging Your Services. There are three ways to get to the top of the heap. You can be truly innovative, which is the most difficult way. The second way is to copy someone else at the top of the heap, which is also difficult. The third way is to repackage present types of services and give them a different name. By creating a new category of service, you make the fee scale more flexible; no one knows what the appropriate charge should be. For instance, almost everyone knows what the square-footage prices are for space planning; but for certain types of design-business analysis none have been established. Therefore they can bring in a higher fee.

Showing a Strong Portfolio. Having an excellent portfolio is another method for setting top fees. The value of good photography cannot be underestimated, and I have seen many designers walk away with major projects just because they had good photographs. They did not necessarily have an excellent background for the job, but they were able to present themselves well and to sell the project appropriately.

Also, if you have a specialty and your portfolio represents that specialty adequately, you have a great entrée to quality work within that specialty.

Offering Something Different. The competition is fierce on larger projects, and most people will bid on a square-foot or a percentage basis. If you can plan a presentation that is different from everyone else's, this gives you a better chance for a larger fee.

In his lectures and books, Frank Stasiowski claims that some jobs with the highest profit are those that are the most innovative, the most unusual, ones that other people are not doing. To get the projects that permit innovation, a firm will often have to do a great deal of marketing research. This means that in the beginning, jobs will principally be research-oriented and not necessarily profitable. Then, when the firm develops skill in that unusual specialty, the profits increase. When competition enters the field, the profits start to drop until they reach the competitive bidding or cutthroat stage.

Offering Better Services. By offering a better or more all-encompassing service, firms can get the competitive edge. Some clients are looking for a multidisciplinary firm—a firm that consists of an interior designer, an architect, an engineer, a landscape architect, and other design professionals who work cooperatively to complete the total project. I have found that in these firms the person who brings in a project is usually the one who controls it. At one time, interior designers waited for architects to team with them; today, however, interior designers are trying to be the ones who write the job so they can have control of the project, including the budget.

Many successful design firms are multidisciplinary and are able to take care of all the design needs of the client. They are able to keep the competition out because they have built a strong team structure. It obviously takes a lot of organizational effort to coordinate a team that works well together; it also requires a tremendous amount of support and charisma on the part of the principals.

Having a Good Reputation. A designer's reputation has a great deal to do with the rates that he or she is able to charge. If someone is well known within a specialty or within a certain social circle, he or she will often be able to charge considerably higher fees than a lesser-known designer.

The charisma of the principals of a design firm has a great deal to do with the size of the fee the firm can command. The value of charisma and ease of social interaction cannot be underestimated. Clients want their projects controlled by a person with whom they feel comfortable. If the design principal or the person selling the project has the ability to gain the confidence of the client, it is amazing the quality and types of jobs that can be secured.

Chapter Nine

WORKING WITH SOURCES AND CONTRACTORS

Interior designers coordinate many different products, suppliers, and outside workers in the course of executing a project. The sources we use—the contractors and craftspeople we engage—are our palette. We have to know how to choose and work with these resources.

SELECTING SOURCES

There are many ways of learning which manufacturers want your business. If you become active in your local ASID chapter's Industry Foundation programs, you will meet companies who are interested in doing interior design work. They are often willing to adapt and adjust their products for you. Some firms are too large to do this; they simply want furniture-store business.

Investigating Source Companies

Know your sources and know them well. Before you consider specifying any material for a project, investigate the company from which you intend to purchase. If it is a new account, talk to other designers to find out what they know about the company. Don't use a firm you have not thoroughly investigated.

Choosing Appropriate Products. When a new catalog comes across your desk, examine it. Be sure it is an appropriate line for your work. Is it the type of material that you would use on a job? For example, if a catalog only lists products for inexpensive contract use and your firm designs very exclusive offices, this catalog probably does not deserve to be in your library. If you decide to keep it, you should store it in a section apart from your usual sources. If you are doing residential work, you should probably not keep contract catalogs, which require quantity purchases.

Review each company's line. If it is appropriate to your work, consider some basic ground rules. Do the products meet your quality standard? Are they products that you would be pleased as a designer to recommend? Find out as much as you can about the product quality, either by personally visiting the company's showrooms or factories, or by visiting an installation that uses the company's product. The company's sales representatives can give you a list of places where you can see their products in use. You should also try to discuss the products with other designers.

Learn whether the company can handle special product work. Many production lines are not in a position to change products as a designer requires. If you want something special, you may need to go to a smaller, more flexible company. Investigate your options carefully when considering changing any product or doing any special design work with an existing product. These variations can be not only expensive, but disastrous as well if the companies you use are not set up to do special design work.

Geographic Convenience. Is the product manufactured within a reasonable distance from your studio or jobs? Freight and administration problems can make long-distance deliveries expensive. Products that are available from your geographic area, or an area nearby, help a project move much more smoothly. Interior design firms are increasingly using neighborhood sources, especially for custom projects.

Jobber versus Manufacturer. Is the source a jobber or a manufacturer? A jobber is a wholesaler who buys in job lots from the manufacturer or importer, and sells on a wholesale basis to interior designers. Quite a number of fabric and accessory lines are sold through jobbers. Generally, designers do not buy fabrics directly from the mills because, in most cases, they do not buy in large enough quantities. Many mills will not sell to interior designers unless the order is for very large lots—hundreds or thousands of yards per item. Jobbers generally charge more than manufacturers, but they provide a method of distribution on a smaller basis that meets the interior designer's needs.

Working Arrangements. Once you have decided that a product is suitable, find out who your contact person at the factory will be. You need a person whom you can contact anytime during working hours to answer your questions about the new product. This person should probably not be the company salesperson. Very often, salespeople are hard to reach except in the evenings or on Saturdays. The more familiar you are with production, the easier it will be for you to talk to the factory workers.

Credit Arrangements. Most interior designers prefer to deal with their suppliers on an open account basis. If you have acquired a good credit standing for your company, you should be able to establish open accounts. It is important to establish your credit at the beginning of a relationship. If you wait until you place an order, it could delay delivery.

Making Sales Reps' Visits Worthwhile

Can designers profit from sales representatives' calls? If you learn to use the time you spend with salespeople properly, they can become a valuable resource. On the other hand, if you don't plan for their visits, sales reps can waste your time and create chaos in your schedule. There are times when you need certain products and times when you don't.

How can you control the situation?

In my firm, we have instituted a few policies that have helped us and could work for you. First, we look on sales representatives as important contributors to our education about sources and the marketplace. We expect them to have information. If they want to sell us anything, we expect them either to have it or to know where to get it and get back to us with precise information. We do not expect them to give us excuses. In this day of so many liability lawsuits, who can afford to take chances? We have to know we're getting the right product.

Setting Aside Space. Our key to controlling the time spent with sales representatives is never to permit them in our work area. First, they disrupt the work schedule. Second, we see no reason for them to see our projects. These representatives visit many other studios in the community. We do not want them discussing our work, much of which is confidential.

We have several rooms on our lower level where we see sales representatives. We make it convenient for them to come right in the door with their sample cases and set up their display for us to see. As soon as they are set up, they let us know and we all come down and look at the line.

Setting a Schedule. Try to schedule sales rep meetings so they don't interrupt time that is scheduled for clients.

We schedule our sales reps visits either early in the day (from 8:30 to 9:00 A.M.), right before lunch (from 11:30 A.M. to 12:00 noon), or late in the day (from 4:30 to 5:00 P.M.) This keeps interruptions at a minimum. We're not making clients wait for us; we're investing time, not losing money. Generally we can see three or four sales rep in each half-hour period. We've found that almost every major fabric line can be reviewed in less than fifteen minutes, and that salespeople with other products can almost always be seen in three to five minutes. There is absolutely nothing wrong with saying, "I don't have anything major for which I can use your line at this time. Keep our catalog up-to-date and when I do have something, I will call you."

I have found that if you make a point never to keep sales reps waiting more than a few minutes, it helps them to respect your schedule. I'm not saying we don't run late; we do, but we try to have it happen only occasionally.

We pay attention to the reps and try to keep them abreast of what we are doing. If a line isn't appropriate for us, we don't take the literature. There's no point in cluttering library shelves with hospital equipment brochures when a firm only designs offices.

Knowing the Line and the Rep. When we take on a new line we want to know more than just what the brochure says. We want to know who the salesperson is, what his or her background is, and how we can reach him or her. We also want to know the history of the company that produces the line. We want to know which designers have used that line, what they think of it, and how they feel about the company offering the line. We ask the sales rep for the names of three designers whom we can call to discuss the product.

Then, if at all possible, I like to visit the factory so I can understand what is easy for the company to produce and what is difficult. So often, the price of a product depends upon the vendor. One company can turn a product out easily and inexpensively, while another company will find it laborious and difficult—and end up charging us three or four times the price we might have paid. If you can match the right vendors with the right projects, you'll find that you can run far more price-effective projects.

Get to know your sales representatives. Offer them respect, but absolutely demand the same from them. I am very straightforward with our sales representatives. I tell them if I like something or not. This frankness saves me from having to see a product I don't like more than once.

Not all designers can see every line, but you should try to make sure you and your staff see what's exceptional. Our staff tries to meet and review new products at least once or twice a week, usually over lunch. Everyone trades information about new catalogs, products, and what we have learned from any of the sales reps or from material received through the mail.

When we buy, we also try to ensure that we know how to reach the reps or a good liaison at the factory at all times. When a problem occurs, we need to have immediate access to them. We always ask, "If something comes up during the day, evening, or on the weekend, how can we reach you?"

Using Design Centers

Design centers are an increasingly important part of the furniture industry. These building complexes where manufacturers of furniture and furnishings show their products became part of the industry in the late 1960s, initially only in New York, Boston, Philadelphia, Atlanta, Miami, Chicago, Dallas, Houston, San Francisco, and Los Angeles. Many more are in operation today; centers are being built and existing ones are increasing their space.

Some design centers are closed to the public, which means that a consumer cannot enter the building unaccompanied by a designer, an architect, or a letter from a design firm. Others permit the individual showrooms to set their own policies, and still others admit the public. In the latter case, a dual pricing system is in effect: interior designers and architects receive a discount, and consumers pay full price. Where the public is allowed free access to the design centers, the center is said to have an "open showroom" policy, as opposed to a "to the trade only" or "closed showroom" policy. From the advertisements in consumer shelter magazines lately, it seems that even centers with closed showroom policies seek to attract the consumer.

Does an open showroom help or hurt the designer? It depends on your methods of fee structuring. For example, most designers who use design centers work on a straight fee basis or a percentage basis. Their fee structure is protected, so it doesn't matter if their clients see two prices on each furniture hangtag. The designer who is hired on a professional fee basis has no worries about the client having pricing information.

To get the best use from a design center, preshop it to determine exactly what you want to show your clients. Otherwise you can spend weeks taking a client shopping. Letting your client see the merchandise you have specified is a good idea because most people cannot visualize; however, you should prepare your client for your visit to the design center. Explain that the purpose of the visit is to see two or three conference tables for his or her new office building, for example, or that he or she must sit in several chairs to see if they are appropriate for the executive offices. This keeps the client from being overwhelmed by the variety and quantity of other merchandise.

DESIGN CENTERS & TRADE MARTS

Arizona

Arizona Design Center
3600 East University
Phoenix, AZ 85034
(602) 232-0032

California

Canyon Creek Design Center of
   San Diego, Inc.
4010 Morena Boulevard, Suite 214
San Diego, CA 92117
(619) 272-1701 or (619) 483-1741

Design Center South
23811 Aliso Creek Road, #151
Laguna Niguel, CA 92656
(714) 643-2929

The LA Mart
1933 South Broadway
Los Angeles, CA 90007
(213) 749-7911

Pacific Design Center
8687 Melrose Avenue
Los Angeles, CA 90069
(213) 657-0800

The Contract Center at Showplace
   Square
600 Townsend
San Francisco, CA 94103
(415) 431-2321 or (415) 864-8541

Showplace Square Design Center
2 Henry Adams Street
San Francisco, CA 94103
(415) 846-1500

Showplace Square East
Rhode Island at 15th
San Francisco, CA 94103
(415) 864-1500

Showplace Square West
550 Fifteenth Street
San Francisco, CA 94103
(415) 552-7475

Canada

Designers Walk
168 Bedford Road, Suite 303
Toronto, Ontario, M5R 2K9
Canada
(416) 961-8577

Place Bonaventure Merchandise Mart
P.O. Box 1000
Place Bonaventure
Montreal, Quebec, H5A 1G1
Canada
(514) 397-2214

The Toronto Design Centre
160 Pears Avenue
Toronto, Ontario, M5R 1T2
Canada
(416) 928-0621

Colorado

Denver Design Center
595 South Broadway
Denver, CO 80209
(303) 733-2455

Denver Merchandise Mart
451 E. 58th Street
Denver, CO 80202
(303) 292-6278

Design Center at the Ice House
1801 Wynkoop Street
Denver, CO 80202
(303) 298-9191

Florida

DCOTA (Design Center of the Americas)
1855 Griffin Road at I-95
Dania, FL 33004
(305) 920-7997

Miami International Merchandise Mart
777 N.W. 72nd Avenue
Miami, FL 33126
(305) 261-2900

Georgia

Atlanta Decorative Arts Center (ADAC)
351 Peachtree Hills Avenue
Atlanta, GA 30305
(414) 231-1720

Atlanta Merchandise Mart
240 Peachtree Street, N.W.
Atlanta, GA 30043
(404) 220-3000

Piedmont Center
10 Piedmont Center, Suite 300
Atlanta, GA 30305
(404) 841-3667

Illinois

The Merchandise Mart
Merchandise Mart Plaza
Chicago, IL 60654
(312) 527-7550

Massachusetts

Boston Design Center
One Design Center Place
Suite 337
Boston, MA 02210
(617) 338-5062

Michigan

Michigan Design Center
1700 Stutz Drive
Troy, MI 48084
(313) 649-4772

Minnesota

International Market Square
275 Market Street
Minneapolis, MN 55405
(612) 338-6250

Missouri

St. Louis Design Center
917 Locust
St. Louis, MO 63101
(314) 621-6446

New York

Architects & Designers Building
150 East 58th Street
New York, NY 10155
(212) 644-6555

Decoration & Design Building
979 Third Avenue
New York, NY 10022
(212) 759-2964

Decorative Arts Center
305 East 63rd Street
New York, NY 10021
(212) 838-7736

The Fine Arts Building
232 East 59th Street
New York, NY 10022
(212) 759-6935

Interior Design Building
306 East 61st Street
New York, NY 10021
(212) 838-7042

International Design Center, N.Y.
  (IDCNY)
29-10 Thomson Avenue
Long Island City, NY 11181
(718) 937-7474

Manhattan Art & Antiques Center
1050 Second Avenue at 56th Street
New York, NY 10022
(212) 355-4400

The New York Gift Building
225 Fifth Avenue
New York, NY 10010
(212) 685-6377

New York Design Center
200 Lexington Avenue
New York, NY 10016
(212) 679-9500

North Carolina

Hamilton Wrenn Community of
  Showrooms
200 North Hamilton Street
High Point, NC 27260
(919) 884-0075

Market Square
305 West High Street
High Point, NC 27260
(919) 889-4464

International Furniture Market Center
210 East Commerce Street
P.O. Box 828
High Point, NC 27261
(919) 889-6144

Ohio

Ohio Design Center
23533 Mercantile Road
Beachwood, OH 44122
(216) 831-1245

Pendleton Square Design Center
1118 Pendleton Square
Cincinnati, OH 45210
(513) 621-7619

Oregon

Design Center at Montgomery Park
2701 N.W. Vaughn Street
Portland, OR 97210
(503) 228-7275

Pennsylvania

The Marketplace
2400 Market Street
Philadelphia, PA 19103
(215) 561-5000

Texas

Dallas Design Center
1025 North Stemmons Freeway
Dallas, TX 75207
(214) 747-2411

Dallas Market Center
2100 Stemmons Freeway
Dallas, TX 75207
(214) 655-6100

Design District (including Dallas
   Decorative Center)
1400 Turtle Creek Blvd.
Dallas, TX 75207
(214) 744-4245

Oak Lawn Design Plaza
1444 Oak Lawn Avenue
Dallas, TX 75207
(214) 689-4222

Decorative Center of Houston
5120 Woodway Drive
Houston, TX 77056
(713) 961-9292

The Resource Center
7026 Old Katy Road, Suite 301
Houston, TX 77024
(713) 861-2114

Utah

Showplace Square
522 South 400 West
Salt Lake City, UT 84101
(801) 355-0519

Washington, D.C.

The Washington Design Center
300 D Street S.W.
Washington, DC 20024
(202) 554-5053

Washington State

Design Center Northwest
5701 Sixth Avenue South
Seattle, WA 98108
(206) 762-1200

Lenora Square Professional
   Design Showrooms
1000 Lenora
Seattle, WA 98121
(206) 621-7500

Seattle Trade Center
2601 Elliott Avenue
Seattle, WA 98121
(206) 441-3000

The 6100 Building
6100 Fourth Avenue South
Seattle, WA 98108
(206) 767-6800

Keeping a Research Sheet

When researching the possible suppliers for a client's project, you can sometimes go through eight or ten catalogs. If the subject and goal are not defined, it's easy to get off track. One way to handle this is to keep a research sheet listing the client's name, the date on which the project was assigned, the date by which you need the information, and the person to whom the research is assigned (see page 221).

Define the subject or the product. Perhaps it is a secretarial desk no longer than sixty inches or a table that must be viewed from a specific angle. Perhaps it is chairs with casters.

State your goals; list the price range, materials, or type of design you need. List the contacts you have made. Document all the companies you have researched, whether by telephone or showroom visit. If a suitable product is located, list the price range. Also state the dates on which phone calls were made and the time they took. At the bottom of the sheet, give the final decision. If at a later date either you or another person picks up this sheet, this research is documented and the results are clearly marked.

Research sheets should be kept in the client's file until the product is ready for processing. You can refer to them to refresh your memory on a project or if you

Research sheet. In researching information that is required for clients, document all the companies you have reviewed, whether by catalog, telephone, or showroom visit. If at a later date either you or another person picks up the file, this research is documented and the result is clearly indicated.

RESEARCH SHEET			
Client:	Date Assigned:	Due Date:	Staff Person:

Subject:

Goal:

Contacts:	Results:	Date/Time:

Final Decision:

© Design Business Monthly

need to change something in the project. For example, if a client's price range changes, you can look at this sheet and quickly see, for example, that a particular sofa you had wanted is going to be too expensive, and that one of the sofas you had originally rejected may be a good choice instead.

Keeping Up-to-Date with Your Sources

Review your sources at least once a year. Fewer than ten years ago, the D & D Building in New York had a completely different makeup. Today, half of the sources there have changed, moved, or gone out of business because it became uneconomical to produce certain merchandise.

WORKING WITH YOUR SUPPLIERS

Make each firm you deal with your ally, not just on exceptionally large projects, but on every project.

When a project has specific needs, enlist your resource company to help find solutions. Define the problem, the type of client, and the probable maintenance as well as the budget and design requirements. With this rundown, the resource company and you can usually come up with a product recommendation to work for the specific situation.

Some firms have laboratories and testing equipment that can help you analyze functional problems or do chemical analyses. Your resource companies' knowledge is an asset, something you could not supply within your own studio, and something that helps make your presentations professional and your designs long-lasting.

Quality Control

Interior designers can be leaders in quality control. We know what clients want. We generally are very good judges of quality. We have researched the product, we know who makes similar products, and we know what the product price should be. We are in a great position of control. It is part of an interior designer's job to monitor quality. First of all, you need to report all problems, even if your clients have not complained. If you see something that is wrong with a product, report to the company that supplies it. Let them know that you are sensitive to quality.

Second, if you receive something that needs a simple repair, you should take care of it so that you don't have to return it. Let companies know that you are willing to make small repairs and touch-ups as required. However, also notify companies when you have had to make repairs and alert them to the situation.

One of the best ways of maintaining your clients is to demand good quality products from your resources. Quality is a commodity. Many excellent designs still use products from top-quality sources, but these can be costly. On occasion, budget compels designers to use mass-market products which discriminating

---

At times, every interior designer has been caught with expensive repair bills for mass-produced furniture. Try to build a safety cushion into each project where you use mass-market products. We had one project where we needed twelve reproduction chairs. One source offered the chairs at $2,100 each, and a source from the mass market had them in the $800 to $900 range. We quoted the client a price for the mass-market chairs, but we added about twenty percent to their actual price to cover any adjustments or refinements that might need to be done when the chairs reached our studio. Quoting the client a variable price—the chairs will cost from $880 to $990—gave us enough leeway within our budget to pay for any necessary repairs. The client has an excellent quality product and never was aware that the product had any shortcomings.

clients will sometimes refuse to accept with even the slightest imperfection. If you must use mass-market products, make a point of having someone from your firm look over these pieces, checking the finish, the upholstery details, and the overall quality. Many times the piece needs work before you can deliver it to your client.

Clients have no idea what happens behind the scenes, and if a job is to run smoothly, they shouldn't have any idea.

Maintenance Programs. Have your sources provide maintenance suggestions. This information is available from the companies supplying the products you purchase. Since factory guarantees are based on maintenance procedures, review these procedures with your resource companies. Find out in advance how the manufacturer wants problems handled and then make appropriate recommendations to your client.

Government Regulations. The government has put a lot of new regulations on the products interior designers handle. Your best source of regulation information is your suppliers. They are required to provide you with flameproofing certificates and other necessary papers to meet state requirements. You, as the designer, are responsible for every product you specify, so be sure to keep abreast of state and federal regulations.

Confidential Work. If your work is confidential, mark it so and explain to the shop from the beginning the reason for this confidentiality so that all of the workers will understand the situation. (See also page 264).

Getting the Best-Quality Performance from Your Suppliers. Interior designers rely heavily on the performance of their craftspeople and suppliers to assure the overall quality of a job. There are ways of improving the quality of this performance. Here are a few methods that have worked for some designers.

1. When you are designing a new project that you expect a shop to build, review the design with the shop before presenting it for pricing or to the client. Let the shop see if there are any ways of improving the design, reducing the cost, or upgrading the quality of the product.

2. As you review the project with the craftspeople, determine what their capabilities are and if there are any areas with which they have difficulty. Is there another resource that you could use for that part of the job? Giving a project to a supplier who is uncomfortable with it only delays the project and can cause problems in the quality of production. Talk it over together carefully. Maybe it would be better to take this project someplace else and bring this shop another project that is more suited to its equipment and abilities. So often, problems in design work are due to the fact that the shops are not appropriately tuned for the work to be done. I have found that giving a woodworking project to a company that specializes in laminates is usually a disaster because that company doesn't want to handle woodworking any longer. Giving a laminate job to someone who is a master woodworker is probably equally foolhardy. Find out what each shop does best and use them for that. Before a shop starts working on a product, make sure that everything is in good condition. Check all of the components that go into the product with the shop that is going to work on it. If there are problems with some aspect, help solve the problems before production begins.

3. Use as few suppliers as you possibly can, and yet still attempt to produce a good job. Giving suppliers priority and letting them know that you are really interested in using them and supporting them is an excellent way of having people perform at a high level for you. If they do a good job for you, reward them. If they do an excellent job for you, show them some form of appreciation: Pay them a little extra money or send them an arrangement of flowers

or a little present. It's amazing what a small gift, especially with a written note, will do to improve the quality of that next job. When you thank your suppliers, send them a letter they will appreciate, one that they can proudly display on their bulletin board.

If you find sources that are not up to standard, replace them. Unfortunately, shops and sources do change for many reasons. Don't put up with a bad situation, look for a new source. There are many more out there.

Attending Markets. When you go to markets, make sure that you meet the people from the factory. Ask them about their products. Try the products. Let them tell you what the strengths and weaknesses are of the individual items; where they should be used, where they should not be used; what the problems and limitations are. These factory people are very good at explaining just how these items should be treated. Often quality is jeopardized by misuse. Everything that you put into a project that doesn't work, or presents a problem, reflects directly on your services.

Visiting Factories. One of the best learning experiences designers can have is to visit the factory of a resource that is important to them. This not only supplies information, but also builds rapport. Here are a few guidelines that can help you get the most from your visit.

▶ Before you go, review the company's catalog and any of its products you have used before. Make sure that you have a general outline of just what your past interests and uses were.

▶ Make a list of questions that you have on various products. Arriving with this list can help you make this trip much more productive. It will let the company know that you are knowledgeable about the product, and you will leave with your questions answered.

▶ Ask to go through the production line to see just how the work is processed. Try to see all of the components that go into the product. This will help you to better explain the product to contractors and clients.

▶ Talk to the people doing the production scheduling, so you can better understand their methods.

▶ Discuss with the factory personnel any documentation you could provide that would be particularly helpful, such as information that they would need for processing special orders.

▶ Review with the factory whether it is willing to do special orders. Find out just what is practical and impractical for them.

▶ Meet the people in the factories. Find out which people are your best contacts. Then, when you call on the phone for your next request (keeping your outline of who you talked to about what functions at hand), you can ask for the right person for the situation and save yourself a lot of time and aggravation. Say hello to workers you may be speaking with later, so that when you call, they will remember you. Building this rapport is immeasurably valuable.

▶ Follow up your visit with a thank-you letter to make sure that the people at the factory will remember that you appreciated their hospitality.

What Suppliers Want

From a source viewpoint, here are some suggested ways to improve communication between designers and sources.

1. Do not duplicate orders by placing them twice. If you do call in an order and follow it up with a written order, be sure that the written order is

clearly marked "Confirming previously called-in order." Suppliers handle hundreds of orders per day and cannot be responsible for identifying identical orders coming to them via two methods of communication. Likewise, if you have mailed in an order and later decide to also call it in, make clear to your source that the order you are calling in is also coming by mail.

2. When ordering, provide complete identification or full specifications. Omissions or abbreviations may lead to misunderstandings about what you want.

3. When inquiring about an order that you have already placed, always mention what products the order called for, rather than just giving an order number. It helps to expedite the order in the event that the original order was never received by the supplier.

4. It is wise to add from five to ten percent to your selling price as protection against possible price increases. Most suppliers bill at the price prevailing at the time of shipment if their products are selling and their inventory is turning over quickly. If you are ordering a substantial quantity of a product it is important to get a firm quotation from the source.

5. When requesting a fabric sample of present stock a supplier is carrying, advise as to the yardage that may be needed. Without knowing what your requirements may be, the source cannot promise that the same stock will be available when a definite order is received. However, most sources will reserve specific yardage for a reasonable length of time if they know what your requirements might be.

6. When attempting to match fabric to paint, or vice versa, always obtain the fabric before painting. A small cutting from present stock can be deceiving. In a larger piece, the intensity of color may look entirely different. The safe practice is to actually have the fabric yardage needed on hand and work from that in determining the paint color.

7. When ordering fabrics for draperies, indicate the size and number of cut lengths needed. For many reasons, suppliers cannot always ship a specific requirement completely free of defects in one length. However, if the source has the details of your requirements, it is often possible for him or her to expedite the shipment.

8. When you need to match a fabric, submit a cutting. Even though you may be ordering a small amount of yardage to supplement a recent shipment, the supplier may not be able to furnish this yardage from the same piece or dye lot as the first shipment. A few suppliers, usually those with smaller lines, may keep a cutting to show what was shipped in the first instance; but most firms do not keep such records.

9. When using a reversible fabric for C.O.M. orders, carefully instruct the manufacturer or fabricator as to which is the face side. It is commonly assumed that the face side is the side that is rolled or folded to the inside. This is not always the case.

10. When suppliers drop ship to a destination other than your studio address, most of them attach a cutting to the invoice that comes to you to show what has been shipped. You are responsible for checking that cutting for accuracy. Do it promptly, before any fabrication can be started.

11. Identify C.O.M. goods sent to a processor. Write to your processor to tell him or her what to expect, from whom the goods are coming, what processing is to be done, and to whom the goods should be shipped when completed. You would be surprised how many times C.O.M. goods sent to a

workroom for quilting, flameproofing, or fabrication sit for days because no one has bothered to say what is to be done with them.

12. When a certificate of flameproofing is required for fabric, request the certificate at the time the fabric order is placed. The detail is then carried out much more smoothly than when the certificate is requested weeks or months later, at which time it is, in fact, sometimes difficult to get.

13. When requesting memo samples by phone, give as much information as possible including a broad description and the ultimate end use. This helps the person selecting the samples to give you the most satisfactory response.

14. When making a remittance, list the invoices being paid. This helps to maintain a mutual understanding of an account. Some suppliers furnish invoices in duplicate; one copy can be returned with your remittance.

15. If there is cause for merchandise to be returned, advise your supplier as to why you are making the return and make the return promptly. It will avoid irritation, confusion, and possible further inconvenience to you.

16. Keep the lines of communication open with your suppliers' credit departments. If you are unable to pay within their terms, notify them. Don't neglect to do this. Credit managers are generally very reasonable people who are anxious to help you in every way they can. Keeping them informed of your situation and intentions is the best way to gain their cooperation.

BUYING METHODS

Today, whom you buy from and how you buy is more involved and more complex than ever. Many companies sell directly to interior designers. Other companies sell only through dealerships or have minimum requirements (usually an annual dollar volume) or the lines are not available. Some of these amounts are substantial yearly expenditures. This, in effect, limits the range of products that can be used.

Since designers like to use different products on each project so that every job does not look alike, it is important to establish buying methods for a project before you actually do the design. The purchasing method needs to be incorporated into the design process.

How can we be sure the client can secure merchandise within the appropriate price range? Only through research. Every project has a different budget and different social and logistic issues. Location affects the availability of products. In a large city, a designer has ready access to a whole variety of products; but a project in a very small community may limit the designer to purchasing paint in gallon cans.

When designing a project, review the purchasing circumstances and consider this part of the budget. Determine which is the most appropriate way for your client to complete the project, and then recommend this method to your client.

Today the way you purchase may strongly affect the quality of your design and the profits on that project. In many instances, designers do all the work and handle all the problems and complaints. The person who acts as purchasing agent only writes up the orders and processes the paper. He or she probably spends one-tenth or less time doing the project as the designer does, doesn't have the client complaints, and is paid three, four, and sometimes ten times as much as the design firm. This needs to be better balanced. It's up to us, as designers, to group together and find methods of establishing equity.

Consider the different possibilities. First of all, if your firm can purchase the merchandise, that puts the firm in the business of merchandising. Your design firm may not be organized for this. In that case, it is better to let someone else do the purchasing, someone who is willing to exert the extra management efforts and to take on any risks involved.

In-house purchasing requires a purchasing division with good expediting policies. The way this is handled can add profits or can bankrupt the firm.

Co-op and Buying Services

Today many designers buy as a co-op, forming organizations to buy together. The volume of purchases gives them access to more varied product choices and gives them the clout to demand and get appropriate quality.

A designer can also use an outside buying service firm to expedite purchasing. Choose the firm just as carefully as you do your clients and sources. Will this company give you the items you specify? Will they notify you if any changes are needed? It should be the designer's decision to make the change, not the purchasing company's.

Methods of handling the project can either enhance or hurt a design. When designers turn projects over to dealerships or expediting companies, some of these later become competitors of the designer and end up taking over the client. The designer never sees the client again. Does the purchasing company have a record of this? Can you trust the head of the firm?

STRENGTHS OF CO-OP AND BUYING SERVICES

A co-op or buying service can:

- Provide better management. Designers are free to design while someone else handles the expediting.

- Reduce the cost of running a small independent studio.

- Give small studios more buying power.

- Give firms better prices and better quality control.

- Give small studios access to more lines.

- Educate designers about quality of products by sharing information.

- Give small firms a better chance to compete with large firms.

- Save time. Jobs can be processed faster because the large volume permits management to use the latest equipment.

- Present fewer problems, as orders are checked and reviewed by another person—one familiar with companies and their ordering procedures.

- Make quicker substitutions. When the desired product is unavailable, the service can suggest suitable alternatives.

Traditional Buying Methods

Interior designers have three traditional ways of buying: through showrooms, from a dealer, and directly from the manufacturer.

Showroom. The showroom fees are included in the prices. For those fees, the designer gets a large variety in furniture and furnishings; but there are some well-known disadvantages. Often, these designer showrooms are run or staffed by former designers who no longer want to deal directly with clients.

As a result, some orders are not relayed to the manufacturers as quickly as they might be and the follow-up is not done on a regular basis. I have found that if you don't badger these people, you hear nothing from them, and there are often great delays in delivery.

A designer who had just opened her own firm told me an all-too-common tale of woe. She had gone into business for herself because she lived in a small community where there was little opportunity for her to test the waters by working for someone else. Within her first month in business, she believed she had been a victim of fraud. A salesman in a showroom had taken her order for a sofa and her $1,200 deposit, but there had been no action. She found out eight months later that he had never ordered the sofa.

Dealer. The second way we buy is through another firm, or another distributor. Sometimes this works and sometimes it doesn't. Because it's an out-of-house account, the follow-through on details isn't always as good as it might be. The arrangement might also be in competition with another dealer in town.

Direct. Finally, we can try to establish individual accounts with manufacturers. This is expensive, time-consuming, and frustrating. You're never really sure you're getting the best price, and each time you use a new vendor, you must spend a lot of time establishing the account. This time could be better spent selling or designing other projects. While the effort is cumulative, the results are not. Even though we spend hours establishing credit each year, we still have to reestablish credit when we start new ventures.

Volume Buying Service: A Proposal for Profitability

Most of us don't have access to all the right lines at the right prices. Many of the lines that we would like to use are only available to dealerships. Others are only available in quantity. We can't buy enough per year to maintain all of the lines, nor do we want to stock the inventory required to do this. Interior designers, unlike furniture dealers, don't want to have every job look alike; therefore, we need many resources or manufacturers.

Each new resource requires us to establish an account for proper pricing and account position. All of this takes time, and many interior designers can't afford the time—or expense—required to run a top-notch purchasing division, as well as to sell jobs. It is unusual for design firms to have an official purchasing agent who handles only these negotiations and who makes sure the firm is buying the right items at the right price. In my own small firm, running a purchasing division costs over $60,000 per year. We know the status of our orders on a weekly basis, and we can negotiate for pricing—but it is quite expensive to do this.

Let's face it; most of us are designers because we enjoy designing and want to design, not to chase papers. We need a streamlined method of dealing with manufacturers—one that will give us access to a diversity in sources without drowning us in credit references and negotiations.

Manufacturers find it very costly to service small accounts. Their sales staff find it unprofitable: credit checks, individual billings, and establishing accounts are all expensive. They often must wait long periods for payment. When they deal with larger firms, dealerships, or showrooms, they are assured of a certain dollar volume and know the payment habits of the account.

The Proposal. What if each designer had one main account? An account for which he or she needed one credit reference and through which he or she could purchase anything that was needed? What if thousands of interior designers established a buying umbrella with manufacturers selected for quality products, at a wide range of prices?

In this ideal situation, the buying umbrella/purchasing firm and the vendors would have cooperative contracts requiring the vendors to send the participating designers first-quality merchandise, to keep them informed on the status of an order, and to agree to adjust and handle problems that occur. Designers would receive regular follow-up reports so that they could keep their clients well informed.

The vendor would have the advantage of dealing with a single purchasing department and maintaining contact with a single individual rather than be harassed by several thousand calls. And there would be only one credit check to be done—the one on the purchasing firm itself. All orders would be shipped directly to the designers or to the designers' receiving warehouses.

I believe that purchasing as we know it is like a dinosaur—its years are numbered. As professional designers we need to be professional business people as we relate to vendors. And I believe we are trained to design, not to track orders. Designers need to band together to make our jobs easier.

Purchase Orders

How precise is your purchase order? Today we can be sued for almost anything, so it is advisable to review your purchase orders and to include on them statements that offer protection from common problems. Freight claims are a time-consuming issue in any office. If a purchase order states that the design firm is responsible for the merchandise *only* after it is received and inspected in the firm's studio, this means that any freight claim is the responsibility of the shipper or resource. This simple declaration on your purchase order can save you a tremendous amount of time and aggravation. I reviewed a large number of purchase orders with several consulting attorneys, and we found that very large firms and firms with high profits have extensive documentation on their purchase orders. Some have qualifying statements of seven pages or more. Is this appropriate or needed? These are big-name firms, and product resources are delighted to service them. I doubt whether small design firms could get away with this amount of disclaimers, but some are in order. As a field, we need to join together and establish appropriate purchasing standards. By working with our resources on this, we can help them realize that designers—their repeat customers—need to be protected. In so many instances the interior designer is the one left holding the bag.

Are your purchase orders easy to understand? Review purchase-order procedures, either with another design firm or with some of your sources. Remember in writing your orders that you are not dealing with another designer, but with a contractor or manufacturer who may not be familiar with your vocabulary. It is easy to say that a firm that wants your business should learn your language, but you must also recognize that the talents that go into production scheduling and manufacturing are not the same talents interior designers must have. Try to find out what your suppliers need to know from you in order to give you what you want.

Learn to be very careful, to recheck to see that everything is properly side-marked and identified. In our firm, purchase order numbers relate to our individual order numbers and our in-house communications, and are as simple as we can make them. We also have a required follow-up procedure. If we have not heard from a company within ten days with a acknowledgment or some comment, we either call or write to the company again. No purchase order simply lies in the files waiting for something to happen. Although we have a set day each week to review purchase orders, every problem regarding those orders is handled on the day it is received.

Purchase orders for certain specialties require different conditions or products and therefore more extensive documentation.

When designing your purchase orders be sure they include the following information; the style and layout may vary according to your system. Most firms require three copies: one for the company from which merchandise is being purchased; one for you, merchandise-on-order file (this may not be needed if your purchasing documents are computerized; and one for your clients file.

The following are the suggested details, terms, and conditions that should be listed on a purchase order from a general design firm.

1. The name of the firm responsible for the purchasing documents. This should include your name, address, and telephone number.

2. Any special information, such as the name of a reference person with whom the supplier should speak with if there are any questions.

3. Your purchase order number. Ask that this number appear on all packages shipped for this order and on all statements and/or correspondence.

4. If there are any special shipping instructions regarding your warehouse (time of receipt, particular location, or directions), these need to be noted.

5. The vendor's listing: the name, address, and any special details of the vendor. Also note if the item should be addressed to anyone's attention.

6. The shipping and billing addresses.

7. The date of the order.

8. The person placing the order and the person responsible for ordering.

9. Any particular payment information and special terms.

10. The direction for the freight bill; whether it is to be prepaid or if freight is to be charged to the bill.

11. The quantity, unit, and description; the unit and total price. It is advisable to provide clear definitions of all details of items. Usually a bit of extra information is far better than too little.

12. If you have standards or other requirements, they should be documented on the back of your purchase order. When you put statements on the back of your purchase order, you should mark clearly on the front of the order that the supplier should refer to the back for performance information regarding the purchase order.

13. All purchase orders should be signed by your purchase agent or other person responsible for approving the order.

Terms and conditions should be clearly printed on the purchase order copy that is sent to the vendor so they will not be missed. If you are printing terms on the back of the form or on other sheets, make sure to provide a clear reference. Review the list of terms and conditions on pages 231–233 to determine which are the most important to your practice. A larger firm will have no problem using all these terms because they have buying clout; smaller firms may be forced to modify their terms. If we all work together, we could make them a standard of the field.

These terms were written by an attorney; before you have your purchase orders printed, have your attorney review the items you find suitable. He will explain their meaning and assist you in determining their value in your practice.

Terms and conditions. Review this list before you have your purchase orders printed to determine which terms and conditions are the most important to your practice.

TERMS AND CONDITIONS

1. This order expressly limits acceptance to the terms stated herein. Any addition or different terms proposed by the Seller (this term is intended to include providers of services) are objected to and hereby rejected, notwithstanding any terms and conditions that may be contained in any acknowledgement, invoice, or other form of Seller, notwithstanding Buyer accepting or paying for any shipment or similar act of Buyer. Shipment of any goods or performance of any services ordered hereunder shall be considered an acceptance of this entire order, including all terms and conditions specified herein.

2. Time and shipping instructions are each of the essence to this contract.

3. It is understood that the cash discount period will date from the receipt of the goods or from the date of the invoice, whichever is later.

4. All goods shall be received subject to Buyer's right of inspection and rejection. Defective goods, or goods not in accordance with Buyer's specifications, will be held for Seller's instructions at Seller's risk and if Seller so directs will be returned at Seller's expense. If inspection discloses that part of the goods received are not in accordance with Buyer's specifications, Buyer shall have the right to cancel any unshipped portion of the order. The Buyer may reject and return at Seller's expense deliveries which exceed or substantially fail to meet the quantity ordered, or deliveries made more than fifteen (15) days in advance of the date required. Our time to inspect the goods and give appropriate notices under the Uniform Commercial Code is hereby extended by sixty (60) days.

5. In addition to any warranty implied in fact or law, Seller expressly warrants all items to be free from defects in design, workmanship, and materials, to conform strictly to applicable specifications, drawings, and approved samples, if any, and to be fit and sufficient for the purpose intended, and to be merchantable. Such warranties, together with all other service warranties of Seller, shall run to Buyer, its successors, assigns, and customers. All warranties shall survive delivery to, inspection, test, acceptance, and payment by Buyer.

6. In the event of breach of this agreement, in addition to the remedies provided by the Uniform Commercial Code, Buyer may either alternatively or cumulatively:
    (a) Return all nonconforming merchandise at Seller's expense for repair or replacement at Buyer's option;
    (b) Repair all nonconforming merchandise at Seller's expense;
    (c) Cover and receive payment therefor at the time Buyer finally learns that Seller will not satisfactorily cure the nonconforming tender;
    (d) Return for credit;
    (e) Terminate this agreement and accordingly reject all further deliveries of goods.

7. No limits may be placed on damages resulting from Seller's breach of this agreement, other than as specified and accepted in writing by us.

8. Seller agrees to indemnify and hold Buyer harmless against any claims or suits arising in connection with the items purchased hereunder for defects in material or workmanship, and for infringement of patent, trademark, or copyright, or other intellectual property rights. Seller will pay, including without limitation, the claim, settlement or judgment, court costs, counsel fees and expenses, and interest; and will refund the price of the goods if Buyer is enjoined from using the same. Buyer shall notify Seller promptly of the initiation of any suit or proceeding, and Buyer may defend or otherwise deal with such matters, if Seller fails to do so after notice, with all costs ultimately paid by Seller.

9. The signature of our receiving clerk is for count of original packages only, and not for correct weight or count, quantity, or condition of contents. Net delivered weight, count, and actual fare shall govern settlement.

10. This purchase order is not valid unless signed by Buyer's authorized representative.

11. Seller agrees to return all physical and intellectual property (whether or not secret or confidential) furnished to him by Buyer or its agents in connection with the execution and billing of this order, and Seller further agrees not to disclose or use such property for the benefit of anyone else. All plans, drawings, specifications, memoranda, or other similar documents prepared by the Buyer, its employees, or its agents, shall be the sole and exclusive property of Buyer, and shall be delivered to Buyer at Buyer's request at any time.

12. If Buyer terminates or breaches this agreement for any reason at any time, Seller must submit an itemized list of all claims within fourteen (14) days.

13. No single or repeated waiver of any default for any period of time shall be construed as a continuing waiver by Buyer, and Buyer's right of termination under this agreement shall remain enforceable at any time any default may exist, no matter how long or how many times that default may have existed.

14. This agreement shall be binding upon and inure to the benefit of the parties hereto, and their respective successors, assigns, heirs, and legal representatives, provided that Seller shall not assign rights arising, nor delegate performance required herein, except to a successor in ownership of substantially the whole of its business.

15. This instrument contains the entire agreement between the parties hereto with respect to the transactions contemplated herein, and may be modified only by a duly executed purchase order change form signed by our authorized representative.

16. This contract shall be interpreted according to the laws of the Commonwealth of Pennsylvania.

17. Seller agrees to provide and maintain comprehensive general liability insurance, including products liability coverage, in an amount not less than $500,000.00 per occurrence for bodily injury or property damage. In addition, Seller shall provide errors and omissions coverage, when applicable, covering contractor's professional liability for any services and/or goods provided for herein with limits of liability which shall not be less than a combined single limit of $500,000.00. Such insurance will apply to all goods supplied under this order. Seller shall furnish Buyer with a certificate of insurance evidencing such coverage prior to shipment of goods. The certificate will provide that ten (10) days prior written notice of cancelation be furnished to Buyer at address listed on this order.

18. Seller shall pay all taxes imposed by the federal or any state or local government on payrolls or compensation of its employees, or any other taxes, fees, or charges on account of this order, the sale of the goods, or the performance of the services.

19. No partial invalidity of this order shall affect the remainder hereof.

20. The price stated in this purchase order shall include the freight costs, unless otherwise stated, however shipment is f.o.b. _____ for delivery to job or to the nearest rail or truck terminal. Title of the goods shall pass from the shipper to the Buyer on receipt by Buyer, or its authorized representatives, subject to any defects or nonconformance as stated above. Buyer shall not be liable for any loss, damage, detention, or delay caused by freight damages, shortages, defective or incorrect material, or by circumstances beyond their control.

21. Buyer does not intend to be bound to Seller based upon any contract which Seller may have with another party. This purchase order is given in good faith for the materials listed on the reverse side, which must be acceptable to Buyer.

WORKING WITH YOUR CONTRACTORS

As designers, we do a lot of work with contractors on projects ranging from the very small ones to costing over a million dollars. In some instances, consulting architects and engineers work with us. By supervising the installation to make jobs run more smoothly, you become a valuable asset to your clients, craftspeople, architects, and engineers.

Finding the Right Contractor

We build our team of contractors through much experience. Often, we lose a contractor because he or she moves away, changes careers, or retires. Finding a new contractor can be one of the most difficult things we do. It's a good idea to talk to the contractor you are losing or to other craftspeople on projects; you can get suggestions from them for other contractors. Someone who does cabinetry will recognize good carpentry. Or a painter will know where he has seen a really clean, well-crafted job.

When you interview a contractor, be sure to take the time to see some of his or her work. Often, contractors will show you photographs, but these often tell very little. Ask any contractor you are seriously considering where you may go to visit one of his or her projects. If he or she is hesitant and does not have ready referrals, think twice about hiring the person.

In smaller communities, contractors are sometimes not familiar with certain new processes and techniques. They will often say, "I can do it!" because they don't fully understand what you have in mind. If you are concerned, you should ask to see a similar project or have them prepare a sample for you before you hire them. You don't want to pay for unqualified contractors to learn on the job.

Designers usually like to be responsible for jobs, and when given the authority, *want* to be responsible. The benefit in hiring a designer is to obtain not only the best quality design but to have it completed with the best quality craftspeople.

In small communities you often must design within the range of what the available craftspeople can handle. You may even have to educate many of them in special techniques to get the results you want, or find components for them that they have never seen before. If all else fails, you may have to bring in someone from out of town. Sometimes you may feel like a teacher, but the time you spend educating your craftspeople will give you a better quality project in the end.

I was raised with the philosophy that you do something right or you don't do it at all. Designers need a great deal of training and exposure to understand all the components of the design craft. The more you understand about the contracting field, the better designs you will be able to create.

Know the size of your contractor's organization, and the type and size of projects he or she handles best—both physically and financially. Giving a small contractor too large of a job, although he or she may really want it, is a mistake. If a contractor doesn't have the ability to perform a job profitably, his or her organization—and your job—will be destroyed.

In my experience with contractors, it is best to give them work they know. A contractor who does good commercial work is usually not likely to understand the requirements of historical restoration. For the restoration of a lovely 150-year-old house, where we knew the client wanted fine quality craftsmanship, we took nine months to find someone appropriate for the project—and that person took a year to complete the project. We had previously done a large, fast-track office-building project for this client. Now we had to make the client understand that the restoration project required a contractor with different abilities and a completely different mindset. We had to explain to the clients that the particular contractor we selected could not be rushed, and that imposing a schedule on him would affect the quality of the project.

When to Use a General Contractor. When should you use a general contractor? It makes sense to use a general contractor on projects that require a number of disciplines that will need management. In situations where the designer must provide every detail of supervision, it is usually easier and simpler to deal directly with the subcontractors.

At my firm we require our contractors to bill us and our clients to pay us. We feel this gives us authority. If we do not handle the money, we assume responsibility for approving all bills and instruct the client not to pay any bill without our approval. Designers often get into difficulties when they are given the responsibility for a job, but not the authority. Without the proper authority a designer cannot maintain the quality control that is so important.

Business Arrangements

It is essential to clarify all legal and financial arrangements with contractors right from the start.

Quotations. Every contractor should understand that you are getting two or three quotations on a job. That keeps them from inflating costs. It is not appropriate to get ten quotations for an average-size job, nor is there time to do so. However, on large projects, you benefit by obtaining as many qualified quotations as possible.

On smaller or medium-size projects, ask contractors to quote within ten percent of their estimated figure. This gives you leeway for adjustments as you get into a project. On highly customized items that a contractor has never done before, it helps him or her to keep estimates more reasonable if he or she knows there is a ten percent play. If you deal with your contractors on a regular basis, and they understand you, you will find that sometimes they use that extra money and sometimes they don't. But everyone feels more comfortable knowing it is there. On special projects clients usually consider estimates within ten percent as reasonable.

Time Schedules. As part of every design, make up a time schedule. Sometimes you develop this with the contractor; other times before meeting the contractor. Coordinate the contractor's schedule and your schedule; your time estimates and his or hers. Then go over the schedule with the client to see how much this work will interfere with his or her personal or business plans. The time factor can affect the cost of a job considerably. With proper preparation, fast-tracking to complete a job in a short period is probably the most economical scheduling in the long run. When you fast-track a job, you can usually afford to have excellent supervision there for several days, which is generally not possible for longer periods.

On every letter, agreement, or contract you send out, include a time schedule. One designer I know writes his schedule on his deposit check alongside the following sentence: "By accepting this deposit, you have agreed to maintain this schedule." When the contractor signs it he or she agrees to meet that schedule. There are many ways of handling this; what is important is that the schedule is in writing and that the contractor understands it is an essential part of your contract.

Written Agreement. Have a written agreement with your contractor (see independent contractors agreement on page 79). Be sure he or she has outlined each and every detail of the project. If anything has been missed on his or her contract, send it back. Be sure he or she acknowledges and initials your drawings and furnishes you with appropriate shop drawings. Our office has an agreement with each and every craftsperson who works for us relating to our standards, our payment procedures, and our insurance and guarantees requirements. For contractors we have used frequently, such as paperhangers and carpenters, we simply get a quotation each time we use them because we keep in our files their statements of conditions.

Financial Arrangements. At our firm, the contractors we use understand our standard structure for financial arrangements. We normally control the money, which means we have a retainer from the client that provides the monies for us to pay the subcontractors as the project progresses. As soon as the project has been approved by our design staff and the client, we see that the contractor is sent his or her check, sometimes within twenty-four hours, sometimes within two or three days. Contractors are very concerned about cash flow these days. We handle this by seeing that they are paid promptly. We will often withhold a certain amount as security until the project is complete, just in case there are any adjustments to be made. When they realize they will have their money when the project is completed and approved, they are more inclined to do the project in a high-quality, timely fashion.

Contractors see that projects are finished to our satisfaction and handle all our complaints because they know that we are going to generate more business for them. If a client pays the contractor directly, the designer loses this control.

Supervision

How much should you supervise a job? This depends on the project and the contractors or craftspeople with whom you are working. If the project is well defined and you know the workers that are assigned to it, then your job may be easy. If this is not the case, you may be required to assign a full-time supervisory person or visit the site several times per day.

It is important to be there to prevent errors, not to require someone to change something that's already been done wrong. There is nothing that destroys the morale of a good craftsperson more than having to redo work to please a client. If changes are required, it is good for you to be there to be sure that the changes are made appropriately and in the least amount of time. Your goal is to have as few change orders as possible on your project.

Don't check a job when it is finished—check it as it goes along. For example, if a plumber has completed his or her work, check to see that the drain is in the appropriate location before the tiling is started. If you wait until the end of the project, you may discover that one of the subcontractors had mismeasured. Check each and every person as the project progresses to control the quality of their work. If an electrical outlet is missing, you want to know it before workers start plastering the wall.

Often it is a good idea to go over your drawings with the electrician or the plumber on the job. You may find that the person who understands the project is away on vacation, and you need to explain the project again to be sure it is properly executed.

Be available. Don't start a project when you won't be around. At my firm we have an understanding with contractors that they may call us anytime. We are readily available from 6:00 A.M. on so they can reach us if they have any problems before starting the project. We also have a policy where, while we will not interrupt a designer to talk to a client or sales rep, we *will* interrupt if a contractor is on a project and has a problem. There are always two or more people in our studio familiar with the project who can answer contractors' questions. We do not want the client paying for lost time on a project, so we make sure we are available to cover any situation at any point.

Ways to Make the Job Easier

To assure that a job is well completed, it is important to have a good relationship with your contractors. There are many facets to the relationship, all of which must be carefully considered.

1. *Perfect your drawings and specifications.* Be sure that your drawings are well done. Include all the fine details that you want to be part of the final project. Your drawings are as much a part of your contract as any other

written form. If you miss a line or misdocument a detail, this is a breach of contract responsibility. If your drawings are clear, your communication with your client and your contractor will be much easier.

Take the time and effort to make your specifications as detailed as possible. Effort spent at this point will pay off later in the project. The contractor will more easily understand the project and will know better how to price it, so you won't have discrepancies throughout the project. Too often, when communication problems occur, it is because the drawings and specifications have not been properly detailed. Before giving your drawings and specifications to your contractors, check to be sure they are easy to understand. Then go over them with the various contractors to be sure that nothing is missing and that they fully understand your format.

2. *Check the availability of all specified items.* Be sure that the items you are selecting are available—and determine from which sources you should order them. Many wonderful products pictured in magazines are either not yet available or are unavailable in your area. Check to be sure you know where a contractor can get an item, and find out the cost. This information will help you to better negotiate the project for your client. If a project involves appliances or similar equipment, investigate who handles repairs and what kind of a maintenance program the client needs. It is much easier to do this research before specifying an item than it is to specify a product that the client cannot have repaired or that will complicate the project.

3. *Be sure your client understands the job to be done.* This is crucial. So often, misunderstandings occur because most clients cannot read blueprints. Take the time to go through the details of a job with the client so that he or she understands what is involved in constructing your design.

Don't create a false impression by downplaying the extent of a project. Forewarn clients about what will be involved, especially on complex projects. Discuss what kind of project it will be, what the time schedule will be, and whether the installation will be dirty. When the installation will be long and involved, suggest when the client should move out of an office space or a residence, or he or she will hate you by the time the project is finished. If a project can be done without major inconvenience to the client, let him or her know which contractors will arrive when. Warn the client about the noise and the hours contractors work. If you surprise a client who sleeps until 9:00 A.M. with a contractor arriving at 5:45 A.M., this can create so many hard feelings that it can harm the project. When clients understand in advance that contractors will begin work at a certain time, they will be prepared—and your likelihood of maintaining a good relationship with your clients will be better.

4. *Be sure all supplies are available before a job starts.* To avoid disrupting time schedules, don't let any contractor begin until you have verified that each item needed for the job is in. At my firm, we send our representative to the suppliers' warehouses to be sure that all the fixtures and items for the job are what we ordered, the correct sizes and the proper quantities. This step helps assure that the job will run smoothly. If you tear up a bathroom or kitchen before your work is ready to begin, hard feelings may develop that can undermine the design project. Often you may have to advance the contractor money to cover the costs of supplies just to be sure that they are there.

5. *Organize permits.* Make permits the responsibility of the contractor and include this in your agreement. In some states the way designers work has been defined as contracting. In our firm we consider ourselves coordinators, not contractors. We use a general contractor who is responsible for liabilities that come under his jurisdiction. All contractors who work for us

must provide us with a certificate of insurance, which we keep in our files, or documentation that they carry insurance for the workers they are using for a project as well as for the client's project itself. Depending upon the situation, we will very often require certain craftspeople to be bonded. These issues must be clarified through our office before we start a project.

6. *Instill pride*. If you know your products and craftspeople and put together the right combination for the job, you will ensure quality control. Problems arise when you inappropriately place contractors on a project they cannot handle. If you choose your contractors properly and create a special pride in projects, you will come up with some of the best quality work you can imagine. Contractors like to work on our projects because they know when they are finished, they will see something they can be proud of.

It is important that your clients and contractors understand the objectives of your project. You may have to take a contractor to other projects you have done so that he or she can understand the quality you want. If you have seen a contractor's projects and he or she has seen yours, standards can be more easily communicated.

7. *Structure communications*. Set a communications structure for your clients and subcontractors. For example, in some projects, especially fast-track ones, you may have to say to your clients, "Please do not talk to the contractors. You may say 'good morning' and that's all. Any communication regarding the project must come through our office. We are on an extremely tight time schedule and it is up to our office to make the decisions if any changes should be considered." There is no way to maintain control of a project if your client makes changes every ten minutes. Make sure that your client understands that the contractor cannot do anything not in the written agreement because he or she is not being paid for it. He is working for you—the designer—and you are responsible for the project.

Instruct the contractor to be sure his or her workers do not discuss the project with the client. There are always problems on a job, and there are ways of solving them if the team works together. There is no point in alarming the client over something you can easily remedy. Once a client feels there are flaws and problems on a project, he or she can lose confidence in you and make the whole project more difficult for everyone. Let the contractor understand that you are always available to discuss the project or any problem, and that he or she should come directly to you.

8. *Delegate responsibility*. Don't let a contractor put the blame on someone else. For example, make sure the painting contractor covers having the carpenter putty holes so they will be ready for painting. If you don't cover these details, the contractor may not remember them. Cover all the fine details and you will save yourself a lot of headaches.

**Chapter
Ten**

MANAGING YOUR OFFICE

Good management involves coordinating your client's goals and those of your design firm and developing a method to reach these goals. Both long-term and short-term issues must be taken into consideration.

MANAGEMENT

In a small firm, one of the principals usually acts as the manager. After a business starts to grow, however, the principals will often hire another person to handle the general management structures so that they can be free to concentrate on marketing or other design issues. Normally, managerial types can be more easily hired than designers or marketing specialists. For this reason, interior designers usually hire managers quite early in setting up their firms.

The day-to-day office management of a small firm may be handled by a secretary with general administrative skills. He or she will handle office procedures such as scheduling, bookkeeping, and other paperwork. As your firm grows larger or expands its line of services, then you will need to establish other management structures. A firm dealing only in professional fees and hourly billings will require less management than a firm that is providing both professional services and selling of products.

The minute a firm starts selling products, the firm requires a total expediting and processing structure for proper management of purchasing and installation processes (see pages 184–85).

The time your firm will devote to managing depends a great deal upon the structure of the firm and its overall objectives. Most design principals try to minimize the time they spend with business administration by hiring someone to handle these processes.

Your accountant and business consultant can help you structure the firm's management format; however, this format may vary, depending on the individual manager hired and his or her education and background. Before hiring a manager, you should outline exactly what his or her management responsibilities will be. Good management is a requirement of a successful business.

There is a great deal of difference between a bookkeeper who does repetitive work and a business manager who can develop new methods for structuring the management of the firm. It is necessary to understand this difference before hiring to determine which type of person your firm needs. For example, if you, as the principal, are closely supervising the management of the company, all the firm may require is a good secretary/bookkeeper who can see that the proper documents and forms you need to see are supplied on a regular basis.

When a firm increases in size, it requires a better qualified person. This person should know the difference between profits that are generated from one base versus another base, their cost to acquire, and some of the other components that lead to bottom-line profits.

Every firm needs to have a good financial management program in place. It is important for management to understand just what the resources and the expenses are within a given design firm. For a good understanding of the business, management must be kept current on these financial issues.

How many management or administrative people does a design firm need? Generally, a firm figures that it must have at least five producing/chargeable people to one administrative person. The better the equipment within an office, the fewer administrative people are required, which is why many design firms are using computers with software strongly adapted to the management of the firm. This enables them to reduce their numbers of support staff.

The business manager can be billable in some instances. If your firm is handling project management, supervising installation, or purchasing, under some programs you may be able to charge your clients for your business management division's services. More design firms are adopting this policy; it enables them to have better qualified personnel in these divisions because the people bring in revenue.

The salary for an office or business manager will vary considerably, depending upon whether the principals maintain most of the responsibilities and controls or the business manager is totally responsible for the firm's management. In the latter case, the business manager is usually paid as well as any of the other vice presidents or principals and has perks and advantages similar to the other principals in the firm.

Interior design firms are finding that if they want to grow and really compete in the mass market, they need to have an excellent business management structure. This normally requires management by a professional with an M.B.A. or a business background who is interested in the business management and financial development of the firm. This person also brings to the firm a different viewpoint; the key is to find someone who appreciates the interior design firm's objectives and can assist the firm in creating a blend of good design and good financial management. It is often difficult to find the right person; but when you do, this coordinated effort can prove to be most profitable.

MANAGEMENT TOOLS

There are many different styles of management. Some design firms work in a cooperative team method, others are very autocratic, and others are very patriarchal. Your particular style of work determines the type of people you will attract. Every interior designer should look at what it takes to be an appropriate manager or a leader. Helping develop the other people within your firm usually creates a stronger firm.

If you want to develop a larger firm, find yourself some good consultants who will assist you with the business management aspects. These outside people can review your firm and see just where you are going. Knowing your objectives, they will consider ways you can improve your management structure and style.

Management must be based on customer service. In order for design firms to continually have repeat business, they must provide excellent services. Firms have learned that it costs five times as much to find a new client as it does to keep an old one. Design firms cannot afford to be constantly getting new clients; they must retain their present client base.

The main aim of management today is to give the customer what he or she wants: good service. The interior design field is very competitive; if one firm doesn't service its customers well, there are many other firms out there ready to do it.

Providing Leadership

The management must motivate staff to do quality work, both for their own benefit and that of their clients. If you are the leader, here are some ways this can be done:

1. *You must emphasize to your staff that clients are the firm's most important commodity.* There must be a constant effort to please the client and give him or her the best possible product.

2. *Management must have the support of the staff.* The employees should like and respect their supervisors. To earn this respect, you must be interested in your employees as well as your clients. This is a message you must constantly broadcast and promote within every area of management.

3. *You must give your employees good information.* They need to know the goals of the firm and their roles in reaching these goals. They need to recognize their strengths and their weaknesses—which areas need improvement and which do not. Employees should feel that they are in control, that they understand just what is going on. Ill-informed employees can be very destructive in a firm.

4. *You must adequately compensate your employees.* They must be paid a reasonable amount. Although many surveys report that financial compensation is not nearly as important to interior designers as the opportunity to do excellent work in an appropriate professional setting, these people still need to support themselves—usually with their salary or income from the design firm. In small firms, where everyone usually knows one another's approximate salaries, offering a reasonable degree of shared profits usually promotes a good company attitude.

5. *You must assemble a staff of high-quality individuals.* You should select individuals who know how to handle their given tasks. Also, be sure any new staff shares your firm's attitude towards clients.

6. *You should create a written job description for each staff member.* As a firm changes, so do the duties and responsibilities of its employees. Ask each staff member to write a job description. Compare your description of each job to the employees' descriptions and determine if changes should be made. Perhaps an employee is spending eighty percent of his or her time performing a task that could be handled by another person in the firm. Maybe there are tasks that a person could be performing that would be more valuable to the firm and give the person the opportunity of holding a better position. Most people like to have a written job description. It helps them know whether what they are doing is on target.

7. *You should have a commitment towards educating management and staff.* Let your employees see that you are interested in learning, as well as in educating them. Don't send only staff to a seminar—go yourself. Try to pick up pointers you can share with your staff.

8. *You should audit constantly.* Make your staff feel important. Make them aware of what is an excellent job, a medium-quality job, or a less-than-quality job by constant evaluation. Document measurements of performance within each given area so that you have a written form that you can go back to next year to determine whether you and your staff met expectations or not. Could performance have been improved? You can use these audits when reviewing your next project to see whether you have improved.

9. *When there are problems, you should discuss performance.* Let your staff realize that there are ways of dealing with problems. Don't just put them aside or forget them. Bring them out, discuss them, and consider how you are going to prevent them on the next project.

10. *You should have a reward system.* Make your employees feel valuable. Design firms have found that receiving a bonus or some kind of a reward periodically is worth much more to an employee than being paid a larger salary on a weekly basis. Let your employees realize that when they do a

good job, they get a reward. It is good to both compliment them on the process and to give them some reward, monetary or otherwise, to show your pleasure.

11. *You should measure customer satisfaction.* Talk to your clients and evaluate your firm's performance levels as you go through a project and after the project is completed. Determine whether your clients are satisfied. If they are not satisfied, find out why. This is a job for you, not a member of your staff. It is up to you to be aware of what the clients need.

12. *You must be aware of staff interaction.* Talk with your staff to see how they are interacting. If you don't have a good team effort within the studio, every client is going to be aware of it. The team must work smoothly. If there are problems with the staff's interaction, there are going to be problems with the projects. Find a way to evaluate staff interaction regularly—both in discussions with individual employees and in group meeting situations. Sometimes, management has to put extra effort into finding out just what is happening, as often employees will try hard to cover up problems and sore points.

13. *You must always be on the scene.* Management can't hide in an ivory tower. Your staff needs to know that you are in there with them working and developing projects. The only way that you can determine how well your firm is being managed is to stay close to what is going on.

14. *When you lose a client, you should call him or her and have an exit interview.* Ask the client what you did wrong—why he or she is going to another firm. Very often clients who leave you will teach you more about your firm than you can learn in any other way. Once a person is no longer your client, you may as well use him or her to find out what you can do to prevent clients from leaving in the future.

15. *You must set high standards.* Keep your standards as high as possible and let everyone know that this effort is a constant. The quality of management must be set by the chief executive officer. This is not something that middle management or support staff can do. It is totally up to the principals to set the firm's standards, and then to put in and construct management systems to provide necessary support.

As designers, we must understand what excellence is and keep striving for it. What is excellent today has to be improved upon tomorrow. The same is true of leadership.

TIME MANAGEMENT

Time is our most valuable commodity. Good time management can make the difference between a profitable year and an unprofitable one. Time is the hardest thing to account for. The perception of passing time is subjective. When we like the job we're working on, time evaporates. If we don't like the job, it seems to take ages. A good time-management schedule and cost-accounting system helps distinguish reality from fantasy.

A creative person can deal with many things at once. A genius is a person who can successfully ignore everything but what he or she is working on at the moment. Interior designers who also own and/or manage small businesses must juggle many things at once. It helps to put these items into categories.

Try first to identify each project. Describe it, and then break it down into its various components. Then determine how much time you expect each part of the project will take and what efforts or additional staff will be needed. Make sure you know what your goals are and keep them written down in the project folder so that every time you work on the project you can go back to your initial description and remind yourself of the expected results. Often, as you get involved in a job you had intended to be profitable or good for marketing, you find that it falls into another category. At that point, reevaluate the job and determine whether it's still worthwhile to pursue, if it should be dropped, or if it should be tied into another project.

Every time you take on a new project, you should either be finishing another one or adjusting your priorities. You just can't keep adding or you'll get nothing done. Scheduling is easier when you limit the number of projects you are working on at any one time, although sometimes it is possible to incorporate several projects for more efficient handling. Setting up a good time-management system takes time, but the payoff is tremendous.

Organizing Your Time

Time management must be planned on a regular basis, at a regular time, each and every week and each and every day. If you don't plan for the day, your time may be frittered away.

To create an appropriate schedule for your personal or your business goals, first outline what is to be accomplished. In order to create any kind of a "to do" list, you need to prioritize your work. Ask yourself what it will take to accomplish each priority and what the chief priorities are within the priorities. Then determine how much time each of these activities will require.

It is usually difficult for executives to preschedule more than fifty percent of the day's time, because they need to reserve time for talking with staff, clients, and other people who call with unexpected priorities. If you schedule your day too tightly, nothing works—there's just not enough time for everything to be accomplished. For major projects, you will need to block out chunks of time and plan a definite change in your schedule.

Establish priority time within the studio schedule. However, recognize that most project work is done in bits and pieces. It is almost impossible to schedule or accomplish any major project within one straight block of time.

Interruptions during creative periods are very disturbing; the exact moment of creativity can never be replaced. However, interior designers also service clients and contractors, so you must expect interruptions and learn to work around them.

Some studios schedule a quiet time each day of two or three hours when the staff is not interrupted and is able to work on a certain project intensely for that block of time. You definitely need careful planning to have the luxury of time such as this.

Creative people often don't believe in time management because they know that sometimes in a matter of three or four minutes, interior designers create an idea that can carry the studio for a year. The sad part is that many designers sit and wait for that next burst of creativity without doing anything productive in the interim. They rely on their creativity to the exclusion of everything else. Wasting time is destructive to morale and long-term profits. Those studios that maintain a regular, disciplined, continuing working structure tend to come up with the most ideas and are the most productive over the years.

The Time Management Chart

What should a time management chart include? The chart should state the goal for billings for the week. It's a good idea to let your staff know just what kind of work they must produce in order to make the company profitable. At the top of the weekly time sheet (see page 245) write the billable amount of work each staff person must do per week in order to be profitable. This must be done on a weekly basis; a daily basis is confusing and any time period longer than a week becomes difficult to recall in detail.

When you take a job, you must budget your time as carefully as you budget the cost of materials, even if you earn your income from percentages or markups from furniture. Calculate the time you plan to spend on the job as if you are selling your hours on a basic hourly rate. You can then compare the money earned from commissions or markups against the time you spent and what your hourly rate would have been.

For each new project, you need to estimate how much time you expect each staff member to spend on the job. Some design firms only pay their staff for the amount of time the firm has allowed for a particular project. Other design firms try for more balance and adjust their charges according to their experience documented on past time sheets.

When judging the pricing of a new project you must separate fact from fantasy. If you don't have time and cost sheets on past projects, you have no way to appropriately estimate a new job. In my firm, we have found many surprises on time sheets. Some of the jobs that we had considered the least glamorous, exciting, and interesting turned out to be the jobs that earned the firm the greatest profits in the shortest periods of time. They made a lot of difference in our end-of-the-year profit statement.

An example of fact versus fantasy is a luxury co-op complex project a firm I know undertook. The job appeared to be a glamour project full of opportunities. In fact, it was really not worth it from a profit-and-loss viewpoint. The firm was called constantly by co-op members who were interested in what was happening or were involved in committees. This, along with the public relations and local publicity requirements, meant that the firm spent many unchargeable hours on this project. The firm was paid for professional services; however, its hours were so much in excess of what had been planned that the project was really difficult and expensive for the firm. It also prevented the firm from doing other projects that year because of all the time required for this one project.

The project turned out beautifully and the members love it. But it was financially, physically, and emotionally taxing for the firm.

Another project that the firm did last year, which almost went unnoticed, turned out to be very financially profitable. It was for a previous client and involved replacing major textiles. Most of the furniture was vintage furniture, some of it antique. The creative demands on the project were minimal—it was a restoration project.

However, the textiles the client wanted were of good quality and provided a reasonable markup. The client had had previous experience with the firm and was easy to work with. When comparing the amount of hours the firm spent on the job and the size of the job, the profit was outstanding. The job was completed in less than three percent of the time that was spent on the co-op complex project and the gross profit was similar. That sounds like an extreme, but it really isn't. When comparing jobs, you will find huge contrasts in the amounts of time, effort, and emotional stress. At the end of the year, these all influence whether or not a designer is looking forward to continuing next year in the design field.

Weekly chargeable hours sheet. Each staff member needs to keep his or her billable work logged on a sheet such as this. The amount of work that needs to be done for the staff member to be profitable should be listed at the top of the sheet. These sheets are usually kept separate from the nonchargeable, or in-house, assignments.

WEEKLY CHARGEABLE HOURS		Staff:		
		Week Ending:		
Day:	Client:	Project:	Code:	Hours:
MON				
TUE				
WED				
THU				
FRI				
SAT				

Refer to time-log category sheet for job codes.

© Design Business Monthly

TIME-LOG CATEGORIES	
Code:	Client-related Activities:
Tr.	Travel – actual time going to/from a client's project or to a location directly associated with a client's project
D.	Design – conceptual work in development of a design project; time spent with a client
DCo.	Design Coordination – planning sequence or scope of activities related to a project; staff-meeting time reviewing a project
R/D.	Research/Development – preparing information for presentation, i.e., gathering samples, product research, pricing, requesting information from supplier
G/D.	Graphic/Drafting – time spent preparing floor plans, renderings, color boards, and other visual-presentation items for a project
DC.	Data Collection – measuring, photographing a client's project, interviewing, reviewing blueprints for measurements, etc.
I.	Installation – activities related to delivering and installing merchandise, including preparation of that merchandise for delivery
M.	Management – writing orders for a specific client; expediting or problem-solving activities for a specific client
Code:	General Operations Activities:
B.	Bookkeeping – all activities related to processing financial records
DS.	Design Support Services – filing samples, catalog information; reviewing new product information and other nonspecific activities related to the design process; meeting with sales representatives and on general product review
MS.	Management Support Services – activities related to the general operation of the company, i.e., maintenance, general administrative duties
MSS.	Merchandise Support Services – upkeep of inventory items, including preparation of items for stock, movement of artwork, etc.
M/P.	Marketing and Promotion – prospecting, interviews with prospective clients, advertising activities, public-relations functions, attendance at community functions
OP.	Order Processing – calls and paperwork associated with clients as a group with minimal time spent on a specific client
P.	Personnel – interviewing, staff evaluation meetings, etc.
T.	Training – attendance at seminars or in-house training sessions

© Design Business Monthly

Project time sheet. Having your staff members keep time logs such as these for each project not only helps you calculate billing, but also helps you keep track of how your staff's time is being spent.

PROJECT TIME SHEET

Project:		Staff:

Date:	Activity:	Time:

Recap:

Design Time:	Research & Devel.:	Drafting & Rend.:	Data Collection:

© Design Business Monthly

Time-Saving Methods and Ideas
The following list suggests ways you can save time at the job:

1. *Realize that you are valuable.* If every designer understands that he or she is a valuable person whose time needs to be treated like a precious commodity, his or her whole attitude in time management changes. Time is such an intangible commodity that sometimes one can forget just what it means to the profit structure of a business.

2. *Use consultants.* There are many specialists who can show you how to do something in one-tenth of the time that you would be able to do it yourself. Using these people when it is appropriate can add professionalism to the job as well as permit you to do the project much more quickly.

3. *Design your studio as carefully as you would a client's office.* Have you thought out all of the details of your office? Does it really function as time-effectively as it should? After all, each time you have to move away from your work at hand to complete another phase of the project, it is a distraction. Review your office and see that its design incorporates the latest time-and-motion studies.

4. *Do a time analysis for two weeks, approximately once a year.* Include for each twenty-four-hour time period how long you sleep, how much time you put into daily maintenance issues, and how much time you spend on fun and relaxation. See that your week is appropriately balanced. This is important in your being highly productive and effective as a designer, as well as as a person.

    It is amazing what you can learn from this intense time/motion study. It is usually well worth the effort.

5. *Learn new techniques.* There are many classes given on special techniques to help designers to do work simpler and faster. Keeping up with your education usually helps save time. Almost every good seminar can teach you something that will pay for the time it required many times over.

6. *Stay abreast of new equipment and technology.* Every design studio needs to understand how to use the latest equipment, which often can save considerable time. Remember, when introducing new equipment or new processes to the studio, it is best to do it at a time when the studio is not under a lot of pressure.

7. *Use computers.* The computer can enable you to save more time than any other tool that has been introduced into the design field for years. However, adapting to this piece of equipment takes time.

    Fortunately, some of the new software programs are very easy to learn. When selecting programs, choose ones that are easy to master. Each person in your firm should have his or her own CRT. At one time designers shared this tool. But today it is considered to be like a telephone or a calculator—everyone has his or her own piece of equipment so that he or she can use it at any time without the interruption of any other person within the office. Refer to the section on computers, pages 66–67, for more details.

8. *Take a time-management course.* You can usually pick up a tip or two that will help save you some extra movements. Because both good and bad habits develop over time, attending a time-management course every few years is usually worthwhile. If there is anyone in your studio who has not attended one recently, you should send him or her.

9. *Realize that other people's time is valuable.* By spending time talking to other workers in the office, you are interrupting and frustrating their work

schedules, as well as detracting from your own. Be friendly, but understand that a staff's most important objective is to work.

10. *Review your work habits.* Developing good work habits is a great way to improve your time management. Habits are subconscious, however, and have been developed over a long period of time; therefore, they need careful reviews. Ask yourself: "Why do I do this first thing in the morning? Should I be opening my mail at this time or is there a better time?" You need to be willing to review your work habits and see if you can find more time-effective ways of working.

11. *Keep a time log.* Although not every hour in the day is chargeable for many designers, just understanding where and how you spend your time permits you to understand how your time will need to be adjusted when taking on a new project. Realize that anytime you take on a new project, you have to eliminate an activity that you were doing in the past. If you have your activities logged, you can easily select which ones should be dropped for more important issues.

12. *Plan telephone calls.* Telephone calls mean business. Allow yourself the time that is required for telephone calls and plan your telephoning in such a way that it will not disturb the whole studio. (Refer to pages 266–76 for additional management ideas.) Planning your telephone calls and letting people know when you can receive them can save an amazing amount of time.

    Often shorter calls can be more effective than longer ones. Learn to make your telephone calls briefer; see whether you can't keep each call down to three minutes. Putting an egg timer in front of you can help you become more aware of the amount of time you spend on each call. Outline your agenda before making a phone call.

13. *Prepare for visitors.* Drop-in visitors can destroy any day. Although you must see some of these visitors, don't see them in your office. See them in another part of the studio so that you have better control over the time you are spending with them. While drop-in visitors can be inconvenient, remember that they are your clients and, therefore, are important.

14. *Learn dictating.* Dictating is an excellent way to save a lot of time. It can help you manage your overall design practice much more time-effectively. See pages 251–53 for an extensive review of dictating techniques.

15. *Reduce paperwork.* When you receive a piece of paper, determine its appropriate value. If it should be kept as a record in the client's file, put it there. If it is a paper that you should refer to until a certain date, date it so that you will throw it away at an appropriate time. Having copies of every paper does not always encourage better management; in fact, sometimes paper can add confusion to the management system.

16. *Instead of writing, make a telephone call.* Usually it is a lot faster to exchange information by telephone. If the call requires some documentation, you can dictate it on your machine and follow it up with a written memo. But try to keep your writing down as much as possible. Writing letters is very expensive. If you can avoid typing by using transmittal sheets or some other method that goes through the office, this will save you considerable time and expense.

17. *Do it yourself.* Review items that you are handling or passing on. Determine whether an issue can be answered by a quick note on a copy of a letter or requires formal correspondence. If there is a way that you can handle something quickly and save the time of other people in the office, obviously this is more time-productive.

18. *Limit forms and procedures.* Only use forms that are productive and make sense to your studio. Some forms are worthwhile and others are not. Designers can spend more time filling out forms than they will spend on designing. Determine just what is appropriate.

19. *Simplify documentation.* Documentation is a requirement of the design field. Find a way to do it simply. Organization of your documentation can be a major time-saver.

20. *Plan sales reps' visits.* Sales reps can take up a lot of time or their visits can be useful and efficient. See pages 214–15 for specific ways to get the most from sales reps' visits.

21. *Use travel time.* When considering taking an out-of-town job, realize that it will take you time to get to and from the job. This time should be factored into every costing procedure. The least expensive and most effective design jobs are close to home, but these jobs are not always available. When you are traveling between your office and a job, try to use that time effectively. Two good ways to use this time are by dictating or using tapes for learning.

22. *Organize your office.* How much time do you spend looking for things? Is everything where you expect it to be? What is the condition of your library and your files? In surveying design studios we have found that the time spent finding what you want at the appropriate time is the single largest time-waster. The organization of your library and your files are primary to your time-effectiveness. Make the investment in time to organize your office, and then require everyone to follow set rules to keep it in order.

23. *Systemize your mail handling.* Many designers use their most valuable part of the day handling the mail. Review how you handle mail handling and determine how you can better manage this time-consuming necessity.

24. *Organize reading and studying.* Designers need to exchange information that can only be learned through reading magazines and other written material. Develop a method of organizing and reviewing this material. Perhaps you might give material to other members of your studio and have each person report back on a particular article at a weekly meeting. This can save a lot of time and bring almost all items to the full review of your staff. Anyone who is particularly interested in the subject can then spend time further analyzing the material. This method is a great way to give other members of the studio an opportunity to explain what they know and to become specialists on certain subjects.

25. *Control crises.* In any design studio there will be crises and problems. However, with proper scheduling, many crises can be prevented. See what you can do with your schedule to prevent most of the crises during any week. This will save you from having your time consumed by such projects.

26. *Learn to delegate.* Delegation can be a time-saver or a time-waster depending upon how it is handled. See pages 256–58 for information on effective delegation methods.

27. *Eliminate indecision.* Many decisions cannot be made until future research is done. However, there are some items that demand immediate decision. Determine which item belongs in which category and make decisions appropriately. During the design process there are many decisions that must be made to keep the job moving. Procrastination can damage any schedule.

Dictation

Learning to dictate into a tape recorder is one of the easiest ways to save time. You can "write" letters, memos, and staff instructions at any odd moment, saving many hours of laborious writing.

I do a lot of dictating every day, all through the day. I am never without a tape recorder or a dictating machine. I carry a small tape recorder with me practically everywhere, whether I am in the car or on a project. I even carry one in the evening, just in case an opportunity to use it arises.

Here are a few tips to make your dictating go more smoothly:

1. *Buy a good machine.* There are many types available—desk-tops, portables, standard sized, and micros. Evaluate which is best for your situation. Most firms have several machines; however, you should try to equip your office with machines that all use the same type of tapes so they can be transcribed from one machine to another.

2. *Become comfortable with your machine.* You must learn how to talk to it. You want to sound natural and relaxed.

3. *Organize whatever you want to dictate.* Work from a list or an outline; this also helps whoever does the transcribing. At our firm, we list the letters or subjects on a tape, number the tape, and, in some cases, code it. For example, a letter can start at 001 and finish at 073. The next item, a memo, starts at 074 and finishes at 110. This system allows our secretary to know how long each item will be and how long it should take to type.

4. *Try to conclude your dictating with instructions.* Tell your typist whether a letter is a rough draft or a final version. If there is punctuation, say how it should appear. Spell out unusual words and words like Naugahyde, which are common to our field, but often unfamiliar to other people. Explain what format you want for the letter. Is it a note? A formal letter? How do you want these notes typed? Do you want space left for additional notations? You may even want to set up a book of samples.

5. *Always spell out a person's name.* There is nothing worse than receiving a letter with your name misspelled. If the person's address might be misspelled, spell it out as well.

6. *Learn to enunciate.* Speak clearly so that your secretary can understand what you are saying and will be able to properly transcribe it.

7. *Develop a speaking pace, and learn to pause.* When you stop to think, stop the recorder, too. A long silence will make the typist think you are finished.

8. *Be very short and to the point.* Do not give a long dissertation that will take seven pages to type when you could accomplish the same objective in one paragraph.

9. *Don't discard tapes unless you are sure that everything on the tape has been completed.* Keep a good library of tapes, if necessary, to make sure that your jobs are thoroughly documented.

When you are on the telephone with a client and he or she is giving extensive details or complaining, tell the client you would like to record the call to make sure that your staff has all the details. At the end of the phone call, put on the tape recorder and review the notes you took during the telephone call and confirm them with the client.

At the end of meetings or interviews with clients, take your tape recorder out and dictate the items that you've covered. Then go down the list and give details

Dictation log. A dictation log similar to this one will assist you and your secretary with the management of your dictating.

DICTATION LOG		
Date:	Tape:	Side:

Addressed to:	Subject:	Inst.:

Instruction Code:

P – Priority	M – Mail	R – Return	D – Rough Draft	E – Edit/Complete

© Design Business Monthly

and instructions to the staff members while the client is there, so he or she will be aware of the exact instructions regarding that stage of the project. Often clients find little points or corrections to add. This procedure works very well in preventing small misunderstandings that can grow into complaints. Your office should send your clients a copy of the transcript as part of the documentation of the project. The transcripts clarify the issues as you go along, helping to avoid legal difficulties.

You may also want to record a total interview with a client. In our firm we often make tapes as we interview support staff for large business projects. We keep a tape of the entire conversation, summarize the contents, and prepare a written summary. Sometimes we give both tape and summary to the workers' manager to review for any discrepancies or unresolved issues.

You can program your answering machine to handle long-distance dictation simply by setting no time limit on the length of messages it can record. This lets you call in a quotation or any details you need typed and mailed in a hurry. You can dictate when phone rates are lowest or during hours that are nonproductive for sales work. Your secretary or typist can transcribe your message the next morning, and it can be on its way before you get back to the office.

Sometimes when I dictate, I listen to my tape and then redo it, just to clean it up and make it easier for the typist to follow. Most often I ask for a rough draft, which I simply edit and rearrange as required. I have all draft copies typed double- or triple-spaced so they are easy to edit.

I also leave taped instructions for my staff when business takes me away from the office. This way they don't wonder what to do. Usually, they can listen to these taped instructions in a matter of a few minutes. I encourage my staff to leave me notes on tapes, and I find that their notations on tape are usually better than their written ones.

This not only saves time, it also eliminates procrastination. Very often in leaving a project and returning to the office, my staff and I put our notes on a tape. If we wait until we get back to the office to tape notes, we sometimes forget certain details. After our notes are transcribed and edited, we make a copy of them to send to the client. We ask if these notes agree with the client's understanding of the project and if there is anything he or she would like to add.

I even dictate to myself. This is a great way of keeping notes when you cannot write something down, as when you are driving a car.

MEETINGS

Your business day is a series of meetings—with your banker, your clients, your staff, your suppliers. Not all meetings are vital interactions, but any meeting that goes on your calendar should have one or more reasons for existing. There are five good ones: to inform, to solve problems, to brainstorm, to plan, and to motivate. Cancel any meeting that has no clearly stated goal or purpose. There is nothing more tedious than sitting in an aimless meeting.

Managing Meetings
Here are some points to consider in managing meetings:

1. *Meet regularly.* Setting a regular time for staff meetings encourages your staff to hold nonurgent topics for discussion at that time, rather than interrupting your day to solve them. Obviously some issues must be dealt with as they occur, but many issues do not merit minute-by-minute updates.

2. *Why are we here today?* A good meeting starts with a stated reason and an agenda. If possible, write out your agenda and have it distributed before the meeting. Send an agenda to a client a day before you get together, or review it with the client's secretary. This gives both parties time to prepare.

3. *Establish the duration of the meeting in advance and include it on the agenda.* Any meeting that takes two hours when you had allowed for fifteen minutes affects your next appointment. When a problem is uncovered during a short meeting and the participants cannot stay to deal with it, set a date and time for a new meeting. If all issues are resolved before the meeting is scheduled to end, break up the meeting and use the extra time for some other activity.

4. *Who's in charge?* Someone must take control of the meeting, but select the leader by issue, not by rank. When the purpose for a meeting is to inform, the person with the information holds the floor. In a planning session, the project director is in charge. The person with the problem directs the problem-solving meeting, and the person who wants and needs ideas directs the brainstorming session. Motivation has to come from the top.

5. *Stick to the issue.* This is a good ground rule for all meetings. Be frank and open and encourage the others to do the same; after all, what goes on at the meeting is confidential. Beating around the bush instead of dealing directly with problems only devours time, and time is money.

6. *Keep the meeting moving.* When talk bogs down or strays too far from the issue at hand, the leader should get the meeting back in pace. Sometimes this is best achieved by interrupting the meeting briefly to serve snacks or to pass around copies of relevant documents. Reintroducing the main topic can also help.

7. *Let participants contribute.* If you bring eight people together for a meeting, make sure all eight have an opportunity to speak and to comment. At a project meeting, it is most effective to include only the staff members directly involved with the project. Not every employee needs to attend every meeting, but if a person is valuable enough for you to hire, he or she should attend *some* meetings.

8. *Take notes.* Three days after a meeting, details tend to fade from memory. Names, dates, decisions, financial details, who made what suggestion, and the resulting agreements all need to be recorded for future reference. I personally recap my meetings by summarizing into a tape recorder as the meeting is about to end. This firms up the issues discussed and gives people a chance to add anything that may have been left out. Later these dictated notes are transcribed and given to the participants. This reinforces the importance of the meeting; the transcript is a visual reminder of the decisions that were made and what must be done before the next meeting.

9. *Make the most of unplanned meetings.* You may bump into a prospective client or a current client anywhere—on a jogging trail, in a locker room, in a ticket line, or at a party. If you discuss business, follow up the chance encounter with a written note. It seals the contact.

10. *Include some humor in each meeting.* It makes everyone relax and helps keep things moving.

Meeting agenda sheet. This sheet can greatly assist in the proper management of meetings.

MEETING AGENDA					Date Sched.:			
					Time:			

Client/Subject:				Location:				

Purpose:

Results Desired:

Scheduled:			Actual:			Meeting Cost:		
Start:	Stop:	Total Hours:	Start:	Stop:	Total Hours:	Billing Rate:	Value Per Hr.:	Total:

Persons Attending:

Agenda:

Items Required for Meeting:	Person Responsible:

© Design Business Monthly

MEETING AGENDA	Page 2
Meeting Notes:	Decisions:

Corporate Board Meetings. All business owners who are part of corporations must have regular meetings, at least once a year. Any change in office, salary, or fringe benefits for one of the business owners must be made as part of this board meeting process. Board meetings must be formalized, which means that records must be kept of any decisions. These records should be reviewed by your corporate lawyer occasionally.

All stockholders and board members must be present at a board meeting. If something happens where you cannot have an official board meeting in person, then an agreement could be reached by letter or telephone. However, to meet the regulations of a corporate structure, it must be documented afterwards.

It is important to keep good minutes of the board meetings. Should the IRS examine your minutes and find any failure of your company to abide by the bylaws or to hold regular meetings, this can be used against you. For example, in setting compensation levels, fringe-benefit programs as well as other employee/owner transactions must be a part of the documentation of board minutes. Ask your lawyer and your financial advisor to check your documents to see that they all conform to standard, especially if any self-interest transactions are covered.

Minutes should be kept on a corporate minutes form (see page 257). Corporations must keep minutes by law, but the appropriate format is not explicitly spelled out. The form provided here can be photocopied. You can fill in the necessary decisions and the names of people who authorized the decisions. By dating it and affixing your corporate seal, you have an official minutes document that can be filed in your book.

DELEGATION

Whether you work for a large company or a small one, your own firm or part of a large corporation, your productivity depends upon your ability to use support staff. Delegation is one of the processes by which you should coordinate your projects with other staff members.

Becoming a skillful delegator will allow you to both save time and develop the abilities of your staff. To be an effective delegator you need to define:

▶ your needs;

▶ your expected results;

▶ your goals;

▶ the specific time by which you need the information;

▶ the general outline of the subject;

▶ what the item is that you're covering.

Your goal may be to locate an item that can be worked into a fast-track project or a product that requires very specialized design detail. Whatever your goals are, make them clear.

Make sure that your staff understands your priorities and knows which items are important to complete first. We all want to do easy projects first, but that may not be appropriate. Keep your schedules coordinated.

Clearly spell out any hidden issues. Often there are certain details about a project, or a client's preferences, that your staff would not know unless you told them. Be very straightforward with your fellow workers. Tell them if the client is truly color blind or can't see farther than two feet.

As you present the projects or items you are going to delegate, ask your staff how long they think the assignment will take and how they intend to handle it. A

Corporate minutes form. This form can be used as an official minutes document as required by law by dating it and affixing your corporate seal to it after you have filled in the details of the meeting.

(Corporation)

I, _____(secretary's name)_____, Secretary of (Corporation),
do hereby certify that at a duly constituted meeting of the Directors
and/or Stockholders of the Corporation held at _____
on _____, 19___, it was upon motion duly made and seconded,
that it be VOTED: (Describe approved corporate action)

It was upon motion made and seconded that it be further VOTED: That
_____(individual)_____ as _____(officer)_____ of the
Corporation be empowered and directed to execute, deliver, and accept
any and all documents reasonably required to accomplish the foregoing
vote, all on such terms and conditions as he or she in his or her
discretion deems to be in best interest of the Corporation.

I further certify that the foregoing votes are in full force without
rescision, as modification or amendment.

Signed this _____ day of _____, 19___.

A TRUE RECORD

ATTEST

                                            Secretary of Corporation

(Corporate Seal)

quick explanation from each person will tell you whether he or she understands your aim. His or her method of handling the project may be off track or inappropriate. This is the time to set the parameters.

Keep in mind your staff's strengths and weaknesses. People are better at some projects than others. You should try to assign projects suited to each individual's strengths. When you must delegate tasks that you know are in areas where your staff is weak, tell them to let you know if they are having problems and offer to help them develop a solution.

Regardless of the abilities of your staff, once you have delegated a task to an employee, suggest that he or she check back with you with a progress report in a set amount of time. There is no point in having someone spend months working in the wrong direction.

Allow for problems. Let your staff know you are aware that everything doesn't run smoothly and, that if there is a problem, you are willing to help be part of the problem-solving process. This does not mean they can simply dump the project back on your desk; they are to tell you what the problem is and their recommendations for handling it. If your staff runs into trouble, they can come back and check with you.

There are certain situations that you should never delegate. They include:

▶ *Any project that is not clearly defined*. To be able to pass on creative assignments to others, you must be able to define the project. If the criteria or specifications have not been determined by the client, wait until they have been set before you delegate the project.

▶ *Crisis situations*. These are difficult to delegate. If there is a crisis, the top management must take care of it.

▶ *Sorting out personality problems*. These should be worked out by the chief executive or management. This is why so many chief executives and management people spend most of their time dealing with personality problems of either staff or clients and not doing interior design.

▶ *Making major changes*. Any change that requires an adjustment of procedures must first be developed by management. You are only going to cause chaos within the organization if you do not make these adjustments yourself.

▶ *Policy making*. This is the responsibility of management. Policy should only be made by the chief executive officer or chief management.

▶ *Making major decisions*. It is your job and responsibility to make decisions such as whether to accept a project.

▶ *Giving congratulations*. Awards and praise are appreciated more when they come from top management. If you can keep the spirits high among your fellow workers, whether they are your own staff or various contractors, this will be one of the most valuable services that you can perform.

HANDLING MAIL

Even in a small firm, handling mail can take a tremendous amount of time. Opening the mail and bringing it to the attention of the right people is not a job for your newest staff members. The person opening the mail must understand what is happening within the corporate structure. In some firms the principal opens all the mail first thing in the morning, before anyone else is in the office. Or the general manager has this responsibility. It is best to route mail to the person who needs to look at it and to review any other mail details either by meeting or note, as required.

When should mail be opened? Open it as soon as it arrives, but not all mail needs the immediate attention of the addressee. Any items that are critical and need immediate attention should get it, but usually critical issues are brought to your attention by telephone or messenger. Schedule a time in your day for reviewing mail; mail should not disrupt the main part of your day.

RECORD KEEPING

Every business today needs to keep good records. Interior design businesses especially need a simple and accurate record-keeping system. It's easy to run one job out of a shopping bag. However, it is very difficult to continue to run job after job, year after year, in this fashion. As businesses grow and change, old methods of record keeping often become inappropriate. You must review new systems of record keeping on a continuing basis.

Computers, especially PCs, are great record-keeping devices. The PC is fast becoming a standard tool for every designer workstation; especially for the record-processing part of the business. Computers enable us to retrieve records and keep documentation in an inexpensive and easy-to-use way.

If you are not computer-oriented, there are other basic record-keeping systems that are simple to use. Any record-keeping system you set up should be designed, or at least approved, by your accountant. It must also be a system that you understand and that is easy for everyone in the studio to use. Make sure you understand the reason for each particular aspect of the record-keeping system. The system must be simple and efficient. Your record-keeping system also must be accurate and have some form of double-checking system to make sure that errors are not made in various categories.

Design firms need good documentation for day-to-day business and in case of an audit. However, there is a lot of information that you don't have time to use or review. There is no point in spending time documenting this type of information. Store and keep only essential information.

Make sure that your system is well defined and functional. You can always add to it later on. Each year, review your system and see how much you use each part of it. Is it possible to delete certain sections? Would this save time?

You must keep your records very up-to-date. Weed your files on a regular basis so that information can be easily retrieved. I believe in good documentation. I have found so many times that having records of a past project or knowing what a client did in another situation prevents problems at a later date. Keep documents throughout every project and make them part of your permanent record. It is a necessary part of every design firm, particularly in these litigious times.

Keep records on a daily basis so that you don't have to worry about documenting orders and other information at a later date, when you often can't remember them entirely. At my firm we make a point of documenting our projects while the clients are there so that they have a chance to go over every detail with us. We review every part of the various contracts so they understand our procedures and know the part they play in this relationship. Good records impress everyone who sees them. Sloppy records are inappropriate in a field that is based on organization.

How long must you keep business records? It depends upon your type of business and style of management, as well as state and other regulatory requirements. For financial records, it is best to check with your accountant or your lawyer for specific scheduling. The length of time you should keep project-management records will vary depending upon your continued interaction with the client or project.

What kind of records should a designer keep to support him in case of a lawsuit? My lawyer said that if you kept extremely complete records of the sort he really likes, you would probably get nothing else done. It is practical to keep a record of all business transactions, copies of all purchase orders and requisitions.

While a job is going on, keep all the correspondence with suppliers and anything written to your client. If you do run into trouble, at that point write a memorandum of every detail you recall about the job. Months later, one does not remember as well. Just keep the documents in an orderly file, and keep the file for six years unless you think the situation involves fraud, which is usually tax-related. Your accountant can also advise you what records to keep and how long to keep them.

There are many other legal issues designers should be aware of: state laws, federal laws, and city laws pertaining to the practice of design, for instance. An attorney can tell you about these, but a better source might be trade or professional associations. Very often things are brought to my attention by the American Society of Interior Designers or by the Chamber of Commerce. I later discuss these with my attorney to see how much importance I should attach to them.

Areas That Require Record Keeping
You are legally required to keep the following for three to seven years:

▶ sales records of contracts acquired

▶ cash receipts for all monies received from all sources, including bank statements and duplicate deposit slips

▶ all cash disbursements, which are the monies paid out by your business.

▶ accounts receivable and accounts payable

▶ tax and payroll records

Daily Diary
A daily diary is a useful addition to the appointment books most of us keep. Here you can record not just appointments, but the actual time spent on each project during the day, phone calls and their outcomes, business that requires follow-through, and anything else that comes up during the day. This saves time when you actually sit down to calculate direct billable hours. Because the records are kept daily and often hourly, the diary is a good method of documentation.

There are designers who find it useful to keep lists of all their phone conversations, client meetings, and other interactions throughout the day. Some of the newer diaries have peel-off sections that make cross-referencing easy. After noting an entry in the diary, you simply peel off the section and place it in your client's file. Now the entry is in two places.

The range and variety of diaries available is quite broad, so you should be able to find one that suits your personal style. More and more designers use them, not just because they are a professional aid and good management tool, but because they simply save time. You don't have to wonder whether you discussed Mrs. A's baroque lamp, because the conversation details are right there on the page.

INVENTORY

Some design firms have no inventory—others need a warehouse. It's a matter of business preference and convenience. Whether maintaining an inventory of furniture and furnishings is practical depends on a number of other factors.

When valuing inventory, determine how it fits into the cash flow of your business. Having a product available when your client wants it means that you can sometimes service a client when another designer cannot. If you have a good turnover, maintaining an inventory can be an advantage in marketing and selling.

Any job that can be done quickly generally has a higher profit margin than one stretched out over a long time. Sometimes a certain amount of inventory is required for this type of project. But is keeping inventory really necessary? Quick-ship programs are becoming increasingly available.

Warehousing is expensive. You pay for using the warehouse and for the energy to heat, air condition, and ventilate the facility. Furniture is relatively fragile and must be kept in a warehouse of reasonable quality or it does not hold up, especially in extreme climates.

Handling inventory can be cost-consuming. It requires good supervision, otherwise the breakage and damage rate is tremendous. Although most of the furnishings you are apt to carry will require considerable care, you cannot always get well-trained labor.

You need to insure against fire and theft for every piece of inventory that you have. This can be quite expensive. Also, extensive burglar-alarm systems may be required, depending upon your location.

Holding inventory of interior design furnishings today usually costs around thirty to thirty-five percent of their worth per year, depending upon such factors as your individual insurance rates and real estate costs. This is expensive. Consider how many projects you have won because you maintain an inventory and determine whether you have made a wise investment. Every item in your warehouse or showroom shows up on your tax bill. Is it worth it?

There are designers I know who claim that most of their income is derived from tremendous markups on antiques they have acquired and later sold. This may be true, but I wonder if the profit margin is as high as they believe. Some pieces sit at a warehouse for eight or ten years before being sold. When you factor in the cost of the repairs and alterations required to make the antiques saleable, the actual cost of the antique becomes quite high.

If you intend to hold inventory, check through it each year and ask your accountant to help you understand what the costs are. Some inventory does appreciate, but interior design is still a fashion industry where a certain amount of stock will not be as appealing next year as it was this year.

FREIGHT CLAIMS

Freight damages are one of an interior designer's greatest problems—or perhaps greatest aggravations. At one time, if you took the normal precautions of documenting your claims with a photograph of the item, and followed shippers' instructions, you would generally get paid for your claim. Sometimes it took several months to a year; but at some point you got paid.

Suddenly, with the changes in trucking regulations, designers are finding it very difficult to collect payment for freight claims. The freight companies use every minor technicality they can to get out of paying them.

Some of our sources now put phrases on their invoices saying they are not responsible for any merchandise once it leaves the factory. But they pack similar merchandise all the time; they should know how to pack the merchandise to survive the freight process. They also should know which carriers will handle their merchandise carefully. It is neither appropriate or fair for designers to be responsible for items over which they have no control.

Design studios have to take a new approach to the problem of freight damage. First of all, you must be sure that any receiving warehouse or studio has the proper procedures for receiving, inspecting, and documenting anything that they receive in our name. Whether the warehouse handlers are a third party or not, you, as the buyer, are responsible for the merchandise even if it is being shipped to them. The address may be in care of that warehouse, but it is your name on the invoice.

Our managing director and I spent many weeks researching this problem with our sources. They have recommended that we make sure that anyone who receives merchandise goes through the standard and appropriate method of inspecting the boxes, looking for crushed corners or other signals that a package may be damaged. If a problem is noticed by our receiver or warehouse person, they are to request that the driver permit them to open the package at that point to check the materials to see if they are in good condition. If they are in good condition, the package or shipment will be accepted. If they are not in good condition, it will be refused. Accept delivery of damaged material only from a freight company with which you have experience and which you know will handle the claim.

Suppose you check an item and it is not in good condition. Some suppliers advise us to simply refuse it, because the company who picked up that freight signed a bill of lading with the manufacturer, saying that they agree to deliver the item to you in good condition. If you accept the item and decide you are going to deal with the freight claim, because perhaps only twenty percent of the merchandise needs replacement, remember that this will require a great amount of documentation.

If freight damage to an item is minor, take care of it in your studio. When the damage is under ten percent of the cost of the item and is something you can handle, it pays you to do so. The merchandise can be repaired in a matter of days and forwarded on to your clients. If you return the merchandise, there might be a delay of three to six months until you get it replaced.

With any damage, it is important that you notify the shipper so that the manufacturer knows whether it is a shipping problem or a manufacturing problem. That way they can do something to prevent this damage the next time. You are their best quality-control engineer.

When you make the decision as to whether or not you are going to accept a shipment, consider how much effort will go into making a freight claim. Photographs are absolutely necessary. Every receiving department and every warehouse must have a camera and facilities to take duplicate (or triplicate) photographs of damaged material. You need to send one photograph to whoever is handling the claim and you must keep one as a record for yourself. You must also keep all packing materials and be able to show the exact condition in which the merchandise arrived. Storing damaged crates can take up a lot of warehouse space.

Any time you make a freight claim, notify the manufacturer or shipper of all the details. Many suppliers realize how difficult freight claims are for receivers to handle and will offer to help handle these claims for you. These are the kind of resources that designers need.

Similar merchandise is usually available from several sources. Find companies who will handle your freight claims and give them your business. They take a lot of the pressure and freight-management problems out of your hands. These companies are also sometimes willing to reship within seven days any items that are damaged at no additional cost to the designer.

As designers we must demand the support and help of our resources in handling freight claims, and there is only one way that we can do it; by all working together. One- and two-day seminars are being given on the topic. There are also agents who will handle your freight claims for a fee. Attorneys will also handle freight claims if they are major.

Receiving Instructions
The receiving instructions on the facing page should either be posted in your warehouse, be made part of your contract with the warehouse serving your firm, and/or be included with purchasing documents when the client or other agent is handling the receiving.

Receiving instructions. These instructions should be posted in your warehouse, be made part of your contract with the warehouse serving your firm, and/or be included with purchasing documents when the client or other agent is handling the receiving. This information has been provided by the SNFCC (Shippers National Freight Claim Counsel)

RECEIVING INSTRUCTIONS

1. Make sure you are signing for the same number of packages as on the delivery slip. If short, note amount received on delivery slip and have the driver sign and date it. *Count all pieces.*

2. *Do not* accept deliveries without inspection. Writing "subject to inspection" on the delivery receipt does not protect you.

3. Open and inspect packages during delivery if at all possible. Insist on opening any package with evidence of damage in the driver's presence.

4. Note any damages on the delivery slip and have the driver sign and date it.

5. If you are not able to open packages at the time of delivery, note any visible damage to the cartons on the delivery slip. Be precise when noting these. (Example: one carton crushed on corners.) *Do not* give opinions as to possible causes of damage; report only the facts.

6. Open package as soon as possible for more complete inspection of goods (within 15 days for reporting concealed damage). After 15 days it may be presumed that *you* caused the damage.

7. Take pictures of damaged merchandise.

8. If damage is discovered after the driver leaves, call the carrier *immediately* for inspection and *confirm in writing* your request for inspection.

9. Keep concealed damaged goods in original packing and set aside.

11. *Do not* reject the shipment to the carrier unless:
   ▶ The shipment is "practically worthless," considering the cost of repair or salvaging.
   ▶ You take pictures.
   ▶ You get the driver to acknowledge and confirm the damage.
   ▶ The shipment may contaminate or damage other freight in your place of business.

12. If carrier does not inspect within 30 days of your request, make a detailed inspection report *with pictures*.

13. If carrier does inspect, request a copy of *all* inspection reports made.

PROTECTING CONFIDENTIAL MATERIAL

How do you protect the confidential material you have in your studio? It's human nature to talk about one's work, and when your staff talks, they could give away many secrets or confidential material that could hurt your project or your business.

First of all, you need to explain to your employees the reason for confidentiality in an overall review of staff policies. At that point you may ask your employees to sign a nondisclosure statement. It is also often valuable to have your vendors, bankers, and consultants sign these statements.

On certain corporate projects, you must sign disclosure statements before you begin the project. More and more companies are requiring this, and not just megafirms such as IBM.

A copyright attorney explained to me that confidential materials must be treated as confidential throughout the design process. They also must be treated as confidential within the office, which means you should not display them on the wall. All confidential drawings must be locked in a special cabinet within the office when they are not in use. They cannot be shown to anyone unless you make a point of first saying the material is confidential. When items go out for quotation, you must mark them accordingly and explain to anyone who touches them that confidentiality is an issue.

Which materials are confidential? Plans and drawings that show an exclusive design or technique should be labeled "confidential" and locked in a safe area. Your customer lists and marketing plans should also be kept confidential; there is nothing of more value to your competitors. Discuss this information only with people you can trust.

Computer software needs to be guarded with caution, as it often holds some of the top secrets of any business. Generally, your computer software packages provide sequential codes or passwords that must be entered before confidential data is displayed or printed.

COPYRIGHTS

Every now and then something you design for a project is not only original, but adaptable to quantity production for limited distribution. When you send this design out to be manufactured, you don't want the manufacturer or shop to copy the item and then sell it all over town. How can you protect the design?

There are very few items that interior designers design that are patentable, but if you have something that is really that creative, it deserves protection. Copyrighting is usually the best safeguard. It is easy, relatively inexpensive, and can be done without incurring legal fees.

To copyright your work, mark "confidential" on each and every design or drawings leaving your shop for either quotation or for manufacturing. At the bottom of every drawing you should put a © (the copyright symbol), the year, and the owner of the copyright, which means the name of the design firm or, in special cases, the individual designer. For example, your drawing would read at the bottom: © 1989 by Business Design, Inc. This is the only way that you can protect your design from being copied by other people who might see it.

Mark any drawings you think might be worth copyrighting in this fashion. Then, as the project progresses, if you find that the item is worth copyrighting, register it.

There are a few reasons to register your copyright with the U.S. Copyright Office. First, it makes your design a matter of public record. Second, registration is necessary if you are going to defend any suits for infringements that might be filed in court.

Copyrighting is very inexpensive. You can do it directly, without an attorney. All you need to do is submit a completed application form, your fee for the application, and a copy of the work being registered. The copy requirements vary, depending upon the type of item that you are registering. To obtain copyright forms write to: The Register of Copyrights, Library of Congress, Washington, D.C. 20559.

When a designer is working for a company, usually the employer, not the employee, is considered the author of a work. This situation is covered under the copyright statute defining "work for hire," which is work that is prepared by an employee when under the employment of a particular company.

Copyrighting is good for the duration of the author's life, plus an additional fifty years after his or her death. If a copyright is registered under a company's auspices, the copyright duration would be seventy-five years from the date of publication, or one-hundred years from the date of creation, whichever is shorter. These units are based on laws that came into effect on January 1, 1978.

Design firms have hundreds of copyrights on various items, and I know design firms who have made more money defending their copyrights than they have on design. Obviously, it doesn't pay to copyright something unless it really is an original work and has copyright value. But it does pay to put the copyright symbol and your name on each and every drawing. It keeps people from copying you without discretion.

USING OFFICE TOOLS

How you use your office tools—the library and telephone in particular—can often be as important as which systems you select.

Managing the Library

Libraries need constant management. They grow, and if not regularly reviewed, can outgrow their space. In most cases, when a library outgrows its space, it is time to review and purge, to get rid of items that have been discontinued or which you no longer use in your practice. Evaluate your library annually. If you don't have the right information, there is no point in having a library.

A library must be organized. It is not professional to have to look through sixteen feet of catalogs to find two product specifications. At the prices designers charge, all time should be spent designing, not searching.

How extensively organized a library is really depends on its size and the number of people working with it. The larger the library and the number of people with access to it, the more structured your categorizing and use regulations must be. Even a small library needs structure. Items must be returned to their positions after being used so they can be easily retrieved the next time they are needed.

Every collection that goes into your library needs an assigned position. Catalogs should be kept together, as should samples. You need open shelving for books, magazines, and catalogs; and standard drawer files for smaller catalogs not in binders, articles, and pages torn from magazines. Product samples come in all shapes and sizes and should be filed according to their physical properties. Lucite trays and drawers are invaluable for some carpet samples, as are standard metal file drawers.

Within your catalog section, catalogs of furniture for contract office spaces should be kept together, apart from catalogs for lighting fixtures or residential furniture.

Magazines. How much are you spending on design books and magazines? This expenditure can run to several thousand dollars. Take the time once a year to review the value of each publication you get. Are your designers and staff people reviewing copies or do they simply fill up shelves in the studio? If you buy magazines, make sure that you use them to keep up-to-date on current products and issues. If they are just cluttering your office you should cancel those subscriptions, whether they are free or paid.

For every publication you decide to keep, ask yourself the following questions:

▶ Who reads it first?

▶ How long should it be kept?

▶ How often must the subscription be renewed?

▶ How often does it come—weekly, monthly, bimonthly, quarterly, or semiannually?

▶ Where will it be stored?

▶ Can you donate old copies to a design school?

To effectively control magazines' circulation and storage, consider using a form similar to the one on page 267. Consult this form to evaluate your magazine buying. Review it once a year and add to it as needed, and you'll probably find it helps you to eliminate some of the clutter and confusion magazines can create in a studio.

Managing the Telephone

Make call handling a top priority in your company. When you look at the time that you spend on it and the value that the phone can bring to your company, it's worth the effort.

The Phone Receptionist. Who should answer the telephone? Should the principal or head designer do this? Probably not. After all, they are among the more expensive people on the payroll and it really doesn't pay to have them answering the telephone. But it should be someone who has a good voice, is friendly, and who likes to build rapport with the person on the other end of the phone. Enthusiasm helps. Make sure the person answering the phone sounds as if he or she is happy to receive the call; not that it's an annoyance or a problem.

Probably the best person to answer your telephone is a person who has been with your firm for a very long time, or an older employee who cannot stand the stress of a field work schedule, but can be hospitable and knows a great deal about the firm.

It is a good idea to have the staff take turns answering the phones so that each person in the studio becomes familiar with client interests and desires. However, you should not let anyone who is not reasonably well informed answer the telephone if you can possibly avoid it. When the person who answers the phone can handle a situation, there is no need to refer to a second or even third person. This saves a lot of staff time and helps develop better rapport with the clients.

Structure your office so the person who answers the phone is pleasant. Any person answering the phone should do so in a polite and professional manner, and not put the client through the third degree. You need information from your clients, but there are good ways and bad ways to get this information.

I have heard of potential clients who decided against a firm because they did not like the way they had been treated over the phone.

Telephone Protocol. Anyone who answers your business telephones must build rapport with your clients. In doing so they must also get basic information, and get it correctly. Sometimes people don't pronounce their names clearly over the telephone. Your phone receptionist must be sure he or she gets the caller's name correctly spelled—even if this requires spelling the name back to the caller to double-check. The receptionist should not put a call through without verifying who the caller is—even if the voice sounds like a person he or she knows.

It is critical for a caller's name to be spelled correctly in the record of each phone call. So often you'll have three or four clients with a similar name. There's

Magazine management sheet. Using a form similar to this one can help you control the circulation and storage of magazines in your firm. It can also help you in evaluating which magazine subscriptions should be continued, discontinued, or added.

MAGAZINES	LOCATION STORED	LENGTH OF TIME	GIVEN TO	CIRCULATION OF STAFF	COST	EXPIRES

nothing more embarrassing and nothing that puts a client off more than your calling with the incorrect name or incorrect information. Your phone receptionist should have in front of him or her a list of clients and their telephone numbers. If the receptionist recognizes the client's voice, he or she can then say, for example, "Yes, Mrs. Jones, are you going to be at your number?" and read Mrs. Jones her number. If the caller says he or she will be at another number, the receptionist should write that number down. He or she should make sure before hanging up that the return number is documented with the message to speed up returning calls.

At one point we had three Mrs. Moores. Each one spelled her name slightly differently. They all had very different projects. They also didn't like each other. In a small community, this was a problem. Two of their voices were not that distinctively different. When a phone call came in, it was very difficult to tell which Mrs. Moore it was unless we compared telephone numbers.

Another time, I received a message to return a call to a name I didn't quite recognize at a number that seemed familiar. I called and got a business office. After getting through to the third secretary with a name that wasn't quite right, I finally realized who I was supposed to be calling. I was embarrassed because this was one of my largest clients whom I obviously should have known well. Fortunately the incident just caused embarrassment to me and was a big joke among the client's secretaries; however, it could have been far worse had my call gone directly to the client.

What is the subject? To whom should a call be directed? It's a kindness not to waste a caller's time. If the call should be returned, the receptionist should find out when the caller is going to be available. If the caller has several telephone numbers, the receptionist needs to get the correct number.

When you're training your receptionist or anyone else in telephone protocol, try to have the person answer each call within two or three rings. Having the phone ring forever is very annoying for the caller. The receptionist must focus on the telephone calls. He or she can't read a magazine or eat lunch and answer the telephone effectively at the same time.

If you can, hire a person whose primary job is answering the telephones; don't expect him or her to do forty other things. Put your receptionist where he or she can concentrate on the telephone and won't be distracted by people passing by.

Not everyone is a good telephone person. If a person really doesn't have good diction or doesn't speak clearly, perhaps he or she need some additional training. It is important that your receptionist's choice of words is appropriate to your business.

Handling Telephone Calls. Many designers tell me that they are constantly harassed by the telephone. Our office is no different. I feel that over fifty percent of your telephone calls—especially the harassing ones—can be eliminated by good phone manners and by checking in regularly with clients and suppliers when you are handling a project. The other fifty percent are very important because they are sales and marketing tools that need to be properly developed.

Every phone call you receive has taken someone time and effort to sit down and call you. Yes, there are clients who call constantly. There are ways of handling this without aggravating the clients. You let them know the specific time when you will return their call, and assure them that you will have the proper information when you call them back. Most of our clients are so very busy that they don't want me to waste their time; but they do want the information. We find that if we respond by gathering the information together and getting back to them at a set time, rather than reacting to suit their moods, we have a better managed and happier office and better informed and happier clients.

Prepare an outline for all of your calls and document everything that is said. Many of us have clients who seem to be lying in wait for us to make a mistake. You should research and prepare solutions for problems before presenting them to a client. You can tell clients about almost any kind of problem if you do it in a controlled, organized manner. If you just present them with the problem, without offering any solution, you'll soon have a bigger problem.

When you realize that a caller is rambling, ask for his or her agenda outline. I'm always prepared to give my outline.

Callers must be kept on track. Many people like to talk about everything under the sun; if you are designing their boardroom, keep the conversation about the boardroom.

Some days do you feel as if you're playing telephone tag with clients? You call them—they call you—you call back, and on it goes. How can you avoid wasting time this way?

If you plan your time so that everyone in your firm knows when you are making phone calls and clients learn when they can reach you, you will save an immeasurable amount of time and keep your dialing to a minimum. I know many designers who refuse to accept telephone calls except during certain hours. If they are interrupted they can't accomplish objectives. I think it is a good idea not to accept phone calls you are unprepared to handle.

I make a special schedule for calls. For example, contractors know that they may reach me between 6:30 and 7:30 every morning. They understand that this is a good time to call me, because if I'm not there, I'll call them back very shortly. This is also the time I will have my files in front of me and be prepared to answer any of their questions. I have other times during the day when I recommend sources or clients to call, depending upon my schedule.

When I am finished with a phone call with a client, I send him or her a written review of any changes or items discussed on that phone call that would affect our original design or documents. When a client realizes that what you've discussed on the phone will be sent to him or her in writing for verification, with the date of the phone call referred to on the transcript, it's much easier to support billing for phone time.

When leaving messages, don't treat secretaries like second-class citizens. Frequently they can help you more than any other person in reaching the person you want. Leave a message that can easily be answered—say what you want and why—so when the person returns your call he or she can be ready with the appropriate information.

If you want a person to call you back, suggest a convenient time. There is no point in having a person call you back when you know you are going to be out on other projects during the day. Your messages should state when you will be available, such as between 4:00 and 5:00 this evening. Usually the secretary knows the schedule of the person you are trying to reach and can help you coordinate this.

When people call you, how do you screen those calls? There are a lot of calls that should never go through to you and just waste your time. You also want to be sure that you've got the right file in hand and are ready to give good information when you take certain calls.

In our office we work as a team. Our clients know that they can speak with any four or five of us and they're going to get excellent information. I feel this develops far more respect for our staff from my clients than if only I gave answers.

The clients know that when it comes to scheduling, several other people know a lot more about it than I do. When it comes to some of the design details, again, someone can give them better information. Therefore not every call is directed toward me, which is a tremendous relief when it comes time to return calls at the end of the day.

Almost all calls can be divided into three groups: those from people you really want to talk to; those from people you surely don't want to talk to; and those that you're not sure about. It's great if someone can screen these calls for you before you pick up the telephone. We try to keep a list in our office of those people we really want to hear from to make sure that they are put through every time. We also keep a list of the pests. My attitude is that certain people should be kept away from me; I want the freedom of not talking to them if at all possible.

Don't let people abuse you with the telephone. I find it's much better to pay for returning a telephone call when it's convenient for me than to have people calling and interrupting me at inappropriate times.

HOW TO END A CALL

Sometimes we have great difficulty because clients call and we just can't get off the phone. We don't want to insult them, but there are other projects to be done. The trick is to convey that you have other obligations but that you are ever so ready to give the client prime attention. The basic story in selling and marketing remains: Give clients attention and they will ordinarily be very happy. Reduce that attention and you have complaints and problems.

If a telephone call gets too long, there are ways of cutting it off. Ask your secretary to ring so the caller hears a buzz. Or simply say, "I'm wanted on another phone. Would you hold the line a moment? Or, better yet, let me get the rest of this information and I'll call you back at four o'clock." Learn to break off calls if they're not productive. Sometimes this can be done by summarizing what you think has been covered and saying you are going to get back to the caller after you check on the points you discussed.

The Phone Log. Every phone call that comes into the office should be recorded in a daily phone log. You should keep a phone log at every phone and list each call, the day and time the call came in, and the subject. This log should be written legibly enough for anyone to be able to pick it up and read it. The log should also include the name of the person to whom the message was given, so that there is a record of who is following up on each message. If three or four days after a call you wonder whether a situation was remedied, you can look up the details of the call in the phone log. The new peel-off message pads make great phone logs, as a copy can be fastened to the client's file pages and become part of your permanent record.

Answering Machines. I used to hate answering machines. Now I think they're one of the greatest things in the world because at least I can leave a message and let someone know that I have responded to a call. Don't apologize for your answering machine in your message. Do make your message short. It's boring for callers to sit through a sixty-second message they've heard ninety times before. Try to have a tape where people can leave long messages and encourage them to do so.

When you're expecting a call but may not be in, instruct your caller to leave his or her details on the message machine so that you can take care of them immediately. Encouraging clients to do this will save you a lot of time.

TELEPHONE RECORD			Date:
			Staff:
Time:	Person:	Purpose of Call:	Results:

© Design Business Monthly

Our policy is that if a client asks for absolutely anything, we attempt to handle it. If a client calls our design studio and asks about a lamp shade, we will help locate it, although this is not really our service. We have clients we have been taking care of for over thirty years. I even help my father's clients—some of whom are now in their nineties—if they call me with a problem. I just take care of it, because I feel that if I were ninety, I would be happy for someone to take care of me. I treat them the way I would like to be treated.

If someone who is not a client calls us for a service we do not provide, we try to find out why the person called us and where he or she found out about us. We can learn from these calls. If people think we are a lamp shop and that is not correct, then we are projecting the wrong image in our marketing. We try to determine why they don't understand what kind of services we really do render.

The Telephone as a Sales Tool. A telephone can be a great sales tool. I must admit that I'd hate to make my living from cold calls. I'm not polished at it, but I have learned a few ways to use the telephone effectively.

1. *Establish rapport with the secretaries.* Ask them questions, such as "Who is in charge of the office-planning division of the company and who does that person report to?" If possible, try to get to this person; you can say that the secretary referred you to them. This gives you a much better chance of getting their attention.

2. *If you're not sure how to pronounce a name, ask the company's telephone operator.* Or ask the secretary. They are usually happy to tell you and it saves a lot of embarrassment later. Make sure you thank them, and to try to develop some common interest with them so that when you call back and you can say, "I spoke with you the other day about such and such and you were kind enough to refer me to Mr. Smith. Is Mr. Smith available now? May I speak with him now?—or do you suggest that I call back at another time when he might not be so pressured?" If someone isn't in, schedule when to call again and be careful to follow through on them. One little trick that often works is to call before 9:00 A.M. or after 5:00 P.M. Very often the staff is not there, but the principal is, and he will answer the phone himself. This is also a strategic time to talk with executives because usually they are less pressured than during the day, and they often don't mind taking a few moments to discuss your marketing objective.

3. *When you make a phone call, ask the person you are calling if he or she has a few minutes to talk with you.* When you're calling someone at home, you never know in what condition you're going to find him or her. There's no worse time to try to make a sale than when a person has stepped out of the bath tub dripping wet to answer the phone. Even at the office, there may be six people in front of the person, making it a very confusing time to talk over the phone.

4. *Keep a daily log of all phone calls and notes in an individual client's file.* I can't tell you how valuable this can be for designers. In fact, on several occasions, when designers I knew had to appear in court in verify certain communications, the judges were very impressed when they saw the record of time and details of phone calls. It was obvious that the logs were accurate because they had been kept on a regular basis in the designer's handwriting.

5. *Make weekly reports by telephone.* One of the most successful sales and marketing techniques is to create good client rapport through frequent telephone communication (see pages 183–84). Make a weekly report on every design project. Confirm with your client at the beginning of a project the appropriate times for this interaction and, at that time each week, have a member of your design team call the client with a full report on the status of his or her design project.

By scheduling your calls, you can be prepared, which makes you appear professional and can add considerably to the overall sales on a project.

Thank people for their kindness. When you make a thank-you telephone call to a factory foreman who's been abused by everybody else that week he'll never forget you. "Congratulations! You've made a beautiful product for us. We're happy we used you and hope to use you again." The time you spend making verbal rewards is not just good manners. You are insuring that you are remembered in a favorable context.

You need to organize to get the most out of your time on the phone, no matter to whom you are talking. Here are some tips.

▶ *Make a written agenda before you make a call.* Skip socializing unless you feel it is necessary for smoothing something over.

▶ *Make sure that the time you are spending in making this call now is important.* Consider whether you could wait and coordinate it with some other issues that you need to discuss tomorrow or the next day.

▶ *Try not to be left on hold.* Try to have an extra project to review while you wait.

▶ *Group similar calls.* Make all calls once or twice during the day and the rest of your day will be more productive. Keep a list of the people you are calling handy so you don't have to look up numbers.

▶ *Direct dial your calls.* Very often it is faster and easier to dial yourself than to use a secretary.

▶ *Plan the time when you are going to make your calls.* Consider when the most convenient times are for both you and the other party.

▶ *Be sure that the telephone call is necessary.*

▶ *Get to the point.* Before you start your business talk, you can still allow that little bit of time for rapport, because most people do appreciate this. Then get to the point; keep focused and concentrate on the subject.

▶ *Learn how to break in, if it's required, but don't interrupt unless it's absolutely necessary.* Then do it in an appropriate manner.

▶ *When you are transferring calls, make sure that the person to whom you are referring the call is ready to take it.* If he or she is not prepared, tell the caller you'll have the person he or she wanted call back in just a few minutes.

▶ *Thank people.* Remember to use the person's name because people like to hear their names.

Using Your Voice to Control a Conversation. On the telephone, your voice tells people who you are. You make a very strong impression within fifteen seconds. Do you sound weak? Hesitant? Wishy-washy? Disorganized? The impression you make can be changed.

To seem businesslike, professional, and strong, speak slowly. The normal telephone conversation pace is about 150 words per minute. If you can reduce this to just about 100 words per minute, you will definitely improve your communication level.

The volume and pace of a conversation is very important in winning a person's confidence. Listen to how the other person is speaking. If you are talking to someone who speaks very slowly, perhaps you need to reduce your pace. In turn, if you're talking to someone who speaks very loudly and rapidly, you may want to reduce his or her pace. When people start screaming at you on the telephone, slow up your pace; speak very quietly and very, very slowly. Many times this calms them down. If you speak loudly and rapidly it will make these people even more emotional. Your diction and enunciation are very important. Over the phone we are judged strictly by our voices.

How can you tell what you sound like? Tape yourself making a call so you can analyze how you sound in different situations. That tape has two purposes; it is both a record of client interaction and a tool for improving your effectiveness on the telephone. If you are going to tape a phone conversation, let the client know you are taping it. Then pay attention to what he or she says, and to what you say in reply. Is what you can say really appropriate?

You should talk with your whole body. Your posture, your expression, and the shape of your mouth affect the way you sound. Your voice is like a window; it expresses everything that is inside of you. Some people stand when they talk on the phone. If you really want to be in control, standing may help.

Remember your facial expression. I once accused a psychologist of being vain for having a very large mirror right across from his desk. Later on I thought it might be a good idea. If we saw how we looked when we were talking on the telephone, perhaps we would change our ways.

There are many signals that people are listening for in your voice. They want to know that you are in control of the situation, that you are managing your own reactions. Don't respond emotionally, but reply to the issues at hand.

More than anything, check your attitude. If you are in a bad mood one day, perhaps you should not answer your own telephone. If you've had a really bad day, perhaps you should have someone hold your calls so you don't accidentally sabotage your relationship with your clients. Your secretary might handle this by saying, "I'm sorry, but she's in a meeting. Would you please let me have her return your call when she has time to go over these details with you?" Give your callers a little positive response when you ask for a delay.

Attitude is really important. We've all had experiences where we're talking with a supplier and fighting for a delivery date and then the next person on the line is one of our very mild-mannered clients. You must answer the phone in the right tone of voice. Take time to restore yourself; poise yourself for that good client.

Many times we're not able to give people the answers that they want to hear. But there are ways of presenting negative news in positive terms. For example, you might say to a client, "How would you like it if we arranged to deliver your furnishings next Friday? We will have our best furniture installers available that day to handle your project." That sounds so much better than saying, "The furniture can't be delivered until next Friday." The first statement makes Friday into a special day.

The goal in any call you make is to establish a true and positive agreement. You want to express feelings at the same time you are covering the facts. Rapport is very important. Use the person's name as you speak. Refer to various experiences that you have had together. Expressing visual and emotional issues verbally is difficult. Creating visual pictures can be helpful.

Say what you mean. Review each day what you have to do so you know what is possible to schedule. Don't say, "I'll take care of it tomorrow," if you know you can't. It's better to say, "I'll look that over in the morning with my associate to see just what it involves and how soon we can do the final detailing."

The Complaint Call. There's at least one way to handle complaints so that angry clients remain clients. Irate clients love to call, full of anger and unreasonable to talk to. What should you do. Do not ignore these calls; if clients can't reach you with a complaint, they'll go to another designer. Encourage people to tell you about problems, and then help them find solutions. But prepare yourself; have your paper in hand ready for note taking. Have yourself in good control. Make sure your posture and everything else about you is perfect, because you're going to need all your ammunition.

Try to learn to separate the facts from the emotions. Usually you hear many more of the latter. This is hard to do when somebody's screaming at you on the other end of the phone.

The way I see it, if there were no problems, the whole design process could be handled by a computer and clients wouldn't need me.

Let angry clients talk. After all, that's why they called. They want to blow off steam. Let them do it, but encourage them to give you the details and define the problem. Ask them what you can do together to solve their problem. Try to involve a client in the solution; if you are successful, you will have developed a partner and a great client for the future.

Try to win clients back by using only positive statements. Make notes of what you will say and change any negatives to positives before you respond.

A few years ago, a client we had worked with extensively called me about a fee on a project. We had billed them a considerable amount of money for the furnishings for their project and they had paid our initial design fee. But, in addition, we had done a great deal of cabinetry and detailing. The client was told he would be billed for the time involved in these areas at our standard rates. This was clearly stated in writing, but the exact amount was left open; he wasn't exactly sure what the bill would be. And when he got the bill he called, irate.

At this point, I said to him, "Here is our story. The furnishings we did, in a sense, sell you, so there is some profit and our design fee in those charges. However, the rest of this project was done by various contractors. We do not receive any compensation except this billing for this part of the job, nor do we accept any kickbacks from any of the contractors. We only bill for our fee. We also negotiated with several contractors to get you the best quality workmen as well as the best price possible. I think you'll agree we did a good job.

"How do you think I should have handled billing for this? You've been a client of ours for probably fifteen years at this point, and we've done a lot of work together. Obviously you feel I've done something wrong. You run a business a lot larger than mine, and if you don't think I did this in the right way, would you explain to me how I could do it better? After all, I can learn a lot from you. You know more about running a business than I do. Most of my career has been spent doing design work".

The client thought about what I had said a little bit and then said, "No, Mary, I think what you did was exactly right." He thanked me for explaining it to him. When we finished talking, he was very calm, and I have done several major jobs for him since.

I used this complaint to *build* confidence rather than to lose a client. In handling a compliant, make sure that you confirm exactly what the client expects from you—what the solution is and what will be done. Then be sure that your staff follows through. Don't promise something that you cannot do.

Long-Distance Savvy. When you're making long-distance phone calls, watch your time zones. They can often work to your advantage because there are places that you can call between 5:00 and 6:00 and even 6:00 and 7:00 in the evening.

You'd be surprised how many mistakes there are in phone bills. We have had as many as four different long-distance services in our offices at one time. Sometimes it's difficult to get lines out of a small community. Check out the services in your area to be sure you won't have a problem getting long-distance lines at primary times.

Conference Calls. The quality of conference calls can vary greatly. You may have a mechanism on your phone that permits you to make conference calls, but you should test it to be sure the communication is coming through clearly.

Have a plan or an outline for every conference call, just as you would for any staff meeting or other kind of conference. A conference call must be well orchestrated, or you're in trouble.

Moderate your conference calls. As the moderator, you should introduce all the participants, including yourself. Give their backgrounds, and let them each make a brief introduction. Address the others by name, and ask each speaker to identify him or herself before speaking so that you're sure exactly who's speaking. When you get four or five people from a factory on a call, you're sometimes not sure if you're talking to the sales manager or the production chief. On a conference call, usually you can't hear as well as you can on a standard two-party call. Talk slowly and clearly.

Mobile Phones. It's not unusual for designers to drive somewhere between 35,000 and 50,000 miles a year. A car phone lets your staff and clients reach you. And it's a safety precaution. You can call someone if you're in trouble.

Cellular phones are expensive, but a vast improvement over earlier mobile phones because they have much clearer reception. But people can listen in, so don't use it to discuss confidential matters. Try to use travel time to make calls that don't need to be documented because it's very hard to be driving, talking on the phone, and taking notes. If something needs documenting at the end of a phone call, ask for permission to tape a summation. At that point, you can put it on your tape recorder and recap the issues of the call on tape, and verify it.

I use my mobile phone for general checking and personal calls. There's no way I would take time out of my day to make personal calls, but I will call a few people on my mobile phone. The speak feature on mobile phones is very nice because it allows you to have both hands free; however, sometimes the voice projection isn't quite as good. Usually I try to use the receiver.

If you sell your car or trade it in, remember that you can always move your mobile phone from car to car.

Chapter Eleven

MASTERING FINANCIAL MANAGEMENT

Good financial management and structure is a requirement for every design firm. More than a few design firms that are excellent at promoting themselves and at getting new business later lose their profit for reasons that could have been avoided. It's hard enough to get profitable projects today; let's find ways to keep that profit.

Profit is a measurement of success in every form of business, including the design business. No one wants to deal with an unprofitable company. Clients instinctively feel that unprofitability jeopardizes their interests. Therefore, in order to have a strong business, you need to understand current financial and business ethics and procedures, and make sure that your relationships with all other companies and people, whether resources or clients, are based on these. No business can continue without a good financial profit structure.

YOUR PROFIT FORECAST

At the beginning of each year, or just before, make up a profit forecast. Consider where your firm is going—what business you expect to acquire during the next year, how your firm will grow, and what monies will be required.

Then work out the necessary methods to handle your growth or change of focus. This is a prerequisite to preparing your budget and preliminary financial plan for the year. Every firm needs a budget, whether the company is new or has been in operation for years. A profit forecast will enable you to budget in the right areas. It also gives you a basis for comparing where you are actually going as opposed to what you expect to do.

CASH MANAGEMENT

The basics of cash management with any interior design firm fall into two areas: cash flow and accounts receivable. Your cash flow projection predicts your expenses for the next several months through to a year. Have your accountant work out the details of your general expenses, including overhead, payroll, and any long-term loans on which you make payments. This will vary from week to week. With this general figure, you will be able to estimate your overall projected expenses. Next, you need to review regularly your accounts receivable, accounts payable, and aging schedules. Each month your bookkeeper or financial manager should give you a list of your accounts receivable and review the payment schedule. Obviously, the closer and tighter control you have on both of these issues and the better informed you are, the easier it will be to run your interior design firm. There will be no surprises or emergencies.

Financial management in a firm with fewer than ten members is generally handled by a bookkeeper/secretary. When the firm grows beyond ten, usually it will require an experienced, full-time bookkeeper. If your firm grows beyond twenty-five, then you will also need a business manager. Computer systems have reduced the staffing required by a firm, but the firm must have an individual in charge of making the decisions and managing the overall practice. Once a firm becomes larger than twenty-five, a person with a strong financial background is needed to be the financial manager. Usually one of the partners fills this role. Firms of every size need to have a certified public accountant available as a consultant and advisor.

The general formats of financial management structures are similar in all firms. Larger firms obviously will require more extensive accounting than small firms, not only because of their higher volume of business but also because there is usually less immediate involvement of the principals on each and every project.

Your accountant will give you a year-end statement; however, it is generally advisable also to have a monthly profit-and-loss statement or a statement showing your financial direction, which includes your cash flow projections and your cash planning for the month, similar to those that are illustrated on page 293. These can be done by your bookkeeper on an in-house basis. Obviously, if you have a financial manager, he or she will want to set up appropriate documents suitable for your firm. With different practices, some of the requirements on these statements may vary slightly, but the ones included here show the general basics.

Cash Flow

Cash flow is more important than profits to the success of a business. And with the cost of money going ever higher, it is becoming even more essential to conserve cash on hand. Two of the areas that eat up funds are inventory and accounts receivable. Also affecting cash flow are profit completion times, buying policies, and the investment of retainer funds. Accounts receivable is such a major factor in cash flow that it is treated separately on pages 279–83.

Inventory. Inventory ties up cash. Are all the items that you have in stock and those you are buying for inventory really worth having? The cost of maintaining inventory each year is approximately thirty-three to thirty-eight percent of the cost of the item, based on the costs of insurance, maintenance, and money. It may be better for you to keep a cash reserve for use in other parts of your business than to maintain a large inventory.

Project Completion Times. Slow project completion times are costly. The sooner you complete a project, the faster you will get paid and the better your cash flow will be. Even though you have retainers for every project you start, you still incur additional costs in doing the job. So the faster you wrap it up, the better.

Buying Policies. Interior designers tend to be cautious about buying policies. There are ways of buying effectively and saving large sums of money. The most successful interior design firms I have seen are those that have very shrewd buying policies. You may want to consider using a service that will negotiate prices for you and make sure that you are getting the best possible prices. I predict that almost every small to medium-sized firm will be using some form of buying service in the near future.

Aim to retain the use of the funds you have for as long as possible. Ask for extended credit from your major resources so you can keep these monies invested and make a profit from them. This is one of the shrewder uses of available funds.

Investments. Any money taken in as retainers on projects should be put into some type of interest-bearing account, such as a money market fund. Some firms earn enough on their money market funds and the amount of interest they charge on overdue accounts receivable to give their employees a very large bonus.

Most firms charge interest on accounts receivable that are overdue. This helps encourage clients to pay promptly; it also reimburses the firm for extending credit. A few years ago I reviewed the books of an interior design firm that was available for purchase. I was amazed as I examined the company's financial statement to find that its major profits came from the interest clients were charged for installment payments. The company's accounts receivable were very large, but the profits from this division were well managed. The company extended a lot of credit, but it was paid well for it.

Accounts Receivable

Accounts receivable are the monies owed you for services or furnishings you supplied to your clients. Good control of accounts receivable is extremely important to the financial profitability of a company. The profit objective is to speed up the whole process of design management. This means that the faster you can process any job through the studio, no matter what kind of service is rendered, the faster it can be billed and the more profitable the project will be. Generally, billings in design firms are done either immediately after the project is completed, when the merchandise is delivered, or within a thirty-day period. Designers who are lax in this area may have no idea how much slow billings cost them on a day-to-day basis.

When establishing and managing accounts receivable, keep in mind that the fewer dollars you have tied up in accounts receivable, the easier it is to manage the cash flow of your business and the less your losses will be. The longer an account remains unpaid, the greater the chances are that it will become uncollectible. The sooner you bring money in, the more you have to work with or reinvest. Often, clients will avoid doing business with a firm to whom they owe money. Therefore, the sooner a client's account is paid, the faster the client will start another project.

Maintaining accounts receivable costs at least one and a half percent a month. This can take a tremendous bite out of your profits. A company whose accounts receivable are current is usually very profitable. Sometimes this requires that you adopt a tougher payment policy. If clients do not pay on time, you should consider stopping work. I know interior designers are reluctant to do this, but it may be your best leverage in getting payment. I know designers who now require payment before delivery, rather than after delivery. Obviously, whether this is suitable depends upon the standards in your part of the country. Progress payments or staged payments are becoming the norm in most billing systems. The faster payments are received, the more profitable the job.

Sadly, many companies with a string of great design jobs have been forced into bankruptcy because they have not properly handled their accounts receivable. It's extremely disheartening to see designers forced out of business because they are unable to collect their accounts receivable.

Credit Checks. Before accepting a job, carefully investigate and analyze the client's ability to pay for the job. Determine exactly what the costs will be and ask the client what his or her position is in handling this expenditure.

Often projects grow as they develop, and the initial budget is not enough to meet the costs. Clients who expected a project to cost perhaps $30,000 may find that with the additions they requested, the work ended up costing $45,000 to $50,000. The client may need to get financing for the additional amount. I recommend making a credit check of the client in the initial or early interview stages while your financial involvement in the project is relatively small. Do not wait until you are into a second or third contracting phase where a lot of money is at stake; it will be too late. If you find that the client does not have the cash available, you can attempt to get it for the client through your sources.

The information that you have collected regarding your client's credit should remain with the project file so that the person responsible for collecting accounts receivable will have it available.

Terms. To establish your accounts receivable terms, you will need to have your accountant, financial advisor, attorney, and marketing consultant make a careful study, as these terms affect every part of your business. If you extend credit, you must have the capital available to support this investment. Every dollar invested must fit into your profit structure. Collection policies affect your future collection and legal costs. Your terms affect your ability to get jobs.

In most instances, designers will ask for a retainer or a deposit on a project. The term "retainer" rather than "deposit" is used because certain states require deposits to be kept in a special account for that particular client's project. These funds cannot be put in your company's general account or used for any other purposes.

The amount of the retainer depends upon the type of work being done. If the project is for professional services, excluding purchasing, and is for a small, private corporation, a normal retainer is half of the estimated cost of the first phase of the project. For a larger project, the retainer is related to the details of the contract. Sometimes a contract alone is considered sufficient and no retainer is required. In other instances, the retainer required could be from one-tenth to one-half of the total fee, depending on the size of the project. For a very large project, the retainer is often as low as ten percent of the total estimated fee. Retainers for smaller projects range from one-third to one-half of the estimated fee. In situations where the billing is based on furnishings, retainers are usually one-third to one-half of the expected invoice total.

Scheduled Payments. In dealing with accounts receivable, it is obviously to the advantage of the design firm to get a retainer followed by scheduled payments throughout the project. If you are billing just for professional service fees, it is best to have a payment schedule outlining the stages and amounts of payments.

The standard method of presenting a payment schedule is to list the stages of completion and to state the percentage of payments that are due at these times.

Stage of Completion	Amount Due
Design	40%
Documentation	40%
Administration	20%

Although more than twenty percent may be spent for administration and supervision, it is always best to collect as much of the fee up front, or at a set point, rather than at the end of the project. Billing on completion requires a considerable amount of bookkeeping and time spent evaluating your hours.

As you define the project to be done, work out a payment schedule and submit it to the client with your initial agreement, so that he or she knows exactly when monies are expected and how much to pay.

Most design firms take from two weeks to thirty days to invoice clients after work is completed. Then it takes the client another thirty days to pay the invoice. With a payment schedule you can often get your payments in much faster. Knowing ahead of time that there is a certain amount due in January, March, and June, for example, the client can then arrange to have funds available.

Extending Credit. Most businesses, including interior design firms, must extend credit. It is important to establish the terms of credit before starting a project. These should be stated at the time of the proposal. Often your company needs to establish a credit policy. It can be changed at any time, but you must start somewhere. Your policy could be that you will receive a retainer of a certain percentage up front, that there will be progressive payments due as the project continues, and that the balance is due ten to thirty days after delivery. You can offer extended terms by use of a bank or other lending institution, or you can make financing available through the firm at a certain rate of cost, depending upon what the state law allows.

Invoicing Methods. Before delivering merchandise, firms notify the client of the date and time they expect to make the delivery and the dollar value of the furnishings, and state when the payment will be due (payments are usually due by the end of the same month). This paves the way for prompt payment because the client knows in advance what you expect. Invoicing is normally done on the day that items are shipped or on a weekly or a monthly basis.

The location of your firm and the business customs of the area will determine somewhat your invoicing methods. In larger cities payment is often expected on delivery. A week prior to the day of a delivery, a firm will send a note saying, for example, "we are going to deliver the furnishings for your facility next Thursday. Enclosed is an invoice for $65,000.00 for the furnishings we will be installing. We shall appreciate having your check available on the day of delivery." In some areas this is not considered proper business courtesy.

When you are doing the billing and dealing with accounts receivable, it is definitely to your advantage to get billing out as soon as possible. In some design firms, it takes thirty days to process a bill, which can be self-defeating to the cash-flow situation. At my firm we aim to send out our invoices within three days of delivery. This requires us to have our data organized. Obviously, there are times when certain items are being shipped or delivered faster than your invoicing procedures can keep up with them, but the sooner you are able to do your billings the better your cash position will be.

Billing should go out within seventy-two hours of the time merchandise is delivered so that clients can easily identify what they are being asked to pay for. If they receive billing a month later, they might not recall what arrived on specific days of the month.

A delay in billing also signals to your client that you do not need the money. Don't delay. It is a foolishly lax business habit that should be nipped in the bud. Billing is best done on a daily or weekly basis. Waiting for the end of the month can be too confusing and too expensive.

Insist that any client billing be checked thoroughly before an invoice is sent out to assure that there are no mistakes. If a client finds errors in the billing, he or she will often question the whole costing procedure. A bit of care in this area can prevent a lot of complaints. If clients find that you are careless in finances, they will worry that you may be careless in other areas too.

Often, designers have difficulty collecting bills because they have not properly documented items or have not kept good contact with their clients. This is absolutely necessary. Regularly scheduled reports by telephone with proper written documentation build rapport.

Check with your bookkeeping department to be sure your invoices are going out regularly. Do not accept excuses. Determine how quickly all of your orders can be processed and shipped. Tightening this lead time can give a boost to your cash flow.

Billing Sheets. When you're preparing to send out bills, a billing sheet is helpful. Ask your bookkeeper to present all the items that are to be billed. The designer or project manager can then compare the amounts that were quoted against the actual costs and determine the appropriate prices to charge. This is an excellent billing method for both professional services and products, even if fees are based on value rather than actual time spent. The data on your billing sheet will give you a basis for determining the costing for your next project.

Require a monthly report from your bookkeeper outlining all accounts and exactly what position they are in. Be sure that the designer or the client coordinator is aware of exactly how these accounts stand.

BILLING SHEET

Order No.:	Item:	Quote: Unit:	Quote: Total:	Cost: Unit:	Cost: Total:	Price: Unit:	Price: Total:
Totals:							

Client: Salesperson: Date:

Deposit Balance on Hand:

Orders in Process:

Sales Tax:

Total Billing:

Less Deposit:

Amount Due:

© Design Business Monthly

Billing sheet. The data on your billing sheet will give you a basis for determining appropriate prices and fees to charge. It will also help you in costing your next project

Delinquent Payments. You must outline your firm's policy for delinquent payments at the beginning of a relationship. Spell out to your client how much and how often you expect to be paid. There are some clients who feel it is fine to pay an invoice in 90 or 120 days; other suppliers have extended them such credit to create a loyalty.

Sometimes the only way to control payments on a project is to have a hard business manner. Stop-work clauses are now becoming common in design contracts. These clauses state that the design firm has the right to stop work on a project if the client is in any way delinquent in making payments. The right to stop work on a design project must be clearly stated in the initial contract.

At the end of each month, review all your accounts receivable that are unpaid for over thirty days, over sixty days, and longer. It is important to check out why they have gone unpaid, which means that your bookkeeper will need to review with each of these clients why the account is overdue.

Collections. Enforcing your accounts receivable procedures does require strict follow-up. You don't harass people, but you do find out why they have not paid their bills and how they intend to handle them. In my firm we will normally make other terms available to a client if he or she cannot pay us promptly. And we do so with tact, explaining that we cannot afford to carry large amounts in our accounts receivable. We also have a delinquency charge. In Pennsylvania, we are permitted to charge one and a half percent of the balance due after thirty days.

Understanding a person's credit situation can help in collecting a payment. It is often useful to have a discussion about the client's payment habits with the other people working on the project.

Collection costs for accounts receivable are very high. Therefore, it is important to find ways to get your monies in ahead of time so you don't need to worry about collections. Although collection agencies can help collect bills, they charge from twenty-five to fifty percent and their success rate is not as great as one would like. Often you can also collect your delinquent accounts through the small claims court and by other legal means. The legal force you can apply will vary, depending upon the size of the claim and the type of legal recourse you have. However, if you are forced to turn over a bill to a collection agency or an attorney, that is usually the last time you will ever see that client.

Some clients are habitually late in paying, even though they are good credit risks. In my firm we ask for payment within thirty days, and we encourage prompt payment by explaining to our clients that the pricing on their job is dependent upon our being paid within thirty days. We ask to be notified if they cannot pay us within thirty days so we can make arrangements accordingly.

Accounts Payable

Accounts payable is the system wherein you record all the liabilities of the firm: materials, equipment, wages, rent, utilities, taxes, and any loans. There are many ways to set up an accounts payable system. The standard ledger system is one.

Accounts Payable Systems. For the last fifteen years I have recommended the one-write check disbursement system for small design firms. When the bookkeeper writes a check, the amount is automatically carboned onto the disbursement journal so that there is no chance for numbers to be transposed; they are automatically entered into the journal and then onto the ledger page. When 500 to 700 checks per month are issued, the one-write system saves an average of two days of office-staff time and eliminates the errors that would normally be made in copying information.

A number of computer systems handle accounts payable beautifully. There is even a computer system based on the one-write system. The computer writes your checks, ledger pages, and journal documentation so that at the end of the month, it is very simple to close out. Other computer systems take this system even further. They start the process when the order is written and have double- and triple-checking functions to assure amounts are correct and payments are appropriate. Interior design firms must be careful to make payments on the right day and not to duplicate payments. Most good computer systems have built-in double-checking systems to take care of these issues.

With traditional bookkeeping, a bookkeeper keeps an individual accounts-payable ledger sheet for every account. Some computer bookkeeping systems automatically do this for you; the extra documentation can be helpful at some points. Many companies operate without individual ledger sheets because having them is so complicated; the firms simply use their filing systems as reference if necessary. Streamline any process and you save time.

Establishing Credit with your Accounts. Today there are several attitudes in handling accounts payable that vary from those of the past. For most small design firms, the top priority is to keep a good credit rating and remain in good standing with their resources.

Establish credit with your resource companies before expecting them to extend it. Before you start placing orders with a resource company, ask what amount of credit the resource is willing to extend to you. If you wait until you place an order, a credit check can delay your project by at least thirty to ninety days. This can cause a lot of problems if you have already quoted your client from the price list and you can't buy directly from the company but have to go through a dealership or another resource. Ask the company what the discounting procedures are and verify buying requirements before you attempt to sell the merchandise. If you only specify merchandise and do not get involved in any purchasing, understanding the credit policies of resource companies lets you reasonably judge how well the dealerships are handling your client's account.

Many of our resources do not like working with small accounts, which is the typical designer account. They much prefer dealerships and large volume accounts because these are less expensive to manage and are safer financial risks.

Unfortunately, because some interior design firms have created problems by not paying their bills on time and neglecting to keep the resource companies properly informed, many resource companies require interior design companies to work on a C.B.D. (Cash Before Delivery) or C.O.D. (Cash On Delivery) basis. Obviously, the larger established firms do not work in this manner. In fact, many of them will not accept any C.B.D. or C.O.D. shipments.

C.O.D.

A new ruling by the U.S. Post Office permits any recipients to pay a C.O.D. bill by check made out to the mailer. The reasoning behind it is that if there is a problem with the merchandise, then the recipient can stop payment on the check. It is important to be aware of this new ruling; in the past when interior designers accepted C.O.D. shipments they had no recourse if the merchandise was damaged.

To be issued credit by a resource company, you must be a large, viable, and valuable account. Manufacturers and dealers will not bother doing the necessary credit checks and establishing the bookkeeping process for an account that means a few hundred dollars worth of business every now and then. This simply

Sample accounts payable and accounts receivable systems. There are many ways to set up these systems. Pictured here are the materials necessary for the one-write check-disbursement and invoicing systems.

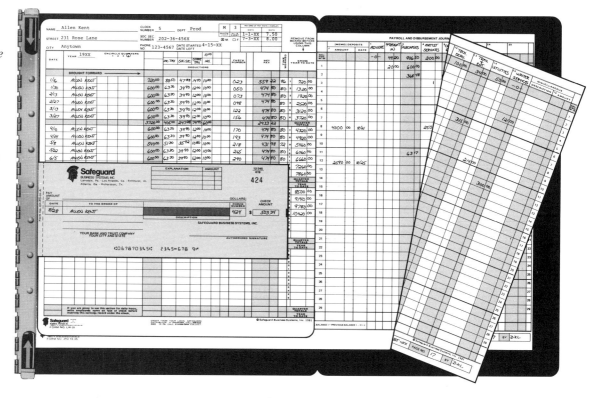

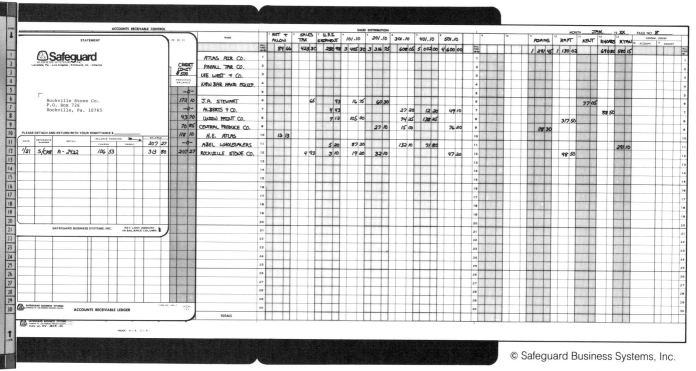

doesn't pay. It costs companies far too much to investigate your company, determine how much credit they should give you, and maintain this relationship.

Credit checks and ongoing evaluations are affordable only for larger volume accounts. When a design firm decides to buy for clients, the firm needs to position itself. A careful review of your financial and corporate position must be made by your accountant, financial advisor, lawyer, and marketing manager. The firm needs to establish an appropriate financial structure for obtaining credit and handling the capital investment required.

There are many other ways design firms can handle the purchasing part of the job, and some of these are proving to be easier to manage and more profitable. Co-op or buying organizations are becoming increasingly popular since they can negotiate from a position of strength.

Obviously you want to be able to go back to a company and say, "We have a problem and what can we do about it?" and have some clout. This must be worked out in the process of establishing your accounts.

Resource companies have financial-management requirements also. They have based their profits on time schedules and turnaround schedules. If design firms don't pay their bills on time, the resources have to protect themselves, which is why they must have strict terms. Companies are constantly notifying us, or even threatening us, with changes in their credit policies. For example:

> Effective April 1st, 1987, we are establishing new credit policies. Any invoice that is not paid within 30 days of the invoice date will be handled on a C.B.D. basis.

The way you handle your finances should take into account major changes in the credit requirements of your suppliers. Don't jeopardize your credit rating by ignoring notices of this kind.

Negotiating Good Credit Terms. The amount of credit that you can get from resources greatly extends the capital you have to run your business. If a supplier wants your business and realizes that you are important in acquiring the contract, he or she will very often extend better terms than would otherwise be available.

The terms you are able to negotiate with your resources greatly affect your cash management. When design firms decide to sell merchandise or handle purchases for clients, the dollar amounts are often very large and the terms and buying conditions that the firms establish have a great deal to do with their profits. Paying your accounts and keeping them up-to-date makes it easier to get merchandise.

You can become a prime account by working closely with a particular resource. A resource may extend large amounts of credit to you if he or she understands the way you work and the types of projects you handle. The first rule in establishing a good relationship with your resources is to inform the companies you buy from about your operation: what type of business you do, how you pay your bills, and how your company is financially structured. Don't expect to get credit without giving valid information and maintaining a standard bill-paying procedure.

Bill-Paying Procedures. When you establish your company's procedure for paying bills, let all of your resources know about it, whether you pay one a month, twice a month, every week, or ten days after receipt of merchandise.

In our company, to keep bookkeeping simple, we try to handle invoices only once. This means if merchandise arrives in good condition, we issue the check for it before the end of the week. Now that we are adapting to using a computer, it is easier for us to extend the period before we pay to the thirty days most invoices state. This gives us the use of this money for two or three additional weeks, and the interest it draws in our money market account enhances our profit picture.

Our company policy is to pay bills promptly even if it means borrowing. We often find this necessary. We have a line of credit at the bank that permits us to borrow on a weekly basis, if we must. We feel it is very important to keep accounts payable up-to-date so we can expect performance from our resources.

It may be expedient to give someone besides yourself the power to sign checks or to commit your company to purchasing contracts. Introduce this staff member to your banker, your accountant, and to your customers and suppliers. Should this person leave your employ, make sure the same people know about it. This can be done tactfully, while introducing the new staff person.

CREDIT TERMS

5–10: If you pay this invoice within ten days, you may take a five percent discount.

2–10: If you pay this invoice within ten days, you may take a two percent discount.

2–30: If you pay this invoice within thirty days, you may take a two percent discount.

N–60: This bill is due at the end of sixty days.

M.O.M. (*Middle of Month*): The billing will be sent out on the fifteenth of the month. This includes all purchases made from the middle of the previous month to the date of billing.

E.O.M. (*End of Month*): The billing will be sent out at the end of the month. This includes all purchases made during the month.

C.W.O. (*Cash with Orders*): Orders that are received will not be processed until payment is made.

C.I.A. (*Cash in Advance*): The same as C.W.O.

C.B.D. (*Cash Before Delivery*): The merchandise will be prepared and packaged, but the shipper will not make shipment until the payment is received.

C.O.D. (*Cash on Delivery*): The amount of the total billing will be collected upon the delivery of the merchandise.

S.D.B.L. (*Sight Draft—Bill of Lading*): A bill of lading will accompany the invoice, and a sight draft will be drawn on the buyer, which is forwarded to the seller by the customer's bank. The bill of lading is then released by the bank to the customer only upon his honoring the draft.

2/10/N/30 R.O.G.: If you pay this invoice within ten days, you make take a two percent discount; the bill is due at the end of thirty days; and the discount period starts at the date of receipt of goods, not the date of shipping or the date of the sale.

2/10/N/30 M.O.M.: If you pay this invoice within ten days, you may take a two percent discount; the bill is due at the end of thirty days; and both periods start from the fifteenth or the middle of the month following the date of the sale.

2/10/N/30 E.O.M.: If you pay this invoice within ten days, you may take a two percent discount; the bill is due at the end of thirty days; and both periods start from the end of the month of sale.

Keep in mind that discounts add up. For example, if you take advantage of a two percent ten-day discount, where the net is due in thirty days, this is worth 36.5 percent per year.

Do not pay for any merchandise until the item is received and inspected. Your purchase orders should explain your payment policy right on them (see pages 231–33). This ensures that your resources know your terms when they receive your order and that when they accept your order, they have accepted it under these conditions.

If problems prevent prompt payment of your bills or you find that you need extended time to pay, call the companies who have billed you and let them know your situation before the bills are due. When resources do not hear from you and do not receive payments or any kind of action, they become concerned, and one can't blame them. Keep your suppliers informed and you'll find that they will work with you in most instances.

Cash Discounts. A number of companies still offer cash discounts. It is amazing how much an interior design firm can earn per year just on the two or five percent discounts allowed them by certain suppliers. Many carpet manufacturers allow us a five percent discount if the invoice is paid within thirty days, with the balance due in sixty days. For just a thirty day period, we could lose a five percent discount. It has paid us to borrow money to be able to pay in time to receive this five percent discount. By taking discounts, we can also keep ourselves in an excellent credit position. But can we afford to offer them to our clients?

A two percent/ten-day cash discount is worth approximately thirty-seven percent on an annual basis. (When you offer discounts it is very difficult to make thirty-seven percent on your money.) Take that into consideration if you offer discounts to your clients. Giving cash discounts usually speeds up your receiving payment; however, there may be other ways of doing this that are less expensive.

Petty Cash. Every company needs to have some cash on hand. Even a straight professional service business has to pay cash for some items occasionally. It's not appropriate, for example, to be without the money to pay for postage or shipping. Most design firms maintain a small petty cash fund.

Try to keep your petty cash fund documented and in order. The fewer people who handle petty cash, the better the chance of keeping it organized; if you put one individual in charge it will run much more smoothly. Documentation of petty cash is required so that the payments can be properly classified for your financial statement. And, a review of petty cash is standard when you are audited by the IRS—they are always interested in how cash is handled.

Petty cash is a simple fund created by drawing a check for a certain amount—$100, for example. All of the items that are paid for out of that $100 are logged and the money is replaced at the end of a given period, possibly on a weekly basis.

Staff Monthly Expenses. In our firm we have our staff submit their expenses for reimbursement on a monthly basis. It is important to keep track of these expenses for many reasons. Not only do they help you in calculating the costs of your staff (see page 289), they also provide important information for the IRS. We have separate envelopes for travel expenses (see page 290).

The travel expense envelope is a practical way to document travel expenses. When a staff member is given an advance, this is clearly noted with the date. The staff member then keeps a record of all types and amounts of expenses, listing food separately (the bookkeeper needs to keep food expenses apart since they are only eighty percent deductible).

The staff member then turns in the envelope to the bookkeeper and it becomes the permanent record for the files. The envelope shows, then, the total reimbursement of expenses, less the advance, the amount due, and the check number that was issued. Any recalculation can be stated on the bottom. This simple envelope form makes management of travel expenses or any kind of expenses that are given out for job projects considerably easier to manage.

Staff monthly expense form. This form can be used to itemize the monthly expenses of your staff. It is a simple way of documenting expenses for reimbursement.

STAFF MONTHLY EXPENSE FORM				
Staff:		Month:		
Date:	Activity:		No. of Miles:	Other Expenses:

Staff Signature:		Total Miles:	
		Allowance:	@
Approved by:	Date Paid:	Subtotals:	
	Check No.:	Total Amount:	

© Design Business Monthly

Travel expense envelope. This envelope is a practical way for staff members to document travel expenses. It is turned in to the bookkeeper when the staff member returns from traveling.

TRAVEL EXPENSES

Staff:	Date:	Advance Amt.:

Summary of Expenses:

Type: (excluding food)	Amt.:
Total $ _____	

Food:	Amt.:
Total $ _____	

Total Reimbursement of Expenses $ _____

Less Advancement $ _____

Due $ _____

Reimbursement $ _____

Check No. _____

Recapitulation: (office use)

© Design Business Monthly

Financial Indicators

A number of years ago I decided I didn't want to spend all my time doing business management because I could hire good people to do this. We now have an excellent managing director in our office who does a top job.-However, I still want to know what's happening. I want to know where we're going, what to worry about, and what I don't need to worry about.

I found that the information our accountant told me I needed to know wasn't exactly what I wanted to know. So through the years I found a way to monitor our company and its directions so that I don't have financial surprises. I can look ahead to see what the trouble spots are going to be or if cash is needed. It's a system so simple our bookkeeper can extrapolate the necessary numbers and put the information on my desk any day of the week that I want it. Usually I get my report on Tuesday mornings, but you decide what day you want it and I am sure your bookkeeper can accommodate you.

From the copy of our monthly reports (see page 293), you can see how simple it is for me to keep abreast of most issues. Some I like to review on a weekly basis, particularly our accounts receivable numbers. I'm interested in whether they are for under thirty days, for thirty days, or for over sixty days because I want to know how well we're doing keeping our accounts current.

It's very easy for me to see whether we have too many accounts that are over sixty days in time to do something about it. Or that our bookkeeper is really doing a great job because everything is under thirty days except for two accounts for which I understand the reasons why.

I also want to know what our client deposit balances are. I call it a deposit balance on our form, although I don't recommend using this term with clients (we usually refer to it as a retainer with clients). But I want to know exactly how much we are holding against purchases or professional fees. Money that in a sense is a debt.

I want to know our checking account balance and our money market balance. With the current banking arrangements, many of you probably do as we do: We deposit most of our money into our money market account and transfer from it to our regular checking account as required.

I want to see what accounts payable are for under thirty days and for over thirty days. Right now we pay our accounts promptly, so anything that is in the over-thirty-day category indicates a problem. Usually if we are having a problem with a company and are not paying them, a client's project is also being affected. Seeing a figure in the over thirty day category is a double alert for me.

I also want to know what our total billing for the month was and how much of it was for product sales and how much for fees. Then I want to know the exact billing of each and every person within the studio. Every designer is responsible for various billings or sales and I want to know what their numbers are.

I then like to see our gross profit figures. (Gross profit is the difference between sales and cost of sales.) We have our accountant do an expense estimate for us on an annual basis and we always compare it to our own. This lets us know what our expenses are per month. Because this doesn't vary a great deal from month to month in our firm, if I see the gross profit figure I have a good idea of exactly how we are doing.

After I have seen the total billings for the month, I look toward the future. What are our sales for the month? What have we written in new contract? In products or professional services fees, exactly what are our numbers and how does this vary per person? Then I want to know the total dollar value of work in progress, and how much of it will be completed within thirty days, sixty days, or over sixty days, because obviously that will bring in revenues.

While this information gives me a forecast of financial issues, I need something more. I want to know exactly what we have sold in new jobs, either professional fees or product sales, for this week, and I like this figure to be ongoing throughout the month. Then I can look at the first, second, and third week and see what we have sold to date.

Then I compare our weekly sales to our inquiry sheet (see page 127). Every phone call or every inquiry that comes in during the month is listed with the name of the client who called, the staff person responsible, and the results.

The trouble with most accounting systems and computer programs is that they give you too much or inappropriate information. Just as our clients get confused by too many design options, we get confused when we have to sift through an overload of financial data to find the information we need. Moreover, financial reports deal with things after the fact; all our training has taught us to look to the future. We're not used to dealing with post mortems.

The monthly financial report on the facing page gives you the information you need to plan and control your company's financial position. It gives you your current financial standing and a ninety-day projection. It allows you to plan for change. Your accountant will need to make adjustments for depreciation and other issues at the end of the year, but this gives you the information that keeps you in daily control.

By looking at the monthly financial report, the sales projections, and inquiries, I can tell not just what the financial picture is, but also what the production schedule is and how we're handling our professional service direction. It's fascinating what these reports will tell you. If I have these on my desk on a regular basis, I know where we are going and I can quickly see areas that need polishing. Even though I might not know exactly why these areas need attention, I can spot the areas and know to focus in on some of the details to see whether we can't make some improvements before a problem develops.

We also see that our bankers are kept properly up-to-date on all of our financial issues so that if we are going to need to borrow money, it's there waiting for us.

I don't like surprises and I feel that we should not permit our staff to place us in a position where we are surprised. You give me these numbers and I'll tell you where any company is going. You can do the same. Forget all about the rest of the numbers that come off of the computer—just look at the important ones and keep them current and regular. Then you will have a reading on the pulse of your business.

How to Use a Financial Statement
On occasion, you will need to read a financial statement, either your own or someone else's. There are many different formulas for interpreting the information available from a financial statement. The following is a list of some of the information that can be derived from a financial statement.

1. *Working Capital Ratio (also referred to as "Current Ratio")*. Working capital is the excess of current assets over current liabilities. The working capital ratio expresses the relation of the amount of current assets to current liabilities and is determined by the following formula:

$$\frac{\text{Total Current Assets}}{\text{Total Current Liabilities}} = \text{Working Capital Ratio}$$

This ratio is a measure of short-term solvency. While no current ratio standard can be applied indiscriminately to all types of businesses, it is generally recognized that for a retail type business, a ratio of 1.5 to 1, or 2 to 1, is desirable.

MONTHLY FINANCIAL REPORT _____, 19_____

C A S H	Accounts Receivable - Total	$ _____
	Under 30 Days	$ _____
	30 to 60 Days	$ _____
	Over 60 Days	$ _____
	Customer's Deposit Balance	$ _____
	Checking Account Balance	$ _____
	Money Market Account Balance	$ _____
	Accounts Payable - Total	$ _____
	Under 30 Days	$ _____
	Over 30 Days	$ _____

BILLING

		Billing	Gross Profit
Total Billing This Month		$ _____	
Products		$ _____	
Fees		$ _____	
Total Gross Profits This Month		$ _____	
Products		$ _____	
Fees		$ _____	
Staff #1 - Products		$ _____	$ _____
- Fees		$ _____	$ _____
Staff #2 - Products		$ _____	$ _____
- Fees		$ _____	$ _____
Staff #3 - Products		$ _____	$ _____
- Fees		$ _____	$ _____
Staff #4 - Products		$ _____	$ _____
- Fees		$ _____	$ _____

SALES

Total Sales Written This Month	$ _____
Staff #1	$ _____
Staff #2	$ _____
Staff #3	$ _____
Staff #4	$ _____

WORK

Total Work in Process	$ _____
Expected Completion - 30 Days	$ _____
- 60 Days	$ _____
- Over 60 Days	$ _____

© Design Business Monthly

2. *The Acid-Test Ratio (sometimes called "Quick Ratio")*. Because inventories must be sold and the proceeds collected before such proceeds can be used to pay current liabilities, many analysts supplement the working capital ratio by the so-called acid-test ratio. This ratio is determined by the following formula:

$$\frac{\text{Cost + Receivables + Marketable Securities}}{\text{Total Current Liabilities}} = \text{Acid-Test Ratio}$$

An acid-test ratio of at least 1 to 1 is usually regarded as desirable.

3. *Working Capital Turnover*. This can indicate the adequacy of the working capital and the number of times it is replenished during a period. It is determined as follows:

$$\frac{\text{Sales for Period}}{\text{Average Working Capital During Period}} = \text{Working Capital Turnover}$$

In my opinion, working capital turnover in itself is of practically no significance because an increase in turnovers may be caused by an increase in the current liabilities, which certainly represents no improvement. A much more meaningful statistic would be the *profitability* per turnover of *current assets*. This is determined by means of two computations:

$$\frac{\text{Cost of Sales and Expenses (excluding depreciation charges)}}{\text{Total Current Assets}} = \text{Number of Current Asset Turnovers}$$

$$\frac{\text{Net Profit}}{\text{Number of Current Asset Turnovers}} = \text{Profit per Turnover}$$

4. *Merchandise Inventory Turnover*. This is the number of times the inventory, on average, was sold or "turned over" during a period. It is determined as follows:

$$\frac{\text{Cost of Goods Sold}}{\text{Average Merchandise Inventory}} = \text{Merchandise Inventory Turnover}$$

Because the inventory quantity may vary substantially throughout the year, a monthly average will produce a more representative statistic. This ratio indicates the tendency to overstock or understock. For this reason, a high turnover is not necessarily good; it may really mean that you do not carry sufficient inventory on hand.

5. *Accounts Receivable Turnover*. This measures the efficiency of collection. It is computed as follows:

$$\frac{\text{Net Credit Sales}}{\text{Average Trade Receivables}} = \text{Accounts Receivable Turnover}$$

6. *Age of Accounts Receivable*. This item represents the average number of days credit sales are in the receivables and is computed as follows:

$$\frac{\text{300 (assuming the business is in operation 300 days per year)}}{\text{Accounts Receivable Turnovers}} = \begin{array}{l}\text{Number of days credit sales} \\ \text{uncollected on average, or} \\ \text{age of accounts receivable}\end{array}$$

Sometimes it may be useful to know the number of days credit sales are in the accounts receivable at the end of a period. In these cases, the accounts receivable at the end of the period would be used instead of the average receivables in computing the turnover. Either way, you can gauge the performance of your collection practices. If the number of days sales go uncollected is ninety, and your credit terms are thirty days, it is obvious that something is wrong. Your collection practices may be at fault or some of your clients may be in trouble, which means you, too, may be in trouble.

Ratios that measure operations and operating results are important management tools. By dividing net sales into each item in the income statement, you can determine exactly what percentage of sales has been spent for each item of cost and expense. By comparing such percentages with those in prior income statements, you can be alerted to your business's trends, both favorable and unfavorable. This comparison enables you to pinpoint weak areas in your operations (such as excessive payroll expenses, or increasing office or travel expenses that may be out of control). If your percentage of gross profit on sales is forty-five percent, and your operating expenses total sixty-five percent, it is obvious that you must reduce expenses somehow, or increase your sale prices (assuming, as is usually the case, that you cannot do much to reduce the cost of sales).

There are a number of other ratios that can be useful, such as the following:

Ratio	Formula for Computation	Result
Return on Owner's Equity	$\dfrac{\text{Net Income}}{\text{Owner's Equity}}$	Measures earnings on resources provided by the owners
Return on Total Assets	$\dfrac{\text{Net Income + Interest Expense}}{\text{Total Assets}}$	Measures earnings on all resources available (from owners and creditors both)
Owner's Equity to Total Liabilities	$\dfrac{\text{Owner's Equity}}{\text{Total Liabilities}}$	Indicates strengths and weaknesses of the financial structure
Fixed Assets to Total Equities	$\dfrac{\text{Fixed Assets (book value)}}{\text{Total Owner's Equity and Liabilities}}$	May indicate excessive real estate and equipment for a retail operation
Ratio of Sales to Fixed Assets	$\dfrac{\text{Net Sales}}{\text{Fixed Assets (book value)}}$	May cast additional light on possible excessive investment in fixed assets

Break-Even Analysis

This tool is used to determine the relationship between your revenue and your costs. Your profit is the difference between the two.

Break-even analysis was developed about forty years ago to help translate very complicated economic theories into a useful management technique. It tells management what it can expect in profits from the various levels of productivity. Whether evaluating the acquisition of a new piece of equipment or adding a new staff member, it is a good idea to do a break-even analysis before making a decision.

Begin by adding up all the fixed expenses related to the project. Fixed expenses are costs that continue even if there is no production. This includes rent, real estate occupancy costs, equipment, salaries, and general overhead.

Next, determine the variable costs or production costs, which become involved when the item is in production. For example, if you buy a new piece of equipment, it will cost you the price of paying for the equipment, the space it takes in the office, and perhaps the salary for an additional person to run it. (In some instances you can simply reassign a person from somewhere else in your firm to work the equipment, so this is a variable.)

After using fixed and variable expenses to determine the total cost per year, then estimate what revenue you can expect as a result of adding that person or piece of equipment. Compare the two, and you will be able to determine where the break-even point is.

Break-even chart. A break-even chart illustrates the relationship between your revenue and your costs. Your profit is the difference between the two.

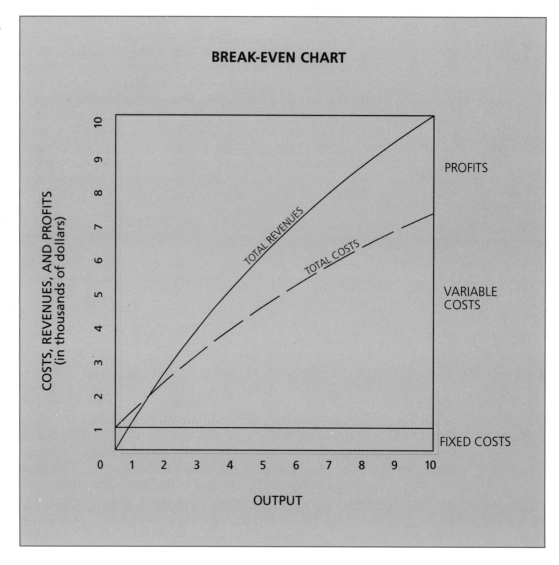

BREAK-EVEN CHART

COSTS, REVENUES, AND PROFITS (in thousands of dollars)

TOTAL REVENUES

TOTAL COSTS

PROFITS

VARIABLE COSTS

FIXED COSTS

OUTPUT

The true definition of break-even is actually cost versus revenue. In any well-run business, one considers the profit figure. Therefore, profit should be added to the total costs when establishing the break-even point. Any average investment can make eight to ten percent, so there is no point in putting money at risk unless there is an opportunity for higher profits.

It is a good idea to create a break-even point for every major expenditure, to determine how long it will take for the item or the person to pay for itself. When making management decisions, this can be helpful in choosing which venture you should do first. Obviously, the more quickly the break-even point can be reached, the more attractive the investment. However, there may be other factors that need to be taken into consideration. Every expenditure does not stand alone, so we need to make comparisons. This visual comparison is a beneficial tool in helping to make that decision.

BANKING RELATIONS

Handling money is an essential part of any business. The interior design business in particular depends a great deal on the ability to handle considerable sums. A solid, supportive relationship with a strong banking institution is crucial. It is much more difficult to establish credit today than it was even five years ago, as money is expensive and banks are more cautious in making loans.

The best way to set up a working relationship with your banking institution is to make that bank part of your business. Banks are only interested in doing business with companies for which they know and understand the purpose and the details of the management structure.

Make that banker and banking institution a part of your company and you will find that he or she will be far more interested in you than you might expect, and will help you in finding ways of financing your business today and in the future.

When you make the initial contact, give your banker the type of information he or she needs to make a proper evaluation of your firm. Here is a checklist of the information that your banker will need:

1. The type of ownership of your firm: corporation, partnership, or sole proprietorship.

2. The product or type of service you offer.

3. The competition in your area.

4. The market available to you.

5. Your sales and service facilities, including any special and unusual services you provide to your customers.

6. Your employees: how many they are, what their qualifications are (including length of service with your company), and what they contribute to the company.

7. Your financial administration: who your certified public accountant is and what your general business administrative structure is.

8. Your current financial statements.

9. A history of your business and financial background.

10. The conditions and details of any outstanding loans.

11. A list of the clients or companies you have worked for and the jobs you have done for them; the dates and approximate size of the jobs.

12. A list of your sources.

13. A list of any banks or lending institutions you have worked with in the past.

14. The goals and objectives of your company. Carefully review these with your banker and update them on a semiannual basis.

15. Your management succession. If something happens to the principal or the major officer, who will take over and how will this be handled? What are the legal methods available to assure business continuity? Who are the people who would take charge and what is their expertise? Are they really capable of sustaining the business?

16. Your insurance. What insurance do you have to cover your company in general and in transition? The bank may require insurance not just as collateral, but to pay off loans. The bank may also want to know if you have insurance to handle any other problems that might come about.

Selecting a Bank

We suggest that you shop the various financial institutions. When you shop, you will want to check out various points such as:

1. What is the average balance versus a straight minimum balance for your firm's checking account? Will they charge you transaction fees (such as deposit items)?

2. What would they give you in terms of a line of credit or a term loan?

3. How many services can they offer your firm?

4. How is the interest compounded and paid on their money market accounts? Their certificates of deposit? You should always ask for the yield as well as the rate so you know what kind of return you will receive on your investment. This applies to certificates or deposit or investment accounts you open for your retirement account (IRA or Keogh) as well.

5. Check with savings institutions as well as commercial banks. Federal deregulations over recent years have allowed savings institutions to offer services to the business world as well as the individual.

How Many Banks Should You Use? Before the days of service charges, many of us dealt with four or five different banks. Today it is too expensive to establish a relationship with a second bank unless you need to borrow large sums of money. Then you might find that you need to use two or three banks to get that amount. But it is probably better, both from a business as well as a financial viewpoint, to give one bank at least the majority of, if not all of, your business; then you can have the clout to request and get certain privileges.

The Bank as a Resource

Your bank can be an excellent resource for services, investment opportunities, and loans. Reexamine your banking services and needs on an annual basis. The banking system changes so rapidly today that your bank may offer new services that you hadn't explored.

You will notice when you are using a bank that you are now charged for certain services that you were not charged for in the past. Banks no longer make their money on the amount of money that you have invested with them; they earn a significant portion of their income from service fees.

You should get to know your business development officer at the bank. This person may also be referred to as an account executive. You don't necessarily meet this person when you're opening your account(s), but you should meet him or her later when your relationship with the bank has been established and the bank knows who to assign to your account.

Your business development officer should review your accounts periodically to determine the suitability of the different investment accounts or other services the bank offers. This person will know your accounts, their size, and your general kind of operation.

Payroll Services. Banks have payroll services that issue checks by preparing an automatic computer tape that debits and credits accounts automatically. When a tape is prepared and goes through, the employees' pay is automatically deposited into the banks they choose; it does not have to be with the bank where the payroll account is established. The funds are debited from the employer's payroll account in that particular bank and issued to the employees' accounts. The bank (or the data processing company the bank uses) writes the withholding checks for the IRS and for any other taxes. The bank then debits the employer's account, and it also does all of the tax reports. You can buy these services from the bank or from an outside source such as ADP (Automatic Data Processing).

The advantage of using a bank is that the bank deposits the money directly into the employees' checking accounts, eliminating in-house paycheck disbursement. A second advantage is that you don't have to run into the bank before noon on the dates the various taxes or withholding payments are due. The bank automatically takes care of those transactions so that your payments are made both accurately and on time. Check with your bank to see what the costs of this service would be and if the bank requires you to have a minimum number of employees.

Your Checking Account. Most banks require that a minimum balance or an average minimum balance be maintained. Some require as little as $300; others may require thousands of dollars. This minimum balance is usually based on an average balance per month since your balance might go down to $300 at one point and up to $10,000 at another.

According to federal law, corporations may not have interest-bearing checking accounts; only personal checking accounts can bear interest. Therefore, you should invest funds in excess of everyday business reimbursements in a money market account or savings account and transfer, as needed, to a checking account.

When you want to stop payment on a check, first call the bank and then either visit the bank within the next fourteen days (the federal regulation) or send a written note. Stop-payment notices are usually good for six months and then need to be renewed if your bank will accept payments for checks that are more than six months old. Usually banks have limits. A sample stop-payment notice is on page 300.

Credit Cards. We issue credit cards to various members of our staff so that they can purchase gas and necessities while traveling for the firm. Keep a record of who has what cards and the card numbers. An easy way to do this is to make a copy of the credit cards on your copying machine. This way, if a credit card is lost, you have a record. This can save you a lot of aggravation.

Money Market Account. A money market account has a daily rate of interest. You can make as many deposits as you want in a money market account. You can also make as many withdrawals as you want as long as you make them in person. However, federal regulations limit other withdrawal transactions, such as telephone transfers or automatic payments, to a maximum of six per month. Normally these six per month will be tracked on a per-statement cycle, rather than by calendar month. You can phone the bank from your office up to six times per month, and can withdraw any amount. At my firm, we normally do this on a weekly basis and then, if we need to do so, we go into the bank in person and make additional withdrawals.

Short-Term Certificates of Deposit. Another way to handle your investment money is short-term certificates of deposit, which are deposits for fourteen days or

Stop payment notice. A letter such as this should be sent to your bank if you wish it to stop payment on a check.

DATE:

TO: (bank name)

Gentlemen:

You are directed to stop payment on the following check:

Name of Payee:

Date of Check:

Amount:

Check Number:

This stop order shall remain in effect until further written notice.

(name of account)

(account number)

By:_____

longer. These usually give you a slightly higher interest rate than the money market accounts. Their disadvantage is that they often require visiting the bank in person to open and to close the certificate. However, your bank may permit you to make other arrangements to open or close certificates of deposit, such as with a letter of instruction bearing your signature or with a special setup where you can phone in your instructions. Short-term certificates often require a minimum opening balance of as little as $100.

Overnight (or Daily Maturing) Repurchase Agreements. These agreements usually require a minimum investment of $5,000. They are an investment in a block of government securities. Any repurchase agreement is a dollar portion of that block of securities. It is not insured by either the Federal Deposit Insurance Corporation (F.D.I.C.) or the Federal Savings and Loan Insurance Corporation (F.S.L.I.C.), but it is "insured" as far as being a government security. These agreements can be held for as short a time as over one night or for as long a term as one might find necessary.

Corporate Investment. Corporate investment requires $50,000 or more. Since the investment is made through the bank's trust department, your money may be invested in diversified securities, such as commercial paper, mutual funds, and areas in which a commercial bank cannot become involved because of S.E.C. regulations. A corporation can invest at a much higher rate by utilizing corporate investments. However, the bank charges an administrative fee to handle these investments for you. The fee structures vary from institution to institution.

Cash Management Services. Cash management services usually require a minimum investment of $50,000. This service invests your available funds by zero-balancing your account to invest every dollar in an overnight repurchase agreement. Although there is a minimum fee of $100 plus transaction costs for managing this account, your company earns more than it would in splitting your funds between a checking account and a money market account because all of the money is being invested together. Once you've reached the corporate level where you have excess cash of $50,000 or more on a consistent basis, you should consider investing in cash-management services instead of money markets.

Individual Retirement Accounts (IRAs). An IRA is an excellent vehicle for an employee to increase his or her retirement fund. Individuals who have no retirement coverage where they work (or if they are covered and have adjusted gross income below $25,000 if single or $40,000 if married) can put up to $2,000 into an IRA and have it fully deductible from their income tax.

No deduction is allowed if individuals are covered by a retirement plan at work and have adjusted gross incomes above $35,000 if single or $50,000 if married. However, if an individual's income is between $25,000 and $35,000 and he or she is single, or if his or her income is between $40,000 and $50,000 and he or she is married, a partial deduction is allowed.

Even if a person is not entitled to a tax deduction, he or she may still put up to $2,000 into an IRA and have the earnings accumulate tax-free until withdrawn.

If one spouse is not employed, the working spouse may put up to $2,250 into a "spousal" IRA, separated into two accounts, and thereby accumulate coverage for the unemployed spouse.

Keogh Plans (also known as H.R. 10 Plans). A Keogh Plan is a retirement plan that may be availed of only by a self-employed person or partnerships for the owners of the business and their employees. As with all employer-sponsored plans, there is a limit for contributions made to the plan for the benefit of the owners. Keoghs, nevertheless, may be worthwhile in certain situations, and should be looked into if a retirement plan or fringe benefits for employees are under consideration.

As with all employer-sponsored plans, the details of Keogh Plans are too complex to discuss adequately here. If you are interested, you should discuss the matter with your accountant or other financial advisor.

401(K) Plans. 401(K) Plans were perhaps the hardest hit of all retirement plans under the Tax Reform Act of 1986. The changes were so drastic that the cost to establish a new plan may be out of proportion to the benefits that can be provided to employees. I include mention of this plan only because some of you may have been considering one without being aware of the changes.

Letters of Credit. A letter of credit is a document issued by a bank, guaranteeing the payment of a customer's draft, up to a specified amount, for a specific period. This letter substitutes the bank's credit for the buyer's and eliminates the seller's risk. It is usually used exclusively for international trade.

A commercial letter of credit is usually drawn up in favor of a third party, called the beneficiary. A confirmed letter of credit is provided by a correspondent bank and guaranteed by the issuing bank. Today these letters of credit are being given to the designer with many out-of-country projects. It is important to realize that they have a specific period of time, which means that they are valid and will be honored only up to a certain date.

Recently, one of the design firms that I work with in New York called me about a letter of credit. The firm had been issued a letter of credit for a project, but the project had been delayed beyond the date listed on the letter, which was in August. The design firm had not realized what this date meant. Because the firm was still waiting for merchandise for the project to be delivered, they had not billed until after the date, and therefore the letter of credit was no longer valid.

When taking a letter of credit, verify its terms. Have your bank approve it and assure you of the handling method for that letter of credit. It is usually a good idea to have this kind of security when dealing with international clients.

Banks also issue a traveling letter of credit for the convenience of the traveling customer. When designers are buying abroad, on occasion, they will carry this traveling letter of credit, which lists the banks at which drafts will be honored. Each country has different laws regarding this lending voucher. You will probably find it best to use an agent for proper handling of a letter of credit.

Borrowing

Although borrowing today is more difficult than it was in the past, there is still some money available. If your situation is presented properly, your chances for getting the loan are much greater. The money will usually be available to you if you have met certain requirements. Before you approach your bank for a loan, review your needs with financial advisors within your company and such outside professionals as your certified public accountant. You need to show that whatever money is borrowed will be used for a good profit, and you need to be able to provide the required collateral. Your accountant and financial manager can help supply this kind of information.

Bank Loans

A banker will want specific information when you are negotiating a loan. I suggest you keep a summary of these points available:

1. The size of the loan required.

2. The purpose of the loan.

3. The time scheduling of when the funds will be needed and for how long.

4. The collateral available to secure the loan.

5. How the loan will be repaid.

6. A cash flow forecast, prepared by your accountant, covering the period of the loan.

7. Personal credit data of the owner or partners or associates of the business.

8. Any life insurance that can be available as collateral for the loan.

9. Any outstanding loans you may have.

10. A history of your business.

11. Your financial statements for this year and for the three to five previous years.

12. Some evidence of your reputation for paying your obligations.

Lines of Credit. When a bank extends a line of credit, the bank makes an advance commitment that it is willing to loan the design firm money under certain conditions, often on a revolving basis. Designers usually find this type of financing advantageous because it is flexible according to their needs. It is on a short-term basis, and it can be more easily controlled according to the design projects. Lines of credit are reviewed annually. You must submit an audited financial statement for the review.

Today, most banks offering lines of credit are charging an annual maintenance fee of approximately one percent of the line of credit, which means that on a $100,000 line of credit, you would be paying $1,000 per year to maintain it. By policy, when you have a line of credit from a bank, the bank is required to review your account and your financial status, usually on a quarterly basis, and this costs money. So when you make your request for a line of credit, make it realistic. If you feel that occasionally you might need something out of the ordinary, handle that more as a term loan rather than a line of credit.

This is why most of us need both a line of a credit and various term loans.

HOW TO KNOW YOUR BANK

It's good to learn something about your bank. Some of the opportunities for getting to know your bank include the following:

1. Attend your bank's seminars. Often banks have seminars on taxes, lending, and other topics that relate to your business. When you attend these, you will find out what your bank's attitudes are towards these issues.

2. Read your bank's annual report so that you know how well the bank is managed. And, if you can, buy some of its stock.

3. Read the literature the bank puts out, whether it is in the form of articles in the paper (either advertising or news items) or brochures they offer. These publications will advise you of any changes in direction and attitude at the bank.

4. Invite your banker to your Christmas party or other social events held at your studio. This familiarizes him or her with your firm and some of your jobs. If there's a new project opening that might be of interest to your banker, invite him or her. This gives your banker a feel for how a design firm runs. By giving your banker first-hand experience with design, you foster better understanding, which can work in your favor the next time you approach the bank for service.

Term Loans. Term loans are usually for up to a ten-year period. Short-term loans are normally for less than a year, sometimes only thirty to sixty days. If a short-term loan goes beyond a year, it is considered a long-term loan. A short-term loan is usually desirable because even though the interest may be higher, it must only be paid over a short period of time. In most cases a short-term loan can be paid off in advance if the project is completed and the monies are available. This type of loan is used for major expenditures. The rates of a long-term loan will vary according to the term of the loan.

Other Sources of Capital

Businesses constantly need money. Whether your firm is a new business or a well-established one, the boundaries of its development are strongly linked to the amount of money available.

There are a number of sources for capital. First of all, borrowing. Where can you borrow money and what are the best sources? Naturally your own money is the first source to consider. You must be ready to invest your monies in your business; otherwise, why should you expect someone else to do so? This is obviously the easiest source of revenue, so if you plan to start a business or to increase your business, try to accumulate some funds to give yourself a base from which to begin.

Your friends or relatives are also a good source of money—probably the second fastest—and they are usually inexpensive. If you borrow from a friend or a relative, however, make this arrangement with caution. You do not want to give away the control of your business, or to cause problems within the family. If you do not want the person you borrow from to participate in your business, set up a loan structure whereby you retain control and the lender does not automatically become a partner.

Banks are usually the best and most preferable sources of capital because a good banking relationship can fill continuing needs. However, there are other sources of capital.

The Small Business Administration. The S.B.A. is a good source for information as well as loans, but S.B.A. loans take a longer time to process than one can imagine. I've seen firms go out of business because they were waiting for an S.B.A. loan to come through. In order to qualify for an S.B.A. loan, you must have good documentation and be ready to meet S.B.A. standards. In general, the S.B.A.'s rates are better and the terms are longer. The S.B.A. will also extend loans in some situations where banks can't. Working with the S.B.A. does take long-term planning, however. If you need financing in a hurry, this is probably not your best resource for money, although they are faster today than they were in the past.

Factoring. This involves selling your accounts receivable to another company or to another party. You get paid upon delivery of your product or services and your customer would then pay the factoring company. This is not the same as accounts receivable loans, which are available through banks. Usually, factoring companies will buy your accounts receivable for less than their value, such as eighty or ninety percent of their worth; you get the additional twenty or ten percent when the company pays. The factoring firm is responsible for checking each client's credit and for determining whether it will be willing to assume the responsibility of that client. Service charges vary.

This type of service was set up primarily for large manufacturers in the 1950s through 1970s, but in the 1980s numerous design firms have used this type of borrowing.

Finance Companies. If you have a large debt or are not able to get financing from a bank, a finance company may be your only recourse. As a rule, this is the least desirable source for money, because you pay a much higher interest rate.

Commercial finance companies will make loans for items such as equipment, and will also act as factors. Although interest rates are high, these loans are usually available at a faster rate than other loans. Sometimes you can obtain a loan within a few days or several weeks, whereas a bank loan or other types of loans will take considerably longer.

Your Suppliers as a Source for Additional Working Capital. Your suppliers will usually grant your terms of either thirty, sixty, or ninety days, but they may extend these terms for a longer time. If you are planning to do a large job and are not able to carry the paper on it, ask your suppliers what they might do to help. Perhaps they will give you additional terms, knowing that it is for a particular project.

It is a good idea, on a biannual basis, to review all of your suppliers and to determine what amounts of credit they are extending to you presently and what you feel you will need over the next six months. By identifying your requirements ahead of time and negotiating with your suppliers, you can often obtain a much larger credit than you might expect. Do not wait until the project is sold; it is then often too late to negotiate. If your sources are aware of your business potential or upcoming objectives, they are usually more than happy to participate by extending additional credit. It's amazing how much this can help a design firm develop its business potential.

Credit Card Loans. This is an easy way to get money up to a specific unit. This type of financing is growing. There are now corporate MasterCards, where if you do not have an account with a certain company, you can charge the money you owe them through your corporate MasterCard. Through a corporate credit card, your bank might extend to you fifty or a hundred thousand dollars worth of credit, permitting you to pay off all of your creditors immediately to get cash discounts from creditors for early payment. You simply pay the bank at the end of thirty or sixty days, as agreed on, and the bank charges you interest if the amount of time your account is outstanding is for over thirty or sixty days. This type of capital resource will be used far more extensively during the next decade. If you don't have a corporate credit card, perhaps you should consider getting one. The card usually doesn't cost you anything until you use it. However, be sure to watch the rates of interest because banks do vary considerably.

Equity Capital Financing. You can sell a portion of your business to another person. If you have a corporation, you would have a stockholder's agreement whereby you would not have to pay back that particular loan, but instead would agree to share with the person making you the loan a certain portion of your profits. This can be a good method of acquiring capital; however, the relationship with the lender must be carefully considered. If the lender thinks he or she owns the business and plans to start controlling it, you may have a problem. In some cases, you may have to relinquish the majority of control. If you are confident of the personal relationship, then discuss this business agreement with your attorney to determine the value of the equity capital. In large corporations, selling stock is an impersonal relationship and these considerations obviously do not apply.

Venture Capital. Venture capital firms or individuals loan their own capital to new businesses. They are usually interested in owning a portion of the business; many insist on owning over fifty percent of the business. There are a lot of venture capitalists and there are firms that put together investors and businesses. They see a lot of proposals and probably reject ninety-five percent of them. Customarily, venture capitalists seek a return of three to five times their investment in five to seven years. Usually they are interested in larger projects, from about $500,000 up to many millions. This is a good source of capital for certain larger projects, but is rarely suitable for the beginning design firm.

SBICs and MESBICs. Small Business Investment Companies (SBICs) and Minority Enterprise Small Business Investment Companies (MESBICs) are both regulated under the Small Business Administration. The government is putting a great deal of capital into these firms. They invest only in young companies or those managed by minorities, and they relax many of the rules in order to accommodate these types of business. SBICs and MESBICs are a great source of long-term loans, which are usually very difficult for the small business to acquire. They often give loans for five to seven years, or even as long as twenty years. It usually takes several months for loans to be approved by these types of organizations.

There are also small business development companies, called SBDCs, which are run in a similar fashion but are not government-owned. They are independently owned. Many times they are run by a local chamber of commerce or a local regional development group attempting to bring businesses into their area. Since these are supported locally, they will make special terms available for the businesses they want to come into the area. Information on these companies can usually be obtained through local chambers of commerce.

Loan Finders. There are many financial consultants or professionals who act as loan finders. They usually charge you a fee, which can be from as low as one percent to as high as fifteen or twenty percent. These finders are often advertised in the financial part of your local newspaper or in the *Wall Street Journal.* If you are going to use a loan finder, make sure that you have clarified the amount of the fee up front and have included this amount within the loan scheduling that you are planning.

Deciding Which Type of Funding to Use. In order to determine which type of resource is best for you, ask yourself these questions when looking for a loan:

▶How much will it cost?

▶What are the projections?

▶Am I sure that by borrowing this amount of money I can make money with it?

▶How much time will it take to get? Developing a loan and working on acquiring it takes a considerable amount of time—months, or even years. Usually small design firms do not have a person that they can assign solely to this task. Therefore it takes the principal's time, and the principal should be out selling or marketing instead of using his time for this particular purpose. Simple bank loans may take less time if you have an established relationship or a regular line of credit.

▶What is the risk that my business will be assuming by taking on this obligation? How will it affect me this year, next year, and in the future?

▶Review the conditions of each individual resource and determine how it will affect your ability to move, grow, or gain additional capital. Can you make changes within your company? Can you progress with your goals for next year? Will you be able to acquire more capital if needed or are you giving up flexibility?

▶Will the control of your business be affected? By taking on that extra investor or partner, are you jeopardizing your position in management of the company? Would this person's contribution be valuable? Weigh the value of the resources against the amount of interaction and control that he or she will want.

▶What sources are available? What are the options? What needs to be done to broaden these options? See whether you can use the very best options available or whether you need to take some that are less advantageous. Look at the value of the overall accomplishment of your project and determine whether it really pays you to borrow.

ESTABLISHING CREDIT

Your credit has a great deal to do with the success of your company. Unfortunately, there are too many interior design-related firms that have bad credit ratings, and their stigma extends to all designers, whether or not our firms are run well. It takes extra effort to establish the financial structure to overcome this.

Caution in planning financial requirements and obligations protects us from being hit with financial demands we cannot meet. Allow for the worst. You will usually be able to do better, which will make you look good to your creditors. If you always plan for the best, and you cannot meet your obligations, then you are in trouble.

Financial planning and forecasting is something that every small-business owner must learn to do; I have included a form for projecting profits from financial indicators on page 293. Understand what you will need one, two, or three months from now, and be prepared.

Your Credit Rating

Once you receive a bad credit report, it is very difficult to work out of that position. If you can avoid getting a bad rating in the first place, this will save you a lot of trouble and will add to the success and growth of your company.

Know what your credit ratings are and learn where you stand with all credit reporting agencies. What are they saying about you? Get your listing from them and verify the information; if it is not correct, furnish the correct information and be sure they make the corrections.

Establish a good rapport with your local bank; your bank is always asked for credit information. Make it a high priority to keep your banker up-to-date with your firm to maintain your good standing.

Forward your financial statements regularly to your bank, Lyons, D & B, and any other credit-related organization that regularly rates you in your geographical area. They will be expecting these statements on an annual basis, so be sure that they get these statements as quickly as possible. If there are issues that you feel these organizations should know about that are not normally on the statement, ask your accountant to add a note explaining these specific issues. This is a better way to provide this information than if it is sent directly from the accounting firm. Also, if you are changing your company's financial priorities, it may be a good idea to let the credit organizations know your objectives.

Ways to Establish Credit

Even if you do not need the money, it is a good idea to borrow from a bank or lending institution so that you can get a good credit record. Make sure that the loan is paid off in advance of its due date. By doing this, you will become familiar to the lending institution and will be recognized as a good credit risk.

Decide which companies and resources are going to be important for your company and build a rapport with them. Establish a good credit standing. Learn which companies give credit reports on you and which ones do not. There are a number of large companies in our field who make a special point of not giving reports on anyone because they are called upon too often. Find out which companies give good reports and attempt to develop a good rapport with them.

When you have established the companies that you feel will be most important to you, talk to them about your payment schedule. Because companies want to develop a rapport with you, they are often willing to extend terms beyond the norm. If this information is established up front, and they agree to carry you for thirty, sixty, or ninety days, your credit report will be excellent if you pay within these terms. If, however, their statement says "payable within ten days" and you do not pay for thirty days, then you are overdue and your credit will be jeopardized.

Sometimes you have a situation where you will not be able to meet a payment because merchandise has been shipped to you too early. Early shipments can create real problems. Often you must store the merchandise in a warehouse for several months before it can be delivered. You may have asked the company to ship the merchandise three months from now, but it came in early, so they shipped it and want immediate payment. If this situation comes up, call your resource immediately and explain the situation. You have the right to refuse delivery of these items at this time or to make payment at the appropriate date, as previously scheduled.

Credit Reporting Agencies
Interior designers need to use credit reporting agencies almost on a daily basis, both to check on prospective clients and to check out resources.

The more you can find out about your clients, the better you are able to protect your business. Therefore it is wise to check the credit history of prospective clients, whether you sought them out as part of your business development or marketing effort, or whether the prospective client approached you. The information gained from credit reports can help you tailor contracts and agreements to the individual client, provided you believe the client is a good risk. Checking in to the credit backgrounds of clients can save you many headaches.

The second reason to use credit organizations is to check out suppliers and resources. Many designers have given large retainers or deposits to companies only to find, when the merchandise was long overdue, that the firm had gone out of business. If the supplier's credit had been checked in advance, these designers would never have extended deposits or retainers. In most instances, the designer is in a responsible position; if the resource defaults, it is up to the designer to make good to the client.

All credit bureaus have regular reporting services, such as newsletters, which are beneficial only if you need constant up-to-date input. Most design services prefer to check credit on an as-needed basis rather than using regular weekly or monthly reporting.

Many of these credit bureaus also have collection divisions, which can be very effective. To ensure appropriately professional handling of collections, you should make sure they are certified by the American Collectors' Association and abide by all federal and state regulations. They generally have a pretty good recovery rate, which they classify as about fifty percent. You should use a collection agency only as a last resort, but it is available as a collection method if all of your other methods fail. Fees generally run thirty percent or more for this type of service.

Local Credit Organizations. These will give you information on individual clients or companies working within that area. This information includes: some background and history; where they were born; how long they have lived in the community; their approximate age; their salaries; their marital status; their number of dependents; and, in some cases, whether they have alimony payments or other obligations. Local credit organizations also report mortgages and other debts that a person might have incurred. With this information, it's easier to tell whether a client will be able to meet the financial requirements of the contract he or she is negotiating. Many designers like to review this information before they go for an initial interview or immediately thereafter. Do not wait to ask for credit information. Get it as early as possible.

Most communities have a local credit bureau. There is usually a membership fee to belong. As a member you can make credit inquiries by telephone at a cost of a few dollars per inquiry, depending upon the type of account you have and the amount that you use the service. In this report you get a person's name, account number, company codes, credit limits, types of accounts, mortgages, revolving charges, reasons for financing, salary, company balance owing, monthly payments, and the number of times the person has been late on payments during the last few years.

A good credit report, however, is not a guarantee that the new account will be satisfactory. It is an indicator, based on the theory that past experience does usually repeat itself.

Dun & Bradstreet. This company specializes in all types of company and corporate reporting. This is your best source for information on your resources and tradespeople, as well as corporate clients. Dun & Bradstreet gathers information regularly from all businesses, and rates them according to size and payment activities. A Dun & Bradstreet report is an analysis of a commercial establishment: its operations, legal structure, payment records, banking relations, financial condition, management history, and business trends.

Dun & Bradstreet has offices in major towns throughout the United States. Manufacturers, wholesalers, retailers, and many businesses and professional services use this organization for their reports. Dun & Bradstreet calls on businesses on a regular basis and interviews the owners and their accountants.

If you requested a large purchase from a vendor, and Dun & Bradstreet was consulted but did not have your records, they would then arrange an interview with you. It is often necessary to refer their investigator to your accountant for detailed information. However, some of the information regarding the functioning and the history of the firm needs to come directly from the managing officers of the firm. The types of information D & B publishes is:

▶ *Your DUNS number.* A nine-digit code which identifies your business name and location in their files.

▶ *A summary.* A quick-reference analysis of the detailed information contained on the report. It includes the business industry standard classification code and function, your product line, the principal executive of your firm, the D & B capital and credit rating (data as to payment habits, sales, worth, number of employees, history, financing, and general conditions and trends).

▶ *Your payment record.* Your firm's payment record, including the amount you owe, or the amount that is past due. The settling terms and time of your last sales are included.

▶ *Your finance record.* A statement of assets, liabilities, sales, expenses, and profits, along with a description of sales and profits trends.

▶ *Your banking record.* Your firm's average balances, previous and current loan activities, lengths of banking relationships, and statement of account satisfaction.

▶ *Your history.* The name, year of birth, and past business experience of the principals or owners of the firm and the legal structure of the business.

▶ *Your operation.* The nature of your business, its premises, products or services, price ranges, classifications of customers, percentages of cash and credit sales, number of accounts, seasonal aspects and number of employees.

▶ *Special events.* Any recent changes of chief executives, the legal structure, partners' control, or location; business discontinuances; criminal proceedings; burglaries; embezzlements; fires; and other events.

▶ *Public filing.* Any public record filing, such as suits or judgments, uniform commercial code filings, tax liens, and record item update and releases.

▶ *D & B capital and credit ratings.* An indicator of estimated strength; a composed credit rating. This information is in the *Dun & Bradstreet Records Book,* published every two months, with a standard industrial classification: the name of the business, the starting year of the operation, and the D & B capital and credit rating.

The Allied Board of Trade. Most designers belong to the Allied Board of Trade (A.B.T.) and are issued a card identifying them as members of the professional design community. This suggests to wholesalers and manufacturers that these are the people who should be purchasing from them on a wholesale basis. Designers who wish to be registered with this board must show proof that they meet minimum professional standards for education and practical experience, and that they actually are in business.

The Allied Board of Trade has been in business since 1925, predating the precursor organization of ASID, the American Institute of Designers. It issues an annual directory with information about design-related businesses. A.B.T. constantly investigates designers and registers newly formed companies. It has a considerable amount of information on specific design companies, although not all of it is published. A.B.T. also tries to put designers in touch with appropriate resources and trades. It publishes a comprehensive reference called *The Green Book*, for members' use. The book contains lists and ratings of all recognized designers and design-related specialists.

Smaller design firms that might not be listed with Dun & Bradstreet usually would be included in *The Green Book* or in the *Lyon Credit Reference Book*, known as the Lyon Red Book.

The Lyon Furniture Mercantile Agency. Founded in 1876, the Lyon Furniture Mercantile Agency has had a major impact in the furniture industry. Interior designers and decorators are listed in the semiannual red *Lyon Credit Reference Book*, but it is dealers, jobbers, furniture manufacturers, and allied tradespeople who maintain service contracts with Lyon.

Designers are contracted by Lyon in response to requests from showrooms and manufacturers. They are asked to furnish current credit and general information, usually by letter.

Lyon also has a registration card for designers. For an annual fee, designers who supply current information are furnished with a validated registration card which can be used as an entrée to the major market buildings and showrooms. You need not purchase the card to be listed in the Red Book.

To find out what your Lyon credit rating is, you must make an appointment with the manager of the Lyon office nearest you (they are in Chicago; Cincinnati; Dallas; High Point, North Carolina; Los Angeles; and Great Neck, New York). Say that you want to look at your report and they will accommodate you without charge. They will not verify it by mail or by phone, and it would be prohibitively expensive for an individual designer to purchase a Lyon service contract.

Do you know what credit organizations are saying about you? There is presently a law that requires them to provide you with all of the information that they are releasing to their clients. Therefore, your credit rating and credit information is available to you at any time. I would suggest that you contact each of the organizations who have you rated on a regular basis and check out your classification. If you have any questions about it, find out what the situation is and talk with them. Some interior designers find themselves with very bad ratings they were unaware of. Take the time and check out just what your position is. If it is not what you think it should be, see what you can do to update it.

TAXES

One of the primary reasons for keeping records is to support our tax documents. There are basically four types of federal taxes: income taxes, social security taxes, unemployment taxes, and excise taxes.

Interior designers are usually involved with the first three taxes. Income taxes depend completely upon the earnings of your company, or you as an individual. The amounts vary according to the type of organizational structure that you choose—a sole proprietorship, a partnership, or a corporation. Your documentation of all exemptions and nonbusiness deductions, and also any credits, will play an important part in the amount of taxes you must pay.

If you are involved in a corporation, then regular income tax will be paid individually on your salary and any other income that you receive from the corporation.

If your company is a sole proprietorship, your taxes will be paid just as if you were working for someone else, even though your income comes from this business instead of from a salary. You file the identical form that any individual taxpayer would file. The only difference is that you file additional forms that identify the expenses and the income of your business. This is Form C on your 1040, which is the profit and loss from your business or profession.

A sole proprietor, since he or she is not an employee, is not subject to social security taxes, as such. He or she is, however, subject to self-employment taxes in lieu of social security taxes. This tax is reported on Schedule SE, which is a part of the individual income tax return.

If you are in a partnership, then you must file a return showing the income and expenses from the business, but you will only report your share of the profit on your own return.

As an individual proprietor or a partner in a partnership, you are required to pay federal self-employment tax as you receive the income. You must file a declaration of estimated tax (Form 1040 ES) on or before April 15 of each year. A partner is subject to self-employment taxes in the same way as a sole proprietor.

This declaration is an estimate of the income and self-employment taxes that you expect to be owing during this coming year. You then make estimated payments each quarter—April 15, June 15, September 15, and January 15. At these times you can adjust each of your estimates according to your actual income.

If you have a regular corporation, and not an S corporation, the corporation pays taxes on its profits and the owner of the corporation pays income taxes on the salary he or she received or the dividends that the corporation paid him or her.

The federal corporation income tax is due 2½ months after the end of your fiscal year. This return is filed just once a year; most corporations pay quarterly. It is important that you make allowances in your money management to be sure that you are prepared to pay these taxes. The Small Business Administration has worksheets for meeting tax obligations which can help you in this documentation if your accountant is not taking care of it for you.

Federal Taxes

There are a number of federal taxes every business will need to consider in addition to "entity" taxes, discussed on pages 46–47.

Withholding Income Taxes. If you have employees, you must, by law, withhold federal income tax. These taxes are transmitted to the government on a regular basis. The process begins the minute you hire any employee. Your employees must sign a W-4 form, an Employee Withholding Allowance Certificate. On this, the employee lists his or her exemptions and any additional withholding allowances that he or she claims. The W-4 certificate is your authorization to withhold tax in accordance with the tables that the Internal Revenue Service has issued. At the end of the year you must complete a W-2 form, which is a statement showing income paid to the employee and taxes withheld. This must be in the employee's hands before January 31 of each year. The employee will then submit this form as part of his or her income tax return. You should send a copy of the W-2s to the IRS using Form W-3 as a transmittal.

Social Security Taxes. As an employer, you must withhold social security contributions for both your employees and yourself. You must then pay an appropriate amount for each employee. The payment is made with the income tax withheld. The social security tax return is due for each calendar quarter on the last day of the month following—April 30, July 31, October 31, and January 31.

Federal Unemployment Taxes. If you pay wages of more than $1,500 in any calendar quarter, or have more than one employee, you must pay federal unemployment taxes. These payments must be deposited with either a commercial bank or a federal reserve bank one month following the quarter. Each deposit must be accompanied by federal unemployment tax deposit form 508. These forms will be furnished to you automatically by the IRS after you have applied for an employer's identification number. If, however, you need extras, you can obtain them from your local IRS office.

Form 1099. Form 1099 is an "Information Return" on which certain business payments are required. Every business enterprise, corporate or otherwise, that makes payments of $600 or more in a calendar year to a nonemployee who is not a corporation, for rents, prizes and awards, fees, commissions, or other compensation, must report the payment. All payments of interest or dividends in the amount of $10 or more in a calendar year must also be reported. A copy of Form 1099 must be issued to the payee no later than January 31 for the preceding calendar year. The original must be filed with the IRS no later than February 28, using Form 1096 as a transmittal slip.

Remitting Taxes. Make deposits with Form 501, a Federal Tax Deposit Form, which is used for withholding income and FICA (social security) taxes. You send this form with your check to the Federal Reserve Bank in your district or to a commercial bank authorized to accept these tax deposits. The dates on these deposits will vary, depending upon the amount due.

State Taxes

Although they vary from state to state, each state usually requires state unemployment tax, income tax, and sales tax. It is important to know what the taxes are within your state.

State Unemployment Taxes. These are required by every state and the rates vary. They are based on the amount of wages your employees are paid and also on the employee turnover in your business.

State Employee Income Taxes. These are also imposed by most states, although the amounts and ways they are collected vary from state to state. Usually the employer is required to collect this tax from the employee.

Sales Tax. Any retailer is required to collect and pay state or local sales taxes when goods are sold to the ultimate consumer. You must get a sales tax identification number or resale permit, as required, in order to collect the taxes.

Sales tax is collected from your client and usually has to be separately stated on your invoice. Use tax must be paid by you and cannot be charged as a tax to your client. A careful review of these tax laws is necessary to avoid problems later.

If you, as a consumer, purchase a taxable item from an out-of-state source that does not collect the tax, you must report and pay a use tax on the purchase.

Penalties for Nonpayment of Taxes

These penalties are very severely and stringently enforced. The fiscal officer may be held personally liable for withholding payroll taxes that are not remitted to the government.

Special Tax Notes

When tax laws change, you need to consult your accountant to avoid the accompanying pitfalls.

Be sure to record every portion of your income; the IRS has no tolerance for unreported income. Of course, try to take every deduction you possibly can, but support them with thorough documentation.

Check with your accountant to make sure you are taking into account every possible deduction. Interior designers can deduct expenditures, but these vary considerably according to your location and the standards in your individual practice.

Interest on Overpaid Taxes. The Internal Revenue Service now pays interest on any amount of taxes that you have overpaid, less one percent of the interest rate they charge you for underpayment. For example, if you have underpaid your taxes, the IRS charges nine percent interest; if you have overpaid, the IRS pays eight percent interest on the amount of overpayment. What this really means is that it does not pay to play games with tax issues. You're better off to pay on time. Even if you overpay, today you're not losing interest as you were in the past.

It's a good idea to review your tax projections with your accountant at the beginning of the year, not at tax time. Let your accountant spell out what he or she thinks your deductions are and compare his or her list with your own. A number of designers I know have been able to deduct their clothing expenses; their accountants received permission from the IRS to do this. On the whole, however, deducting for clothing is not appropriate because the IRS feels that we are not wearing a uniform, since we usually wear standard clothing that could be worn somewhere else. Therefore it's not deductible. But clothing damaged on a construction job can be deducted if details and costs are documented.

Travel Expenses. Beginning in 1987, the IRS has instituted more stringent requirements for travel and entertainment expenses. You may deduct only eighty percent on meals and entertainment expenses. The records must be much more specific for both the employer and the employee.

Receipts are necessary for all lodging, and for meals over $25. For expenses under $25, you don't need a receipt, but you must keep a record in your diary. When you are traveling, keep track of every single expense. I find that if I do this on a daily basis, I'm accurate. If I wait until the end of the week, I can never remember how much I spent for what or when. So I do my record keeping religiously, several times a day. When I'm in a taxi, or waiting for someone, I will mark down exactly what I have spent. I have an envelope in which I keep my receipts and an account of everything that I have spent on that particular trip. The IRS requires that the records be maintained as the expenses are incurred.

A most important IRS requirement concerns business-connected expenditures. For every meal or entertainment expense you list, you must be able to document the person you were with and the business subject you discussed. A good-will dinner with a long-standing customer is no longer deductible unless current business is discussed either before, during, or after the meal. However, if this meal is one in which business is discussed, then the traditional eighty-percent rule applies.

If money is advanced, or expenses reimbursed, to an employee who is a stockholder and the transaction is not clearly documented, the IRS may declare this payment to be a dividend, taxable to the employee but not deductible by the employer. If you give an employee a flat expense allowance and do not require the employee to account for those expenses, you must include it on the employee's W-2 form; otherwise, the company will lose the tax deduction.

The IRS is also looking at owners' expense accounts more carefully and requiring that all travel and entertainment expenses be itemized. An owner may no longer declare a per diem amount on meals or lodging. This law also applies to any other family member, owner, or stockholder of the business.

If you give your employees a flat rate for expenses, IRS limits the basic rate. There are some special cities that have higher rates, such as New York City and Los Angeles. This per diem rate covers all lodging, meals, and incidental expenses. Transportation is a separate deduction.

If an employee goes out of town for the day, but does not stay overnight, extra expenses, such as dry cleaning, cannot be deduced by his employer unless the payment is considered added salary, which would make it taxable income to the employee.

There are two ways you may reimburse an employee for travel in his or her own car: with repayment of all expenses incurred, which means that the company would pay for the gas, oil, and maintenance of the car, or with a flat-rate method based on miles traveled.

The IRS allows reimbursement up to a fixed amount per mile, plus expenses for parking or tolls. If you reimburse an employee more than the allowance per mile, then the entire amount of the reimbursement must be shown on his or her W-2 form and taxes must be paid on that amount.

Automobile expenses and receipts must be kept to verify all the prices and costs (the base cost of the automobile, plus cost for maintenance, gas, oil, and so forth). You must also keep a detailed mileage log, which records all the usage of the company car, including the person's name, the purpose of the trip, the miles driven, and the date of each trip. A mileage log also needs to record any personal use of the car.

It is important to see that all expenses are turned in on a regular basis and not permitted to accumulate because there is no way accurate documentation can be done on a long-term basis. It must be kept current. In our firm we have had great success with travel expense envelopes (see page 290). We give our employees their traveling expense advances in these envelopes and have them document their expenses on the outside of the envelope and put all their receipts inside the envelope. We think that this envelope is much easier to use for the person who makes an occasional trip and perhaps doesn't keep a weekly or daily account. It also makes our record keeping much simpler by having all the receipts in this envelope.

Tax Audits

What should you do if you are being audited by the IRS or any other tax agency? First, notify your accountant. Then ask the agent conducting the audit to get in touch with your accountant. Do not answer any questions relating to the audit and do not discuss anything with the agent. Leave it to your accountant to handle all matters with the agent. It is best, in fact, if you are absent during the conducting of the audit.

If you have followed your accountant's direction, you will have good records and will be prepared for this kind of audit. Your accountant will let you know exactly how to present the information required.

Ask your accountant to control the audit. I find that it is important for one person to be in control, and it is usually best if that person is your accountant. Let him or her select the location.

Just recently, a design firm I know had a state sales tax audit, which took a considerable amount of time. The auditor arrived with two other men whom he was training, and he asked for certain papers, which the firm's accountant had reviewed and were ready. The auditors established themselves in the conference room, which is a very pleasant room with coffee and refreshments convenient to it. They came each day for approximately five weeks, during which time they continually asked for additional materials and items. This kept two, and sometimes three, staff members busy reviewing or pulling records and information for them. When the auditor and his men were finished, they found that the records were in reasonably good order. The only tax that they were able to collect was some use tax the firm had inadvertently not paid on items purchased for office use. The company from whom the items had been purchased had not charged sales tax; therefore the design firm was responsible for the use tax. The auditors' total tax collection was less than $2,000 after reviewing six years of taxes over a five week period.

The definitions of sales and use tax are not clearly defined within many states. Another designer told me of a similar situation he had had a few weeks earlier, where auditors had asked to see his records for the past two years. He related the following:

"As you can probably guess, our records are not very well kept because bookkeeping is not one of our specialties. Our bookkeeper had just left and I had no idea where things were, so my accountant gave me the following instructions. He told me to take an enormous cardboard box and to put all of our records in it—everything that we could find to fill the box with as many papers as possible—and to put this box in our station wagon and deliver it to the tax auditor's office. We did exactly as he said, and when we arrived, the auditors looked at the box and said 'Sorry, I think we've changed our minds; we do not want to audit you'— and we weren't audited."

So where the first firm went through considerable expense and harassment, he was able to get out of his audit completely because of his method of presentation. The first firm was very cooperative; but sometimes I wonder which approach is the most effective.

After the audit is completed, you and your accountant should discuss the audit and make notes of any weak spots in your records. Ask your accountant how these can be remedied for the future. Review all the disallowed items to determine the reason for disallowance. If you found you had inadequate records, now is the time to edit and revise your record-keeping system. What adjustments can be made on future schedules? After this review, file all your documents again properly so that you are ready for the next audit.

It is now the practice of the IRS to examine the tax returns of all related parties. For example, in the examination of a partnership, the returns of all of the partners will be examined. If there are related corporations (subsidiaries or brother-sister corporations, for example), their returns, too, will be examined. In an examination of a corporation, the returns of the principals will be at least scanned.

In an independent contractor relationship, the IRS will look very carefully into the working relationship in order to determine it is really a bonafide independent contractors situation or in reality an employer-employee relationship and thus subject to employee payroll tax requirements.

If the IRS agent is a special agent as opposed to a revenue agent, this means that you are involved in a criminal investigation and you need to hire a lawyer immediately. Let your lawyer work with your accountant or let him or her hire the accountant to properly defend you. An accountant who works for a lawyer is legally protected by the lawyer-client privilege. If your accountant is working for you, he is not protected by this privilege.

A final cautionary word: It must be kept in mind that taxes are subject to frequent changes. Accordingly, it is most important whenever the tax effect of a contemplated transaction will be significant that you and your advisors be aware of the tax laws as then in force.

INSURANCE

No design firm can afford to be without a good insurance program.

Insurance Advisor

Your insurance consultant is an important part of your financial advisory group and should work with your accountant and your attorney. Select someone who will be available to you at all times and who is compatible with the rest of the group. This working rapport is just as important as the insurance consultant's ability and the knowledge he or she will offer you.

How do you select an insurance advisor? It is important to find someone you can work with. Another businessperson or one of the financial professionals in your advisory group might be able to help you select a competent and capable professional. A very large corporation would hire an advisor or an independent insurance consultant. A small company, like many interior design firms, would use an agent or a broker.

An insurance agent normally represents one insurance company. A broker will represent a number of companies and can negotiate to determine the best coverage for you and the best price on that coverage. In most instances, you are better off with a broker or a person who is both an agent and a broker. The agent/broker is allied with one or several companies, but has other lines available to you so that he or she can handle your whole package. This person is the middle-man between you and the insurance market, and he or she earns a commission for handling your insurance programs.

Unless the insurance agent understands the interior design field, it is very hard for him or her to define your needs. He or she should talk with your accountant and attorney; together they will define the particular needs of your company so that the agent can match you with an appropriate coverage package.

In today's world it is sometimes necessary to go to several difference sources to get the coverage you need. Use your insurance advisor as a coordinator so that he or she can review the policies and prevent overlap of coverage. By combining various policies, you often reduce the expense of coverage and get a more all-encompassing package. But for certain insurance, such as for errors and omissions and other special liabilities (usually obtained through professional associations such as ASID), you must go to a specialist. I have found that it is more valuable to keep my insurance advisor on a local basis if I can, even though I must use several out-of-town resources for specialities. He is more aware of what is happening locally and what my needs are.

Selecting Insurance

Several companies offer an insurance package that includes coverage for all-risk special property, comprehensive general liability, and professional liability, or errors and omissions in design. Because this is packaged, it may be less expensive and more encompassing than when policies are purchased individually. If you are a member of ASID, or another professional organization, you need to evaluate the policies offered by your organization. In some cases they offer better coverage than you can purchase from your regular insurance agents.

Ask your agent or broker to provide information on the financial condition of the companies he or she is using. In 1986 more than a hundred insurance companies went bankrupt (as did banks and savings and loan associations); more companies are expected to do the same. Exercise every caution you can to make sure the company (or companies) you select will be in business to pay your long-term claims, such as those that arise in workmen's compensation and product liability. A current illustration of this is the billions of dollars being paid by insurance companies on asbestos claims for exposures which occurred over thirty years ago. In Pennsylvania, for example, the employer is responsible for payment of all employee medical expenses without limit as to their amount for as long as they occur during the lifetime of the employee. In addition, income must be paid to an employee as long as he or she lives and suffers disability. Remember: The obligation is the designer's, not the insurance company's, according to law. The designer uses insurance to transfer the risk to the insurance company. The transfer of risk ceases to exist when an insurance company goes bankrupt.

Insurance demands differ considerably from state to state and from area to area, not necessarily because of legal or business requirements, but because of the attitudes of people in the areas. In some areas people are far more litigious on certain issues, and therefore you may require additional insurance of a particular type because you are in New York and not in Ohio. Your local advisor will know the state laws as well as the social issues of your community.

In the interior design business you are often exposed to possible litigation. There are four methods of handling the various exposures you face:

1. *Eliminate the exposure.*

2. *Assume the exposure yourself.* This method can only be selected after you have measured what financial impact or burden a loss would create for your business.

3. *Reduce the exposure.* This method allows you to establish a loss-prevention program. Such a program helps your organization identify and reduce those hazards which cause losses.

4. *Transfer the exposure.* This method allows you and your organization to transfer the risk to an insurance company.

There are three essentials to remember in buying proper insurance:

1. Never risk more than you can afford to lose.

2. Do not risk too much for too little.

3. Know the odds of sustaining loss.

Types of Insurance
There are a number of types of insurance you should consider.

Building Property Insurance. Property coverage insures against many risks to your buildings and premises. Very often a company will write a package policy that saves you money. The package policy works best when it is custom-designed for your particular needs, rather than as a regular prepackaged policy.

The two general ways in which this type coverage is set up are: (1) insuring for reimbursement losses due to specific perils such as fire and (2) insuring on a special or all-risk basis whereby reimbursement is made for all losses except those that are excluded under the policy. If the special or all-risk basis is available in your coverage, the small additional premium required for this more complete protection is usually well worth spending.

Clarify the way your policy is written. I have had several experiences where replacement value was interpreted in different ways by the adjusters. In one case—a country club project—the claim was adjusted before we started the project. Part of the claim involved chairs and stacking chairs, which were stored on the third floor. Although they had not been used for many years, they were evaluated at today's current replacement value and the club was given this full value in cash.

In the second case—a church project—the evaluation was based on replacement value also, but it was interpreted differently. In this case, the insurance adjuster decided that since the church had, for example, wool carpeting worth about $60 a yard, we were permitted to buy carpeting priced at up to $60 a yard. However, we could not buy carpeting for $30 a yard and then spend the rest of the money on lighting fixtures. The replacement money was to be only spent on the particular item specified in the church's claim.

It is a good idea to clarify this value in advance, if you can. Most designers are interested in making changes and updating at the time of a disaster; they don't always want to replace exactly the same items. This can be a problem at the time of a claim.

If you are assisting a client in handling a claim, check the individual company's practice in regard to replacement costs. The General Adjustment Bureau gives guidelines, but claim practices vary. Be sure you know the ground rules as to the procedures for repair or replacement. It would be unwise for you to make a commitment before having solid information as to the specific insurance company's settlement procedures.

Definition of loss: The insured considers a loss to be the amount paid for the repair of a fire-damaged building. The policy includes depreciation in determining the amount to be paid the insured. For example, the contractor's bill of $50,000 could be considered as the amount of loss by the insured. However, the policy determination of the loss would be $50,000 less $10,000, or $40,000. Depreciation used would be determined by various factors such as age and condition of the building and in some cases use and type of the structure.

Use of the replacement basis of loss settlement eliminates the foregoing in that the insured is paid the actual cost of replacement or repair (if possible), whichever is lower.

You will probably need insurance in some of the following areas:

1. *Fire Insurance*. This is an important consideration for the interior design business. You must have an adequate appraisal for the value of your building and its contents. There are a number of types of fire insurance written today. One is written for depreciated value and the other for replacement value. It is wiser to have replacement value insurance, despite its additional cost, since prices do fluctuate and you will need funds to replace what you lose at the time of loss.

2. *Building and Contents*. This insurance applies to the described structures and the permanent fixtures belonging to and constituting a part of the building. Machinery used in the building—such as air conditioning systems, boilers, and elevators—is covered under the policy. The location of your building will affect the premium of this particular policy.

3. *Contents and Personal Property*. Insurance should be carried on all furniture, fixtures, and inventory. General coverage is similar to the building property coverage.

4. *Replacement Costs Endorsement.* This insurance provides for the full reimbursement of the actual costs of repair or replacement of the insured building without any deduction for depreciation.

5. *Extended Coverage Endorsement.* This insurance covers your property for the same amount as that of your fire policy against all direct loss or damage caused by windstorms, hail, explosions, riots and civil commotion, aircraft, vehicles, and smoke.

6. *Vandalism and Malicious Mischief.* You can get endorsements on your policy to cover loss and damages caused by vandalism and malicious mischief.

7. *Flood Insurance.* This protects the owner of a dwelling and contents against financial loss in catastrophic floods; it includes coverage against inundation from mudslides. Flood insurance is available in areas declared eligible by the federal government, and coverage can be obtained through your local broker through the National Flood Insurance Program. Because the cost of this policy is partially covered by the federal government, it is still very economical. A small number of insurance companies are now writing this coverage.

8. *Computers and Software.* Ordinary insurance does not adequately cover losses involving computers. Special coverage is available for software as well as hardware.

Business Operations Insurance. You can also purchase insurance that can help protect your business operations.

1. *Accounts Receivable Policy.* This policy protects the insured against loss related to the inability to collect accounts receivable when books and records have been destroyed, lost, or damaged. Coverage can be extended to cover loss off of the premises of your business.

2. *Valuable Papers.* This policy covers the loss or destruction of valuable papers such as mortgages, records, financial data, product specifications, merchandise records, customer lists, blueprints, and plans and specifications.

3. *Transportation Floater.* This floater provides an all-risk coverage for the designer's property while it is in transit—either while being delivered to your customer or while en route from your source to the client.

4. *Bailee Customer Floater.* This floater insures against the loss of a customer's property from fire, burglary, hold-up and windstorms. It covers any articles or materials you have accepted from your client for renovation, repair, or any other reason. It covers the client's property while in the possession of the interior designer or craftspeople. It does not cover damage to articles while they are being repaired.

5. *Transportation Damage Insurance.* This insurance is offered by many resources and is popular with companies offering breakable or fragile merchandise. It can be well worth the cost.

    Different types of coverage are offered by various vendors. Under one plan, you do not file a claim with the carrier for merchandise damaged in transit. For an additional charge of two percent of the net invoice, any covered merchandise that is damaged in transit will be replaced at no charge or credited to your account, as you prefer. Certain restrictions do apply. This insurance is available from vendors only.

6. *Business Interruption*. This policy reimburses the designer for the profits he would have earned if a fire or other hazard had not occurred. It includes reimbursement for continued expenses, including payroll, for a specific time or number of days.

7. *Earnings Insurance*. This is a simplified business interruption policy. It is suitable for small businesses whose earnings are not regular and are difficult to forecast. It is based on a predetermined expected profit amount. Extra expense, earnings, and business interruption coverages are now often included under the policy provision termed "Business Income."

8. *General Liability Insurance*. Interior designers and other professionals are subject to the threat of third-party claims. Injury exists as long as there is a client on the premises. It does not terminate when the doors are closed. The designer and the manufacturer are often named jointly in suits alleging injuries caused by defective products. There are policies designed to cover the interior designer in most issues where protection is required against injury or property damage.

   It is extremely important to use the same insurance company for both workmen's compensation insurance and general liability insurance. This prevents litigation between two different carriers if a person is injured. It frequently occurs that when different companies are used, you, as both the insured party and the employer, are caught in litigation that can take years to be resolved.

9. *Comprehensive General Liability*. This insures against all declared existing hazards, plus unknown hazards occurring during the policy term, that might come from the designer's offices or business operations. It is a good idea to have this policy written in conjunction with your automobile policy and your product liability policy, so that the company covering you will provide as complete coverage as possible.

10. *Personal Injury*. This insurance is popularly called the "false arrest insurance." It is often added as an endorsement to the general liability insurance policy. It insures against libel, slander, or defamation of character against the designer or an employee.

11. *Medical Payments*. This policy pays up to a certain amount, with specified limits, to customers and other members of the public injured on the premises as a result of the insured party's business operations. Payments are made to the injured party on a voluntary basis regardless of the insured's liability. It is an excellent way to create good will for the very small premium that is involved.

12. *Workers' Compensation*. This insures all employees, including officers active in the business operations, due to the statutory liability resulting from personal injury or death suffered in the course of employment. This coverage is mandatory in most states. Benefits are payable in accordance with the program of each state. Employer's liability coverage is usually offered in conjunction with workers' compensation. Coverage can be endorsed for employees living and operating in all states except for Nevada, North Dakota, Washington, West Virginia, and Wyoming. The states excepted operate monopolistic funds, and coverage can be obtained only through the state funds. (Note: In some states the employer is responsible not only for occupational disabilities but also for nonoccupational disabilities.)

13. *Motor Vehicle Insurance*. If you provide delivery service, you must insure your trucks and other delivery vehicles against damage or loss. The same is

true of any passenger cars your company uses. It is most important to have high liability coverage for all vehicles used in the interest of business. (See also General Liability Insurance, page 320.)

14. *Automobile Liability*. This insures you against loss or damages for reason of liability or bodily injury; it also provides property damage coverage to members of the public for any operation of the business autos or delivery trucks. Claims arising out of the use, ownership, and maintenance of company-owned vehicles. Defense costs are paid on behalf of the insured regardless of liability. Some states have mandatory (compulsory) liability regulations. Insurance requirements vary from state to state. It is vital that your policy meets the requirements of any U.S. states and provinces of Canada in which an accident occurs. Special conditions also exist for operation of your vehicles in Mexico. The type or form of business under which you operate dictates the use of various provisions to provide proper coverage.

15. *Employer's Nonownership Liability*. This covers your business against claims in situations where employees are using their own cars for business purposes.

16. *Hired Car Insurance*. This covers the use of any hired cares, such as additional delivery trucks that are rented or leased. A minimum premium is usually required under this policy.

17. *Collision Insurance*. This insures you against loss due to collision or upset of your motor vehicle while in use for your business.

18. *Comprehensive Automobile Insurance*. This insures the interior designer's own business automobiles and other motor vehicles against loss, fire or theft, or other physical damage hazards, including glass breakage. This coverage reimburses you for loss or damage to owned vehicles regardless of fault for such claims as fire, flood, theft, vandalism, windstorm, tornado, glass damage, and similar losses.

19. *Professional Liability Insurance*. This is now available for interior designers through ASID. It covers liability for claims resulting from the commission or omission of professional acts. Such claims are often without merit; nevertheless, they are troublesome and expensive to defend. This new policy protects you against these claims.

20. *Product Liability Insurance*. This is designed to provide coverage against claims resulting from misuse or use of products installed by interior designers. Product liability insurance addresses claims for accidents arising after the insured has completed repairs or installations and has departed from the client's premises.

21. *Group Life Insurance*. This may be purchased by businesses for the benefit of their employees. It may be written to provide minimal amounts of insurance for each employee, subject to increases as to the individual's period of employment lengthens.

22. *Disability Insurance*. This insurance is available from both casualty insurance and life insurance companies. Most interior designers work on their own or with small firms, and should have good disability insurance. In my own situation, it has proved very helpful. I recommend that every designer have some sort of disability policy to provide a form of income during any time that he or she may be disabled by illness or accident. Benefits are available on both occupational and nonoccupational bases. The noncancelable or guaranteed renewable policies are the most desirable ones to

have, although their premiums are somewhat higher. With these, restrictive endorsements cannot be later issued to prevent reimbursement for claims recurring from the same cause or for unusual claim activity. The noncancelable form premiums at issuance cannot be increased. Premium increases can be made under a guaranteed renewable policy for various reasons but are normally done on a class rather than an individual basis.

23. *Group Hospitalization Insurance*. This provides you and your employees with coverage for hospital confinement periods. The benefits are similar to those offered under Blue Cross/Blue Shield plans. This coverage normally pays for nonoccupational sickness and injury.

24. *Major Medical Insurance*. This insurance pays for medical expenses arising from illnesses and accidents, up to a specified amount. These policies are often purchased in coordination with your group hospitalization insurance.

25. *Pensions*. Employees value pension benefits. Only group hospitalization, life, and disability benefits are valued more. There are so many types of financial programs available that it is difficult to decide which method, if any, is the best for your employees. In providing pension benefits you make a long-term commitment. In most cases, it is against the law to change the basic elements of your pension program. If your business in later years cannot make the required contributions to the plan, and you plead your inability to continue to the government, your pleas will fall on deaf ears. Unless you are going out of business, or filing for bankruptcy, you will find it very difficult to make such a change. Profit-sharing plans used for pension purposes provide the employer relief in that the amount of the profits determine the employer's contribution. Thus, in a year in which no profits were made, the plan would not require a contribution from the employer.

26. *Key Personnel Life Insurance*. This is commonly used to enable a business to offset the financial loss of a person vital to its continued profitable operation. Owners also use life insurance to finance buy-sell agreements involving the business. Corporations can accumulate money on a tax-deferred basis to provide for retirement of themselves, as well as key personnel.

Many interior designers serve on volunteer boards. Check with your insurance agent to see if you are covered for liability you might incur when serving on volunteer boards. Often this coverage is included under your homeowners' umbrella policy. This insurance would not cover your liability on boards for which you are financially compensated.

Care, Custody, and Control

We need insurance today for things we never dreamed could become an issue. Almost every designer I know has liability insurance and daily policies on items handled for clients, and most have a variety of other liability insurances. I thought we were very well covered until a broken chandelier showed us otherwise.

One of our designers was decorating a chandelier when the chandelier fell from the thirty-foot ceiling. It hit a marble floor, a number of other accessories, and did considerable damage along the way. He immediately called the office. Our managing director directed him to clean up the damage and take care of everything he could. We would notify our insurance company, as we were sure that we had very good coverage.

There was a small, but very important, phrase in our insurance policy called "Care, Custody, and Control," which means that any item that a designer or a staff person has his or her hands on is not in any way covered. According to our policy, the marble floor and the other items that were damaged by the chandelier were covered, but the item our designer was working on—the chandelier—was not. It was considered under our "care, custody, and control."

When I heard this, I became very concerned. Not just about this $15,000 fixture, for which we had to pay, but about all of our projects. I thought of the many costly items we handled on a day-to-day basis. When clients move, we are always there assisting. In some cases we take the complete responsibility for the move. Our staff people are on location on the day that the furniture is transferred. When the furniture arrives, they see that it is arranged properly so that when the client arrives at the new location, everything is in place.

When I think of the hundreds of thousands of dollars of merchandise our firm handles in a year, I find the prospect of being held liable for it chilling. I know enough about art and porcelain to tell the difference between a $50 vase and a $500 vase, but I have no way of knowing the value of rare and unusual antiques or art objects.

After the incident with the chandelier, in trying to diminish our future liability, my eyes became opened to a lot of risks. I consulted with our attorney and insurance broker, and also with two other attorneys who handle nothing but insurance work for large companies such as Equitable. I checked with the brokers and agents who handle Lloyd's of London and found that there is no way that we, as designers, can insure our client's furniture or art objects, simply because we do not know their value. If you, as an individual, wanted to insure a piece of jewelry or furniture, the procedure is simple. You have the item appraised and present the appraisal to your insurance company, and they in turn insure it for you. But they can't possibly sell you insurance on an unknown item of undetermined value.

My solution is to require our client, at the start of a project, to sign a "Lease of Liens." This document states that since we do not know the value of the objects on the client's property, our firm can only be responsible for items that are valued at $500 or less.

We ask the client to notify our staff of all items worth more than $500 so that they will not touch or handle these items. We also ask the client to notify their insurance company to have these items covered during our redesigning or construction project. Most policies do include this coverage.

It's sad to realize that my doing something kind for a client—many times without charge—makes me legally liable for damages way beyond my ability to afford. In self-protection, we now notify the clients so that they can see to it that their policies cover these items, or remove these items from the area while our staff is working. Therefore, we feel this is the only safe way to handle the situation.

Ways of Saving Money
It is not practical for interior designers to carry all the insurance that they might like to have. It is important that your insurance advisor, your accountant, and your attorney, as well as your business advisor, give you some advice as to which areas present your greatest loss potentials, which losses you should insure, and which losses should be covered by self-insurance. If the maximum amount of loss potentials is a small, calculable amount, it is usually preferable to self-insure. Your business can self-insure small claims less expensively than it would cost to pay insurance company premiums. Where the probability of loss isn't great, but the potential loss cannot be calculated or controlled (such as liability claims), the risk should be transferred to your insurance company.

Taking Higher Deductibles
By taking higher deductibles on certain insurance policies and doing some self-insuring, you can reduce premiums. The amount of the deductible and/or the uninsured loss is considered as an income tax deduction.

Using high deductibles is advised on property insurance of all types, in bonding employees, and on automobile insurance; but *not* on anything that involves liability insurance, because of third-party involvement.

Look over all your insurance for the last five years. See which policies you normally do not have claims on. Check with your company to see whether you can save yourself a considerable amount of money by raising the deductible on these policies.

THE HIGH COST OF LIABILITY INSURANCE

Katya Gonscharoff, in writing for the *New York Times*, reported that architects are buying liability premiums at a disaster level. A large number of architectural firms are having problems with liability insurance rates, many of which have increased over the past few years by as much as 700 percent, according to the American Institute of Architects. The AIA New York Chapter's liability coverage for smaller firms—those with gross fees of less than $500,000—averaged 5.7 percent of gross fees. They were 2.3 percent in 1981.

Gonscharoff explains that many firms run the risk of bankruptcy. Either they pay the heavy insurance fees, which many firms feel they cannot afford to do, or they open themselves up to the possibility that they could be sued and the partners would be totally financially liable. A lot of firms are considering doing without insurance because they find that many of the suits seem to be based on the amount of insurance the architects have. Architects are also considering a team insurance; with this insurance if any error is made the entire building team—the designer and the builders—are covered by the developer. Larger firms are considering self-insurance.

The problems that architects are having are similar to those which interior designers experience. A chief management officer of a large architectural firm from Philadelphia said he had discovered, in reviewing his company's work over the past three years, that there was not one job that his office had done that had not had some form of a lawsuit. For construction firms the situation is similar. We are living in a litigious time and good liability, malpractice, or errors and omissions insurance must definitely be part of our insurance package.

How to Lower Your Insurance Rates

In a round-table discussion at our Harrisburg Chamber of Commerce, representatives from the Pennsylvania Insurance Department recommended ways interior designers can lower insurance rates.

1. First, reexamine the coverage you have now to see that it includes the full scope of your business. If you make changes in your business, discuss them with your insurance advisor. Many people are not going into certain businesses or are limiting their areas of work because they can't get good insurance coverage. In my own business, I have stopped extending certain services, or am requiring signed releases from clients, just because I cannot get proper coverage.

2. How well trained your employees are affects your insurance rates. If you can't get well-trained employees, don't do the job. You're better off to hire it out and let someone else be liable, rather than to jeopardize the relationship you have with your client and, in turn, your financial position. If

necessary, send your employees to school or require them to have extra training that might help them do the job well.

3. Is your firm safety-conscious? Have training sessions for safety. I know one firm that holds Saturday training sessions in safety-awareness for its management. Anyone who doesn't show up doesn't have a job. Do whatever is necessary to be sure that your people understand what they can do to prevent accidents and avoid claims.

4. Make your staff responsible for any damages they do. For example, a number of firms now make staff members responsible for the first $100 on an auto claim. This way, the employees are much more careful in the way they handle a company vehicle—and save the firm a lot of expense.

5. It was also recommended that you give a bonus at the end of the year if there have been no damages or suits. Have a party. Celebrate. Make your staff aware that avoiding suits is a very important issue.

PRODUCT LIABILITY BILLS

In the last few years there have been many product liability bills before the Senate, on national and state levels. Interior designers should support these bills, since most of them are attempting to ease the product liability situation. In other words, if a company manufactures an item and it fails, they alone could be sued. The designer, the architect, the contractors, the distributors, or other intermediate people could not be named in the suits. This would reduce malpractice insurance rates considerably since responsibility would automatically be assigned.

These bills would also give statute of limitation rights, which in some states do not exist. Whether the designer sells or specifies merchandise, he or she is still liable. Liability insurance is required for each situation. Therefore interior designers need to define the services that are being offered to the given client when purchasing the appropriate amount of liability insurance, as well as errors and omissions insurance.

Insurance Claims
If you do have to use your insurance, these guidelines may help you in handling your claims.

Calculating Losses. Calculate your losses accurately. Many business people cannot determine the extent of their losses because their accounting system and record-keeping procedures are not in order. Interior designers have a better opportunity than most professionals to calculate losses. At most times, we do know the cost of replacing or restoring whatever property losses we might have.

If you overstate your loss, you automatically raise many questions and delay getting the claim settled. Be careful also not to understate value; this is just as inaccurate as an overstatement.

Present the claim properly. Review your claim with your accountant and insurance agent before presenting it to the adjuster. If it is not presented properly, you will not get the results you seek.

Coordination. Be sure that the coordination between your office and the insurance company is handled by one person. Have this person follow through carefully to be sure that there is a record of all of the necessary details and that all interaction between you and the insurance company is documented for future reference.

As designers, we know what contractors we want to use in restoring a project or who the merchandise came from initially. Present this to your insurance adjuster. Normally you will be able to use the person you want.

Use your insurance consultant or agent as one of your negotiating group. He or she has a very strong play with the insurance company since he or she is purchasing the insurance in your name. Let him or her take your stand. Be sure he or she is aware of each and every detail of the negotiation. This is an excellent opportunity to find out the value of an insurance agent.

You can't live without liability insurance. I never thought I'd have to worry about being sued for things that had nothing to do with my interior design performance. My eyes were opened a few years ago when I was involved in a small country club project. The club had been destroyed through arson, and our design team designed, built, furnished, and completed the new club within a year. We more than tripled its size and certainly made it more efficient to run as well as more attractive. It opened in June, in good time for the club's season.

That winter was very cold. I recall that on Christmas Day everyone's battery was dead, including mine. You couldn't go anywhere on Christmas Day because you couldn't get your car fixed. Over that particular holiday the country club decided to close and, for some reason, no one walked into the club for over thirty days.

During that time, the water pipes in the building froze. The sprinkler system broke, flooding both levels of the clubhouse. The water in the lower level then froze, creating over four feet of ice. Doors had to be broken down in order to get into the office.

I was not the specifier of the sprinkler system. I may have suggested moving a head or two because of interference with a lighting fixture, but that was all I had to do with the sprinkler system. Nevertheless, I was one of the design consultants, so our firm was included in the suit. Our attorney found a way to remove me from the claim; however, it cost me a good bit of money, time, anguish, and aggravation.

It's just amazing. You don't have to do anything to get sued, which is one of the reasons that liability insurance and proper documentation of projects are really critical.

What can we do to protect ourselves? First, we must have reasonable contracts and documents. Compare yours with what other firms are using. This is something for you to discuss with your attorney. But this is only part of the process. The kind of relationship you have with your client is crucial. Ideally, your relationship is one where you work together with mutual respect. If that respect is lost, or if that client feels that he or she is not getting attention, that's very often when problems begin.

In lawsuits, what it boils down to is not whether you made a mistake or were careless, but if you can be held responsible for the problem. Proper documentation of each stage of the project can help greatly in establishing your position.

On a project like the country club job I did, you probably cannot avoid a suit because when a person is going to sue one design professional, he or she will sue all those that are on the team. However, there are many individual suits against interior designers, and your chances of winning are not very good. There are states, I am told by an experienced source, in which there has never been a case against an interior designer where the interior designer won. When I hear statistics like this, I realize that we must assume that juries and judges are not exactly on our side. Few understand what we do. The simplest way to protect yourself is to have positive rapport with your client. As I mentioned earlier, if you find someone who is litigious, probably you're going to be the next one to be sued. So look for another client.

RULES OF RECORD KEEPING

Here are a few guidelines for maintaining a worry-free financial system:

1. *Always pay your bills by check, or through your petty cash fund.* Don't pay for anything out of pocket; try to keep payments restricted to these two individual funds. Restrict petty cash payments to incidental expenses.

2. *Never pay any form of disbursement in cash.* If you happen to take in cash, don't make any disbursement out of it; deposit the cash and write a check for the disbursement.

3. *Be sure that all money that is taken in is properly reported.* This applies to both cash and checks.

4. *Never take any money out of the company for your personal use.* Pay yourself a salary instead. A lot of small businesses run very loosely, which can be quite a problem, especially during an IRS audit. Use separate banking accounts for your design firm and your other businesses or personal funds.

5. *Have your accountant create your record-keeping system.* A system runs most smoothly when your accountant is comfortable with it.

Chapter Twelve

GROWING AS A PROFESSIONAL

Success and advancement in interior design are closely related to additional education. So often it isn't what you do while at work, but what you do on your own time that affects your future positioning in a field. This applies especially to the interior design field; it is a discipline that demands novelty in the best sense of that word. When you enter this field, you embark on a continuing-education process—just as medical practitioners do.

CONTINUING EDUCATION

Tuition is tax-deductible if it is for additional education within your professional discipline. This includes professional seminars, conventions, and formal university education. The IRS does not allow deductions of expense incurred in learning about a new field, but you can deduct anything related to your own field.

You can also deduct your automobile expenses in traveling to seminars, up to a maximum of 26.5 cents per mile. This mileage is now unlimited.

Aside from attending seminars and going back to school, there is a lot you can do to keep yourself up to date on current issues affecting your business.

Learning on the Job

If you plan to start a business, first work for someone else in as similar a business as possible and learn at his or her expense. This is the best investment you can make. So many businesses fail because the people running them have to learn on the job.

Hire smart people. You will learn from them and they will help you develop your business. You do not have the time or energy to train everyone, and it's far too expensive. Be willing to pay them for skill and talent.

Lunch is sometimes the most valuable time that our staff has together. During a shared meal, we talk about the problems of the day and what can be done to make things better. We try to use mealtime as a creative problem-solving time, and learn a lot from each other in this casual atmosphere.

Create a board of advisors. Most people are hesitant to be on a board of directors unless they are provided with good liability insurance coverage, and this gets very involved for a small company. But they *will* sit on your board of advisors. A number of past clients and several outstanding businesspeople in the community sit with my firm and review our progress and goals. We learn a great deal from having this outside point of view.

Surround yourself by people you think are good for you.

Talk to your suppliers. Find out what they are doing. They will also be able to tell you what your competitors are doing. It's amazing what you can learn from your suppliers. They'll show you what is selling and help you understand why.

Bring in experts. Every time there is someone visiting our area who we think knows something about our business, we try to have the person in for lunch so that the whole staff gets to meet him or her. If a designer is visiting from another community, we invite him or her to the office. We ask the designer to show us what he or she is doing. This is a great way of keeping everybody in our staff on top of changes in our field.

Prepare a list of consultants on every major design issue you might encounter, so that when a project comes up you don't have to scramble to create a design team.

For younger people I think additional education in business is very good. However, after you reach a certain age and position, probably you are far better off to use consultants. You can get much more out of your time and it will be directed to your particular needs.

You can also learn from your customers' complaints. Most of our clients are very well educated. If they complain, generally there is some reason.

Learning from Friends and Acquaintances

Anytime you meet someone from whom you would like to learn more, offer to take the person to breakfast, lunch, or dinner. I usually make it either breakfast or dinner because I have a hard time getting away from my office for lunch in the middle of the day. This is a good way to pick people's brains. You learn things that they would not tell you otherwise, and it develops a relationship for future exchange of ideas.

Your family members and friends can be very valuable. Everyone is an expert in his or her own life and lifestyle. Usually these people are more than willing to give you information. Reasonable courtesies can bring you information of great value.

For the last thirty years I've had a practice of having one night a week on which I invite a group of my friends in to talk about business issues. These are usually people whom I respect. I cook for them at my house and we talk about what is progressive and new in business. Some of the same people come almost every week, others only occasionally. These days this practice is called networking (see pages 109–10).

Join any great club that is of value to you. Of course ASID and some of the major design associations are very worthwhile. The Chamber of Commerce is a must, as is any group where you can find people in a similar position to yours. For women, this is sometimes difficult because some organizations, such as the Rotary Club, are for men only.

Business Courses

While many colleges offer business courses, often designers do not have the time to attend. This does not mean you can't learn about business. Many radio and television programs have business courses; see what the subjects are and listen to or watch them. A number of topics such as real estate, accounts receivable, and money management have been covered on these media and have been very helpful to me in running my business.

Listen to tapes. In an average week, I listen to twelve to thirty hours of tapes. I drive over 40,000 miles a year; this gives me a great deal of tape-listening time. I have a large library of tapes and never go anywhere without a program of tapes. By listening to tapes, you can hear a lot of relevant information with minimal effort on your part.

Check what the Small Business Administration (SBA) is doing. It sponsors business courses, sometimes through colleges, and will keep you attuned to economic developments.

Reading

I believe in reading. I read over 150 publications per month, plus four newspapers per day. I don't read every word, but I find that even a cursory reading is critical in keeping abreast of issues. Learn what publications are really useful for you to read, and then see if you can't follow them on a regular basis.

Getting Other Points of View

Tap into older people. Retired people who are interested in their fields have a lot to offer. They are not in competition, and they're curious about what you can do. They often come up with good tips, information, and methods that can be very beneficial.

Watch what other people are doing and find a way to do it better. It's so much easier than creating the whole idea yourself. Look around when you're visiting other areas. Visit other design firms and see what they're doing. There's always some idea there that you can adapt to fit your needs.

Asking questions is the single best way to learn, so don't worry about whether the question is silly or irrelevant. If you want to know something, ask. The more you learn, the better able you are to evaluate the information you have already received.

EDUCATING YOUR STAFF

Make your employees better than they were when they came to work for you. Educate them, develop them, polish them. Of course they will often leave you and go onto something else; however, no one wants employees around who are the same now as they were when they started. Polish them up; make them succeed and it will generally be much better for your firm.

ATTENDING SEMINARS

A designer's education is never really complete, and attending seminars is a relatively painless way to take in new information or to earn continuing education units (CEUs). Most professionals today require their members to complete a certain number of CEU credits each year. In the design profession, CEUs are increasingly important and need to be scheduled into every designer's life. Doctors and attorneys reserve several days a month for attending seminars, and designers must do the same.

Usually a day spent in a seminar is more rewarding than a day of independent study because you are with people whose interests are similar. It is an efficient use of time in that you learn the latest information, and you see how other people solve problems like your own. It's also often fun. Attending a seminar can lend a new perspective to some of your day-to-day activities. Interior design is a constantly changing field. You need to update your knowledge, evaluate your position in the field, and determine where you are going. The results of a seminar can be reassuring, or they might well be an incentive to go home and do better.

Selecting the Right Seminars

Seminars are an investment. You measure the worth of a seminar by this guideline: You should make from six to ten times the price of the seminar from the information gained there. Sometimes the company pays for these seminars. If so, put in written requests to your firm for each seminar you wish to attend, and do it early. Try to work out how many days you can devote to seminars and continuing education throughout the year and then determine which areas of information are important to you and gear your seminar choices accordingly.

Brochure write-ups are so glowing that it is hard to tell good programs from bad ones until after you've spent your money and sat through that seminar. Make sure it's a good program by checking references. You might contact the sponsor and ask for some names and addresses of people who attended past seminars. Ask for their telephone numbers as well, so you can check with them personally. Then go on their recommendations. It is highly unlikely that the sponsors would refuse to give you past references, but if this happens, ask for a copy of the evaluations of this seminar. There is no point in wasting your time in a seminar that is not worthwhile.

Paying for Seminars

Seminars cost more than just the admission fee. Each day you are away from the office, even at an inexpensive seminar, costs the firm at least $1,000. If your employer pays for you to attend a seminar, send him or her a copy of your summary and highlight what you feel you learned by attending. If there is evidence that the seminar was useful, your employer will be more likely to send you and other employees to other programs.

Preparing for Seminars

Before you go to a seminar, list your goals. Outline just what you would like to get out of a particular seminar when you first sign up for it.

Plan ahead for the seminar. Make sure you know where it is, and how much time it will take you to get there. It's best to arrive about twenty minutes to a half hour early so that you can select your seat and meet other participants. It's also a good time to introduce yourself to the speaker and to mention some of your primary reasons for coming to the seminar.

Benefiting from the Seminar

During the seminar, assess its value to you. What are the good ideas that are coming from this program and how can you use them? Try to make note of several good points. Even if you find, in reviewing your notes, that you have thirty or forty ideas, select the one, two, or three that are the best and try out those ideas within twenty-four hours. If you do this, statistics tell us that you will probably make these changes a part of your life and they will continue to be of value to you. If you try to do too many things, you'll find that nothing is accomplished. After you've incorporated the first few ideas into your practice, you can always refer to your notes to see which others might be profitable in other situations.

Buy the books or tapes that relate to the seminar. Normally, we forget about ninety percent of anything we learn within two weeks; books and tapes are good reference materials. Tapes are especially good because you can play them in your car or while you are doing something else.

Don't call the office while you are at a seminar. Devote your energies to the topic at hand and get all you possibly can from it. It's most likely that your call to the office won't really do any good anyhow. Program yourself and your staff to understand that you will just not be available for that seven- or eight-hour period.

Participate in the seminar. Don't be afraid to ask questions. This is your chance to try things out. It's much better to make a mistake here in the seminar atmosphere than it is out there on the job. Take good notes that you can read later; most of us never have time to rewrite seminar notes, but we may need to refer to them later on.

A seminar is also an opportunity to make contacts. I always try to meet at least one new person during a seminar who may be important to me later on. This is a chance to expand your networking circle. Mingle. Exchange cards with the people you meet; you will later be able to call them and review other issues.

Summarize what you got out of the day. Keep a copy of this summary for yourself in your CEU file; I recommend you keep a reference book or a file on any continuing education courses that you attend. It may become necessary documentation of professional standing. In addition, it's useful to know what seminars you have attended and what you got from them as you consider what to attend in the future. This summary will help you evaluate what the day was worth.

Allied Board of Trade
550 Mamaroneck Avenue
Harrison, NY 10528
(914) 381-5200
(212) 473-3877

American Hardware Manufacturers
  Association
931 North Plum Grove Road
Schaumburg, IL 60173-4796
(708) 605-1025

American Hotel & Motel Association
1201 New York Avenue, N.W.
Washington, DC 20005
(202) 289-3100

American Institute of Architects (AIA)
1735 New York Avenue, N.W.
Washington, DC 20006
(202) 626-7300

American Society of Furniture Designers
  (ASFD)
521 Hamilton
High Point, NC 27261
(919) 884-4074

American Society of Interior Designers
  (ASID)
608 Massachusetts Avenue
Washington, DC 20002
(202) 546-3480

American Society of Landscape
  Architects (ASLA)
4401 Connecticut Avenue, N.W.
Washington, DC 20008
(202) 686-2752

American Society for Testing of Materials
  (ASTM)
1916 Race Street
Philadelphia, PA 19103
(215) 299-5400

Art Deco Society of Los Angeles
P.O. Box 972
Hollywood, CA 90078
(213) 659-DECO

Art Deco Society of New York
90 West Street
New York, NY 10006
(212) 925-4946

Art & Antique Dealers League of
  America
1020 Madison Avenue
New York, NY 10021
(212) 879-7558

Associated Landscape Contractors of
  America
405 North Washington Street
Falls Church, VA 22046
(703) 241-4004

Association of Registered Interior
  Designers of Ontario
168 Bedford Road
Toronto, Ontario M5R 2K9
Canada
(416) 921-2127

Association of University Interior
  Designers
Miami University
Cook Place
Oxford, OH 45056
(513) 529-3730

Better Fabrics Testing Bureau, Inc.
101 West 31st Street
New York, NY 10001
(212) 868-7090

Brick Institute of America
11490 Commerce Park Drive
Reston, VA 22091
(703) 620-0100

Business & Institutional Furniture
  Manufacturers' Association (BIFMA)
2335 Burton, S.E.
Grand Rapids, MI 49506
(616) 243-1681

California Redwood Association
405 Enfrente Drive
Novato, CA 94949
(415) 382-0662

The Carpet & Rug Institute
Box 2048
Dalton, GA 30722-2048
(404) 278-3176

Center for Fire Research
National Institute of Standards &
  Technology
A247 Polymers Building
Gaithersburg, MD 20899
(301) 975-6850

Color Association of the United States
409 West 44th Street
New York, NY 10036
(212) 582-6884

Color Marketing Group
4001 North Ninth Street
Arlington, VA 22203
(703) 528-7666

Contract Furnishings Council
1190 Merchandise Mart
Chicago, IL 60654
(312) 321-0563

Foundation for Interior Design
　Education Research
60 Monore Center, N.W.
Grand Rapids, MI 49503
(616) 458-0400

Illuminating Engineering Society of
　North America
345 East 47th Street
New York, NY 10017
(212) 705-7926

Interior Design Educators Council
　(IDEC)
14252 Culver Drive
Irvine, CA 92714
(714) 551-0100

Institute of Business Designers (IBD)
341 Merchandise Mart
Chicago, IL 60654
(312) 467-1950

International Association of Lighting
　Designers
18 East 16th Street
New York, NY 10003
(212) 206-1281

International Facility Management
　Association
1 Greenway Plaza, Suite 1410
Houston, TX 77046
(616) 772-IFMA

Marble Institute of America
33505 State Street
Farmington, MI 48335
(313) 476-5558

National Association of Display
　Industries
470 Park Avenue South
New York, NY 10016
(212) 213-2662

National Council of Acoustical
　Consultants
P.O. Box 359
66 Morris Avenue
Springfield, NJ 07081
(201) 379-1100

National Council of Interior Design
　Qualification (NCIDQ)
118 East 25th Street
New York, NY 10010
(212) 473-1188

National Fire Protection Association
Batterymarch Park
Quincy, MA 02269
(617) 770-3000

National Institute of Governmental
　Purchasing
115 Hillwood Avenue
Falls Church, VA 22046
(703) 533-7300

National Office Products Association
　(NOPA)
301 North Fairfax Street
Alexandria, VA 22314
(703) 549-9040

National Restaurant Association
1200 17th Street, N.W.
Washington, DC 20036
(202) 331-5900

National Trust for Historic Preservation
1785 Massachusetts Avenue, N.W.
Washington, DC 20036
(202) 673-4000

Society for Marketing Professional
　Services
99 Canal Center Plaza
Alexandria, VA 22314
(703) 549-6117

Tile Council of America
P.O. Box 326
Princeton, NJ 08542-0326
(609) 921-7050

Upholstered Furniture Action Council
　(UFAC)
P.O. Box 2436
High Point, NC 27261
(919) 885-5065

The Wool Bureau
Atlanta Merchandise Mart
240 Peachtree Street, N.W.
Atlanta, GA 30303
(404) 524-0512

EPILOGUE

This book has been dedicated to the paper process rather than the computer because it is important that the designer or the design business manager understand exactly how things are done manually before adapting them to computer.

In the past few years many software packages that are very simple and easy to use have appeared on the market. Computers and computer software are definitely part of, or the core of, many design practices. Review several business software packages before making your decision. There are even programs based on this book.

Today we must use every method modern technology affords to make our firms as efficient as possible, because a major emphasis in the future will be on how to accomplish jobs accurately and well yet remain price effective. The issue of costing is going to become far more important in this next decade than ever before. Designers have a lot of competition and we must perform at the highest possible levels.

We also need to be able to give our clients what they want, which is why so many of the forms and interview techniques deal with communication. It is crucial to communicate appropriately so we understand each other, our clients, and our workrooms. Communicating with resources is quite different from communicating with clients. One of our key professional functions as designers is to translate our clients' vocabulary into language our resources will understand.

This book emphasizes simple, familiar procedures that can make some of this communication routine rather than something that requires constant thought and effort. Many of the forms presented here may need alteration to fit your individual practice, but at least you and your staff have a starting point, a ready reference.

The industry has changed since the 1980s. Our clients are more educated. They know far more about interior design than ever before. A great deal of the mystique is gone. They know what you do, how you charge, what products cost. They feel in many instances that they can do things almost as well as the professional designer. The design profession must raise its standards to the point where designers can do things that others cannot. We must demonstrate this higher level of professionalism to maintain our clients.

Competition comes from many sources, not just other design professionals, but other people who sell products and services—in many cases, not even charging for design services. They are our competition and will continue to be so. Interior design sources are exceedingly varied. Always study the competition; you need to know where people can buy what we sell.

Budgets are larger than ever before, and this trend will continue. With monumental budgets, our responsibilities also increase. We must learn to manage these financial aspects with great care and accuracy, because the way the monies are managed during the design process can make a great deal of difference to our profit picture.

There is also increased risk because the projects are more involved. These are very litigious times and will continue to be so. Interior designers must improve and develop their paper tracking to provide a well-documented project for the client and resources and for self-protection. Documentation is part of communication; maintaining good communications is one of the best ways to eliminate or minimize legal threats.

Today there is better design for everyone. There are wonderful products of great quality in almost every price range. Design is not just for the very wealthy; excellent design is becoming part of every lifestyle.

Master builders, people who know how to finish a job completely, will be increasingly important in the future. There are designers who work with or are even responsible for the manufacture of many of the products that go into their projects. Clients want more than just design; they want a completed product. The question is, how can we create our design for good control of the finished project?

How should we position ourselves properly for this next decade? It is important to understand the position of the interior designer and how we fit in with our clients' expectations. What do they want from us and how do they see us?

Part of the positioning answer is specialization. Today interior design is a complex and broad-spectrum discipline. As professionals we have the time, energy, and expertise to excel in only one aspect of interior design. Selecting a specialty and then dedicating your education to developing that specialty will give you a special edge.

Associating with other designers in various ways also strengthens our positions. As partners, teams, and organizations, we can support each other and achieve a business system that provides clients with benefits impossible for the single practitioner.

Increasing our use of design consultants also strengthens our position. The quality of your group of consultants affects the type and size of the projects your firm is able to attract.

THE LIBRARY

If you don't have a great library, you can't function in today's design world. The demands on the design library are increasing constantly, and individual library collections within studios may not be adequate for most practices. Fortunately several new library systems are available: master research libraries, video libraries, computerized manufacturers' catalogues, and library update services.

In many major cities, large research libraries boasting 30,000 and more manufacturers' catalogs of materials for architectural and interior design projects are being developed in or near the design centers. Maintaining a collection of this size requires professional management and can be expensive, making it impractical for the average design studio. Master libraries for design research make membership available to professionals in the design field. Some charge membership fees; some do not.

In some larger cities, library specialists will set up a design library in your office or studio, customizing it to your specialty. The service includes weekly on-site updates and maintenance. Because this is their specialty, they are able to keep your library up to date efficiently and cost effectively all the time.

Several services extend the reach of the studio design library. Large manufacturers now provide computerized library systems, including all details needed for layout and specification of their line. Weekly updates keep the systems current. There is also a system to send color photographs of products via modem, but in most areas present phone lines cannot accommodate it.

Video libraries are available from many manufacturers. These give us the opportunity to present products to clients in perspective. These images can be incorporated into our own video presentations for special clients. Designers who use this process make slides or videos of special items when visiting markets, showrooms, or factories.

Videos are also used to show how products are made, answering the question of what makes one product different from a competing product. Another use of videos is for training staff where no live trainer is available. They are not as effective as interactive training but are certainly better than nothing.

At one time, it was enough to update your catalog library twice a year. Now, weekly or even daily is more appropriate. In this high-tech age, speed is a requirement.

In smaller cities, this opportunity to build a quality library is a good reason to develop a co-op or team group practice.

PHOTOGRAPHY

Because of advanced technology, magazines have become less exacting in their photography requirements. Computer retouching can cure many ills, and a skilled computer graphics technician can crop and enlarge details to enhance the photo. Slides are acceptable to most editors.

Still, the best way to learn what kind of photography a magazine wants is to look at the masthead, get the editor's name, and write a letter asking for photography requirements. In most cases, you will receive a form letter listing the magazine's needs.

SERVICE

Interior design is a dedicated-service industry. Most designers are heavily involved in servicing their clients. One of the unique reasons clients come to a designer is that they want special attention. They view their designers as being responsible for coordinating the service of the project, even if the company provides only the design concept. Clients expect and believe that if the designer does a good job, the design will be easy to produce.

Meeting the client's expectations is not always easy; they often have very different ideas from the designer. One of the most important ways to build a strong relationship is to find out what the client really wants. Put into your client management system an interviewing structure that will let you clarify the client's needs and desires. There is an example on pages 197–202, the Design Service Outline. Review it, and then add to it.

The outline of services has a number of uses. As a marketing and sales tool, it shows clients the range of design services available. It also helps you define what clients actually need by eliminating those services they don't need.

Time spent learning about a client's preferences is critical to a successful job. Some designers delve deeply into the client's lifestyles, personal and color preferences, and the client's history of environmental experiences.

Clients today expect a designer to make the job happen. They are not interested in buying beautifully presented boards. Our professional organizations and our legal advisers suggest that "professional designers" should only sell services, not product. Why? Professional control and fear of litigation. I do strongly believe the greatest safeguard in today's litigious climate is to be careful not to overextend yourself or your firm. Be sure you have good control over whatever part of a job you take responsibility for.

You do this by defining the project carefully. State exactly what you can do and what you will be responsible for. Don't tell the client that you can take care of everything. That was part of the design mystique of the past, but today's clients are more sophisticated. They want results, not just mystique. So often we try to do more than is possible. You know many of the limitations of the project, so use care in defining what you can and will do. Of course, what and how to be properly compensated for your services is also the basis of your business success.

PROFESSIONAL ORGANIZATIONS

To keep abreast of current issues in your specialty, you may need to belong to more than one professional organization. This is an effective way to keep up-to-date and to meet and talk with others whose work and interests are similar. These organizations also provide services, such as health insurance and liability/errors and omissions insurance, that may be less expensive and better dedicated to our needs because they were geared for the design community.

Make the time and effort to learn about the organization, because the rewards are commensurate. If you attend the meetings and conferences and ask for the published material, you get more benefit from your membership. Networking is only one of the advantages of membership.

Some organizations give you more prestige simply by associating your name with their initials. They have gained credibility with the public and in the design industry by requiring their membership to pass tests of knowledge and skill. The American Society of Interior Designers and the Institute of Business Designers now require all potential members to pass the National Council for Interior Design Qualification (NCIDQ) exam.

Organizations that do not require proficiency exams may be useful simply because of the broad range of people who belong. For instance, the International Furnishings and Design Association (IFDA) has members from all segments of the design industry, including designers, publicists, journalists, manufacturers, and distribution specialists. This is an excellent organization in which to network and learn what is happening in the field.

PLANNING

"Vision without systems thinking ends up painting lovely pictures of the future with no deep understanding of the forces that must be mastered to move from here to there." (Peter M. Senge, *The Fifth Dimension,* p. 12. New York: Doubleday, 1990.)

Today it is easier than ever to become just another firm offering design services. This underscores the value of planning.

Planning is establishing priorities. Planning provides a map and direction for the activities that lead us to achieve our goals. I find a visual map of the processes needed a great help in accomplishing goals.

Planning makes decision making simpler because it provides a yardstick to measure against. Without a plan, it is easier to fall into the habit of making no decisions, of being pushed and pulled by events.

Sometimes we don't plan because we are afraid of failure. We don't want to measure the levels of success for fear it will show we have none. But the only wrong decision is no decision. One day each year should be spent on planning, either by hiring a personal consultant to work with your firm or by attending a workshop to learn the techniques of the planning process.

EDUCATION

"A learning organization is a place where people are continually discovering how they create their reality and how they can change it." (Peter M. Senge, *The Fifth Dimension,* p. 13. New York: Doubleday, 1990.)

Most consultants will tell you that at least one day per week of education is needed to keep you sufficiently up-to-date to meet the standards of your field and to keep you competitive. If you expect to earn a high income, you must have the knowledge that enables you to work at levels that keep you interested and stimulated.

Professional organizations in the design industry see education as a key concern and are offering more Continuing Education Unit (CEU) courses. Some programs are sponsored by manufacturers. Some firms bring in the best training specialists they can find to empower their staff. There is more material to know than ever before. Program time for education into your schedule on a regular basis.

During the last few years, the demand for specialized knowledge has grown considerably. Designers who have been practicing for many years are now going back to universities to restudy design. Their background and training is so different from the way design is presented today that the new vantage point renews their excitement and pleasure in their careers. The classroom mix of practicing designers and young students helps both groups. College study is definitely not only for the young.

This era of changing information and resource overload has made necessary a specialist with the company structure, the human resource manager or human resource development director. It is a challenging job involving training and empowering the staff with the systems they need to achieve the creative visions of the firm.

Today's successful company is a learning organization. Clients come to us for up-to-date information. Designers, when selecting the firm they want to be associated with, are looking for firms that provide the best conditions for developing and enriching their careers and lifestyles as design professionals.

BIBLIOGRAPHY

This compilation includes books, magazines, and journals that have been read to advantage and, in some cases, used repeatedly as reference resources. It is not intended to be all-inclusive. Some of the books are now out of print, but all are available through libraries.

INTERIOR DESIGN BUSINESS AND PRACTICE MANAGEMENT BOOKS

Alderman, Robert L. *How to Make More Money at Interior Design*. New York: Interior Design Books, 1982. Distributed by Van Nostrand Reinhold.

Burden, Ernest. *Design Communication: Developing Promotional Material for Design Professionals*. New York: McGraw-Hill, 1987.

Ching, Frank. *Illustrated Guide to Interior Architecture*. New York: Van Nostrand Reinhold, 1987.

Cochrane, Diane. *This Business of Art*. New, revised edition. New York: Watson-Guptill, 1988.

Cooper, David G. *Architectural and Engineering Salesmanship*. New York: John Wiley & Sons, 1978.

Coxe, Weld, David Maister, and The Coxe Group. *Success Strategies for Design Professionals*. New York: McGraw-Hill, 1987.

Crawford, Tad. *Legal Guide for the Visual Artist*. New York: Madison Square Press, 1977.

Dell'Isola, Alphonse, and Stephen J. Kirk. *Life Cycle Costing for Design Professionals*. New York: McGraw-Hill, 1981.

Epstein, Lee. *Legal Forms for the Designer*. New York: Design Publications, 1977.

Foxhall, William B., ed. *Techniques of Successful Practice for Architects and Engineers*. New York: McGraw-Hill, 1975.

Getz, Lowell, and Frank Stasiowski. *Financial Management for the Design Professional*. New York: Whitney Library of Design, 1982.

Jones, Gerre. *How to Market Professional Design Services*. New York: McGraw-Hill, 1983.

Kennedy, E. Lee. *CAD Drawing, Design, Data Management*. New York: Whitney Library of Design, 1986.

Kliment, Stephen A. *Creative Communication for a Successful Design Practice*. New York: Whitney Library of Design, 1977.

Knackstedt, Mary V. *Interior Design for Profit*. New York: Kobro Publications, 1980.

Knackstedt, Mary V., with Laura J. Haney. *Profitable Careers Options for Interiors Designers*. New York: Kobro Publications, 1985.

Lewis, Jack R. *Architects and Engineers Office Practice Guide*. Englewood Cliffs, N.J.: Prentice-Hall, 1978.

Loebelson, *How to Profit in Contract Design*. New York: Interior Design Books, 1983. Distributed by Van Nostrand Reinhold.

Mattox, Robert F. *Financial Management for Architects*. Washington, D.C.: American Institute of Architects, 1980.

McGrath, Norman. *Photographing Buildings Inside and Out*. New York: Whitney Library of Design, 1987.

Morgan, Jim. *Marketing for the Small Design Firm*. New York: Whitney Library of Design, 1984.

Panero, Julius, and Martin Zelnick. *Human Dimension & Interior Space*. New York: Whitney Library of Design, 1979.

Pegler, Martin M. *Dictionary of Interior Design*. New York: Fairchild, 1983.

Preiser, Wolfgang, et al. *Post-Occupancy Evaluation*. New York: Van Nostrand Reinhold, 1987.

Reznikoff, S. C. *Interior Graphic and Design Standards*. New York: Whitney Library of Design, 1986.

———. *Specifications for Commercial Interiors*. New York: Whitney Library of Design, 1979.

Rose, Stuart W. *Achieving Excellence in Your Design Practice*. New York: Whitney Library of Design, 1987.

Siegel, Harry. *Business Guide for Interior Designers: A Practical Checklist for Analyzing the Various Conditions of a Design Project and the Related Clauses for a Letter of Agreement*. New York: Whitney Library of Design, 1976.

———. *This Business of Interior Design*. New York: Whitney Library of Design, 1976.

Siegel, Harry, and Alan Siegel. *A Guide to Business Principles and Practices for Interior Designers*. Revised edition. New York: Whitney Library of Design, 1982.

Stasiowski, Frank. *Negotiating Higher Design Fees*. New York: Whitney Library of Design, 1985.

Stasiowski, Frank, and David Burstein. *Project Management for the Design Professional*. New York: Whitney Library of Design, 1984.

Stitt, Fred A., ed. *Design Office Management Handbook*. Santa Monica: Art & Architecture Press, 1986.

GENERAL BUSINESS AND MANAGEMENT BOOKS

Albrecht, Karl, and Ron Zemke. *Service America: Doing Business in the New Economy*. Homewood, Ill.: Dow-Jones-Irwin, 1985.

Berenyi, John. *The Modern American Business Dictionary*. New York: William Morrow, 1982.

Bliss, Edwin C. *Getting Things Done: The ABC's of Time Management*. New York: Charles Scribner's Sons, 1976.

Brooks, Earl, and George S. Odiorne. *Managing by Negotiation*. New York: Van Nostrand Reinhold, 1984.

Broom, H. N. et al. *Small Business Management*. 7th ed. Cincinnati: South-Western, 1987.

Cohen, William A. *How to Sell to the Government*. New York: John Wiley & Sons, 1981.

Cresci, Martha W. *Complete Book of Model Business Letters*. West Nyack, N.Y.: Parker Publishing Co., 1976. Distributed by Prentice-Hall.

Drucker, Peter F. *The Effective Executive*. New York: Harper & Row, 1967.

_____. *The Frontiers of Management*. New York: Truman Talley Books, 1986.

_____. *Innovation and Entrepreneurship: Practice and Principles*. New York: Harper & Row, 1985.

_____. *Management: Tasks, Practices, Responsibilities*. Abbreviated and revised edition. New York: Harper & Row, 1985.

Fallon, W., ed. *American Management Association Management Handbook*. 2nd edition. New York: AMACOM, 1983.

Fink, Steven. *Crisis Management: Planning for the Inevitable*. New York: AMACOM, 1986.

Fisher, Robert, and William Ury. *Getting to Yes: Negotiating Agreements Without Giving In*. Boston: Houghton Mifflin, 1981.

Frank, Milo O. *How to Get Your Point Across in 30 Seconds—or Less*. New York: Simon & Schuster, 1986.

Funkhouser, G. Ray. *The Power of Persuasion: Giving Up Control on the Way to Power*. New York: Times Books, 1986.

Geneen, Harold, with Alvin Moscow. *Managing*. New York: Doubleday, 1984.

Gumpert, David E. and Jeffrey A. Timmons. *The Encyclopedia of Small Business Resources*. New York: Harper & Row, 1984.

Heller, Robert. *The Supermanagers*. New York: McGraw-Hill, 1985.

Hennig, Margaret, and Anne Jardim. *The Managerial Woman*. New York: Anchor Press/Doubleday, 1981.

Heyl, Carl. *The Encyclopedia of Management*. 3rd edition. New York: Van Nostrand Reinhold, 1983.

Heyl, Carl, and Belden Menkus. *Handbook of Management for the Growing Business*. New York: Van Nostrand Reinhold, 1987.

Holcomb, Marya A. *Presentations for Decision Makers*. New York: Van Nostrand Reinhold, 1983.

Lowry, Albert J. *How to Become Financially Successful by Owning Your Own Business*. New York: Simon & Schuster, 1981.

Nagelschmidt, Joseph S. *The Public Affairs Handbook*. New York: AMACOM, 1982.

Nickerson, Clarence B. *Accounting Handbook for Nonaccountants*. 3rd edition. New York: Van Nostrand Reinhold, 1985.

Ouchi, William G. *The M-Form Society*. Reading, Mass.: Addison-Wesley, 1984.

Peters, Thomas J. and Nancy Austin. *A Passion for Excellence: The Leadership Difference*. New York: Random House, 1985.

Peters, Thomas J., and Robert H. Waterman, Jr. *In Search of Excellence*. New York: Harper & Row, 1982.

Peters, Tom. *Thriving on Chaos: A Revolutionary Agenda for Today's Manager*. New York: Knopf, 1987.

Rosenberg, Jerry M. *Dictionary of Business and Management*. 2nd edition. New York: John Wiley & Sons, 1983.

Scott, Dru. *How to Put More Time in Your Life*. New York: Rawson, Wade, 1980.

Steiner, George A. *The New CEO*. New York: Free Press, 1983.

Tropman, John E. *Meetings: How to Make Them Work for You*. New York: Van Nostrand Reinhold, 1985.

Weston, J. Fred and Eugene F. Brigham. *Essentials of Managerial Finance*. 7th edition. Hinsdale, Ill.: The Dryden Press, 1985.

Winston, Stephanie. *The Organized Executive*. New York: Norton, 1983.

Winter, Elmer L. *A Complete Guide to Preparing a Corporate Annual Report*. New York: Van Nostrand Reinhold, 1985.

DESIGN MAGAZINES AND JOURNALS

Architecture
994 Old Eagle School Road
Suite 1000
Wayne, PA 19087

Architecture Minnesota
275 Market Street, Suite 54
Minneapolis, MN 55405

Architectural Record
1221 Avenue of the Americas
New York, NY 10020

ASID Report
608 Massachusetts Avenue N.E.
Washington, DC 20002

Canadian Interiors
777 Bay Street
Toronto, Ontario M5W 1A7
Canada

Contract
1515 Broadway, 24th Floor
New York, NY 10036

Design South
3201 Griffin Road, Suite 204
Ft. Lauderdale, FL 33312

Design Times
715 Boylston
Boston, MA 02116

The Designer/Specifier
401 North Broad Street
Philadelphia, PA 19108

Designers West
8914 Santa Monica Boulevard
Los Angeles, CA 90069

Facilities Design & Management
1515 Broadway
New York, NY 10036

ID International (Industrial Design)
330 West 42nd Street
New York, NY 10036

I.D.E.A.S.
P.O. Box 343392
Miami, FL 33114

IDH (Interior Design Handbook)
370 Lexington Avenue
New York, NY 10164

Interior Design
249 West 17th Street
New York, NY 10011

Interiors
1515 Broadway
New York, NY 10036

Interiors & Sources
450 Skokie Boulevard, #507
Northbrook, IL 60062

Interiorscape
3023 Eastland Boulevard
Clearwater, FL 34621

*Journal of Interior Design
    Education and Research (JIDER)*
College of Human Resources
University of Delaware
Newark, DE 19716

Metropolis
177 East 87th Street
New York, NY 10128

Progressive Architecture
600 Summer Street
P.O. Box 1361
Stamford, CT 06904

Architectural Digest
5900 Wilshire Boulevard
Los Angeles, CA 90036

Better Homes and Gardens
1761 Locust Street
Des Moines, IA 50336

Canadian Hotel & Restaurant
777 Bay Street
Toronto, Ontario M5W 1A7
Canada

Catering Today
P.O. Box 222
Santa Claus, IN 47579

Colonial Homes
1790 Broadway
New York, NY 10019

Elle Decor
1633 Broadway
New York, NY 10019

Fine Homebuilding
P.O. Box 5506
63 South Main Street
Newtown, CT 06470

Florida Home & Garden
800 Douglas Road, Suite 500
Coral Gables, FL 33134

*Food Services Equipment and
    Supplies Specialist*
1350 East Touhy Avenue
Des Plaines, IL 60601

Gifts & Decorative Accessories
51 Madison Avenue
New York, NY 10010

Hotel & Motel Management
7500 Old Oak Boulevard
Cleveland, OH 44130

Hotel & Resort Industry
488 Madison Avenue
New York, NY 10022

House Beautiful
1700 Broadway
New York, NY 10019

Houston Metropolitan
5615 Kirby Drive
Houston, TX 77265

Kitchen & Bath Concepts
20 East Jackson
Chicago, IL 60604

Kitchen & Bath Design News
2 University Plaza, Suite 11
Hackensack, NJ 07601

Lighting Design & Application
345 East 47th Street
New York, NY 10017

Lighting Dimensions
135 Fifth Avenue
New York, NY 10010

Lodging Hospitality
1100 Superior Avenue
Cleveland, OH 44114

Metropolitan Home
750 Third Avenue
New York, NY 10017

Modern Office Technology
1100 Superior Avenue
Cleveland, OH 44114

Northern California Home & Garden
656 Bair Island Road
Redwood City, CA 94063

The Office
600 Summer Street
P.O. Box 1231
Stamford, CT 06904

Old House Journal
435 Ninth Street
Brooklyn, NY 11215

1001 Home Ideas
3 Park Avenue
New York, NY 10016

Phoenix Home & Garden
Suite A-100
4041 North Central Avenue
Phoenix, AZ 85012

Practical Homeowner
825 Seventh Avenue
New York, NY 10019

Restaurant Hospitality
100 Superior Avenue
Cleveland, OH 44114

Southern Accents
2100 Lakeshore Drive
Birmingham, AL 35209

Southern California Home & Garden
656 Bair Island Road
Redwood City, CA 94063

Southern Living
2100 Lakeshore Drive
Birmingham, AL 35209

*Southern Prestigious Homes &
   Interiors*
P.O. Box 306
Mt. Pleasant, SC 29465

Southwest Sampler
707 Kautz Road
St. Charles, IL 60174

Texas Homes
3988 North Central Expressway
Suite 1200
Dallas, TX 75204

The Source for Interiors
5339 Alpha Road, #105
Dallas, TX 75240

BUSINESS PUBLICATIONS

*Barron's—National Business and
   Financial Weekly*
420 Lexington Avenue
New York, NY 10170

Boardroom Reports
330 West 42nd Street
New York, NY 10036

Business Week
1221 Avenue of the Americas
New York, NY 10020

D & B Reports
299 Park Avenue South
New York, NY 10171

Forbes
60 Fifth Avenue
New York, NY 10011

Fortune
Time & Life Building
Rockefeller Center
New York, NY 10020

Industry Week
1100 Superior Avenue
Cleveland, OH 44114

Nation's Business
(Chamber of Commerce)
1615 H Street N.W.
Washington, DC 20062

Voice of Small Business
(National Small Business
   Association)
1604 K Street, N.W.
Washington, DC 20006

The Wall Street Journal
420 Lexington Avenue
New York, NY 10170

INDEX

401(K) Plans, 302
Freelancers, 77
Freight damage, 261–64
Furniture/furnishings
    design, 20, 23
    design centers, 215–20
    installation of, 187–88
    mass-produced, 222
    wrappings, 191
Furniture, furnishings, and equipment
        specifications sheet, 181

General partnership, 41–42
Good will, 39
Government
    as client, 108
    market information from, 111
    product regulation by, 223
Graphic design, 20
Green Book, The, 310
Greenhouse design, 20
Gross lease, 62

Hardware design, 20
Health benefits, 90
Health club, 20
Hearing/vision impairment, design for, 18
High-Flex Society, The (Choate), 90
Historic preservation and adaptive re-use,
    20
Home studio, 63–64
Hospital design, 20
    psychiatric, 25
Hospitality design, 21
Hourly fee, 208
    calculating, 205, 206, 207
    plus percentage, 209
Human resource consultants, 103
Human resource manager, 75–76

Import and export specialists, 103
In Search of Excellence (Peters and
    Waterman), 74
Income tax, 46, 47, 312
    withholding, 311–12
    See also Taxes
Independent designer, 13
Individual retirement accounts (IRAs), 301
Installation
    assembly process in, 185
    day of, 190–91
    of furnishings, 187–88
    maintenance manual supplied at, 192
    preparation for, 186
        of site, 187
    records, 188–90
    supervision of, 186–87
Installation sheet, 188, 189
Installation specialist, 76
Insurance, 45, 90, 191
    business operations, 319–22
        liability, 320, 321, 322–23, 324, 326
    claims, 325–26
    key person, 91–92, 322
    property, 317–19
    saving money on, 323–25
    selection of, 316–17

Insurance advisor, 36, 103, 316, 326
Interior design(er)
    charges of. *See* Fee
    and continuing education, 328–31
    income levels of, 88
    job search by, 29–30
    measures of success for, 30
    personal goals of, 50–51
    personal traits of, 11–12
    phases of. *See* Project management
    relationship with client, 12–13, 194, 237
        See also Client
    specialization and specialties of, 14–29
    trade associations of, 332–36
    working arrangements of, 13–14, 210
        See also Design firm; Design studio;
        specific subjects
Inventory, 261, 278, 294
Investment, 278
    corporate, 301
Invoicing methods, 281–83

Job description, 78, 80, 241
Job site, preparation of, 187
Jobber, 214
Joint ventures and associations, 48–49

Kennel design, 21
Keogh Plans (H.R. 10 Plans), 301–2
Kitchen design, 21
    restaurant, 26

Landscaping, interior, 21
Lawsuits, 135–36, 259–60, 317, 326
Lawyer, 36, 40, 45, 52, 101–2, 259–60, 315–
    16, 323
Leadership consultants, 103–4
Leases/leasing, 62–63
Legal office, design for, 21
Letter of agreement, 156, 157–72, 174
    See also Contract
Letter of commendation, 116, 117
Letter of credit, 302
Letter of interest, 114, 115
Letter of resignation, 93, 96, 97
Letter of transmittal, 182
Liability insurance, 320, 321, 322–23, 324, 326
Librarian, 76
Library, design studio
    collection of, 68–71
    management of, 265
Library design, 21
Licenses and permits, 47, 237
Licensing, 22
Life insurance
    group, 321
    key personnel, 322
Lighting design, 22
Lighting fixture design, 22
Limited partnerships, 42
Liturgical design, 22
Loans
    bank, 302–4
    sources of, 304–6
Location, design firm, 39
    evaluating, 59–61
Long-distance calls, 275